# OXFORD THEOLOGICAL MONOGRAPHS

# OXFORD THEOLOGICAL MONOGRAPHS

*Frontispiece* St Macarius of Egypt (Community of St John the Baptist, Tolleshunt Knights, Essex).

# The Macarian Legacy

## *The Place of Macarius-Symeon in the Eastern Christian Tradition*

MARCUS PLESTED

OXFORD

UNIVERSITY PRESS

# OXFORD

UNIVERSITY PRESS

Great Clarendon Street, Oxford OX2 6DP

Oxford University Press is a department of the University of Oxford.
It furthers the University's objective of excellence in research, scholarship,
and education by publishing worldwide in

Oxford New York.

Auckland Bangkok Buenos Aires Cape Town Chennai
Dar es Salaam Delhi Hong Kong Istanbul Karachi Kolkata
Kuala Lumpur Madrid Melbourne Mexico City Mumbai Nairobi
São Paulo Shanghai Taipei Tokyo Toronto

Oxford is a registered trade mark of Oxford University Press
in the UK and in certain other countries

Published in the United States
by Oxford University Press Inc., New York

© Marcus Plested 2004

The moral rights of the author have been asserted
Database right Oxford University Press (maker)

First published 2004

British Library Cataloguing in Publication Data

Data available

Library of Congress Cataloging in Publication Data

Data available

ISBN-19-926779-0

1 3 5 7 9 10 8 6 4 2

Typeset by Kolam Information Service Pvt. Ltd, Pondicherry, India
Printed in Great Britain on acid-free paper by
Biddles Ltd, King's Lynn.

For my grandfather,
the Reverend Ronald Crowther (1922–99).
*Αἰωνία ἡ μνήμη!*

# ACKNOWLEDGEMENTS

I should like first of all to extend my sincerest thanks to my doctoral supervisor, the Right Reverend Dr Kallistos Ware, for his sure guidance, unfailing encouragement and, above all, his example. I have also benefited from discussing elements of my work with a number of other scholars, amongst whom are Ysabel de Andia, Fr Alexander Golitzin, Jean-Claude Larchet, and Fr Anthony Meredith. A special debt of thanks must go to Fr Vincent Desprez, who has been extremely generous and gracious both with his time and with the materials to which he has given me access. My examiners, Dr Sebastian Brock and Professor Andrew Louth, both gave me a great deal of constructive advice that greatly facilitated the passage from thesis to book. Needless to say, the many errors that doubtless remain are all my own. On a more material level, I must acknowledge the indispensable support of the British Academy for the funding that made possible the work on which this book is based. I should also like to express my gratitude to the Warden and Fellows of Merton College, to the staff of the Theology Faculty Library in Oxford and, particularly, to my family who consistently supported me despite not always knowing precisely what it was I was doing those several years spent among the spires and dusty tomes of Oxford. I am also grateful to the Community of St John Baptist at Tolleshunt Knights, both for permission to reproduce the icon that serves as frontispiece to this book and for the advice and encouragement given over the years by several of its members. In considering the thanks I owe to so many people, I am reminded of the wise remark of Pascal which ought always to be borne in mind in the compilation of acknowledgements: 'Certains auteurs, parlant de leurs ouvrages, disent: "Mon livre, mon commentaire, mon histoire, etc." [ . . . ] Ils feraient mieux de dire: "Notre livre, notre commentaire, notre histoire, etc." vu que d'ordinaire, il y a plus en cela du bien d'autrui que du leur.'

*Cambridge*
*January 2004*
*Feast of St Macarius of Egypt*

# CONTENTS

# ABBREVIATIONS

## Primary Sources

| | |
|---|---|
| *ACO* | Ecumenical Councils. E. Schwartz, *Acta conciliorum oecumenicorum* (Berlin 1914– ) |
| *AP* (Alph.) | Apophthegmata patrum. Alphabetical Collection in PG 65 72–440 |
| Basil, *Ep.* | Basil of Caesarea. Y. Courtonne, *Lettres*, 3 vols. (Paris 1957–66) |
| Clement, *Paed.* | Clement of Alexandria. O. Stählin *et al.*, *Paedagogus* (GCS 12.3; Berlin 1972) |
| Clement, *Prot.* | Clement of Alexandria. O. Stählin *et al.*, *Protrepticus* (GCS 12.3; Berlin 1972) |
| Clement, *Strom.* | Clement of Alexandria. O. Stählin *et al.*, *Stromata* I–VI (GCS 52.4; Berlin 1985); VII–VIII (GCS 17.2; Berlin 1970) |
| Diadochus, *GC* | Diadochus of Photice. *Gnostic Chapters*, in É. Des Places, *Œuvres spirituelles* (SC 5.3; Paris 1966) |
| Dionysius, *DN* | Dionysius the Areopagite. *De divinis nominibus* (PG 3 585–984; PTS 33) |
| Dionysius, *CH* | Dionysius the Areopagite. *De cœlesti hierarchia* (PG 3 120–340; PTS 36) |
| Dionysius, *EH* | Dionysius the Areopagite. *De ecclesiastica hierarchia* (PG 3 369–569; PTS 36) |
| Dionysius, *Ep.* | Dionysius the Areopagite. *Epistulae* (PG 3 1065–1120; PTS 36) |

| | |
|---|---|
| Dionysius, *MT* | Dionysius the Areopagite. *De mystica theologia* (PG 3 997–1048; PTS 36) |
| Evagrius, *Ad Monachos* | Evagrius of Pontus. J. Driscoll, *The 'Ad Monachos' of Evagrius Ponticus: Its Structure and a Select Commentary* (Studia Anselmia 104; Rome 1991) |
| Evagrius, *Ad Monachos* (Add.) | Evagrius of Pontus. J. Muyldermans, 'Evagriana: Le vatic. Barb. Graecus 515', *Le Muséon* 51 (1938), 200–3 |
| Evagrius, *Admonition on Prayer* | Evagrius of Pontus. In S. P. Brock (tr.), *The Syriac Fathers on Prayer and the Spiritual Life* (Kalamazoo 1987) |
| Evagrius, *Advice to a Virgin* | Evagrius of Pontus. H. Gressmann, *Nonnenspiegel* (TU 39 (4); Leipzig 1913), 146–51 |
| Evagrius, *Gnostikos* | Evagrius of Pontus. A. and C. Guillaumont, *Le Gnostique* (SC 356; Paris 1989) |
| Evagrius, *KG* | Evagrius of Pontus. A. Guillaumont, *Les Six Centuries des 'Kephalaia Gnostica' d'Évagre le Pontique* (PO 28; Paris 1958) |
| Evagrius, *OP* | Evagrius of Pontus. *De oratione capitula* (PG 79 1165–1200) |
| Evagrius, *Praktikos* | Evagrius of Pontus. A. and C. Guillaumont, *Traité pratique ou le moine*, 2 vols. (SC 170–1; Paris 1971) |
| Evagrius, *Schol. Eccl.* | Evagrius of Pontus. P. Géhin, *Scholies à l'Ecclésiaste* (SC 397; Paris 1993) |
| Evagrius, *Schol. Prov.* | Evagrius of Pontus. P. Géhin, *Scholies aux Proverbes* (SC 340; Paris 1987) |

Evagrius, *Skemmata*

Evagrius of Pontus. J. Muyldermans, 'Note Additionelle à *Evagriana*', *Le Muséon* 44 (1931), 374–80.
Reprinted in idem, *Evagriana,
Extrait de la revue Le Muséon 44,
augmenté de: Nouveaux fragments grecs
inédits* (Paris 1931), 38–44

Evagrius, *Thoughts*

Evagrius of Pontus. P. Géhin,
with A. and C. Guillaumont, *Sur
les pensées* (SC 438; Paris 1998)

GNO

Gregory of Nyssa. *Gregorii Nysseni
Opera* (gen. ed. W. Jaeger; Leiden
1960–)

Gregory, *Cant.*

Gregory of Nyssa. H. Langerbeck, *Homiliae in Canticum canticorum* (GNO 6)

Gregory, *De instituto christiano*

Gregory of Nyssa. R. Staats,
*Makarios-Symeon: Epistola Magna*
(Göttingen 1984)

Gregory, *Or.*

Gregory Nazianzen. J. Bernardi
*et al.*, *Orationes* 1–12, 20–43 (SC
247, 309, 405, 270, 284, 250, 318,
358, 384; Paris 1978–95); *Orationes*
13–19 (PG 35)

Gregory, *Or. cat.*

Gregory of Nyssa. E. Mühlenberg, *Oratio catechetica* (GNO 3 (4))

Gregory, *Virg.*

Gregory of Nyssa. J. Cavarnos, *De
virginitate* (GNO 8 (1))

HM

A.-J. Festugière, *Historia monachorum in Aegypto* (Subsidia Hagiographica 34; Brussels 1961)

Irenaeus, *AH*

Irenaeus of Lyons. A. Rousseau *et
al.*, *Contre les hérésies* 1–v (SC 263–4
(1), SC 293–4 (11), SC 210–11 (111),
SC 100 (1v), SC 152–3 (v); Paris
1965–79)

Isaiah, G

Abba Isaiah. D. J. Chitty,
Working text of the Greek *Asceti-*

|  | *con*, MS held in the library of the House of SS Gregory and Macrina, Oxford |
|---|---|
| Isaiah, S | Abba Isaiah. R. Draguet, *Les Cinq Recensions de l'Ascéticon syriaque d'abba Isaïe* (CSCO 289–90 (text), 293–4 (translation))—the common Syriac recension |
| Isaiah, Sa | Abba Isaiah. R. Draguet, *Les Cinq Recensions de l'Ascéticon syriaque d'abba Isaïe* (CSCO 289–90 (text), 293–4 (translation))—the earliest Syriac recension |
| John Cassian, *Conf.* | E. Pichery, *Conférences* (SC 42 (i–vii), SC 54 (viii–xvii), SC 64 (xviii–xxiv); Paris 1955–9) |
| John Cassian, *Inst.* | J.-C. Guy, *Institutions cénobitiques* (SC 109; Paris 1965) |
| J | John of Damascus. B. Kotter, *De haeresibus* (PTS 22; Berlin 1981), 41–8 |
| *LG* | *Liber Graduum.* M. Kmosko, *Liber graduum* (PS 3; Paris 1926) |
| Macarius, i | Macarius-Symeon. H. Berthold, *Makarios/Symeon, Reden und Briefe. Die Sammlung I des Vaticanus Graecus 694 (B)*, 2 vols. (GCS 55–6; Berlin 1973) |
| Macarius, ii | Macarius-Symeon. (i–50): H. Dörries, E. Klostermann, and M. Kroeger, *Die 50 Geistlichen Homilien des Makarios* (PTS 4; Berlin 1964); (51–7): G. L. Marriott, *Macarii Anecdota: Seven Unpublished Homilies of Macarius* (Harvard Theological Studies 5; Cambridge, Mass. 1918) |
| Macarius, iii | Macarius-Symeon. V. Desprez, *Pseudo-Macaire: Oeuvres spirituelles,* |

|                              |                                                                                                                                                                                                                 |
| ---------------------------- | --------------------------------------------------------------------------------------------------------------------------------------------------------------------------------------------------------------- |
|                              | i: *Homélies propres à la Collection III* (SC 275; Paris 1980); E. Klostermann and H. Berthold, *Neue Homilien des Makarius/Symeon*, i: *Aus Typus III* (TU 72; Berlin 1961)                                      |
| Macarius, *EM*               | Macarius-Symeon. R. Staats, *Makarios-Symeon: Epistola Magna. Eine messalianische Mönchsregel und ihre Umschrift in Gregors von Nyssa 'De Instituto Christiano'* (Göttingen 1984)                                 |
| Macarius, *Syr.*             | Macarius-Symeon. W. Strothmann, *Die syrische Überlieferung der Schriften des Makarios*, 2 vols. (Göttinger Orientforschungen, Series 1: Syriaca 21; Wiesbaden 1981)                                              |
| Macarius, The 150 Chapters   | Macarius-Symeon. Nicodemus the Haghiorite and Macarius of Corinth, Φιλοκαλία τῶν ἱερῶν νηπτικῶν πατέρων, 5 vols. (3rd edn. Athens 1957–63), iii. 169–234                                                          |
| Macarius, TV                 | Macarius-Symeon. W. Strothmann, *Makarios/Symeon: das arabische Sondergut* (Göttinger Orientforschungen, Series 1: Syriaca 11; Wiesbaden 1975)                                                                   |
| Mark the Monk, i–v, vii–viii, x–xi | *Opuscula* i–v, vii–viii, x–xi, in G. M. de Durand, *Marc le Moine: Traités*, 2 vols. (SC 445, 455; Paris 1999, 2000)                                                                                        |
| Maximus, *Amb.*              | Maximus the Confessor. *Ambigua* (PG 91 1031–1418)                                                                                                                                                               |
| Maximus, *CC*                | Maximus the Confessor. A. Ceresa-Gastaldo, *Capitoli sulla carità* (Verba seniorum 3; Rome 1963)                                                                                                                 |
| Maximus, *CT*                | Maximus the Confessor. *Capita theologiae et oeconomiae* (PG 90 1033–1176)                                                                                                                                       |

| | |
|---|---|
| Maximus, *Ep.* | Maximus the Confessor. *Epistulae* (PG 91 362–650) |
| Maximus, *Exp. Ps. LIX; LP* | Maximus the Confessor. P. Van Deun, *Opuscula exegetica duo: Expositio in Psalmum LIX; Expositio orationis dominicae* (CCSG 23; Louvain 1991) |
| Maximus, *Myst.* | Maximus the Confessor. *Mystagogia* (PG 91 658–718) |
| Maximus, *QD* | Maximus the Confessor. J. Declerck, *Quaestiones et dubia* (CCSG 10; Louvain 1982) |
| Maximus, *QT* | Maximus the Confessor. C. Laga and C. Steel, *Quaestiones ad Thalassium* (CCSG 7, 22; Louvain 1980, 1990) |
| Palladius, *LH* | C. Butler, *The Lausiac History of Palladius* (Cambridge 1898–1904) |
| Photius, *Bibliotheca* | R. Henry, *La Bibliothèque de Photius*, 5 vols. (Collection Byzantine; Paris 1959) |
| T | Timothy of Constantinople. *De iis qui ad ecclesiam ab haereticis accedunt* (PG 86 12–68), 48A–52C |
| Theodoret, *Haer. fab. comp.* | Theodoret of Cyrrhus. *Haereticarum fabularum compendium* (PG 83 336–556) |
| Theodoret, *HE* | Theodoret of Cyrrhus. F. Parmentier, *Historia ecclesiastica* (GCS 44; Berlin 1954) |
| *VA* | Athanasius of Alexandria. G. J. M. Bartelink, *Vie d'Antoine* (SC 400; Paris 1994) |
| *VH* | Callinicus. Bartelink, G. J. M., *Vie d'Hypatios* (SC 177; Paris 1971) |
| *VP* | F. Halkin, *Sancti Pachomii vitae Graecae* (Subsidia hagiographica 19; Brussels 1932) |

## General and Secondary Sources

| | |
|---|---|
| CCSG | Corpus christianorum series graeca |
| *CPG* | *Clavis patrum graecorum* |
| CSCO | Corpus scriptorum christianorum orientalium |
| CSEL | Corpus scriptorum ecclesiasticorum latinorum |
| *DS* | *Dictionnaire de spiritualité* |
| *ECR* | *Eastern Churches Review* |
| GCS | Die griechischen christlichen Schriftsteller der ersten drei Jahrhunderte |
| *JEH* | *Journal of Ecclesiastical History* |
| *JTS* | *Journal of Theological Studies* |
| Lampe | G. W. H. Lampe, *A Patristic Greek Lexicon* |
| LS | H. Liddell and R. Scott, *A Greek–English Lexicon* |
| OCA | Orientalia christiana analecta |
| *OCP* | *Orientalia christiana periodica* |
| Payne-Smith | J. Payne-Smith, *A Compendious Syriac Dictionary* |
| PG | Migne, Patrologia graeca |
| PL | Migne, Patrologia latina |
| PO | Patrologia orientalis |
| PS | Patrologia syriaca |
| PTS | Patristische Texte und Studien |
| *RAM* | *Revue d'ascétique et de mystique* |
| SC | Sources Chrétiennes |
| *SVQ* | *St Vladimir's Theological Quarterly* |
| TLG | *Thesaurus Linguae Graecae* |
| TU | Texte und Untersuchungen |
| *VC* | *Vigiliae christianae* |

# Introduction

Christianity has always experienced a certain tension between the priestly and prophetic ministries, between the institutional Church and the charismatic tradition. The Macarian writings lie very much at the centre of this often constructive, sometimes destructive tension, offering a peculiarly vivid insight into the nature of the complex relationship between those who would be the mediators of grace and those who claim direct access to it. The Macarian writings are one of the principal fountainheads of the Christian ascetic and mystical tradition. Issuing from the spiritual, intellectual, and political ferment of fourth-century Syria, they bring us to the heart of the confrontation between the burgeoning ascetic movement and the ecclesiastical hierarchy, most notably in that groups associated with the author were condemned as heretical 'Messalians'. They also bring us to the centre of the ongoing encounter between Hellenic and Semitic thought-worlds, between Greek and Syriac expressions of the Christian revelation.

The writings were rapidly translated and widely circulated. They exercised a profound and formative influence upon the Eastern Christian spiritual tradition, an influence quite as decisive as that of Dionysius the Areopagite or Evagrius of Pontus. The Macarian legacy is clearly discernible in, for example, SS Mark the Monk, Diadochus of Photice, Maximus the Confessor, Symeon the New Theologian, and Gregory Palamas.[1] The writings have also had a remarkable odyssey within the Western Christian tradition, providing a link between, amongst others, Dante, Wesley, the Society of Jesus, and German Pietism.[2] This is a distinctly ecumenical legacy.

---

[1] For Mark, Diadochus, and Maximus, see the relevant chapters below. For Symeon and Gregory, see n. 5.

[2] For Dante, see *Paradiso* 22: St Benedict points to SS Romuald and Macarius in the highest sphere of contemplation. For Wesley, see his *Diary* for 30 July 1736: at sea off Carolina he 'read Macarius and sang'; see also Outler, *John Wesley*, 9 n. 6, 274–5. The *Institutum societatis Jesu*, iii. 121, recommend the Macarian Homilies (the most popular and widespread collection of the writings) to novices, a recommendation going back to

What is it about the Macarian writings that has proved so attractive to posterity? While the book as a whole stands as a response to this question, a short answer would point to the timeless and cross-confessional appeal of the central message of the writings—a call to every Christian, without exception, to seek out and directly experience the life-giving and perfecting action of the triune God. Such experience is deemed to constitute the very essence of Christianity: 'The reality of Christianity is this: the taste of truth, the eating and drinking of truth' (Macarius, II 17. 7).[3] The focus on the unmediated experience of the divine is one of the outstanding characteristics of the Macarian corpus. While not advocating any sort of merely individualistic mysticism, divorced from society and the Church, the writings are remarkably effective as a wake-up call, a *reveille* for the somnambulant soul, an exhortation to taste and know the truth. The writings are quite uncompromising in their insistence that all Christians must strive towards perfection. In this respect the title of the first English translation of the Homilies, published in 1721, neatly, if not concisely, conveys their *leitmotif*: *Primitive Morality or the Spiritual Homilies of St Macarius the Egyptian; Full of very profitable instructions concerning that Perfection which is Expected from Christians and which it is their Duty to Endeavour after.*[4]

The tone in which this call to perfection is made is engaging, distinctive, and encouraging. The writings are warm, vivid, and expansive, making use of a veritable riot of colour, imagery, and metaphor. They combine to remarkable effect the philosophical reflection of the Greek Fathers with the vibrant symbolism and poetry of the Syriac tradition. The author observes with great finesse the workings of sin and grace within the human person and speaks with extraordinary intensity and colour of the progressive

---

Mercurian's *Regula* (1580). The Jesuits do not appear ever to have taken account of the condemnation of the Homilies by the Spanish Inquisition (in 1631, 1707, and 1736). For this condemnation, see Nieto Ibáñez, 'Ortodoxos, humanistas y protestantes ante la espiritualidad bizantina: el enigma de San Macario', 34–5, and, idem., *Pedro de Valencia: Obras completas*, IX.1: *Escritos espirituales: San Macario*, 77–8. Johann Arndt knew the Homilies by heart, and paraphrases sections of them in his *True Christianity*. For Gottfried Arnold, see Dörries, *Geist und Geschichte bei Gottfried Arnold*. For a more general account, see Benz, *Die protestantische Thebais: zur Nachwirkung Makarius des Ägypters in Europa und Amerika*. Lastly, again on the Protestant inheritance, see van de Bank, *Macarius en zijn involfed in de Nederlanden*.

[3] For conventions of citation, see Abbreviations, pp. xiii–xiv.

[4] The writings were long ascribed to St Macarius of Egypt, the founder of the monastic community at Scetis. I explain the difficulties behind this ascription below (p. 12-17).

sanctification and deification of the Christian. The accuracy of his observations, the warmth and vividness of his teaching, and the clarity of his message have combined to make them remarkably accessible and appealing to Christians of all persuasions.

But while the influence of the Macarian writings has long been recognized and spoken of, few attempts have been made to determine in what exactly that influence consists, and in what manner it was transmitted. As regards the Eastern Christian tradition, we have only a number of monographs dealing with John Cassian, Mark the Monk, Diadochus of Photice, and Symeon the New Theologian.[5] No systematic attempt has yet been made to assess the Macarian legacy in anything like its totality.[6] This study exists to remedy, at least in part, that deficiency.

The book is divided into two parts. Part I—'The Background'—(Chapters 1–4) is essentially introductory, its primary purpose being to situate the writings within their immediate theological and historical context. Chapter 1 gives an account of the manuscript tradition and of the authorship, dating, and location of the corpus. It also deals with the fundamental question of Macarius' relationship with the Messalian tendency, a question which forms a recurring theme of the book as a whole. In it I offer some new observations as to the nature of that relationship. Chapter 2 provides a summary of the spiritual teaching of the writings, adumbrating some of the themes that were to prove so attractive to later writers. Chapter 3 explores the connection between

---

[5] Kemmer, *Charisma Maximum: Untersuchung zu Cassians Vollkommenheitslehre und seiner Stellung zum Messalianismus*; Hesse, 'Markos Eremites und Symeon von Mesopotamien: Untersuchung und Vergleich ihrer Lehren zur Taufe und zur Askese'; Dörr, *Diadochus von Photike und die Messalianer*; Dörries, 'Diadochus und Symeon: Das Verhältnis der κεφάλαια γνωστικά zum Messalianismus'; Hatzopoulos, *Two Outstanding Cases in Byzantine Spirituality: The Macarian Writings and Symeon the New Theologian*. Alfeyev, *St Symeon the New Theologian and Orthodox Tradition* and Meyendorff, *A Study of Gregory Palamas*, also contain some observations on the Macarian legacy in their respective subjects. Beulay, *La Lumière sans forme*, gives a somewhat idiosyncratic sketch of the Macarian legacy in the Syrian tradition, focusing his attentions on the mystics of the Church of the East. Kemmer's thesis is deeply flawed; he equates Messalianism with the Macarian corpus and the *Liber graduum*, taking these as representative of a kind of Eastern Semi-Pelagianism—hence an extra stick with which to beat Cassian. My own study of Cassian has not convinced me of direct Macarian influence, *pace* Kemmer. The works on Mark and Diadochus are discussed in the relevant chapters. Hatzopoulos' examination places Symeon within the Macarian tradition but remains, surprisingly, agnostic as to whether Symeon actually knew the Macarian corpus.

[6] Cf. Desprez with Canévet, 'Pseudo-Macaire (Syméon)', 39: 'une étude d'ensemble manque encore'.

Macarius and the Cappadocian Fathers, while Chapter 4 attempts a re-evaluation of the dichotomy often perceived between the Macarian and Evagrian spiritual traditions. Part I is designed so as to provide a firm basis for the chief concern of this work, the evaluation of the Macarian legacy in the later tradition carried out in Part II.

Part II—'The Legacy'—(Chapters 5–8) contains an examination of the relations obtaining between the Macarian writings and the works of Mark the Monk, Diadochus of Photice, Abba Isaiah, and Maximus the Confessor. These writers have been selected as being the most significant in terms of the assessment of the Macarian legacy in the Eastern Christian tradition up to the close of the seventh century. A survey of the Macarian legacy could, of course, be almost infinitely extended; some delimitation of subject matter has proved inevitable. Thus even within the chronological boundaries of this work, I have not been able to include a study of the possible Macarian influence in, to name but the most obvious examples, John Cassian, Barsanuphius and John, Dorotheus of Gaza, John Climacus, Anastasius of Sinai, and Isaac of Nineveh—all of whom merit close attention in this respect.

My methodology is relatively straightforward, consisting in an examination of the linguistic, theological, and exegetical parallels existing between the works of Macarius and those of the various authors examined. I have been very wary of assuming any sort of mechanistic pattern of influence, of supposing that the fact that a given author borrows from Macarius of itself constitutes subscription to Macarius' teaching as a whole. I have therefore consistently attempted to set the various parallels discovered within the wider context of the spiritual teaching of the authors in question, so as to produce not only a quantitative but also a qualitative assessment of the Macarian legacy within those authors.

I have been acutely aware of the influence of commonplaces and coincidences, allowing for these in each parallel adduced. *Quellenforschung* is, at root, an inexact science, frequently relying on cumulative arguments, the weighing up of relative probabilities, and common sense. This is particularly the case when concerned with ascetic writers almost inextricably bound up within a shared and predominately oral tradition. I hope, however, to have brought to this particular example of the genre as much precision as lies in my power.

All the authors dealt with in this book belong to a living tradition; they do not draw upon authors such as Macarius so as to produce a kind of 'scissors and paste' spirituality, a patchwork compilation of received authorities. They draw upon him rather as a confirmation and enrichment of their own lived experience of God. While this study is concerned with the Macarian tradition in particular, it hopes also to shed some light on the nature of the Christian tradition in general.

# PART I

# The Background

# The Macarian Writings and their Historical Context

## 1.1 The Manuscript Tradition

Jumping straight in at the deep end, we may begin with a brief account of the physical nature of the Macarian corpus. The Macarian writings make up an extensive body of material containing over a hundred pieces in the form of discussions, homilies, treatises, and letters. The manuscript tradition is, it must be admitted, rather complex and remains unclear in many respects. For instance, we know very little about the transmission of the writings prior to the eleventh century and are still guessing about the exact nature of the relationship between the various collections of Macarian material. What follows is essentially a summary of the main forms in which the Macarian writings have come down to us. The Greek manuscript tradition gives us four principal collections. These collections each contain a substantial amount of overlapping material and are conventionally numbered in reverse order of antiquity.[1]

Collection I is the largest collection, comprising sixty-four Logoi. Logos 1 is the *Epistola magna*, or *Great Letter*, which has been separately edited by Jaeger and by Staats. The *Epistola magna* is particularly interesting in that it attracted the attention of Gregory of Nyssa, who paid it the compliment of reworking it as his *De instituto christiano*. A forthcoming edition by Desprez promises to rely more heavily than Staats on the most ancient manuscripts.[2]

[1] On the manuscript tradition, Dörries, *Symeon von Mesopotamien*, remains the standard work. See also the introductions to the critical editions of the Macariana cited below and *CPG* ii. 2410–27 (and Supplement 2411–27).

[2] Jaeger, *Two Rediscovered Works of Ancient Christian Literature: Gregory of Nyssa and Macarius*; Staats, *Makarios-Symeon: Epistola Magna*. Staats's edition relies on a wider manuscript base than that of Jaeger and conveniently provides parallel texts of the *Epistola Magna* and Gregory of Nyssa's *De instituto christiano*. References are according to Staats's numbering, prefixed *EM*. We shall return to the question of the relationship between the *Epistola magna*

Logoi 2–64 have been edited by Berthold, largely on the basis of two thirteenth-century manuscripts.[3]

Collection II, the fifty spiritual homilies, has proved to be the most popular collection, widely attested in the manuscript tradition and the subject of the vast majority of printed editions and modern translations. Its earliest manuscript witness is from the eleventh or twelfth century. It has been edited by Dörries, Klostermann, and Kroeger.[4] An appendix to two manuscripts of Collection II gives a further seven homilies which have been provisionally edited by Marriott.[5]

Collection III comprises forty-three Logoi. Roughly one-half of its material is unique to it. The Logoi not duplicated in Collection II have been edited by Klostermann and Berthold. Their text, with the additional omission of those Logoi duplicated in Collection I, is reproduced by Desprez.[6] The earliest manuscript witness to this collection dates from the eleventh century.

Collection IV, comprising twenty-six Logoi, has not been separately edited. It is wholly contained within Collection I. Its form

and the *De instituto christiano* below, Ch. 3. Desprez expects to give greater weight to the Greek Ephrem and the witness of Collection IV. I owe thanks to him for kindly updating me on his plans.

[3] Berthold, *Makarios/Symeon, Reden und Briefe. Die Sammlung I des Vaticanus Graecus 694 (B)*. The other main MS used is Atheniensis graecus 423 (b). References are given as: 1, Logos, section, subsection (where applicable), according to Berthold's numbering. Logos 1 62.1-22 is not authentic. References to Collection I normally refer to material unique to that collection. A recent German translation exists: Fitschen, *Pseudo-Macarius, Reden und Briefe*.

[4] Dörries, Klostermann, and Kroeger, *Die 50 Geistlichen Homilien des Makarios*. References will be to this edition in the form: II, Homily, section. Strothmann, *Textcritische Anmerkungen zu den geistlichen Homilien des Makarios/Symeon*, should also be consulted when examining texts also found in the other collections. Collection II was first printed in 1559 by Picus in Paris. The English translation of Thomas Haywood was published in 1721 as *Primitive Morality, or the Spiritual Homilies of St Macarius the Egyptian*. The volume also includes a fascinating introduction. Part of this translation was re-published by John Wesley as volume i (a signal honour) of his *Christian Library*. Of the more recent English translations, that of Mason, *Fifty Spiritual Homilies of St Macarius the Egyptian*, is to be preferred over that of Maloney, *The Fifty Spiritual Homilies and Great Letter*—although it too is often rather loose. Perhaps the best modern translation is the French of Fr Placide Deseille, *Les Homélies spirituelles de saint Macaire*. The Italian of Cremaschi can also be recommended.

[5] Marriott, *Macarii Anecdota: Seven Unpublished Homilies of Macarius*. See also Baker, 'Corrections in Macarii Anecdota'. Homilies 54 (Palladius) and 57 (Ammonas) are certainly not by our author. Homilies 56 and 53 (§§8–13a) may also be inauthentic. References will be given as: II, Homily, section, as given by Marriott. Deseille, *Les Homélies spirituelles*, provides a translation. These Homilies were noticed by Haywood, but left untranslated.

[6] Klostermann and Berthold, *Neue Homilien des Makarius/Symeon*, i: *Aus Typus III*; Desprez, *Pseudo-Macaire: Oeuvres spirituelles*, i: *Homélies propres à la Collection III*. References to Collection III will be to Desprez's numbering and given as: III, Logos, section, subsection.

may be pieced together from the critical apparatus of that Collection. Like Collection I, Collection IV begins with the *Epistola magna*. Collection IV is attested in Georgian translation before 1028, and in Arabic in 1055.[7] The earliest Greek manuscript appears to date from 1044–5.[8] An edition by Desprez is forthcoming in Sources Chrétiennes.

In the absence, for the time being, of a separate edition of Collection IV, we are assisted not only by the apparatus of Collection I, but also by the indirect Greek tradition. Amongst the various collections of extracts, the most influential has been the 150 Chapters found, perhaps most notably, in the *Philokalia*.[9] Symeon Metaphrastes is credited with the compilation of this collection, but not by the oldest manuscripts. The compilation is derived from Collection IV. Chapters 1–32 draw upon the *Epistola magna*, whilst Chapters 33–150 continue systematically through Logoi 2–26.[10] It is an intelligent compilation which preserves and, in its conciseness, even enhances the freshness, insight, and vigour of the original.

A certain amount of Macarian material has also been transmitted outside the main collections under various ascriptions. The eight Logoi contained within the Greek Ephrem and edited by Strothmann are particularly interesting in that they provide material unique to this collection.[11] Other material is to be found under the names of Basil, Evagrius, Mark, and Isaiah.[12]

---

[7] See Desprez, *Oeuvres spirituelles*, 23–4. The Arabic MS in question is Vaticanus arabicus 84 (1055) (W). It is attributed to 'Macarius'.

[8] Note that this MS (Parisinus graecus 973) (X) came to light too late to be fully utilized in the preparation of the apparatus of Collection I. See Desprez with Canévet, 'Pseudo-Macaire (Syméon)', 21.

[9] *Φιλοκαλία τῶν ἱερῶν νηπτικῶν πατέρων*, ed. Nicodemus the Haghiorite and Macarius of Corinth. English translation by Palmer, Sherrard, and Ware, in *The Philokalia*, vol. iii. The extracts in the *Philokalia* correspond to *Opuscula* 11–vii as given by Migne (PG 34 841–965). The *Opuscula* have been translated by Penn as *Institutes of Christian Perfection*. Desprez, *Oeuvres spirituelles*, 18 n. 2, reports the finding of Julien Leroy that Paul Evergetinos (d. 1054) transcribed portions of *Opuscula* i–iii and v–vii in his *Catecheses*.

[10] See the tables provided by Desprez in Jacques Touraille (tr.), *Philocalie des Pères neptiques* (fascicule 5), 89–96. In fact the text of the 150 Chapters appears to rely on a version of Collection IV more ancient than that of the common subarchetype of the extant MSS. See Staats, *Makarios-Symeon: Epistola Magna*, 53–5. Thanks to Fr Desprez for drawing my attention to this point.

[11] Strothmann, *Schriften des Makarios/Symeon unter dem Namen des Ephraem*.

[12] For Basil and Evagrius, see Desprez, *Oeuvres spirituelles*, 19–20. For Mark and Isaiah, see Chs. 5 and 7 below.

Amongst the various translations, the Syriac and Arabic are particularly important. The Syriac includes the earliest known manuscript witness to the Macarian corpus, dated 534.[13] The Syriac corpus attributes the works variously to either Macarius of Egypt or Macarius of Alexandria. The Syriac Macarius has been edited and translated by Strothmann.[14] A Greek manuscript has recently come to light which provides a partial basis for the form of the Syriac collection.[15] The Arabic Collection TV contains, in addition to elements from Collections I, II, and III, material that is not duplicated elsewhere.[16] There is no extant Greek witness for the form of this Collection. The TV Collection is attributed to Symeon the Ascetic or to Symeon the Stylite.

The complexity of the manuscript tradition is in itself a testimony to the popularity and wide circulation of the Macarian writings. These were evidently highly valued and sought-after works. But whose works are they? This, as we shall see, is a question that remains decidedly open.

## 1.2    The Authorship, Date, and Immediate Milieu of the Macarian Writings

The question of authorship is a thorny one. The ascription to Macarius of Egypt, Macarius of Alexandria, or Macarius *tout court* is well established, being made by all the principal Greek collections, the earliest extant Syriac MSS, and the Arabic version of Collection IV. The fact that the Arabic Collection TV is ascribed to Symeon, either the Ascetic or the Stylite, as are certain manuscripts of the appendix to Collection II, must, however, be taken into account. In addition, Géhin has recently signalled the existence of a Greek manuscript of the tenth or eleventh century ascribed to 'Saint Symeon' and containing extracts which corres-

---

[13] British Library, Additional MS 12 175.

[14] Strothmann, *Die syrische Überlieferung der Schriften des Makarios*. See also his 'Makarios und die Makariosschriften in der syrischen literatur'.

[15] See Géhin, 'Le Dossier Macarien de l'Atheniensis 2492'.

[16] The material unique to TV has been translated by Strothmann in his *Makarios/ Symeon: das arabische Sondergut*. See also Dörries, *Symeon von Mesopotamien*, 337–77, 410–15, and 471–86.

pond to Logoi 7 and 4 of Collection I.[17] It remains to be seen whether this could be a Greek basis for TV, and therefore an indication that the ascription to Symeon is not original to the Arabic. Working from the principal attributions of the manuscript traditions, the author can conveniently be referred to as Macarius-Symeon. The ascription to Macarius of Egypt is, as we shall see, untenable.

Internal evidence provides only very scanty information as to the date and location of the author, but is sufficient to establish a Syrian, rather than an Egyptian, milieu.[18] The only river to be mentioned by name is the Euphrates (I 8.4.2, 14.26), referred to in such a way as to make clear that it is the principal river of the region. The author also observes how 'in a severe winter even the great rivers freeze over, especially in northern parts' (I 50.1.10)—ruling out Egypt and suggesting the upper course of the Euphrates.[19] The mention of wars between Rome and Persia (II 15.46, 27.22) may refer to the wars culminating in the disastrous campaign and death of the Emperor Julian in 363. It may also imply a location in border territory, perhaps in Mesopotamia, although this reference to the 'superpowers' of the ancient world might have been made by any resident of the Eastern Roman Empire. He also refers to missionary activity in India (I 34.7), and to incursions of Indians and Saracens (I 34.8)—but these *topoi* provide little help in our attempt to locate the author.[20] His mention of wars against the

[17] Géhin, 'Evagriana d'un manuscrit basilien'. The MS is Vaticanus graecus 2028 (10th/11th cent.). Note that Baroccianus 213 (16th cent.), the basis of Marriott's edition of H, presents the additional homilies as 'The Second Epistle of the same Divine Father Macarius to Abba Symeon the Ascetic of Mesopotamia in Syria and to the Brethren with him'. This is intriguing, but is not supported by the earlier MS M (Mosquensis 177 (12th cent.)), which gives 'Symeon' as the author. Coislinianus 193 (11th cent.), however, does ascribe the material to 'Macarius'. See Géhin, 'Un recueil d'extraits patristiques: les Miscellanea Coisliniana (*Parisinus Coislinianus* 193 et *Sinaiticus graecus* 461)'. Thanks, again, to Fr Desprez for this reference.

[18] The best survey of the question of date and location is now Fitschen, *Messalianismus und Antimessalianismus*, 162–70.

[19] On occasion, the whole Euphrates was known to freeze, as in the winter of 608/9 in which 'There was a great deal of snow everywhere and it was so cold that the entire Euphrates froze on the night of Epiphany and rafts of ice were floating on it for six days so that ferries could not cross it.' Cited in Palmer, *The Seventh Century in the West-Syrian Chronicles*, 17. Many thanks to Garth Fowden for this reference.

[20] Macarius-Symeon writes of a city taken by 'Indians and Saracens' and subsequently restored to imperial control as a type of the reclaiming of the soul by Christ. Fitschen, *Messalianismus und Antimessalianismus* 167–8, takes this reference as an indication that Macarius-Symeon was aware of the siege and capture of Amida in 359 by Shapur II and its return

Goths (I 34.11) is slightly more promising in that it may suggest the period following the defeat of the Emperor Valens by the Goths at the battle of Adrianopole in 378, when the Gothic threat would be very much in the minds of all imperial citizens. The author also refers to the 'first month of Xanthikos, which is called April' (II 5.9), a use of the Macedonian calendar which may help connect him with the region of Antioch.[21] He claims to have known two confessors of the faith who suffered persecution prior to the advent of the peace of the Church (II 27.14–15) (i.e. before 324 in the Eastern Empire). In this case, the author can hardly have lived far beyond the close of the fourth century.

The author draws upon many traditional motifs of Syrian Christianity.[22] His graphic and poetic symbolism recalls the thought-world of Ephrem and Aphrahat. A good case has also been made for his use of Gospel citations in the form found in the Diatessaron and of apocrypha of Syrian origin, such as the Acts and Gospel of Thomas.[23]

The Syrian is, however, by no means the only milieu to have influenced our author. Much of his culture is deeply Hellenic. His Greek is competent and fluent, if not elegant; it is certainly his mother tongue. Many aspects of his thought are rooted in the Alexandrine theological tradition, doubtless due in part to the influence of the Cappadocian Fathers, within whose orbit he

to imperial control under the Emperor Julian in 363. This suggestion, however attractive, seems to me to be pushing the evidence a little too far. Some of the troops and allies of Shapur as described in the principal source for these events, Ammianus Marcellinus, could indeed be called Indians and Saracens, but the city was quite unambiguously taken by the Persians, under the direct command of the Shahenshah himself. If Macarius-Symeon had been thinking of Amida, he would surely have mentioned the Persians, to whom he refers quite freely elsewhere.

[21] In the critical edition, the editors comment that this usage 'schließt Kleinasien nicht aus und legt höchstens nahe, den Ursprung im (weiteren) Umkreis von Antiochien zu suchen, wo der Xanthikos am 1. April beginnt'.

[22] Columba Stewart, *'Working the Earth of the Heart'*, provides an excellent summary of Macarius-Symeon's Syrian background, especially 9–11 and 84–6. For a short but perceptive survey see also Vööbus, *On the Historical Importance of the Legacy of Pseudo-Macarius: New Observations about its Syriac Provenance*. The Syrian element in the Macariana will be discussed further below, Ch. 2.1.

[23] See Quispel, *Makarius, das Thomasevangelium und das Lied von der Perle* and 'The Syrian Thomas and the Syrian Macarius'; Baker, 'Pseudo-Macarius and the Gospel of Thomas' and 'Syriac and the Scriptural Quotations of Pseudo-Macarius'; Klijn, 'Some Remarks on the Quotations of the Gospels in Gregory of Nyssa's *De instituto christiano* and Macarius' *Epistola Magna*'; Staats, *Gregor von Nyssa und die Messalianer*, 94–100.

certainly fell. He is possessed of a diffused philosophical culture, making extensive use of elements drawn from Platonic and Stoic philosophy.[24]

He is familiar with the workings of an imperial palace and the structures of civil administration (III 4.1). He refers to the Roman educational system (II 15.42) and to Roman law (III 21.3.3).[25] He is definitely a citizen of the Empire. There are also some possible links with the Egyptian monastic tradition, as witnessed, in particular, by the affinity between elements of his works and the *Epistles* of Anthony.[26]

Other indications as to context and dating can be gleaned from the relationship between Macarius-Symeon's *Epistola magna* and the *De instituto christiano* of Gregory of Nyssa. If we accept the authenticity of the *De instituto*, and follow the now universal recognition of the anteriority of the *Epistola magna*, both treatises may be dated to between 381 and 394.[27]

Macarius-Symeon acted as the spiritual guide of more than one ascetic community. The community to which the *Epistola magna*, for example, is addressed is designated either a 'brotherhood' or a 'monastery' (*EM* 6.2). It is guided by 'superiors' ($\pi\rho o\epsilon\sigma\tau\hat{\omega}\tau\epsilon\varsigma$)—implying some sort of collegiate leadership (*EM* 6.5). He also refers to 'the monasteries of the brotherhood'—suggesting a network of communities (*EM* 6.1). He constantly urges unity within the community (II 3.1–2) and holds that the brethren should consider themselves to be members of one body (I 4.30.13). While he praises the solitary life (*EM* 5.1, 6.1), he also emphasizes the advantages of the coenobitic model: a monk who leaves the community under

[24] His Hellenic culture and connection with the Cappadocians will be explored further in Chs. 2 and 3.

[25] III 4.1 gives a detailed account of the administrative structure of an imperial palace, describing the various ranks within; II 15.42 deals with the educational system of the Empire; III 21.3.3 speaks of Roman law. Desprez, *Oeuvres spirituelles*, 36 n., gives examples of a number of Latinisms in the writings.

[26] Compare, for example, Anthony, *Ep.* 6.72–7 and Macarius-Symeon, II 31.5, given below, Ch. 6.4 Note also the frequent description of the soul as $\nu o\epsilon\rho\grave{a}$ $o\mathring{v}\sigma\acute{\iota}a$ in both writers (e.g. Anthony, *Ep.* 2.28 (p. 205) and Macarius, II 25.1). This unusual appellation is not readily paralleled in other monastic writers. It is, however, also found in Philo, *De specialibus legibus* 4. 123; Eusebius of Caesarea, *Praeparatio evangelica* 7. 10 (PG 21 533D); Gregory of Nyssa, *Contra Eunomium* 3. 6 (GNO 2, p. 213); *De anima et resurrectione* (PG 46 29B); and *De infantibus praemature abreptis* (GNO 3 (2), p. 78). The usage thus also stands as a further sign of the affinity between Gregory and Macarius-Symeon.

[27] The dates are those of the Council of Constantinople and the (approximate) death of Gregory. The question is discussed further in Ch. 3.

the pretext of seeking solitude for prayer is like an amputated limb (TV 10.18–20).[28] He mentions a community of thirty monks (II 3.1) and a 'monastery of Christians', built on a remote and rather wild mountain and which offers up 'ceaseless psalms, hymns, and spiritual songs' (I 21.2).[29] Monks of his acquaintance wore a distinctive outer garment (III 10.3.4). Dörries suggests that Macarius-Symeon's immediate circle practised errancy much as those of Alexander the Acemite.[30] This suggestion is not, however, borne out by the writings themselves.

In summary, Macarius-Symeon remains an elusive figure. Much of the evidence suggests a location in Osrhoene or the region around Antioch and a late fourth-century dating. He may, perhaps, have retired into the Syrian hinterland after a spell in imperial service at Antioch. The suggestion made by Dörries in his early work, *Symeon von Mesopotamien*, that the author was the eponymous Messalian leader, about whom we know virtually nothing, was effectively dropped in his later *Die Theologie des Makarios-Symeon*. For the purposes of this study, we shall follow the bulk of the manuscript tradition and refer simply to Macarius, 'the blessed one'.[31]

## 1.3   The Messalian Connection

The most telling argument against the authorship of Macarius of Egypt has been the discovery of themes in work related to the Messalian movement. Suspicions about this connection are by no means a modern phenomenon. Darrouzès has drawn attention to a query made in the margin of a thirteenth-century manuscript of

---

[28] Dörries, *Die Theologie*, 448, overlooks the coenobitic strain in Macarius-Symeon's teaching.

[29] The designation of monks as 'Christians' is one of the many points of contact between the ascetic vocabulary and teaching of Macarius-Symeon and Basil. For further discussion of this, see below, Ch. 3. Macarius-Symeon regularly speaks of the ascetic as ὁ μονάζων (I 50.4.13; II 15.51, 38.1, 48.6), and, much less frequently, ὁ μοναχός (I 29.1.8, 30.4). In his terminology, he preserves some of the sense of the Syriac *iḥidaya* (single one, single-minded, close to the only-begotten one).

[30] Dörries, *Die Theologie*, 448.

[31] The title 'blessed one' was, in any case, very common in the Syrian tradition. The anonymous author of the *Liber graduum*, for example, is also given the title. It is quite conceivable that the works initially circulated with the simple designation τοῦ μακαρίου with the epithet 'of Egypt' being added later to bolster their authority.

Collection I making precisely this connection.[32] In the eighteenth century, Neophytos Kausokalyvites concluded from the relations between Collection II and the condemned Messalian propositions reported by Timothy of Constantinople and John of Damascus that the ascription to Macarius of Egypt could not possibly be correct.[33] More recently, Villecourt has asserted that the Messalian connection warrants the identification of some form of the Macarian corpus with the Messalian *Asceticon* condemned at the Ecumenical Council of Ephesus in 431.[34]

In view of the importance of the Messalian question in any evaluation of the Macariana, some account must be made of the issues involved. The material relating to the Messalian connection has been studied at length elsewhere, particularly in Columba Stewart's '*Working the Earth of the Heart*' and, more recently, Klaus Fitschen's *Messalianismus und Antimessalianismus*.[35] Without wishing to repeat the labours of these scholars or pretending to supersede them, I propose in this section simply to provide a résumé and a brief discussion of the *status quaestionis*—a discussion which, for all its brevity, does hope to open up some new insights into this difficult area. I should stress that this is not a book about Messalianism as such and I shall not, therefore, be able to engage in any minute detail with the arguments of either Stewart or Fitschen.

The Messalians are first recorded within the Syrian orbit. Ephrem makes a passing reference to them in *Madrasa* 22 of his *Against the Heresies* (AD 363–73).[36] He ends a list of heresies with: 'And the Messalians who live in debauchery—good is he who leads them back to his fold.' The term 'Messalian' derives from the Syriac root *ṣl'* (to incline) which in the pa'el conjugation bears the meaning 'to pray'. 'Messalians' can thus be translated 'the praying ones' or 'the pray-ers'. It passes into Greek as εὐχῖται (Euchites).

[32] *Atheniensis graecus* 423 (13th cent.). See Darrouzès, 'Notes sur les Homélies du Pseudo-Macaire'. Darrouzès reports that the query is in a late thirteenth- or early fourteenth-century hand.

[33] See Darrouzès, 'Notes'.

[34] Villecourt, 'La Date et l'origine des "Homélies spirituelles" attribuées à Macaire'.

[35] On the Messalian question see also Gribomont, 'Le Dossier des origines du Messalianisme'; Kmosko, *Liber graduum*, cxvi–ccxciii; Desprez with Canévet, 'Pseudo-Macaire (Syméon)'; Guillaumont, 'Messaliens'; Staats, *Gregor von Nyssa und die Messalianer*. Fitschen's is now the most complete treatment of the subject.

[36] CSCO 169, p. 79. Dates refer to the fall of Nisibis and death of Ephrem (but cf. Stewart, '*Working the Earth of the Heart*', 15 n).

Ephrem's brief notice tells us very little. Its chief significance is that it constitutes the first use of the term in question and an indication of the Syrian origin of the Messalians. As yet we know nothing of any suspect doctrine, but simply a vague reference to a debauched lifestyle, a stock accusation that might be levelled against any group viewed as heretical. It is, moreover, the only place Ephrem mentions the Messalians—they were evidently not a pressing concern.

Epiphanius of Salamis produces a rather confused description of the Messalians. Like Ephrem, he is writing a piece of heresiology and, also like Ephrem, places the Messalians last in his lists of heresies, indicating that they are a recent phenomenon. He deals with the Messalians in his *Ancoratus* and *Panarion*. The *Ancoratus* (c.374) concludes with, 'and the Messalians with whom are associated, from among the Greeks, Martyrians, Euphemites, and Satanians'.[37] The *Panarion* (c.377) goes into rather greater detail as to the nature of the crimes of the Messalians.[38] Again the Messalians are associated with pagan heresies of the post-Constantinian period. Epiphanius transliterates the Syriac as μασσαλιανοί and explains it to his Greek audience as εὐχόμενοι (80.1.2). He evidently wishes to convey a common link between these groups, apparently consisting in an excessive emphasis on prayer. Equally, he goes on to speak of another group of Messalians, who purport to be Christian, and whom he obviously wishes to link with the pagan Messalians (80.2). This link is fanciful, as he himself implicitly admits in his complaint that they have: 'neither beginning nor end, nor head nor root, but who are entirely unstable and anarchic and deceived, utterly lacking the fixity of name or regulation or rule or legislation' (80.3.3). Expanding upon their lawlessness, his first concern is that their men and women sleep together 'in the same place', which he uses, predictably, as the basis of an accusation of debauchery—notwithstanding his own admission that he has no evidence to support this charge. He bemoans

---

[37] GCS 25, p. 22. John of Damascus picks up this same association in his anti-Messalian list, *De haeresibus* 80 (PTS 22, p. 41). Timothy of Constantinople associates the Messalians or Euchites with 'Marcianites, Enthusiasts, Choreuites, Lampetians, Adelphians, and Eustathians' (PG 86 45C–48A). The difficulty the heresiologists have in pinning down the Messalians to any one name, let alone a coherent set of beliefs, is an indication of the fundamentally artificial nature of their enterprise.

[38] *Panarion* 80 (GCS 37, pp. 484–96).

their willingness to accept any name one might give them—whether prophet or Christ or patriarch or angel. He criticizes their irregular habits of eating and their failure to observe the fasts. He attacks their radical poverty and irresponsible mendicancy, using this as a cue for an excursus upon the necessity for work and a suggestion that Messalian laziness may derive from Mani (80.4.3).[39]

Epiphanius has little success in making the various charges stick: only the accusation of disdain for manual labour was to play a major role in the subsequent condemnation of the Messalians. On the question of sexual impropriety, he admits the existence of continent persons within the communities, yet claims that they are such only out of 'ignorance'. Many of his accusations recall those he makes against Eustathius and his followers.[40] His account bears the traits of a second-hand condemnation of a form of asceticism with which he is both unfamiliar and uncomfortable. It may be accepted only in broad outline and his various inferences must be considered to be of dubious validity. Perhaps his main contribution is the remark that there were Messalians in Antioch, and that they had originated in Mesopotamia. We appear to have in Epiphanius a hazy description of early Mesopotamian asceticism, already viewed with suspicion by the Greek ecclesiastical hierarchy.

The remainder of our evidence centres on a series of anti-Messalian synods and councils held between *c.*390 and 431. These councils reflect an instinctive suspicion similar to that noted in Epiphanius. We have few details directly from the councils. The bulk of our material is drawn from writers working at various intervals after the events. As will be shown, this evidence is highly problematic and is not as illuminating as might be desired.

Photius, working in the ninth century from a sixth-century codex, provides our first scrap of information: 'Read the synod held at Side against the heresy of the Messalians or Euchites or Adelphians. Amphilochius of Iconium presided over the synod;

---

[39] This alleged link with Mani helps elucidate the association with the Satanians, whom Epiphanius holds to teach the superior strength of evil. Theodoret also writes of the Euchites as 'suffering from the illness of the Manichaeans' (*History of the Monks of Syria* III.16: SC 234, p. 278). John of Damascus presents them as holding 'that things are evil by nature' (J 13).

[40] *Panarion* 75 (GCS 37, pp. 333–40).

twenty-five other bishops sat with him.'[41] This is the sole historical reference to the synod of Side. It is generally dated to *c*.390. Photius continues:

Read in the same book the synodical letter of the same council to the great Flavian of Antioch, giving an account of the things that were done. Thereupon [Flavian] himself gathered a synod against the same heretics, together with three bishops, Bizos of Seleucia, Marouthas of the Sufarene peoples, and Samus; thirty priests and deacons also attended.[42]

Photius records the condemnation of the Messalian leader Adelphius and his companions Sabbas, 'the usurper of the monastic habit, called the castrate', the other Sabbas, Eustathius of Edessa, Dadoes, and Symeon. Antioch is presented by Photius as the launch of a concerted campaign against the Messalians directed by the indefatigable Flavian.[43] Photius does not, however, record any doctrinal issues. For this we must turn to Theodoret, who provides some very vivid descriptions. In the *Ecclesiastical History* (AD 440s) he records the ruse used by Flavian to coax the elderly Messalian leader Adelphius, whom he'd had brought from Edessa, to reveal his suspect doctrine, allegedly eliciting the following response:

[Adelphius] said, 'In truth holy baptism procures no benefit in those to whom it is accorded; only assiduous prayer (τὴν σπουδαίαν εὐχήν) is able to expel the indwelling demon. For all who are born draw from the first father along with their nature a servitude to demons. When these demons are expelled by assiduous prayer, then the All-Holy Spirit visits and manifests his presence both sensibly and visibly, freeing the body from the movement of passions and entirely liberating the soul from inclination towards base things; being thus entirely loosed, the body no longer needs the coercion of fasting, nor the bridle of teaching [...].

---

[41] *Bibliotheca* 52 (Henry, vol. i, pp. 36–7). On the dating of the codex see Gribomont, 'Le Dossier', 614.

[42] *Bibliotheca* 52 (Henry, vol. i, p. 37). Marouthas' see was Maiperqat/Martyropolis in Armenia. Bizos was bishop of Seleucia near Antioch, Samus of Seleucia in Isauria (see Stewart, '*Working the Earth of the Heart*', 30. On Marouthas see also Elizabeth Key Fowden, *The Barbarian Plain*, 44–59). The dating is problematic; Stewart argues for the anteriority and greater importance of Antioch over Side, *pace* Dörries. It would certainly make sense for the ecclesiastical campaign to begin from Antioch and to proceed to Side, the gateway to Asia Minor, particularly as this accords with Theodoret's account of the expulsion of the Messalians from Syria and their taking refuge in Pamphylia (*HE* IV.II: GCS 44, p. 231).

[43] *Bibliotheca* 52 (Henry, vol. i, pp. 37–8).

[Such a one] sees future things clearly and sees the Divine Trinity with his own eyes.' (*HE* IV.11)[44]

Theodoret notes the leaders of the sect as, 'Dadoes, Sabbas, Adelphius, Symeon, Hermas, and others' (ibid.). He also mentions certain other deviant features: their being possessed by a demon they think to be the Holy Spirit, their lack of enthusiasm for manual work, and their claim of a prophetic quality to their dreams. This characterization of Messalianism is repeated in all its essentials in his *Haereticarum fabularum compendium* IV.11 (AD 453).[45]

The synods of Side and Antioch evidently proved unable to control the Messalians, notwithstanding the best efforts of Flavian and other like-minded bishops. The tumour was, it seemed, malignant, and was proving increasingly difficult to define, isolate, and remove. None of our immediate sources are able to provide a convincing picture of the nature of Messalianism. We know *that* Messalianism was; we do not know *what* it was. We are led to the conclusion that 'Messalianism' was little more than a sobriquet for a radical ascetic tendency stemming from the Syrian East, and, at this stage, little welcomed or understood by the Greek bishops who confronted it.[46] The amorphous quality of the tendency made it extremely difficult to control. The only apparent solution was to extract evidence of doctrinal deviation in order to secure its condemnation as a specific heresy. It is in this context that we may understand the condemnation of Constantinople (426), as confirmed and amplified by the Third Ecumenical Council of Ephesus (431).

Patriarch Atticus (406–25) wrote to the bishops of Pamphylia demanding the expulsion of the Messalians.[47] The Council of Constantinople which took place on the occasion of the enthronement of his successor, Sisinnius, continued this policy with enthusiasm, marking a noticeable intensification of the anti-Messalian campaign. The council produced a synodical letter condemning

[44] GCS 44, pp. 229–31. Note that some editions (e.g. PG) have a different numbering here.

[45] PG 83 429–32.

[46] The term 'tendency' is used advisedly: 'movement' or 'sect' implies a greater degree of cohesion than is in evidence. Equally the term 'Greek' is used in its linguistic and cultural sense—not, of course, in its ethnic sense.

[47] Photius, *Bibliotheca* 52 (Henry, vol. i, p. 38).

the Messalians, signed by Sisinnius and Theodotus of Antioch, again directed primarily at Pamphylia.[48] The condemnation was enforced by imperial decree in 428 and confirmed by the Council of Ephesus. The question of the Messalians was raised at Ephesus by Valerian of Iconium and Amphilochius of Side, bishops of the infected regions of Lycaonia and Pamphylia. The Definition of the council against the Messalians commends the work of these bishops against the 'so-called Messalians or Euchites or Enthusiasts, or whatever name this most filthy heresy goes under'. The synodical letter of Constantinople was read out and reconfirmed, with reference also being made to actions taken in Alexandria.[49] The Definition orders that those suspected of Messalianism must anathematize the heresy 'according to things contained in the aforementioned synodical letter'. Valerian is then recorded as having presented to the council a Messalian *Asceticon*, which was duly anathematized—along with anything 'savouring of like impiety'.[50] Photius, in his account of the council, centres the action squarely on the *Asceticon*, telling us that 'the blasphemous and heretical propositions contained in their ascetic book were struck with anathema'.[51]

We do not have any definite record of the precise nature of the charges on which the condemnations of the Messalians at Constantinople and Ephesus were secured. It is, however, commonly assumed that elements, at least, of the charges have been

---

[48] Ibid., pp. 38–9.

[49] The reference to Alexandria seems to be a way of confirming the legitimacy of Cyril's somewhat less harsh approach to the Messalians (see the footnote following).

[50] The Definition is given in Kmosko, *Liber graduum*, clxxxiv–clxxxvi; Schwartz (*ACO* i.1.7, pp. 117–18), and also in Tanner's splendidly handy edition and translation (vol. i, pp. 66–7). Cyril of Alexandria was accused, by the Antiochene party led by John of Antioch, of exercising too much leniency towards the Messalians, even receiving into communion these heretics 'who think like Celestius and Pelagius' and cynically packing the council with, amongst others, Pamphylian Messalians (Schwartz, *ACO* i.1.3, p. 39; i.1.5, p. 126). The mention of the Pelagians is doubtless largely a counter to Cyril's attempts to tar Nestorius with a Pelagian brush and has similarly scant justification. The idea that Cyril brought Messalians to Ephesus is clearly absurd, given the condemnation of the Messalians effected at the council. In his *Epistola ad Amphilochium* (*Ep.* 82) (PG 77 376AB), Cyril urges Amphilochius of Side to be satisfied with a simple abjuration of the heresy of the Messalians and to avoid taxing simple people with subtle questions about specific propositions. It is this kind of pastoral concern that may have led to the suspicions of the dissenting party at Ephesus— suspicions which may have prompted the specific reference in the Definition to actions taken against the Messalians in Alexandria. *AP* (Alph.), Lucius 1 (PG 65 253BC), provides further evidence of a Messalian presence in Egypt before *c.*450.

[51] *Bibliotheca* 52 (Henry, vol. i, p. 39).

preserved in the anti-Messalian lists of Timothy of Constantinople (*c*.600) and of John of Damascus (before 750).[52] Both sets of lists are based on earlier documents and are structured around the same central themes as those recorded by Theodoret. It should be recognized that these lists supply, with Theodoret, almost all the specific information we have as to the nature of the Messalian heresy: in other words, it is they who tell us, or purport to tell us, what Messalianism is. Certain propositions contained in the lists, particularly in that of John, do indeed correspond in varying degrees to parts of the Macarian corpus. This correspondence has been the basis of the twentieth-century exposure of Macarius as a Messalian (and indeed of his writings as the infamous *Asceticon*). It must, however, be acknowledged that the very foundation of our evidence is deeply problematic. Stewart has carefully noted the very substantial difficulties raised by the available evidence. An obvious danger, he argues, is that of circularity: the anti-Messalian lists supply virtually all our detailed information as to the exact nature of the Messalian tendency. The anti-Messalian lists correspond in some degree to the Macarian writings. Therefore, so it is argued, Macarius is Messalian. As Stewart points out, it makes as much sense, on this basis, to call the Messalians Macarian, as it does to call Macarius Messalian. We simply do not have a reliable criterion by which to judge the supposedly 'Messalian' character of the Macarian writings. In the absence of such a criterion, the term 'Messalian' bears no technical precision. Certainly to speak of Messalianism as a coherent movement with a definable creed is stretching the evidence. What, therefore, are we to make of the Messalian question? Is it truly, as Kallistos Ware once put it in conversation, 'a swamp from which there is no apparent exit'?

---

[52] Timothy of Constantinople, *De iis qui ad ecclesiam ab haereticis accedunt* (Kmosko, *Liber graduum*, ccxxi–ccxxx; PG 86 48A–52C) [ = T ]. John of Damascus, *De haeresibus* 80 (Kmosko ccxxx–ccxli; PTS 22 42–6) [ = J ]. References to these lists will be in simple numerical order. The only complication comes in the later sections of John's list (J 19–37) which form a block of text rather than a straightforward list. Here I follow the subdivisons adopted by Kmosko, running them on to produce a list of thirty-seven propositions in total. Although this sounds complicated, it should present no difficulties to the reader when working from the text. Stewart, '*Working the Earth of the Heart*', has performed the great service of arranging these lists thematically in an appendix and provided a table of correspondences with the Macarian corpus. The most complete treatment of the relation between the lists and the works of Macarius-Symeon is that of Fitschen, *Messalianismus und Antimessalianismus*.

To answer this we must begin by turning back to the anti-Messalian lists. Quite apart from the warning concerning circularity, it must be emphasized that the correspondence between the lists and the Macarian writings is by no means straightforward. Many passages in the Macarian corpus formally contradict the central Messalian propositions recorded in the lists. This is particularly clear on the question of the efficacy of the sacraments (T 2, 12; J 4–6, 22, 25), the importance of manual labour (T 13; J 19), the place of dreams and visions in the spiritual life (T 14), the understanding of *apatheia* (T 9, 16; J 27–8), the prospect of a bodily vision of the Holy Trinity (T 5) and the nature of evil (J 13). On all these points Macarius addresses precisely the same concerns as those reflected in the lists, albeit from a rather different perspective.[53] Furthermore, many propositions have no correspondence whatsoever with the works of Macarius, for example the idea of fire as a demiurge (J 11), willingness to dissolve marriages and receive runaway slaves (J 31), and the promotion of women to positions of authority (T 18). In other propositions, we are presented simply with analogous language or imagery, such as the use of nuptial imagery or the picturing of demons as smoke or serpents. At most, we are dealing with elements wrenched from their context, simplified, and distorted. In the majority of cases such points of contact only serve to illustrate the shared ascetic milieu of Macarius and the Messalian tendency.[54]

Only in a very few cases, principally in John's list, is the correspondence between the condemned propositions and the Macarian writings at all clear.[55] Even in these instances, the distortion is

---

[53] This question of the relationship between the anti-Messalian lists and the works of Macarius is a major sub-theme of this work. All the themes mentioned will be returned to in the course of this study.

[54] For example, the indwelling demon which remains lodged within after baptism and is expelled only by prayer. This may be linked to Macarius' teaching on the enduring legacy of indwelling sin persisting even after baptism and the initial experience of grace. His teaching is, as we shall see, balanced by a very positive evaluation of baptism and insistence on the insufficiency of human effort in the spiritual struggle. One has to suppose either a wilful misunderstanding of Macarius (by the Messalians) or a misrepresentation (by the ecclesiastical hierarchy) if one is to make such a link. It is simpler and probably more correct to suppose that we are dealing in this case with evidence of a shared milieu rather than attempting to force a connection with Macarius.

[55] This fits with John's claim that his list has been gathered 'from the book' of the Messalians (PTS 22, p. 42). Note the alternative reading 'books' in PG and in Kmosko, *Liber graduum*.

patent. For example, T 7 and J 15 have it that: 'they say that seed and word fell into Mary'. This is a corruption of the Macarian 'the divine seed is the Word, who fell into Mary the Theotokos' (II 52.3). Clearly there has been an attempt here to produce a Christological heresy by the insertion of the 'and'.[56] In other instances, no attempt is made to explain why a given proposition should be deemed heretical, as in the case of the assertions that man must acquire two souls (J 16), that participation in the Holy Spirit be 'in all perception and plenitude' (ἐν αἰσθήσει πάσῃ καὶ πληροφορίᾳ) (J 7),[57] and that 'the Cross in light can be revealed to those that pray and that at one time a man was found standing by the altar and that three loaves mixed with oil were brought to him'(J 18).

If the elements in the lists that do closely correspond with the Macariana accurately reflect the Ephesine condemnation of the *Asceticon*—a big 'if', but we do need some way of explaining their presence in the lists—then we may allow that this book, an ascetic florilegium compiled by the Messalians, did indeed contain a selection of Macarian material. It can only have been an unrepresentative selection, a series of extracts wrenched from their context and heavily distorted.[58] This 'ascetic book' was, in this scenario, read by the Church hierarchy at Ephesus with the aim of detecting affinities with an already established construct of the nature of the

---

[56] Similarly, T 6, following a charge of unitarianism without any foundation in the Macarian writings: 'that the divine nature is altered and changes into whatever it has willed and desired, so that it can be co-mingled with souls worthy of itself'. This is essentially a misrepresentation of the Macarian teaching on the extension of the mystery of the Incarnation in the souls of the worthy and the related explanation of the Old Testament theophanies (II 4.9–13). The same pattern of misrepresentation is also evident in T 11, a distortion of the perfectly traditional doctrine of *theosis*.

[57] In this instance, the phrase is being associated with the Messalian claim that the visitation of the Holy Spirit is sensible *and* visible (T 3; Theodoret, *HE* IV.11, cited above).

[58] This fits with Fitschen's presentation, in his *Messalianismus und Antimessalianismus*, of Adelphius as the bridge between the Macarian circle and the Messalian heresy, an adept of Macarian theology responsible for a radical interpretation and selective manipulation of Macarius' teaching—hence the bridge between Macarius and Messalianism. Macarius was, in short, the 'unfreiwilliger Stichwortgeber der Bewegung'. Fitschen recognizes that Macarius consciously set himself against the kind of teaching propagated by Adelphius, but submits that Macarius is anti-Messalian only in the sense that he opposes the nascent abnormalities of the movement and not as a reformer of fully-fledged Messalianism. He is, therefore, best understood as being 'pre-Messalian'. I find a substantial congruity between Fitschen's analysis and my own, yet I would hesitate to be quite so confident in speaking about Messalianism and pre-Messalianism, given that we know so little about the real nature of Messalianism, let alone that of pre-Messalianism.

Messalian heresy. That is to say, the *Asceticon* was judged by its affinities with an established list of condemned propositions, built up from Side to Constantinople. Those elements in the anti-Messalian lists that do correspond closely to the Macariana may have been extracted from the *Asceticon* in order to provide additional confirmation of its Messalian character. Thus the specific propositions that Photius records as having been taken from the *Asceticon* and condemned at Ephesus may be seen as constituting an additional layer of anti-Messalian material, one drawn in part, ironically enough, from the chief force for reform within the Messalian tendency itself. One important supporting argument for this theory is the presence in John's list of the theme of the coexistence of sin and grace (J 3), a theme which contradicts the central Messalian proposition that the sensible advent of grace brings one from a state of demonic infestation to one of inalienable *apatheia*. It is precisely this black-and-white schema which Macarius and the anti-Messalian lists attack. The contradiction within John's list supports the claim that the palpably Macarian material contained in the lists represents an additional layer of material, selected because of its superficial affinities with the earlier material, and on at least one point inconsistent with that material.[59]

It is clear that Constantinople–Ephesus represents the culmination of an attempt to systematize, and thereby to destroy, an ascetic tendency deemed to be deviant. In short, the formation of heresy from a form-less tendency. As part of this process, some portion of Macarian material can plausibly be argued to have been condemned at Ephesus within the Messalian *Asceticon*. If this is the case, it would represent a curb upon certain of the less guarded statements of Macarius as understood by the more radical elements within the Messalian tendency and, implicitly, a rejection of the Macarian approach to reform of that tendency. What we do not have is a direct condemnation of Macarius as a Messalian in any meaningful sense. At most, a very partial and unrepresentative selection of Macarian material came into play in the last stage of an attempt to systematize an extreme ascetic tendency. That this attempt was to some extent an artificial one,

---

[59] Here I disagree with Stewart, '*Working the Earth of the Heart*', 58: 'One can do no more than note that that the Ps-Macarian material in John's list does not contradict the other lists.'

is indicated by the persistence of groups labelled 'Messalian' into the later fifth century and beyond. The term eventually becomes a sobriquet meaning little more than a perceived excessive emphasis on the conscious experience of God in prayer.[60] Messalianism may never have been much more than a broad experiential tendency with little internal coherence. Our sources give us no exact information as to its nature, but only supply details of its formalization into heresy. As pointed out above, the circularity of the evidence makes it rather pointless to speak of the 'Messalianism' of Macarius, even if the correlation between Macarius and the Messalian propositions were more straightforward than it in fact appears to be.[61] How, therefore, are we to escape from this 'swamp'? The answer, I submit, is to look beyond the Messalian controversy, and to examine the reception of the Macarian corpus within the wider Christian tradition. This, I believe, will provide the 'exit' for which we are searching.

## 1.4 Additional Note: The *Vita Hypatii*

Gribomont suggests, purely as a hypothesis, that the *Asceticon* may have been brought to Constantinople by Alexander the Acemite, and there fallen into Valerian's hands.[62] To support this claim

[60] For instance as applied to SS Symeon the New Theologian and Gregory Palamas. By this time, the term Messalian was used as a synonym for Bogomil. It is a characteristic of heresiology to stigmatize newer heresies with the name of an older heresy, see for example the exposure of one of the priests of the Blachernae palace as a 'Messalian' in the reign of Emperor Alexius Comnenus (Anna Comnena, *Alexiad* x.2). It is almost certain that this priest was a Bogomil; Bogomilism was at that time enjoying something of a vogue in Constantinople, see Obolensky, *The Byzantine Commonwealth*, 126. On the Bogomils, see also Runciman, *The Medieval Manichee* and Obolensky, *The Bogomils*. The alleged Manichaean dualism of the Messalians helps explain this connection.

[61] In this respect, the remark of Irénée Hausherr, 'the great spiritual heresy of the Christian East is Messalianism', in 'L'Erreur fondamentale et la logique du Messalianisme', appears to be based on a false set of presuppositions. In selecting the excessive emphasis on the conscious experience of God in prayer as the fundamental error of Messalianism, Hausherr goes beyond the evidence, producing from the condemned propositions a systematization of what was already a systematization. Compare Karl Rahner, 'Ein messalianisches Fragment über die Taufe', 262. Rahner defines the 'Grundanschauung' of Messalianism as 'consisting in the identification of what man actually and essentially is [...] with his subjective experience in a pseudo-mystical psychological empiricism'. This attempt to define a 'governing principle' of Messalianism, like that of Hausherr, goes beyond the evidence. Such definitions have contributed to the 'pan-Messalian' attitude that spots Messalianism wherever the conscious experience of grace is mentioned.

[62] 'Le Dossier', 617–19 and 625, 'Note additionelle'.

he cites Nilus of Ancyra's association of Alexander with Adelphius
(*De voluntaria paupertate* 21). The only grounds adduced for this
association are a common disdain for manual labour. The fact
that Alexander's band of itinerant monks disturbed and were
expelled from Constantinople precisely in 426 is, as Gribomont
observes, 'plus qu'une coïncidence'.[63] This troublesome band
were given refuge by Hypatius, abbot of the monastery of the
Rufinianae, south of Chalcedon (*VH* 41). In a postscript to his
article, Gribomont notes the discovery by Bartelink, editor of the
*Vita Hypatii*, of certain parallels between the Macariana and the
*Vita*.[64] Bartelink is inclined to connect these parallels to the Syrian
origin of the author of the *Vita*, Callinicus, whereas Gribomont
suggests that the parallels may rather be explained by supposing
that it was in fact Alexander who introduced the Macariana to
Hypatius and his community.

In view of the historical interest of the question, some account
can be made here of the relation between the *Vita* and the
Macariana. Bartelink adduces a parallel between Macarius, II
27.4: Οὐκ ἔστιν οὖν τὸ τυχὸν ὁ Χριστιανισμός and *VH* 48.1:
Τεκνία, οὐκ ἔστι τὸ τυχὸν Χριστιανισμός. This affirmation that
Christianity is 'no common thing' may have been a common
slogan within oral monastic culture, but is not preserved in writing
elsewhere. A second parallel concerns the constant hope for deliverance—if not today, then tomorrow. Macarius, II 26.11 advises
one to tell oneself: ἐὰν σήμερον οὐκ ἐλυτρώθην, αὔριον λυτροῦμαι.
This advice is repeated word for word in *VH* 63.20: κἂν μὴ
σήμερον ἐλυτρώθην, αὔριον λυτροῦμαι. Other parallels can be
readily accessed in Bartelink's work. To these can be added *VH*
48.25: the illumination of the inner man ἐν τῷ κρυπτῷ τῆς καρδίας
ἐργαστηρίῳ and Macarius, I 2.4.4: demonic activity ἐν τῷ κρυπτῷ
τῆς καρδίας ἐργαστηρίῳ. Notwithstanding the different agencies
presented as acting upon this 'hidden workshop of the heart', this

---

[63] Note that the *Life* of Alexander (ed. Stoop) tells us that he had already angered
Theodotus of Antioch, the chief co-signatory of the synodical letter of 426, during a recent
spell in that city (38–40). Alexander is also recorded in his *Life* as having been accused of
heresy in Constantinople (48). Given his Syrian background, emphasis on unceasing
prayer, eschewal of manual labour, and lack of respect for civil and ecclesiastical authority,
it can be assumed that the heresy in question was Messalianism. On Alexander, see also
Gatier, 'Un moine sur la frontière, Alexandre l'Acémète en Syrie'.

[64] Bartelink, 'Text Parallels between the *Vita Hypatii* of Callinicus and the Pseudo-
Macariana', reiterated in his *Vie d'Hypatios*, 38–41.

unusual and arresting phrase provides a strong indication of a Macarian connection.

All the parallels mentioned occur in the discourses of Hypatius preserved in the *Vita*. They represent occasional felicitous borrowings from an author held in esteem and are not central to Hypatius' teaching. Nevertheless, they constitute a strong case for the presence of a collection of Macarian material at the Rufinianae. If brought by Callinicus, who had arrived before the Alexander episode, or by Alexander himself, the writings will have reached the Rufinianae before or during 426. While the hypothesis linking these events to Valerian's acquisition of the *Asceticon* remains purely speculative, the parallels given do provide useful evidence as to the early circulation of the Macarian writings—to the actual teaching of which we may now turn.

# 2

# The Lineaments of the Macarian Vision

Macarius is far from systematic in his teaching, yet is remarkably consistent in his language and imagery.[1] He has relatively few 'master themes', pursued with ever increasing ingenuity and virtuosity. The present chapter is a short outline of these central themes, given as a prelude to the investigation of the place of the Macarian writings within the wider Christian tradition.

## 2.1  Sources

No Christian author writes in isolation, and Macarius is no exception. He is reticent as to his sources but is by no means unusual in this. The only texts quoted are either biblical or apocryphal; the only non-scriptural characters mentioned are Aristotle, Plato, and Isocrates: great cities of knowledge laid waste because of the absence of the Spirit of God (II 42.1). Macarius certainly draws much from the Syriac Christian tradition: the feminine quality ascribed to the Holy Spirit, the tradition of poetic symbolism, the extensive use of clothing metaphors and nuptial imagery, and the concept of the two souls. The Syriac background is, however, by no means the only thought-world to have influenced him. Macarius is often presented as an example of biblical or Semitic Christianity, over and against the Hellenizing current associated with Origen and Evagrius. The attempt to juxtapose and hold apart these 'currents' does not stand up to analysis in the case of Macarius. Much of his thought-world is fundamentally Hellenic in inspiration. He works within the type–antitype, noetic–sensible framework, more typical of the Hellenic than the pre-fifth-century Syriac tradition. His pattern of exegesis and Christology is that of

---

[1] The fullest work on the Macarian teaching remains Dörries, *Die Theologie des Makarios-Symeon*. It is, however, somewhat limited by its peculiarly restricted choice of themes and by its decidedly Lutheran perspective.

the Alexandrine tradition. His understanding of the place of light in the spiritual life is, like that of Evagrius, strongly marked by Origen. His anthropology is centred upon the heart, a Semitic insight, yet he also gives full rein to the νοῦς, the 'spiritual intellect', and to noetic contemplation.[2]

## 2.2 The Mutual Indwelling of Man and God

The compiler of Collection II placed at its head a quite remarkable piece of exegesis which reflects one of the guiding principles of the Macarian writings: the prospect of the mutual indwelling of man and God. Hence the vision of the prophet Ezekiel (Ezek. 1, 10) is of the soul become the 'throne of glory', the 'dwelling-place' of God (II 1.2).[3] In this divine indwelling the purpose of man's creation is fulfilled (II 46.4). Macarius stresses that the movement is a double one. As he puts it in II 6.5: 'the throne of the Godhead is our intellect, and again, the throne of our intellect is the Godhead and the Spirit'. Similarly: 'God serves the soul in the city of the body and it serves God in the heavenly city. The soul has inherited God in heaven and God has inherited the soul upon the earth. The Lord has become the inheritance of the soul and the soul the inheritance of the Lord' (II 46.4). This mutuality does not, however, imply confusion of nature:

He is God, the soul is not God. He is Lord, it a servant. He is Creator, it a creature. He is maker, it a thing made. There is nothing in common between his nature and that of the soul. But through his infinite, ineffable, and inconceivable love and compassion, he has been pleased to dwell in this thing of his making, this intellectual creation, this precious and especial work. (II 49.4)

Thus God's love bridges the ontological gap between creature and Creator.

---

[2] We shall return to the supposed Hellenic–Semitic dichotomy below, particularly in Ch. 4. More detailed explorations of Macarius' sources will be undertaken as they arise.

[3] Note the obvious link with the Jewish *merkabah* tradition. Intriguingly, Macarius draws on the chariot image from Plato's *Phaedrus* in his treatment of Ezekiel's vision. This is a nice sign, at the very opening of the most widespread collection of the homilies, of Macarius' double inheritance.

## 2.3   Cosmology and Anthropology

While the distinction between Creator and creature remains the
primary division of the Macarian universe, the writings also
employ a noetic–sensible framework, thus: 'the world of phenomena is a type and icon and pattern of the invisible and eternal
world of the Godhead' (i 28.1.7); 'all visible things are shadows of
invisible things' (i 23.1.3); and 'the root of every sensible thing is
the noetic' (i 41.3). This framework informs the whole pattern of
Macarian exegesis. Thus the vision of Ezekiel also prefigured,
besides the outer reality, 'a hidden and divine reality' (ii 1.1).
Scripture is constantly said to indicate a given truth 'hiddenly'
(i 28.1.1, 10.2.1, 61.2.1) or to invite us to a 'higher contemplation'
(*EM* 7.11). It must be understood 'spiritually' and not 'according to
the flesh' (i 24.1). Paul's injunction that women be veiled in
church, for example, came as part of the general call to temperance made by the early Church, but its deeper meaning is as
a figure of the Holy Spirit's protective veiling of the Church
(ii 12.15).

The noetic–sensible framework is also used in an anagogical
way, recalling the speech of Diotima in Plato's *Symposium*: by
directing the 'invisible and intellectual eye of the mind' it is
possible to receive 'intellection (κατανόησις) from visible things of
heavenly good things' (iii 16.6.1). It also underlies the doctrine
of the spiritual senses, namely the understanding that there are in
man faculties corresponding in some way with the five senses, yet
capable of apprehending divine realities.[4] The noetic–sensible
framework, albeit less significant than the Creator–creation distinction, is nevertheless one of the principal structures of the
Macarian world-view. Allied to the symbolism of the Syriac
tradition, this framework explains the abundance of images, parallels, and vivid similes in the writings. As Macarius puts it in iii
16.3.1: 'All these things I have described with the use of visible
things, through birds and beasts and all things which are seen,
since it is impossible to express or to explain spiritual things
otherwise.'

---

[4] An element he owes to Origen, see Rahner, 'Le Début d'une doctrine des cinq sens
spirituels chez Origène' and Fraigneau-Julien, *Les Sens spirituels et la vision de Dieu selon Syméon
le nouveau théologien*.

Macarian anthropology is marked by the location of the intellect in the heart:

The heart governs and rules the whole bodily organ; and when grace takes hold of the pastures of the heart, it rules over all the members and the thoughts. For there is the intellect, and all the thoughts of the soul and its expectation, thus [through the heart] grace penetrates to all the members of the body. (II 15.20)

The heart is the centre of the human person, the point at which the soul and body meet. As a physical organ it is linked to all the members of the body; as the spiritual centre of the human person it is connected with all the faculties of the soul.[5] The heart is the deep self, a vast and shifting domain of which we have only a dim apprehension:

The heart has infinite depth. In it are dining rooms and bedchambers, doors and porches, many service rooms and passageways. In it is the workshop of righteousness and that of unrighteousness, death and life, good commerce and the contrary. (II 15.32)

Although the heart is a small vessel, it contains dragons and lions, venomous beasts and all the stockpiles of evil, rough and uneven paths and chasms. Likewise God and the angels are there, as are life and the Kingdom, light and the apostles, the heavenly cities and the treasuries of grace. All things are there. (II 43.7)

The heart is far more than simply the physical organ or the seat of the emotions and affections. It is both of these, yet also much more, principally because it is seen to be the dwelling-place of the intellect. The intellect is the 'governor' of the heart (II 15.33). It directs the heart as the charioteer his chariot (II 15.34). It is at the very centre of the heart as the pupil is in the eye (II 43.7). This location of the intellect in the heart has some affinities with Stoic thought although Macarius doubtless simply draws it directly from the Bible. By virtue of his understanding of the place of the heart, Macarius is able to affirm the unity of the human person and the participation of the body in the spiritual life. To illustrate this he takes the Transfiguration as his paradigm:

As the body of the Lord, when he went up onto the mountain, was glorified and transfigured into the divine glory and infinite light, so also

---

[5] On the heart, see Guillaumont, 'Le Coeur chez les spirituels grecs' and 'Les Sens des noms du coeur dans l'Antiquité'.

are the bodies of the saints glorified and resplendent. For just as the inner glory of Christ covered his body and shone forth, so in the same way, on that day, the power of Christ which the saints [now] have within, will be poured out upon their bodies.   (II 15.38)

Similarly, the light that shone from the face of Moses is taken as a prefiguration of the resurrection glory of the body (II 5.10). The eschaton is not historicized in Macarius; it is realized in this life in the soul, but is manifested outwardly only at the general resurrection.

Macarius associates the image of God principally with the soul. He observes: 'It was not of Michael and Gabriel, the archangels, that God said, "Let us make [man] after our image and likeness", but of the intellective essence (νοερὰ οὐσία) of man, that is, his immortal soul' (II 15.22). Its dignity is supreme: the entire creation cannot equal the worth of a single soul (I 27.2.6; II 15.43). The body is in a sense the icon of the soul, the image of the *imago Dei* (I 18.7.1–3). The soul is composed of four ruling faculties: the will, the conscience, the intellect, and the capacity to love (II 1.3). Macarius expressly links the faculty of will to the image and emphasizes that the soul is in balance:

You are [created] 'according to the image and likeness', because just as God is self-determining, and does what he wills [...], so you are self-determining, even, if you so choose, to your own destruction.   (II 15.23)

For the soul is neither of the nature of the Godhead, nor of the nature of the darkness of evil, but is an intellectual, comely, great, wonderful, and beautiful creature, the image and likeness of God.   (II 1.7)

The soul is also in some sense a 'subtle body':

Now each thing—whether angel, soul, or demon—is, in conformity with its own nature, a body. No matter how subtle it may be, each thing possesses a body whose subtlety of substance, form, and image, corresponds to the subtlety of its nature. Just as the body is gross in substance so the soul is subtle by nature [...] and the soul has clothed itself in the whole visible body and all its members, becoming co-mingled with them, and through them accomplishing everything it does in this life.   (II 4.9)[6]

This notion of subtlety recalls Stoic materialism. It is evidently an idea to which Macarius attaches great importance, calling it 'a

---

[6] Cf. Origen, *De Principiis* 2.2.1 (GCS 22, pp. III–12).

subject which is both subtle and profound' (II 4.9). One should not, however, conclude that Macarius' anthropology is crudely materialistic. He also calls the soul 'bodiless' (II 15.28, 53.6) and speaks of it with terms such as εὔπτερος (well-winged), ἐλαφρός (light), and εὐκίνητος (swiftly moving) (III 26.6.3, 26.7.2). The concept of the 'subtle body' in Macarius would seem to correspond to the Platonic ὄχημα, or vehicle, of the soul.[7] Macarius goes on to exhort:

> Let no one suppose that the soul is some small thing, given that it dwells in a small body and is entirely within that body. See, it is in the body, yet also outside of the body, wholly in it but also wholly outside it in its mind and its thoughts. [...] The [purified] soul serves Christ in heaven entirely in spirit and also serves him entirely in its body. The soul dilates in mind such that it is everywhere, and serves the Lord when and where it wishes.   (III 26.4.3–6.3).

It is clear that in his anthropology Macarius makes full use of the complementary dimensions of heart and intellect.

## 2.4   The Fall

Macarius has a keen awareness of the tragedy of the Fall. Adam lost his glory, and was clothed in darkness and enslaved by the prince of darkness (II 30.7). Satan has covered the soul of man with 'the purple of darkness', thereby also subjecting the body to suffering and corruption (II 2.1). The power of Satan has filled the hearts of all the sons and daughters of Adam and covered their wills as with smoke (III 1.3.3). All humanity has been affected by the Fall: the closing of Paradise, the placing of the flaming sword and the Cherubim at its gates to deny man entry 'must be regarded as actual events, but they are also realities encountered inwardly by each soul; for the veil of darkness—the fire of the worldly spirit—surrounds the heart, preventing the intellect from communing with God' (I 2.3.12–13). This 'veil' prevents the soul from grasping its true nature and from perceiving its Creator (III 26.4.4). The soul was to have progressed and grown to full maturity, but through the transgression 'plunged into a sea of

---

[7] Cf. Dodds, *Proclus: The Elements of Theology*, 205 f. Dodds discusses the roots of the concept of the vehicle of the soul in the classical tradition in Appendix II of the same work.

unknowing, an ocean of forgetfulness and a mass of delusion'
(I 3.5.6). It lapsed into a state of savagery (III 8.3.5), lost in desert
places and guided only by the 'bestial, wild and material intellect'
(III 4.2.2). In such a condition man was almost entirely given over
to evil, unaware of his true nature and wholly the slave of delusion.
Christ came to call man back from the abyss:

He dispelled the abyss of unknowing, the forgetfulness, and the delusion.
He broke through the closed gates of Hell and entered the deluded soul,
so that the soul, taking him as its model, might follow the commandment
and return to the first image.    (I 3.5.8)

Through the coming of Christ, mankind reaches, through the power of
baptism, the first measure of Adam, having become the master of
demons and passions, 'the last enemy which is death', laid 'under the
feet' of Adam.    (III 1.2.1)

The advent of Christ and the gift of baptism bring man out of
subjection to evil, to the stage where sin and grace coexist, to the
stage of spiritual warfare. Salvation is not a *fiat*, a compulsory
recapitulation of Adam; it also requires the co-operation of man.

## 2.5   The Coexistence of Sin and Grace: Unseen Warfare

In this stage the soul is in balance and has the capacity to determine its own fate. It is no longer enslaved to evil: 'Our intellect is
well matched, having the power to subdue evil impulses and
shameful desires through the vigour of its thought' (II 15.23).
Whilst affirming the inward struggle between sin and grace,
Macarius does not suppose an ontological dualism of good and
evil: 'Those who say that evil is a subsistent reality know nothing'
(II 16.1). He continues, 'To God there is no such thing as subsistent
evil [ . . . ]. But to us, evil is [a reality], because it dwells and acts in
the heart suggesting evil and defiling thoughts and not allowing
[us] to pray purely but rather imprisoning the intellect in this
world' (II 16.5–6). Macarius is well aware of the essentially Platonic perception of the non-subsistence of evil, yet this in no way
diminishes his keen sense of sin and spiritual struggle. He is a
deeply practical theologian. No matter what the ontological basis
of evil thoughts, such thoughts do assail the baptized Christian
and must therefore be treated very seriously. The experience of sin

and grace is allowed for good reason: 'So that by its experience of the two natures, tasting frequently both the bitterness of sin and the sweetness of grace, the soul might become more perceptive and more vigilant, so as to flee evil entirely and to attach itself wholly to the Lord' (III 12.2.2). If the soul knew only sweetness, rest, and joy, it would easily become negligent, being unaware of the immensity of the gift. Only by experiencing the bitterness of sin can the soul manifest its free will and turn to the Lord. The coexistence of sin and grace is permitted so as to educate and to form the soul.

This process gives rise to some of the most vivid metaphors of the Macarian writings. Macarius calls this struggle 'invisible warfare' (ἀόρατος πόλεμος) (I 19.1.4): his is a profoundly militant Christianity. His writings are a call to arms against the enemy powers, an exhortation to fight for an experience of grace 'in all perception and plenitude' (ἐν αἰσθήσει πάσῃ καὶ πληροφορίᾳ). The soul must undergo its own passover, tasting both the sweetness of the lamb and the bitterness of the herbs, ever being pursued by the noetic Pharaoh (II 47.7–14). At times Macarius' teaching anticipates the dark night of the soul of St John of the Cross: 'Blessed are they that pass through the fearful places of that darkness, the dread night (τὴν δεινὴν νύκτα), the dry places, and the pestilential airs of sin, and who enter into rest and joy in the gladness of the Holy Spirit' (II 55.4).

The soul must in some sense be slain (II 1.6). In order to share in the glory of the Lord, it must also participate in his sufferings:

The Lord shows himself to the soul in two aspects (ἐν δυσὶ προσώποις), with his wounds and in the glory of his light. The soul contemplates the sufferings which he suffered for it; but it also contemplates the dazzling glory of his divine light and is transfigured from glory to glory in this same image, according to [the action of] the Spirit of the Lord, and grows in both aspects—in that of the sufferings and in that of the glorious light [...]. (III 3.3.2)

Macarius is one of few writers in East or West to unite so cogently the themes of Transfiguration and Crucifixion, integrating them with the theme of the pedagogy of sin and grace in the soul. Macarius expresses devotion to 'the mystery of the cross' (II 25.4), of bearing the sign of the cross in the heart and intellect (II 15.42), and of experiencing the stigmata and sufferings of the

Lord (II 53.17; I 40.2.10).[8] The faithful soul is ever 'nailed to the Cross of Christ' (II 10.1). Such a soul shares in the Crucifxion, imitating Christ's patient acceptance of his torments and crying loudly to the one who can deliver us from death (I 3.5.10).

Sufferings are an integral part of the spiritual life, the mark of Christian endeavour (III 1.3.4). They are an essential aspect of the process whereby the soul is configured to the image of Christ (II 10.4). It is not enough to simply believe in Christ; one must also suffer with him (I 40.2.9). Although Macarius is acutely aware of the severity of the struggles that afflict all Christians, his is essentially a message of hope. We must never despair of our salvation or give up hope. Despair is, in fact, a ruse of the devil (I 60.1.1–3; II 4.24). The experienced soul, when faced with temptations, 'does not consider it strange, nor does it give up hope, for it knows that it is permitted under sufferance to be tried and educated by evil' (II 16.3). Hope founded upon experience pervades the writings. Notwithstanding their very sombre estimation of the power of evil, the tone remains profoundly positive and encouraging. Indeed, Macarius knows of certain solitaries: 'who go down into the depths of the sea of evil and into the abyss of darkness, and from the depths take hold of and bring up precious stones suitable for the crown of Christ, for the heavenly Church, for a new world, a city of light and an angelic people' (II 15.51). In all this one is reminded of the saying of a twentieth-century ascetic, St Silouan the Athonite: 'Keep thy mind in hell, and despair not.'[9]

## 2.6 Prayer and the Sacraments: The Visible and Invisible Church

In the stage of spiritual struggle, man is called upon to exercise his free will to turn from sin and to call for divine grace. This determination may be manifested in two main ways, through inner prayer and through participation in the sacraments. Collection II,

---

[8] Here we meet with an interesting parallel in the Coptic *Virtues of Saint Macarius*, in which a cherubim appeared to Macarius of Scetis, took the measure of his chest and 'crucified him upon the earth'. It is quite conceivable that material from the Macarian writings influenced this seventh- or eighth-century collection of material. The text is given in Regnault, *Les Sentences des pères du désert*, iii. 151-2.

[9] Archimandrite Sophrony, *Saint Silouan the Athonite*, 42.

the most widespread collection, tends to give the impression that Macarius marginalizes the sacraments to the point of irrelevance; this impression is, however, corrected by recourse to material from the other main collections.

Macarius' understanding of the relationship between inward struggle and participation in the mysteries is developed in his detailed treatment of the analogy between the visible and invisible Church, preserved as Logos 52 of Collection I. It is worth quoting in some detail:

> The whole visible dispensation of the Church of God came about for the sake of the living and intellectual essence of the rational soul, made in the image of God, which is the living and true Church of God. [ . . . ] For just as the worship and way of life of the Law were a shadow of the present Church of Christ, so the present visible Church is a shadow of the rational and true inner man: for the whole visible dispensation and the service of the mysteries of the Church will pass away in the final consummation, while the rational and intellectual essence of the inner man will endure [ . . . ]. (I 52.1.1–2)

One must not, therefore, put one's trust in surface appearances. True Christianity requires one to penetrate beneath the superficial and to seek out the active participation of the inner man:

> So, for this reason, God gave the Holy Spirit to the holy catholic Church, ordaining that he be present at the holy altar and in the water of holy baptism; and the Saviour granted through the apostles that the Spirit, the Comforter, should preside over (ἐπιπολάζειν) and participate in all the service of the holy Church of God according to the Lord's own words: 'And lo, I am with you always, to the end of the age.' This is so that from baptism, the altar, the eucharist of bread, and from all the mystical worship that is in the Church, believing hearts might be powerfully acted upon by the Holy Spirit [ . . . ]. (I 52.1.4)

Unworthy hearts, for their part, do not receive such divine activity—Macarius makes this quite clear. He then goes on to develop a fascinating analogy between the eucharistic offering of the Church and the ascetic offering of each Christian: 'In the visible Church, unless the readings, psalmody and gathering (σύναξις) of the people and all the ecclesiastical ordinance of the service are first accomplished, the priest does not accomplish this divine mystery of the body and blood of Christ, and the mystical communion of the believers does not take place.' Equally, the mystery is not brought to a conclusion if the 'whole ecclesiastical canon' is not first observed (1 52.2.2). The same applies to the Christian: he will not receive the gift of the Spirit without proper discipline and preparation. But it is also true if he has 'fasting, vigils, psalmody, all *ascesis* and all virtue, but the hidden activity of the Spirit is not accomplished by grace upon the altar of his heart in all perception and spiritual rest, then all his ascetic effort is in vain' (1 52.2.3).

In both examples the pattern is the same: without preparation, the consecration does not take place; without the consecration, the preparation is in vain. The treatise appears to be both a response to outside criticism and an attempt to restrain the crudely anti-sacramental leanings of the Messalian tendency. The deliberate emphasis on the parallel importance of personal ascetic effort alongside participation in the sacraments, the warning that divine grace will not embrace those unworthy of it, and the implication of the possibility of direct experience of the Holy Spirit outside the ecclesiastical structure would not, perhaps, have mollified a hierarch looking for signs of heresy, the 'savour of impiety' of which the *Acta* of Ephesus had spoken.[10] Nevertheless, Macarius leaves us in no doubt as to his adherence to the sacraments of the Church: the Holy Spirit is present in all the Church's ministry, most especially at the eucharist and in 'all the mystagogy of holy baptism' (1 52.1.5). Of the ecclesiastical hierarchy, Macarius declares: 'All bishops and ministers who hold fast to the Lord and speak in harmony with the Gospels and the apostles form, so to say, one edifice, for they build on the foundation. But if they do not speak in harmony with [the Gospels and apostles], then they are pseudo-apostles and pseudo-prophets' (1 34.16).

Macarius' understanding of the ministry of the visible Church is perfectly orthodox. It is, however, not so much an apology as a challenge.[11] He is fighting a battle on two fronts: against Messalian anti-sacramentalism and against a complacent faith in the merely outward structures of the Church. It is, however, clear that his primary interest lies with the inner struggle of the Christian, a struggle manifested most clearly in prayer.

For Macarius, prayer is the centre and focus of the spiritual life. It is given detailed attention in the course of the writings,

---

[10] Cf. above, p. 22.

[11] In contrast to, say, the *Liber graduum*, Memra 12 (PS 3 285–304).

particularly in the treatise known as the *Epistola magna* or *Great Letter*. Whilst he allows a distinction within ascetic communities between those who pray and those who work, it is equally clear that he does not regard prayer as excluding the practical virtues. All the virtues are linked: prayer to love, love to joy, joy to gentleness, and so on (*EM* 8.1). The part of Mary is superior to that of Martha, and the apostles appointed men to serve so that they might devote themselves to the ministry of the word and to prayer, preferring first things to the secondary, but both prayer and work 'spring from the same good root' (*EM* 11.10–11). Prayer is the chief pursuit of all, yet without the other virtues, it is dead (11 53.3). There is no prospect of going beyond service to the neighbour; love for God and love for the neighbour are mutually dependent (*EM* 7.2–3).

Macarius calls prayer 'sending the intellect to God' (1 6.1) and 'converse' with God (11 56.6). It can never be forced (11 19.4); it is the work of the Holy Spirit in us (11 19.9). Prayer is to be a ceaseless activity (11 33.4). The soul may hold concourse with God even in the theatre (11 15.8). The Christian should preserve the remembrance of God not only in the place of prayer, 'but in walking and speaking and eating' (11 43.3). It is to become rooted in us as though inherent in us (1 29.1.1). It must be free of all material images: we must 'estrange ourselves from every earthly thought and turn from every material conception' (1 29.1.4). Macarius warns that, 'All visible things are imaginations and the delusion of the eyes' (111 1.3.1); and that, 'The whole struggle and effort of the adversary [ ... ] is that he might distract the intellect from the remembrance of God and from the fear and love of the Lord' (*EM* 7.9).

Divested from all earthly forms, the intellect will see God's glory: 'The perfectly purified intellect continually sees the glory of the light of Christ, and is with the Lord night and day' (11 17.4). The delicate balance of Macarian anthropology, however, prevents him from lapsing into a rarefied intellectualism, as the following citation indicates:

[There are times when] someone simply comes in and kneels down and his heart is filled with divine energy and his soul rejoices in the Lord as a bride with the bridegroom [ ... ]. A man may be occupied throughout the day, and give but one hour to prayer and yet be carried away by it in the inner man, entering into the infinite depths of the other world in intense delight. His intellect is then wholly removed [from this world], raised up and carried away in such a way that it forgets all earthly thoughts, its thoughts rather being filled with and captivated by divine and heavenly things, by boundless and incomprehensible realities, by marvels which cannot be uttered by the mouth of man. In that hour he prays saying, 'Would that my soul be taken up with my prayer.'    (I 4.8)

We have here a particularly cogent example of the application of a holistic anthropology to prayer, and of the grace received by the whole human person. This brings us to the theme that unites the visible and invisible Church: both provide the occasion for grace to act.

Ascetic effort constitutes an offering: 'the first and highest elements of our whole composite nature—the intellect, the conscience, the disposition, the upright thought, the loving power of the soul—[...] must always first of all be offered to God as a holy sacrifice' (*EM* 7.11). Like the first stages of the eucharist, human endeavour constitutes a stage of preparation. The sacrifice is accomplished only by the Holy Spirit, yet for this to happen, the offering must first be made. The process is one of co-operation:

We receive salvation by grace and divine gift. But to advance to the perfect measure of spiritual maturity we also need faith and love, and to struggle to exercise our free will. Thus we become inheritors of eternal life by grace and by justice. We do not advance through divine power and grace alone, without human co-operation and effort; but neither on the other hand do we attain to the will of God and the final measure of freedom and purity as a result of our own power, effort, and strength alone, without the co-operation and assistance of the Holy Spirit.  (*EM* 3.1)

Man is called upon to express his free will, to make the offering and thereby to provide the occasion (πρόφασις) for divine grace to act (III 26.2.4). Just as a bedridden man is able to cry out for help, so is man able to call for his salvation (III 26.3.2).

## 2.7  The Trinitarian Dynamic of Salvation

The Macarian writings are profoundly Trinitarian. This dimension fits squarely within the context of the Trinitarian controversies of the fourth century. In particular, the writings provide a striking attestation of the divinity of the Holy Spirit, both anticipating and confirming the recognition of the full and equal divinity of the Spirit proclaimed at the Ecumenical Council of Constantinople (381).

We have already noted the Christocentrism of the Macarian writings, in particular his devotion to the Cross and emphasis on the *imitatio Christi*. His Christology is very much of the Alexandrine tradition. Struggling to express the two natures, he declares:

> He is God, and he is man; he is the one who lives, and he is the one who dies; he is the Lord of all, and he is the servant of all; he is the lamb, and he is the sacrifice; he is the sacrificial calf, and he is the high priest who performs the sacrifice; he is the one who suffers, and he is the one who cannot suffer. (II 52.7)

Only on one occasion does he attempt a more cataphatic approach, asserting that, 'The ensouled flesh and the Godhead became one thing, even though they are two' (I 10.4.5). In a remarkably original and precise metaphorical and theological formulation he explains:

> As wool dyed in purple results in one beautiful form (εἶδος), even though it comes from two (ἐκ δύο) natures and hypostases—and it is no longer possible for the wool to be separated from the dye, nor the dye from the wool—so the flesh with the soul united to the divinity results in one thing, that is to say one hypostasis: the heavenly God worshipped with the flesh. (I 10.4.6)[12]

Christology is not, however, Macarius' chief concern—he is far more interested in the actual purpose of the Incarnation. Summing this up he declares that the Incarnation 'has restored to mankind the original nature of Adam and in addition bestowed upon it the heavenly inheritance of the Holy Spirit' (I 61.1.1). Thus the economy of the Son prepares the way for the economy of the Spirit.

One of the clearest witnesses to Macarius' contacts with the Syriac Christian tradition is his understanding of the maternal character of the ministry of the Spirit. Souls still in this world should call upon the 'heavenly mother', the Holy Spirit, in order that she might, by her grace, 'come to the souls that seek her and take them in her arms of life, warm them with the spiritual and

---

[12] On this theme see also my, 'The Christology of Macarius-Symeon'. Note the stress on the human soul of Christ, something that puts us very much in the context of the Apollinarian controversy.

heavenly food of the delicious, desirable, holy, spiritual, and pure milk' (III 27.4.2).[13]

The passages describing the activity of the Spirit are amongst the most remarkable of the corpus. The following is a fine example:

Those who have been found worthy to become children of God, to be born from above in the Spirit and to have Christ shining forth and reposing in them are guided in varied and differing qualities of the Spirit. They are steered by grace in spiritual repose within the heart [ . . . ]. Sometimes it seems that they are a royal banquet rejoicing and exulting in an inexpressible joy and happiness. [ . . . ] Sometimes they are as if drunk with wine, drunk with the divine and spiritual drunkenness of the Spirit in heavenly mysteries. And then at other times they are full of weeping and lamentation as they intercede for man's salvation. For burning with the love of the Spirit for all mankind, they take to themselves the sorrow and grief of the whole Adam. [ . . . ] Grace guides the soul in very many different ways [ . . . ] so as to present it perfect, spotless and pure to the heavenly Father. [ . . . ]

When the soul attains spiritual perfection, totally purged of all the passions and perfectly united to and mingled with the Spirit, the Para-clete, in ineffable communion, then the soul is itself vouchsafed to become spirit, being commingled with the Spirit. It then becomes all light, all spirit, all joy, all repose, all gladness, all love, all compassion, all goodness and kindness. It is as though it had been swallowed up in the virtues of the Holy Spirit as a stone in the depths of the sea is surrounded by water. Such people are totally mingled with and embraced by the Spirit, united to the grace of Christ, and assimilated to Christ.   (I 13.2.1–4)[14]

---

[13] Macarius uses this kind of maternal imagery frequently in his writings. It is a marked feature of early Syriac literature, being found in, for example, the *Odes of Solomon*, the *Acts of Thomas* and the works of Aphrahat the Persian Sage. It tended to drop out of common currency from the beginning of the fifth century. This fall from grace was marked by the fact that while the word 'spirit' is in Syriac, as in all Semitic languages, a feminine, the title 'Holy Spirit' began to be construed as a masculine. While Macarius certainly has a sense of the Spirit as representing the feminine in God, he does, on one occasion, speak of the Holy Spirit in masculine terms, as the 'bridegroom' of the soul (III 20.1.2). He thus reminds us of the inadequacy of human gender categories when speaking of God.

[14] Cf. II 1.2: the soul that becomes the throne of God is 'all eye, all light, all face, all glory, and all spirit'. This bears comparison with *AP* (Alph.) Bessarion 11 (PG 65 141D): 'The monk ought to be as the Cherubim and the Seraphim: all eye.' Grant, *Irenaeus of Lyons*, 44–5, gives examples of similar 'all eye' imagery applied to God in Irenaeus of Lyons and Clement of Alexandria (Irenaeus, *AH* I.12.2 (SC 264, p. 184) and II.13.3 (SC 294, pp. 114–16); Clement, *Strom.* VII. 5. 5 (GCS 17, p. 7) and VII. 37.6 (p. 29)). The ascetic tradition has, typically, transposed the image from the plane of theology to that of the soul.

This union does not imply confusion of natures, as the distinction between the stone and water indicates. The ontological gap always endures: 'The Spirit is not of our nature for we are created, while he is uncreated' (I 50.1.7). Man may be deified, but he is not thereby lost in the Godhead. At the resurrection:

All the members become translucent, all are plunged into light and fire, and transformed; they are not, as some say, destroyed, they do not become fire, their own nature ceasing to subsist. For Peter remains Peter, and Paul remains Paul, and Philip remains Philip. Each retains his own nature and hypostasis, filled by the Spirit. (II 15.10)

The theme of deification brings us back to the theme with which we started, the mutual indwelling of man and God: 'The holy and venerable Trinity dwells in the purified man [...] not as it is in itself—for the Trinity cannot be contained by any created thing—but according to the capacity and receptivity of the one in whom it has been well-pleased' (I 52.2.6). Neither God's dwelling in man nor man's dwelling in God eradicates the ontological gap between their respective natures. Man's nature is not swallowed up into the Godhead; God remains infinite and inapprehensible. Macarius is struggling to express the reality of the union of man and God, without compromising their ontological discontinuity. The tension produced by this attempt runs throughout the Macarian writings.

# 3

# Macarius and the Cappadocians

The connection between Macarius and the Cappadocian Fathers makes a natural starting-point for our discussion of the influence of the Macarian writings in the later Eastern Christian tradition. This connection is clearest in the case of Gregory of Nyssa, where we have a substantial textual parallel between his *De instituto christiano* and Macarius' *Great Letter*. But to understand Gregory of Nyssa's approach to Macarian material, we should begin by examining the links between Basil and Macarius.[1] The connection is not at first sight an obvious one; the predominantly sober and careful tone of Basil contrasts greatly with the experiential approach and exuberant imagery of Macarius. Some form of connection cannot, however, be ruled out. Basil had first-hand experience of the ascetic traditions of Coele Syria and Mesopotamia.[2] Macarius, for his part, is no stranger to the Greek-speaking world, and may even have passed through Cappadocia.[3] While we have no direct evidence of personal contact or even of mutual awareness, there are a number of significant theological and ascetic parallels in their respective works that deserve notice.

To set these parallels in context, we can begin by summarizing the monastic background of the period.[4] The pioneer of monasticism in Asia Minor is generally held to be Eustathius of Sebaste, against whom the Council of Gangra (*c*.341) was directed. A list of twenty propositions attack the anarchic character of Eustathian communities, in particular their negative attitude to marriage, their lack of consideration for earthly ties of family and social

---

[1] On this question see especially Desprez, 'Les Relations entre le Pseudo-Macaire et S. Basile', and Dörries, *Die Theologie*, 435–45.

[2] Basil, *Ep.* 223 (Courtonne, vol. iii, pp. 10–11). Gribomont argues for the profound effect of the visit upon Basil's ascetic theology, 'Eustathe le Philosophe et les voyages du jeune Basile de Césarée'.

[3] The one possible suggestion of this comes in iii 15.3, in which he mentions hollowed-out rock dwellings similar to those of Cappadocia.

[4] For the background see Gribomont, 'Le Monachisme au IVe s. en Asie Mineure: De Gangres au Messalianisme'.

status, and their ecclesial separatism.[5] Basil appears to have taken
no notice of the council, possibly because it was chaired by the
Arian Eusebius of Nicomedia. Moreover, Basil did not break with
Eustathius until 371–2, and did so on the question of the divinity of
the Spirit and not the proper conduct of ascetics. Basil's
programme of monastic reform commends as much as it criticizes
the Eustathian communities.[6] A very broad parallel with
Eustathian monasticism may be detected in the Messalian tendency, although there is no evidence to suggest that they were
directly linked. In the eyes of concerned ecclesiastical authorities,
however, these radical ascetic tendencies were often conflated.
Epiphanius' complaints against the Messalians, as we have
noted, recall those he directed against the Eustathians. Amphilochius of Iconium may have seen his work at Side simply as a
continuation of Basil's charge to deal with the Encratites, Sacco-
phores, and Hydroparastates.[7] Likewise, Timothy of Constantinople's list opens with an equation of the Messalians with the
Eustathians.[8]

Basil's approach to monastic reform demonstrates that condemnation was not the only option open to the Church authorities and
that the more positive elements of the radical ascetic tendencies
could be integrated within the ecclesiastical mainstream. Both
Macarius and Basil were in contact with the incipient 'wild-man'
element of early monasticism, and may be argued to have approached its reform in a complementary fashion.[9] Despite the
Council of Gangra, and despite his break with Eustathius in 373,
Basil's approach to monastic reform remained irenic and ecumenical. He avoids direct confrontation with Eustathian groups, preferring to channel their energies into the wider Church structure.
His strategy is firm but flexible, advising against the holding of

---

[5] Sozomen, *Ecclesiastical History* 3.14.31. The *acta* of the council are given in Mansi,
*Sacrorum conciliorum*, ii. 1095–1122.

[6] On Basil's reforms in general, see Gribomont, *Saint Basile: Évangile et église* and *Commandements du Seigneur et liberté évangélique*, 81–138; Rousseau, *Basil of Caesarea*, 190–232; Elm,
'*Virgins of God*', 60–77.

[7] Basil, *Ep.* 199 (Courtonne, vol. ii, p. 163).

[8] PG 86 48A. Gribomont, 'Le Monachisme', presents the Messalians as 'des héritiers
d'Eustathe'. In fact the Messalians can be seen as heirs to the Eustathians only in a very
loose sense.

[9] On this theme see especially Gribomont, 'Saint Basile et le monachisme enthousiaste'
and Meyendorff, 'St Basil, Messalianism and Byzantine Christianity'.

separate assemblies, yet under certain circumstances admitting the
dissolution of marriage in order to pursue the ascetic life.[10] It
seems clear that Basil was concerned to commend the zeal of the
Eustathian communities, and to encourage their integration
within the ecclesial community. By doing so, he set a pattern
whereby the charismatic and eschatological vision of monasticism
might be integrated within an ecclesiastical framework.

Macarius is by no means as systematic or as subtle as Basil. It is,
however, clear from his writings that he undertook a thorough
critique of the Messalian tendency, warning against hasty declarations of *apatheia*, ostentatious practices of prayer, and the deni-
gration of the sacraments. The frequent occurrence of the
question–answer format is, as in Basil, often a pretext for a revision of an extremist position.[11] In the *Great Letter*, the fullest account Macarius gives of the organization of ascetic communities,
he echoes Basil in emphasizing due obedience to and supervision
by the college of superiors and in insisting on unity within the
community—whatever one's function in that community might
be. Like Basil, Macarius is sympathetic to, but not uncritical of,
the radical ascetic tendencies. Basil's approach is certainly far
more systematic and detached than that of Macarius, yet both
approach the extremist tendencies with sympathy and with restraint. The parallel between their respective approaches to monasticism helps explain the inclusion of Homily 11 25 of Macarius
as the *Ascetic Prologue* separating the *Longer* and *Shorter Rules* in the
Vulgate recension of Basil's *Asceticon*.[12]

Certain features of ascetic vocabulary correspond closely. Most
significantly, both use the designation 'Christians' in preference to
that of 'monks'.[13] The coincidence is important; in both cases it
implies a restraint upon a sectarian conception of monasticism in
its refusal to separate ascetics from the wider Church community.
It also emphasizes the fact that with both Basil and Macarius, we
are dealing with an ascetic context anterior to the general ascend-
ancy of specifically Egyptian forms of monasticism.

---

[10] Basil, *Shorter Rules* 310 (PG 31 1304BC); *Longer Rules* 12 (PG 31 948C–949A).

[11] See for example 11 7, in which Homily Macarius revises a Messalian understanding of
*apatheia* and corrects the incipient dualism of his interlocutor.

[12] See Desprez, *Oeuvres spirituelles*, 19 n. 4.

[13] Basil, *Longer Rules* 17.2 (PG 31 964C); 20.1–2 (972C–973A). Macarius, 1 21.2, 48.3.11.

A further important point of correspondence is on the use of the noun πληροφορία and the verb πληροφορέω.[14] Basil uses one or other over thirty-five times in his moral and ascetic works. Most often he does so to convey a sense of conviction, confidence, and certitude—for example in relation to the promises of God or the infallibility of Scripture.[15] He also uses the term to designate the fullness of faith with which we must receive the eucharist, and the assurance brought by the sense of the presence of God.[16] Basil uses the concept more often than any previous author, and indeed than either of the two Gregories. Macarius uses it with even greater frequency. On at least ten occasions he does so with Basil's sense of conviction or of certitude. More often he uses it to mean 'full measure', for example the 'full reality' of the Christian life (*EM* 3.12) and, especially, the sense of spiritual plenitude (e.g. I 2.12.17, 30.7, 28.2.5). His 'trademark', as it were, is the use of the word in combination, with activity (twice), with faith (six times), with power (eight times), and with αἴσθησις (eleven times).[17] Macarius gives what had been in Basil a means of expressing conviction an explicitly mystical dimension.

Both Basil and Macarius recommend implicit remembrance of God over the continual vocal prayer practised by the Messalians. In the *Homily on the Martyr Julitta* Basil interprets the command 'pray without ceasing' of 1 Thessalonians 5: 17 not as the repetition of syllables, but as a life dedicated to the service of God. To demonstrate this Basil selects 1 Corinthians 10: 31, 'whether you eat or drink or whatever you do, do all to the glory of God'.[18] In the *Great Letter*, and indeed elsewhere, Macarius expounds substantially the same point of view:

All of you must pursue all the practices of the commandments, this hidden struggle, this meditation upon the Lord, this day and night labour, whether you are praying or serving, whether you are eating or drinking, or whatever you are doing, so that everything you do

---

[14] See Miquel and Desprez, 'Plèrophoria', and Stewart, '*Working the Earth of the Heart*', 96–116. I rely greatly on both for the material in this paragraph. The word πληροφορία is biblical in origin (Heb. 6: 11; 10: 22; 1 Thess. 1: 5; Col. 2: 2), but has no discernible pedigree in classical Greek. Both these studies reveal that Macarius' systematic use of the term to convey the experience of spiritual fullness or plenitude is original to him.

[15] See, for example, *On Faith* 1 (PG 31 677D–680A) and *Moralia* 8.1 (PG 31 712C).

[16] *Shorter Rules* 172 (PG 31 1196A); *Shorter Rules* 34 (1105A).

[17] Exact references in Miquel and Desprez, 'Plèrophoria', 1813–21.

[18] *Homily on the Martyr Julitta* (PG 31 244AB).

becomes a good practice of virtue to the glory of God [...]. For the whole sequence of the commandments is sanctified when accomplished by you in purity and through unceasing remembrance of the Lord. (*EM* 7.8)

Macarius uses or refers to the same two Pauline verses treated by Basil, 1 Corinthians 10: 31 and 1 Thessalonians 5: 17. Macarius, like Basil, understands continual prayer to imply continual remembrance of God in all aspects of life and not continual vocal prayer.[19]

To turn to doctrine, the insistence upon the salvific function of the Holy Spirit in Macarius perfectly accords with the Cappadocian polemic in defence of the divinity of the Holy Spirit. As we have seen, for Macarius it is the Spirit who incorporates us into the life of the Godhead. His insistence on the divine and deifying quality of the Holy Spirit makes a conscious contribution to the Trinitarian controversies of the day. His affirmation that the Spirit is 'uncreated' (1 50.1.7) is a patent refutation of the claim of the Pneumatomachi that the Spirit was to be ranked with the creatures.[20] Notwithstanding their different starting-points—Basil approaches the subject from the perspective of Trinitarian theology, Macarius from the personal experience of the sanctifying power of the Spirit, wrenching out the passions imbedded in us—our authors reach precisely the same conclusion.[21]

The question of the relations obtaining between Macarius and Gregory of Nyssa is dominated by the connection between Macarius' *Great Letter* and Gregory's *De instituto christiano*. This question is a complex one and has been the basis of much scholarly argument in recent decades. It is quite certain that one of the texts depends

[19] See also Macarius, II 43.3: 'The Christian should always guard the remembrance of God, for it is written, "you shall love the Lord your God with all your heart", so that you should not love God only when you go to the place of prayer but that you should have the remembrance of God and love and affection for him when walking and talking and eating.' Compare the amusing treatment by Abba Lucius of an erstwhile group of Euchites in *AP* (Alph.) Lucius 1 (PG 65 253BC).

[20] Dörries, *Die Theologie*, 445 n. 16, observes: 'Sein Bekenntis zur Gottheit des Heiligen Geistes ist der unmittelbare Ausdruck der Erfahrung, deren Zeuge er war.'

[21] Dörries, *Die Theologie*, 440, points to a marked difference between Basil's and Macarius' understanding of the activity of the Holy Spirit. Macarius, owing to his acute sense of the power of indwelling sin, focuses upon the liberation from the inhering passions effected by the Spirit; Basil tends to present the reception of the Spirit as the term of the Christian life, hence *Shorter Rules* 204 (1217B): 'If we do not accomplish all the commandments of the Lord [...] we cannot expect to be held worthy of the Holy Spirit.'

upon the other. We shall begin with a summary of the debate concerning this parallel and go on to study certain other correspondences between Gregory and Macarius.

The debate concerning the relation between the *De instituto christiano* and the *Great Letter* was sparked off by Jaeger's work on the critical edition of Gregory. Jaeger produced an edition of both pieces, affirming the priority of the *De instituto christiano*. His thesis was initially widely accepted. Gribomont, however, dissented from this view, pointing out that the various correspondences could equally well support the priority of the *Great Letter*. This line of enquiry was followed up by Staats in his *Gregor von Nyssa und die Messalianer* and in his parallel edition of the texts. Staats's arguments have effectively overturned the thesis of Jaeger as to the priority of the Gregorian text. A new twist to the controversy was added by the suggestion by Canévet that the *De instituto christiano* itself may not be authentic, but this remains very much a minority position.[22]

The *Great Letter* is a kind of manifesto: Macarius' fullest statement of his vision of authentic monasticism (i.e. authentic Christianity).[23] It is a call for monasticism based on inward experience and not on outward and essentially ostentatious ascetic practices, a rallying cry for a renewal of the charismatic gifts of the primitive Church, produced in an era in which the zeal of the golden age of monasticism had begun to wane.

The proemium to the *Great Letter* lays down certain theological principles, including a statement of faith in

the divine and holy declaration that has rightly been laid down concerning the exact and pious opinion and faith: one revered Godhead of the co-essential Trinity, one will, one glory, and one worship of the one tri-hypostatic Godhead. This is in accordance with our pious affirmation of the good confession before many witnesses in the mystery of holy baptism. (*EM* 1.3)[24]

---

[22] The relevant texts are, in the order given above: Jaeger, *Two Rediscovered Works of Ancient Christian Literature*; Gribomont, 'Le De instituto christiano et le Messalianisme de Grégoire de Nysse'; Staats, *Gregor von Nyssa und die Messalianer* and *Makarios-Symeon: Epistola magna*; Canévet, 'Le "De instituto christiano" est-il de Grégoire de Nysse?'

[23] The *Great Letter* edited by Jaeger, and subsequently by Staats, must be distinguished from the gravely corrupted version edited by Floss and contained in Migne (PG 34 420C–441A). Maloney, *Spiritual Homilies*, inexplicably chooses to translate the PG version.

[24] Basil had also linked the baptismal confession of faith with the argument for the divinity of the Holy Spirit, *De Spiritu Sancto* 12.28 (PG 32 117B).

This confession of the three hypostases of the one Godhead is Cappadocian Trinitarian theology at its clearest. It also clearly indicates an awareness of the decisions of the Ecumenical Council of Constantinople.[25]

Macarius goes on to present the goal of the ascetic life as the expulsion of the passions and the perfect acquisition of the Spirit—to be attained through the development of baptismal grace (*EM* 2). The Christian must advance through the synergy of divine grace and human effort to 'the purification and sanctification of the heart that comes about by the participation of the perfect and divine Spirit, accomplished in all perception and plenitude' (*EM* 3.1–2). Macarius proceeds to discuss the regulation of the community. He stresses internal discipline—focusing on the ministry of the college of superiors (προεστῶτες) (*EM* 6). He insists that all the virtues are linked to one another in a sacred chain in the order: prayer–love–joy–gentleness–humility–service–hope–faith–obedience–simplicity (*EM* 8.1). Perseverance in prayer is the 'head of all good effort and crown of the virtues' (*EM* 8.3), but cannot be separated from the other virtues. Macarius allows for certain monks to dedicate themselves entirely to prayer (*EM* 9) but is, as we have seen, clear that all are called to dedicate themselves to the remembrance of God, whatever their function within the community. Those who are as yet unable to pray undistractedly should, as a stage of preparation, commit themselves to tasks of service (*EM* 10.1). In allowing this fluid distinction between those that work and those that pray, Macarius is at pains to underline the importance and integrity of work. In a critique of Messalian spiritual elitism and disdain for work, Macarius stresses the value placed upon service in the Gospel, paraphrasing 2 Thessalonians 3: 10: 'let not the idler eat' (*EM* 10.6). Service and prayer are complementary; the part of Mary may be superior to that of Martha, 'but both spring from the same good root' (*EM* 11.11). *EM* 12 rounds off with a restatement of the principle that Macarius' manifesto is essentially a call to realize the promises contained in Scripture. *EM* 13 is a form of apology, possibly a later addition, and answering to the charge that his teaching calls for an experience of things beyond the capacity of man's

---

[25] This allows us to date the treatise to between 381 and 394 (i.e. between the Council of Constantinople and Gregory's death).

nature.[26] Those who bring such a charge, argues Macarius, deny the promises of Scripture. Perfect purity is possible, contrary to what such gainsayers say, albeit only by grace, for what is impossible to man is possible to God. Such perfection consists in freedom from the sinful passions and the perceptible action of the Holy Spirit in the pure heart. Thus body and soul are perfectly sanctified, becoming a pure dwelling-place of God. The treatise is thus concluded in inimitable fashion, bringing together several of the most distinctive themes of the Macarian writings.

The *De instituto christiano* parallels the *Great Letter* model up to *EM* 10.4, introducing but not expanding upon the theme of the relation between prayer and work. When presented with one text more polished, concise, and sophisticated than the other, one must concur with Gribomont's observation: 'on s'explique mal le passage du correct à l'incorrect'. Jaeger's suggestion that Macarius has consciously removed the grammatical niceties of Gregory produces an unlikely picture of deliberate rustification. Gribomont's supposition of 'un correcteur qui enrichit le premier jet et retouche le vocabulaire pour le rendre plus classique' is far more plausible.[27] Attempts have been made to set the question of priority on a firmer basis than that of style, in particular by looking at the idiomatic Gospel quotations found in both treatises.[28] Although we cannot here explore all the intricacies of the question, it is clear that the evidence points firmly to the anteriority of the *Great Letter*. Gregory's reworking is subtle and concise, ironing out the inelegancies of Macarius' style and presenting in a more cultured and philosophical style all the essentials of Macarius' treatise.

The emphasis on the primacy of prayer and the gift of the Spirit in the *De instituto christiano* certainly stands out in the Gregorian

---

[26] On the later portion see Baker, 'The Great Letter of Pseudo-Macarius and Gregory of Nyssa', 381 n. 5. Baker argues that this portion, like the proemium, has been added to the treatise.

[27] See Gribomont, 'Le De instituto christiano et le Messalianisme de Grégoire de Nysse', 316–17.

[28] See, for example, Quispel, 'The Syrian Thomas and the Syrian Macarius' and Baker, 'The Great Letter of Pseudo-Macarius and Gregory of Nyssa'. In his 'Some Remarks on the Quotations of the Gospels in Gregory of Nyssa's *De instituto christiano* and Macarius' *Epistola magna*', Klijn responded that the parallels do not necessarily help establish priority. Baker replied with 'Pseudo-Macarius and Gregory of Nyssa', in which he deals with eight variant readings, seven of which are, he argues, typically Macarian. See also the excursus in Staats, *Gregor von Nyssa und die Messalianer*, 94–100.

corpus, as does the theme of spiritual plenitude. While the prominence given to the ministry of the Holy Spirit accords perfectly
with Cappadocian Trinitarian theology, Gregory has also taken
on board Macarius' sense of the inward operation of the Spirit.[29]
The unusual stress given to certain themes in comparison with the
rest of the Gregorian corpus should not be taken as evidence of the
inauthenticity of the *De instituto christiano*. These may readily be
explained by his dependence upon the Macarian model.

Gregory was evidently impressed by the ascetic teaching of the
*Great Letter* and indeed by its organizational considerations. He
gladly reworked Macarius' text, thereby giving his sincerest possible approval of Macarian teaching and ensuring that, under his
name, it would circulate far more widely than would otherwise
have been the case.[30]

The exact nature of the links between the sophisticated Cappadocian circle and that gathered around Macarius is difficult to
determine. Staats very plausibly argues that Gregory is speaking of
ascetic groups associated with Macarius in his warm praise of
certain 'Mesopotamians' given in his *In Gregorii ordinationem* (or *In
suam ordinationem*).[31] Gregory credits these Mesopotamians with
renewing the gifts of the early Church. 'They have', he writes,
'like Abraham left their country, their family and the world at
large. They look to heaven; they cut themselves off, so to say, from
human life; they are superior to the passions of nature [ ... ]. They
do not struggle with words, they do not study rhetoric; but they
have such power over the spirits [ ... ] that they expel demons not
through syllogistic arts but through the power of faith [ ... ].'[32]

---

[29] Note that Gregory has a much keener sense than Basil of the strength of the hold of
the passions upon us, hence *De anima et resurrectione* (PG 46 160c): '[ ... ] the passions sprung
from evil, which are so hard for the soul to get rid of, when they have infused themselves
into the very substance of its entire nature and become one with it [ ... ].' It is precisely this
kind of understanding that may have disposed him to take so seriously Macarius' focus on
the uprooting of the passions effected by the Spirit.

[30] We may also note Henry Chadwick's detection of a close affinity between the exegesis
of Luke 15: 8–9 (the widow's lost coin) in Macarius, 11 11.4 and Gregory's *De virginitate* 12.3.
He makes this point in his review of Staats's *Gregor von Nyssa und die Messalianer*.

[31] Ed. Gebhardt, GNO 9. One MS entitles it *To Evagrius on the Deity*. See Staats, 'Die
Asketen aus Mesopotamien in der Rede des Gregor von Nyssa *In suam ordinationem*'. Staats
had argued for a date of 394, a view rightly challenged by May, 'Die Datierung der Rede *In
suam ordinationem* des Gregor von Nyssa'. The context is clearly that of the council of 381, as
Staats was later to accept.

[32] Basil had also heard of the 'holy and blessed' ascetics of Mesopotamia, *Ep.* 207
(Courtonne, vol. ii, p. 185).

This commendation, made in the context of the controversy surrounding the Pneumatomachi, is quite conceivably a reference to Macarius and his circle, valued by Gregory for their experiential confirmation of the divinity of the Holy Spirit. His description certainly fits with Macarius' critique of merely academic theology and his emphasis on the need to expel indwelling evil. Equally, the Mesopotamian label can easily be squared with what we know of the geographical location of Macarius. While we cannot be sure that Gregory is here referring specifically to Macarius and his circle, his praise confirms his enthusiasm for the zeal of the radical asceticism of Syria.

The Cappadocian polemic against the neo-Arians combined the defence of the divinity of the Holy Spirit and of Christ with an assertion of the incomprehensibility of God. One of Gregory's most striking rejoinders to neo-Arian rationalism is the connection he makes between the incomprehensibility of God and that of man. Just as God is unknowable, so also is his image, man, by nature unknowable.[33] Macarius uses essentially the same argument. Asked in what the image of God consists, he replies that just as God is incomprehensible, so also is our own intellect (I 18.7.1). Even the Greek philosophers with all their wisdom, he tells us, were unable to understand the workings of the soul (II 49.4). We cannot even enumerate the thoughts we have in the course of one single day; how therefore can we pretend to know the thoughts of God? (II 12.11).

The analogy between the incomprehensibility of God and that of the soul is a distinctive feature of the Cappadocian apophatic theology developed in response to Eunomian rationalism. To find the same analogy in Macarius is significant. Whilst it is not to be ruled out that Macarius came to this conclusion independently, the analogy is sufficiently distinctive to make it reasonable to suppose that Macarius is here appropriating a feature of Cappadocian apophatic theology and impressing it upon groups close to him. Our information on the Messalians suggests that they were preoccupied with the vision of the soul and prone to making unguarded statements as to the possibility of the bodily vision of God. Cappadocian apophatic theology provided an antidote to such speculations, an antidote Macarius was only too glad to employ.

---

[33] *De hominis opificio* 11 (PG 46 156B).

The most striking contrast between the apophaticism of Macarius and that of Gregory is that Macarius does not take up the motif of the divine darkness. While Macarius frequently dwells upon the revelation of God to Moses on Mount Sinai, he speaks only of the light that streamed from the face of Moses on his descent. The light is spoken of as a pledge of immortality, a prefiguration of the resurrection glory of the saints:

The blessed Moses showed in a type, through the glory of the Spirit which was upon his face and which no one was able to behold, how at the resurrection of the righteous the bodies of the worthy will be glorified with the glory that holy and faithful souls are even now granted to possess in the inner man. For, as [St Paul] says, 'with unveiled face', that is to say in the inner man, 'we reflect as in a mirror the glory of the Lord, and we are transfigured into the same image from glory to glory [2 Cor. 3: 18]'. (II 5.10)

It is significant that Macarius links the glory that shone on and from the face of Moses to certain themes dear to Gregory and contained in the citation from 2 Corinthians: the soul as mirror of God and the theme of *epektasis*.[34] It remains, however, that Macarius chooses to concentrate upon the light of the descent of Moses in Exodus 34: 29–35, over the ascent into the divine darkness of Exodus 20: 21 f. This concentration on light rather than darkness does not constitute a fundamental distinction between the apophaticism of Gregory and that of Macarius. The use of one or other motif does not of itself determine a given author's approach to the question of the knowledge of God. To take but one example, Gregory of Nazianzus is deeply apophatic, as is abundantly clear in the *Theological Orations*, without ever having recourse to the motif of the divine darkness.

A further parallel between Macarius and the Cappadocians is the balance between affirmative and negative theology, the view that while God is unknowable in himself, he is yet revealed *ad extra* in his operations. Macarius asserts that God may, if he so chooses, reveal both himself and the nature of the soul (III 18.1.1–2). The nature of that revelation is dealt with in more detail in Logos 22 of the same collection. We may not know the nature of God, and

---

[34] Elsewhere he develops the idea of the intellect as a mirror in which one can contemplate the form of Christ (II 25.3). For the theme of *epektasis* see also I 21.10, 34.9–12; II 8.6, 10.1; III 7.4.2–5.3.

neither human reason nor biblical images are sufficient to apprehend the truth. What we may know, as St Paul testifies, is that
which God grants us to know (III 22.2.1, citing 1 Cor. 2: 12–13). We
should 'seek the Lord and he will guide us and teach us so that we
may be given to know the hidden things of God in so far as it is
possible for man to know them and not as God is [in himself]' (III
22.2.2). The Cappadocians work within the same basic schema.
Basil puts it that God is both hidden and revealed, inaccessible in
his essence, but knowable in his energies or operations.[35] Gregory
of Nyssa takes the same line: 'For he is invisible by nature, but
becomes visible in his energies, for he may be contemplated in the
things that are referred to him.'[36] The apophaticism of the Cappadocians and of Macarius is balanced by their acute sense of the
revelation of God *ad extra*.

To conclude, the relationship between Macarius and the Cappadocians centres upon monastic reform and Trinitarian theology. Gregory of Nyssa's irenic and sympathetic approach to
aberrant forms of monasticism perfectly accords with that of
Basil, contrasting greatly with the ecclesiastical condemnations
issued at Side, Antioch, and subsequent councils. The *De instituto
christiano* affords evidence of Gregory's willingness to make use of a
moderating influence within the amorphous Messalian tendency.
Gregory took the *Great Letter* as a model for a treatise combining
the pneumatological and eschatological insights of that tendency
with an insistence on peaceful relations and discipline within the
monastic community. Gregory's respect for his model was such as
to allow him to incorporate the positive aspects of ascetic enthusiasm within his own teaching. Gregory gives his model a more
philosophical form and corrects its literary deficiencies, yet retains
its most distinctive qualities. His ability to take on board the
charismatic aspects of the radical ascetic tendency reveals, as
Gribomont puts it, 'combien reste, en réalité, secondaire le vête-
ment platonicien sous lequel il représente son Christianisme'.[37]
This instance of appropriation confirms the Cappadocian attempt
to integrate the religious enthusiasm of radical asceticism into the

---

[35] *Ep.* 234 (Courtonne, vol. iii, p. 43).
[36] *On the Beatitudes* 6 (GNO 7 (2), p. 141). Cf. also Athanasius: 'God is in all things
according to his own bounty, and outside of all things according to his own nature', *De
decretis* 11 (PG 25 433D (NB misprinted as 441)).
[37] 'Le De instituto christiano et le Messalianisme de Grégoire de Nysse', 322.

structures of the wider Church community. Gregory fully recognized the capacity of the Macarian writings to contribute to
this process of integration and eagerly marshalled them to that
end. The connection between Macarius and the Cappadocians
extends, as we have seen, beyond monastic reform, to the defence
of the divinity of the Holy Spirit and the use of apophatic theology.
I would suggest, to finish, that the connection between Macarius
and the Cappadocians, witnessed by the example of the *De instituto
christiano* and the parallel in Trinitarian theology, has been instru-
mental in the preservation of the Macarian writings within the
mainstream Christian tradition. The Cappadocian approach has
been shown to be both constructive and enduring—much more so
than the often specious condemnations issued from Side to Ephesus.[38] When seeking to discover the 'place' of the Macarian
writings in the Eastern Christian tradition, the association with
the Cappadocians is fundamental.

---

[38] It is even possible that Gregory's absence had to be secured to allow the condemnation of Side to go through, or that it took place after his death (*c.*394): see Gribomont, 'Le
Dossier', 623; Desprez, *Oeuvres spirituelles*, 51.

# 4

# Macarius and Evagrius

Hausherr made a bold and influential attempt in 1935 to classify certain distinct 'currents of spirituality' within the Eastern Christian tradition. His article, 'Les Grands Courants de la spiritualité orientale', has made it conventional to oppose, or at least to juxtapose, the 'spiritualité intellectualiste' of Evagrius of Pontus and the 'école du sentiment ou de surnaturel conscient' associated with the anonymous author of the writings ascribed to Macarius the Great, elder of Egypt. Hausherr does not insist on this classification, admitting that this schema is simply an abstract working tool; to add the facts would be 'une autre conférence à faire, plus intéressante sans doute que le schématisme trop abstrait que vous venez d'entendre'.[1] A later article presents a somewhat subtler analysis, maintaining the basic intellective–affective distinction yet distinguishing within the latter group, within those who yearned for a *conscious* experience of the Holy Spirit, two further 'orientations':

l'une qui se rapproche des intellectuels [i.e. the two Gregories and Evagrius] tout en appuyant fortement sur le sentiment et qui dépend sans doute pour une part d'Origène: le porte-parole en est le pseudo-Macaire; l'autre ignorant tout le vocabulaire savant et se basant uniquement sur la révélation de l'Esprit promise dans l'Écriture [e.g. Ammonas].

Hausherr presents Macarius as an intermediary between the learned and 'l'esthétisme des simples' and describes his 'mystique de la lumière' as 'une vulgarisation à l'usage d'une foule qui *non ascendit ad sublimia*'. He also makes the important point that this double aspect in Macarius makes him susceptible to two differing interpretations, 'une plus philosophique et une plus commune et matérielle'.[2]

---

[1] Hence, perhaps, its not being included in the two volumes of Hausherr's collected writings. His 'L'Erreur fondamentale', which works with precisely the same schema, is, however, included.

[2] 'Contemplation chez les grecs et autres orientaux chrétiens', 1849–51.

This schema is rather more satisfactory than that of 1935 in that it recognizes the distinct philosophical culture running through the work of Macarius, yet remains attached to the basic supposition of the original article that Macarius and Evagrius are rightly to be held in contradistinction. This supposition is also that of many Orthodox scholars. Vladimir Lossky shares something with the revised schema in his pointing out of two main spiritual deviations:

the intellectualism of Evagrius with its source in Origen and the latter's Platonic spiritualism, and the Messalians' sensual experience of God. [...] Between the two there is the mysticism of affection, of grace that is felt, experienced, the mysticism of the 'Spiritual Homilies' attributed to St Macarius, and the doctrine of contemplation of St Diadochus of Photice, more sober than that of Macarius, suspicious of all sensible depiction, but alien to the intellectualism of Evagrius.[3]

Lossky's approach gives a rather one-sided picture of Evagrius and tends to minimize the Evagrian impact on Diadochus. The schema, like that of Hausherr, puts undue confidence in its categorization of distinct currents of spirituality. Nevertheless, the location of the affective mysticism of Macarius and Diadochus somewhere between Evagrian 'intellectualism' and Messalian 'materialism' is worth consideration.

John Meyendorff, on the other hand, reflects the more straightforward contrast of Hausherr's 1935 article. His analysis of the sources of St Gregory Palamas attaches great significance to the contrast between Evagrius and Macarius. If we look at the Macarian writings, Meyendorff argues,

We easily see that, for readers from the fifth to the fourteenth centuries these writings opposed a Biblical terminology and a Biblical doctrine concerning man—with perhaps some Stoic connections—to a Platonic terminology and Evagrius' spiritualizing doctrine of man. These two doctrines concerning man are latent in the history of hesychasm, and writers can be rightly classified as disciples of Evagrius or of Macarius, provided, of course, that that classification is not applied too strictly and, especially, too much stress is not put on the terminology which tends to get the two schools confused even when they most preserve their peculiar characteristics.

---

[3] *The Vision of God*, 114.

Meyendorff gave no quarter in his bid to present the issue as a straight choice between the anthropology of Plato and that of the Bible. He argued that even the adoption of Evagrian vocabulary within Macarian circles—viz. the location of the *nous*, or spiritual intellect, in the heart—did not alter the irreconcilability of the Platonic and biblical doctrines of man. He presented the choice between the two as follows:

Is man only an intelligence imprisoned in matter and longing to be free, or is he a psycho-physiological whole to whom God brought salvation by his Incarnation? Does grace only touch the mind (*nous*) purified not only of all passion but also of all material attachment, or does the whole man, by virtue of the baptismal water into which he is plunged, receive the first fruits of bodily resurrection?[4]

One or other alternative had to be plumped for, Evagrius chose the former, his doctrine of 'pure prayer' being 'a sort of gnosis foreign to the piety of which Jesus Christ is the centre', Macarius, conversely, chose the latter, and stands, therefore, as the principal forerunner of the Hesychast doctrine of man.

Despite starting from different angles and exhibiting markedly divergent preferences, these authors have contributed to the development of a tendency to discuss the development of Eastern Christian spirituality in terms of an Evagrian–Macarian contrast. Whilst this contrast is rarely expressed bluntly, it is nevertheless latent in so much discussion of this area as to merit closer consideration.

One of the very few people to seriously detract from what we might call the 'dichotomist viewpoint' has been Alexander Golitzin. After summarizing the conventional contrast between Macarius and Evagrius as represented, in this case, by Meyendorff, he writes:

The contradistinction of 'mind' and 'heart' reflects the Medieval Western opposition between 'intellective' and 'affective' mysticisms a little too much for my comfort. Evagrius is not an Eckhardt, nor is Macarius a Bernard of Clairvaux [...]. Then too, the contrast implicit in this definition between a 'biblical' and a 'platonizing' Christianity strikes me as very questionable. Plato and company were quite as much involved in first-century Palestine as they were anywhere else in the Graeco-Roman world, and the 'Greeks' thus had a say in the formation

---

[4] *A Study of Gregory Palamas*, 137–8.

of both Christianity and of rabbinic Judaism. I do not, in short, believe that Evagrius' *nous* and Macarius' *kardia* are all that different from each other.[5]

These remarks come as something of a breath of fresh air after the over-familiar contrast between Evagrius and Macarius. They are helpful in that they point out within this contrast the latent suspicion of an insidious Hellenizing force corrupting the purely Semitic Christianity of the Bible, a suspicion evident in Harnack and much early twentieth-century biblical criticism. The point about the head–heart disjunction is, I feel, highly justified. It is debatable whether either of the authors with whom we are dealing perceived any opposition between 'head' and 'heart', between 'intellective' and 'affective' mysticisms.[6] But while whole-heartedly agreeing with Golitzin in general, his closing statement is, it must be said, too simple. In fact, Evagrius' *nous* is contained within Macarius' *kardia*—as we shall see.

Having summarized certain paradigmatic models of this critical period in the development of the Eastern Christian spiritual tradition, I hope to have opened up the whole Macarian–Evagrian question somewhat. I intend in what follows to offer my analysis—which can only be partial—of the validity of the opposition or juxtaposition of the two authors. The purpose of this chapter is not so much to refute or uphold any particular schema, but to tentatively suggest that the opposition between the two authors may, in some respects, be more apparent than real.

Apart from his birth in 345–6 in Pontic Ibora to the family of a rural bishop, we know very little as to the circumstances of Evagrius' early life, yet from the sophistication of his writings we can affirm that he was well educated. He had his theological formation from the Cappadocians, being ordained reader by Basil and deacon by Gregory of Nazianzus. His link with Gregory seems to have been particularly close; Evagrius described Gregory as the one who had 'planted' him.[7] Evagrius accompanied Gregory to

[5] 'Hierarchy versus Anarchy', 153. See also Kallistos Ware, 'Prayer in Evagrius and the Macarian Homilies'.

[6] Such an opposition may be seen, much later, in Bernard of Clairvaux: 'there are two kinds of contemplation, one seated in the intellect, the other in the heart's disposition, the one is accompanied by light, the other by warmth, the one consists in perception, the other in devotion'. *On the Song of Songs*, 49 (PL 183 1018) quoted in Brock, 'The Prayer of the Heart in the Syriac Tradition'.

[7] *Praktikos*, Epilogue (SC 171, p. 712).

the Council of Constantinople in 381, but fled the capital shortly after for fear of scandal. After a brief period in Jerusalem, Evagrius spent the rest of his life in the Egyptian desert, becoming a monk in Nitria and dying in Kellia in 399. In Egypt, he was in close contact with the greatest elders of the day, particularly with Macarius of Alexandria at Kellia, and Macarius of Egypt, the founder of the community at Scetis.[8] From the living experience of the Egyptian desert, Evagrius drew the substance of his teaching on the practical ascetic life. He came to acquire one of the finest faculties of observation and discernment to be found in the ascetic literature of the Eastern Christian tradition. Evagrius himself seems to have perceived a certain tension in his combination of a sophisticated philosophical culture with the spirituality of the Egyptian desert.[9]

Evagrius' systematization of the spiritual life is presented in a kind of trilogy: the *Praktikos*, one hundred chapters on the ascetic struggle; the *Gnostikos*, fifty chapters of advice on the proper conduct of the true gnostic; and the *Kephalaia Gnostika*, comprising six centuries, each of ninety chapters, dealing with the some of more speculative aspects of his thought.[10] The system reproduces and reifies the cosmological speculations of Origen.[11] Evagrius develops the theory of the pre-existence of a Henad of pure intellects engaged in the contemplation of God. A rupture is produced by the fall of these beings from contemplation, due to satiety or negligence. The fall brings about a second, material, creation, each intellect being given a body in accordance with the degree of its fall. The second creation is seen as a providential

[8] See Bunge, 'Évagre le Pontique et les deux Macaire'. Bunge is one of the few authors to attempt to present Evagrius' work as an organic whole. See also his excellent *Akèdia: La Doctrine spirituelle d'Évagre le Pontique sur l'acédie*.

[9] See Budge, *The Book of Paradise*, 882 f: 'On one occasion Abba Evagrius said to Abba Arsenius: "Since we are not without learning according to the world [ . . . ] [how is it that] the Egyptian villagers possess such excellences?" Abba Arsenius replied to him: "We possess nothing whatever from the learning of the world but these Egyptian villagers have acquired spiritual excellences through their labours." '

[10] The *Gnostikos* and the *Kephalaia Gnostika* had disappeared from the Greek tradition by the seventh century, largely as a result of the condemnations secured by the Emperor Justinian at the time of the Fifth Ecumenical Council (553). The practical aspect of Evagrius' teaching has always been highly valued in the Christian tradition, transmitted to the West by John Cassian and often preserved in the East under various pseudonyms, particularly that of Nilus.

[11] For Evagrius' cosmology, see the standard work of Guillaumont, *Les 'Kephalaia Gnostica' d'Évagre le Pontique et l'histoire de l'Origénisme chez les Grecs et chez les Syriens*.

measure of God, dictated neither by necessity nor by punishment, but as a way of return. Christ, the one intellect not to fall, has taken a body in order to demonstrate the means whereby each intellect may return to God. Evagrius' work is chiefly concerned with this stage of return. The path back shown by Christ requires a conscious turning from materiality, both in body (the struggle against the passions) and in intellect (the divestment of forms). The opening of the *Praktikos* describes the pattern with admirable conciseness: 'Christianity is the doctrine of our Saviour Christ, composed of the practical, the natural and the theological.'[12] The struggle against the passions produces the state of *apatheia*, which in turn gives rise to love.[13] From the practice of the commandments, the intellect is to proceed to secondary natural contemplation, to perceive the *logoi* of visible phenomena, and then to primary natural contemplation, to the contemplation of the rational intelligences, and, ultimately, to contemplation of the Holy Trinity, to the stage of true theology. Each of these stages requires a proportionate divestment of the intellect from all forms, material and immaterial, until it is perfectly 'naked' and reunited to unoriginate intellect. Thus the original state of all things is restored and the *apokatastasis* accomplished.

The contrast between Evagrian and Macarian conceptions of the spiritual life could, at first sight, hardly be more striking. Evagrius is a staunch Origenist and a sophisticated philosopher in his own right; Macarius less cultivated and to a great degree the product of the vivid and emotive world of Syrian asceticism. Against the meta-historical cycle of rest–movement–return of Evagrius, we have in Macarius far more clearly the historical drama of Fall and redemption. Against the 'naked intellect' of Evagrius, we have a wealth of colour and imagery. Against Evagrian gnosis we have a form of spirituality centred far more evidently upon Christ and the Holy Spirit. It would seem natural to contrast the Hellenic intellect of Evagrius with the biblical-Semitic heart of Macarius. This black-and-white picture must, however, be nuanced. In this respect the comment of Gribomont provides a useful starting-point:

Évagre est cultivé, philosophe, ésotérique; Syméon abonde en images plastiques et très personnelles, il est plus proche du peuple. Mais Évagre

---

[12] *Praktikos* 1 (SC 171, p. 498).   [13] Ibid. 78 (p. 666), 81 (p. 670).

a tenu à s'humilier, 'apprenant l'alphabet des paysans coptes' qui l'initiaient à leur ascèse; et Syméon a acquis, lui aussi, une telle finesse d'observation des mouvements du coeur qu'il mérite sans aucun doute un doctorat *honoris causa* en psychologie.[14]

Gribomont implies a condescension on the part of Evagrius to the experience of the desert, and an ascension through *ascesis* of Macarius-Symeon to a degree of observation comparable to that of Evagrius. His observation highlights the substantial common ground between the two authors in terms of their treatment of the psychology of temptation. I would suggest, however, that Macarius and Evagrius are compatible in a more fundamental way than even this framework would imply. In order to substantiate this, I shall treat each author in turn, pointing out some of their more unfamiliar characteristics that tend to be obscured if the contrast between them is pushed too far.

We have already noted many aspects of Macarius' teaching which underline his philosophical culture, and drawn attention to the complementarity of heart and intellect in his understanding of the nature of the human person.[15] We may also note some additional indicators of this neglected aspect of his thought:

Because of the Fall the soul has been overpowered by material and unclean thoughts and has become quite witless. It is no small thing for it to rise out of such materiality and to grasp the subtlety of evil, so that it can co-mingle with unoriginate intellect. (I 3.6.1)

The heart is a tomb and there our thoughts and our intellect are buried, imprisoned in heavy darkness. And so Christ comes to the souls in Hell that call upon him, descending, that is to say, into the depths of the heart. [...] Then lifting up the heavy stone that covers the soul, and opening the tomb, he grants us resurrection—for we were truly dead—and releases our imprisoned soul from its lightless prison. (II 11.11)

The spiritual intellect is given great freedom in the Macarian writings; there is no indication that its location in the heart suggested in passages such as II 15.20 implies a material restriction upon its activity. Indeed, the fact that Macarius can speak of the intellect 'rising out of materiality' and of the heart as a 'tomb' makes it plain that his 'mystique du coeur' contains a form of spirituality that emphasizes the direct apprehension by the intellect of divine realities, without explicit reference to the body.

---

[14] 'Mystique et orthodoxie: Évagre et Syméon', 107.    [15] See esp. Ch. 2.3.

The intellectual-immaterial element in Macarius served as a corrective to the crudely material understanding of spiritual experience characteristic of the Messalians. This element allows him to speak of the Fall as 'forgetfulness' (I 3.5.6), as the loss of the 'immaterial and deathless senses' (I 58.3.3) and as the 'blinding' of the intellect (III 20.2.1). It informs his understanding of perfection as the purification of the intellect through the gathering of the dispersed and multiple thoughts of the soul by the 'wings' of the Spirit 'into one single divine thought' (III 18.2.2), and as an ascent from materiality to 'co-mingle with unoriginate intellect' (I 3.6.1).

Evagrius is equally ill-served by the pressing of the contrast between himself and Macarius; he tends to come out of it as a rarefied intellectual or as a crypto-Gnostic. His anthropology, for example, is rather more nuanced than Meyendorff's set of choices would allow. It is misleading to depict Evagrius' *nous* as straining to be released from the material creation—the body and soul are there to help the intellect and not to hinder it. Evagrius insists that to denigrate the body is to blaspheme the Creator and to deny the workings of providence.[16] Evagrius has, in his own way, a unified understanding of the human person. Intellect, soul, and body form a whole: the intellect is directly linked to the rational part of the soul, the body to the irascible and desiring parts of the soul. Thus the soul constitutes the bond uniting the human person, taking a comparable role to that of the heart in Macarius. Furthermore, the quest for *apatheia* does not entail the quenching but rather the harnessing of the passionate parts of the soul—a Platonic insight—so that the soul desires knowledge and virtue and is angry and fights against the thoughts. Hence, as Evagrius' *On Prayer* puts it, pure prayer includes an element of joy and of longing: 'The state of prayer is one of freedom from passions, which by virtue of the most intense love transports to the noetic realm the intellect that longs for wisdom.'[17] The spiritual life is not a struggle to transcend but to transform body and soul. This process is fulfilled in the eschaton. As he writes to Melania: 'There will be a time when the human body, soul, and mind cease to be separate, with their own names and their plurality, because the body and soul

---

[16] *Schol. Prov.* 215 (SC 340, p. 310).
[17] *OP* 52 (PG 79 1177C). For the element of joy see also *OP* 61 (1180C).

will be raised to the rank of *nous*. This may be concluded from the text "That they may be one even as we are one".[18] The classification of Evagrius as an 'intellectualist' ought to be further qualified with reference to passages in which Evagrius deals with the heart:

Allow the Spirit of God to dwell within you; then in his love he will come and make a habitation with you: he will reside in you and live in you. If your heart is pure you will see him and he will sow in you the good seed of reflection upon his actions and wonder at his majesty. This will happen if you take the trouble to weed out from your soul the undergrowth of desires, along with the thorns and tares of bad habits.[19]

In this passage Evagrius picks up on certain themes more commonly associated with Macarius, most obviously the indwelling of the Spirit, the biblical theme of purity of heart, and, to some extent, even the theme of working the earth of the heart. Evagrius was certainly well aware of the biblical understanding of the place of the heart. The *Kephalaia Gnostika* make this clear: 'According to the word of Solomon, the *nous* is joined with the heart.'[20]

Elsewhere, Evagrius makes further use of the dimension of the heart, noticeably in the *Ad monachos*, in which he consciously imitates biblical Wisdom literature. Here he links the heart with knowledge (24, 27, 94, 117) and with wisdom (31, 131). He treats it as the place of thoughts (37, 45, 58, 59) and as the locus of spiritual warfare (36, 60, 62, 66, 100). The most interesting examples are perhaps 135–6:

> Contemplation of worlds enlarges the heart;
> principles of providence and judgement lift it up.
>
> Knowledge of incorporeals raises the intellect
> and sets it before the Holy Trinity.

Were it not for these passages, one might assume that in imitating Solomon, Evagrius has simply substituted the word 'heart' where he would normally use 'intellect'. In fact he seems here to be drawing a distinction between the specific functions of heart and intellect, treating secondary natural contemplation as the proper

---

[18] *Epistula ad Melaniam* 4 (Frankenberg, *Euagrius Ponticus*, p. 617).
[19] *Admonition on Prayer*, tr. Brock, in *Syriac Fathers on Prayer and the Spiritual Life*, 68.
[20] *KG* vi.87 (PO 28, p. 255).

sphere of the heart and primary natural contemplation, the stage prior to true theology, as the proper sphere of the intellect.

These references do not amount to a developed understanding of the place of the heart in the spiritual life and are not easy to fit into any conventional schematization of Evagrian doctrine. The heart is certainly less integrated into the Evagrian teaching than is the intellect in the Macarian. These instances should, however, give pause for thought whenever one is tempted to portray Evagrius as a mere intellectualist.

These sketches of certain of the less familiar aspects of these two exponents of early monastic spirituality should not obscure the very real differences remaining between the two writers. In terms of cosmology they are quite distinct. Certain elements in Macarius such as a hint of the two-fold creation of man (III 26.7.2) and a reference to the distribution of bodies of differing quantity (II 4.9) do recall Origenist cosmology and anthropology, yet neither is taken by Macarius as an indication of a pre-cosmic fall. Macarius does not distinguish the stages of the spiritual life so clearly as does Evagrius. Non-iconic prayer is not found in any developed form in Macarius; he requires only that prayer be undistracted and free of all material images. Our authors may also be distinguished on the question of the nature of the light witnessed in prayer. Evagrius speaks of the light of prayer most often as the light of the human intellect: 'When the intellect has shed its fallen state and acquired the state of grace, then during prayer it will see its own nature like sapphire or the colour of the sky. In Scripture this is called the realm of God that was seen by the elders on Mount Sinai.'[21]

When the *intellect* reaches such a state it truly becomes the dwelling-place of God: 'From holy David we have learnt clearly what the "place of God" is. For he says that: "His place has been in peace, and his dwelling place from Sion" [Ps. 75: 3 LXX]. The place of God therefore is the rational soul, and his "dwelling place" the luminous intellect.'[22] The luminous intellect is the inner Sinai, the place of God's self-revelation. This light is, presumably, created, yet it should be noted that Evagrius also speaks

---

[21] *Thoughts* 39 (pp. 286–8). On this theme see Guillaumont, 'La Vision de l'intellect par lui-même dans la mystique évagrienne'; Bunge, *Das Geistgebet. Studien zum Traktat De Oratione des Evagrios Pontikos*, ch. 4: 'Zustand des Intellektes'.

[22] *Skemmata* 25 (p. 377).

of the uncreated light of the Holy Trinity[23] and suggests that these lights are in some sense 'cognate'.[24]

Macarius is generally wary of the narcissistic connotations of the quest for the vision of one's own intellect or soul: taxed on this issue he gives a distinctly wary answer, allowing the possibility and stating that the image of the soul is like that of the angels, but stresses the rarity of such visions. The interlocutor has to ask the question twice in order to elicit even this response (ii 7.5–7). Elsewhere, he treats our inability to see our own soul as a product of the Fall (iii 26.4.4). When illumined one will be granted to see the rational nature of the soul (i 39.1.3). On one occasion he even describes the soul as 'shining all round like a bright pearl or precious stone' (i 5.1)—a description that, in a less explicit way than Evagrius, associates the light of the soul with the divine *shekinah*. Like Evagrius, he seems to perceive a certain connection between the light of the soul and the divine light; speaking of his own mystical experience he describes how 'the very light which shines in the heart opened up to a more inward, deeper and hidden light' (ii 8.3). It is this deeper light that he focuses on, rather than the created light of the soul. He stresses that this deeper light is the very light of the divinity shining within man: 'The perfect mystery of the Christian faith [ ... ] is the effulgence of celestial light in the revelation and power of the Spirit. [ ... ] The illumination of grace is not merely a revelation on the level of conceptual images. It is the true and hypostatic effulgence of the eternal light in the soul' (i 58.1.1–2.1).

Notwithstanding the distinction in their respective approaches to the nature of the light perceived in prayer, Macarius and Evagrius are united in their concentration upon light as opposed to the dimension of the divine darkness focused on by Gregory of Nyssa after Clement and Philo. It is possible that neither Evagrius nor Macarius were familiar with the later works of Gregory of Nyssa dealing with this motif. Both follow rather the tradition of Origen, whose commentaries on the Old Testament pass over the theme of the divine darkness. It is quite possible that Macarius was simply not aware of Gregory's development of the theme.

---

[23] *KG* 11.29 (p. 73); *Thoughts* 42 (p. 296); *Skemmata* 27 (p. 377).
[24] *Skemmata* 2 (p. 374). As will have been noted, his descriptions of the light of the intellect deliberately evoke the divine *shekinah*.

Similarly, we may presume that the contact between Evagrius and the Cappadocians lessened after Evagrius' departure from Constantinople in 382, and thus he too may have been unfamiliar with the later works of Gregory of Nyssa, such as, most notably, the *Life of Moses*.[25] Whatever the fact of the matter, it should again be noted that the motif of light does not in itself preclude an apophatic approach to the knowledge of God.

Whilst many points of convergence and divergence remain to be explored, those mentioned should be sufficient to make the point that the distinction between Evagrius and Macarius is a subtler and more complex issue than is generally appreciated.[26] The area of anthropology is the key one—each may take heart or intellect as their primary motif, yet each is also aware of the complementary dimension. Evagrius is familiar with the world of the heart from the Bible and the traditions of the Egyptian desert, while Macarius has picked up on the concept of the intellect from the Hellenic tradition. Although Macarius has integrated the intellect within his teaching far more profoundly than has Evagrius the heart (allowing us to assert that Evagrius' *nous* is contained within Macarius' *kardia*), both may be seen as groping towards the expression of the same spiritual reality. The chief difference lies in the greater balance and breadth of Macarian over Evagrian anthropology—not in any fundamental polarity between the two treatments.

In this light the Byzantine reading of Macarius and Evagrius (often under the guise of Nilus) becomes more readily comprehensible. Far from distinguishing 'currents of spirituality' the classical Byzantine approach was one of synthesis. This approach is epitomized in Diadochus, Maximus, and the fourteenth-century Hesychasts. It might not be too bold to argue that the interaction

---

[25] There are always controversies concerning the dating of Gregory's works: Jean Daniélou suggests in his edition of the *Life of Moses* a rough dating of 392 (SC 1 bis, p. ix).

[26] We may also note that both stress the concept of *apatheia*. Both also treat deification as the goal of the Christian life. Hence Evagrius, *KG* v.81 (p. 211): 'When the *nous* will receive essential science, then it also will be called God, because it also will be able to found various worlds.' Cf. Macarius, II 34.2: 'All are changed into a divine nature, having become Christs and gods and children of God.' Both approaches to exegesis are related to that of Origen. Evagrius' three levels of interpretation (as in *Gnostikos* 18 (p. 117)) correspond only to the two higher levels envisaged by Origen. Evagrius does not allow for the literal meaning of a given text in his schema. Macarius speaks both of the literal and of the 'hidden' meaning of scriptural texts (see above, Ch. 2.3). In this respect, it might be argued that Macarius is in fact closer to Origen's pattern of exegesis than is Evagrius.

of the legacies of Evagrius and Macarius shaped the emergence of a distinctively 'Orthodox' spiritual tradition.

This interaction was not one of opposing—or even sharply contrasting—spiritual currents, but rather the interplay of distinctive yet complementary insights into the nature of the Christian life. Despite coming from very different angles, the teachings of our authors—both of whom have nourished many generations of Christians despite varying degrees of ecclesiastical censure—are far from incompatible.

# PART II

# The Legacy

# 5

# Mark the Monk

## 5.1 Introduction

Mark the Monk, also known, less correctly, as the Hermit or the Ascetic, is a difficult figure to place.[1] In some respects he is more elusive even than the author of the Macarian writings. Our only advantage with Mark is that we can be sure about his name. We have very few clues as to his location or position. In his *To Nicholas*, he writes of his having retired into the desert 'with the true labourers and athletes of Christ', but gives no clues as to where that desert was (v 1029B).[2] The *Controversy with an Advocate* suggests that Mark was at some stage the superior of a monastic community—again with no reference to the location of that community.

We have slightly more information as to Mark's dates. The *terminus ad quem* for his writings is 534, the date of a Syriac MS containing a translation of a selection of his writings.[3] Another

[1] On Mark in general, see the Introduction of Kallistos Ware to the French translation of the authentic works of Mark: *Marc le Moine: Traités spirituels et théologiques* (tr. Sr Claire-Agnes Zirnheld). The Marcan corpus given in Migne (PG 65 905–1140) is in parts gravely corrupted. Thankfully, a critical edition has recently appeared: de Durand, *Marc le Moine: Traités*, 2 vols. (SC 445 and 455). The authentic works of Mark are: *Op.* I, *On the Spiritual Law*; *Op.* II, *On Those who Think that they are Justified by their Works*; *Op.* III, *On Penitence*; *Op.* IV, *On Baptism*; *Op.* V, *To Nicholas*; *Op.* VII, *Controversy with an Advocate*; *Op.* VIII, *Discussion of the Intellect with its own Soul*; *Op.* X, *On Melchizedek*; *Op.* XI, *Against the Nestorians* (or, *On the Hypostatic Union*). Several of the spurious *Opuscula* given in Migne are, incidentally, Macarian. See Gribomont, 'Marc le Moine', for a summary of the widespread confusion of the Marcan and Macarian MS traditions.

[2] References to Mark give the number of the Marcan *opusculum* in Roman numerals followed by their place in Migne. While the text is that given by de Durand, I have, for the sake of general convenience, maintained the Migne numbering, which is given in parallel by de Durand. The only exception is *Op.* XI, not given in Migne, where I give the section number in de Durand followed by the numbering of Kunze's edition in brackets. *Opuscula* I and II (which take the form of short chapters) also have their chapter number as given in de Durand (corresponding closely but not exactly to the numbering in Migne).

[3] British Library, Additional MS 12 175, ff. 145ᵛ–155. The manuscript also contains the earliest dated Syriac translation from the Macariana (211ʳ–225ʳ).

clue is given by the fact that he speaks of the hypostatic union
with some frequency in his works *On Melchizedek* (*Op.* x) and
*Against the Nestorians* (or, *On the Hypostatic Union*) (*Op.* xi).[4] The
concept is first attested with certainty in Cyril of Alexandria's
*Second Letter to Nestorius* (430). Mark treats it as an acceptable
concept, requiring no defence or explanation, indicating that he
is here relying on Cyril. This gives a *post quem*, for *Opuscula* x and
xi at least, of *c*.430–1. The fact that he nowhere uses the title
*Theotokos* is odd in a post-Ephesine writer with decidedly Cyrilline
sympathies. Kunze suggested that Mark's failure to use the title
allows us to place him in the early fifth century, composing
*Opusculum* xi on the eve of the Council of Ephesus. This is
stretching the evidence and, of course, arguing from silence.
I am, furthermore, not convinced by the arguments of Grillmeier
that would have Mark attacking an Origenist Christology in the
context of the anti-Origenist campaign of 399–400, or indeed by
those of Gribomont, who agrees on the target of *Opusculum* xi, but
switches the context to early sixth-century Palestine. If Mark is
indeed attacking an Origenist Christology, it is odd in the extreme
that he should give so little attention to the question of Christ's
human soul.[5]

Allowing a certain amount of time for filtration into the Syriac
world and subsequent translation, we may assume that Mark was
active in the latter two-thirds of the fifth century.[6] We may therefore exclude the possibility that the connections explored in this
chapter result from Mark's influence upon Macarius. Mark is a
key figure in this study, not least because he has been widely
regarded as an anti-Messalian writer. The fact that he appears
to have been deeply indebted to the Macarian writings must
further nuance our understanding of the relation between Macarius and the Messalian tendency.

---

[4] *Op.* x (1124B); *Op.* xi. 13 (8), 17 (10), 21 (13), 26 (15) (× 2), 30 (16), 34 (20), 42 (23).

[5] Kunze, *Marcus Eremita* (discussed by Ware, in the Introduction to Zirnheld (tr.), *Marc le
Moine*, xiii); Grillmeier, 'Marco Eremita e l'origenismo'; Gribomont, 'Marc l'Ermite et la
christologie évagrienne'. See also below, Ch. 5.9, on Mark's Christology.

[6] Note also the ingenious suggestion of Henry Chadwick, in 'The Identity and Date of
Mark the Monk', that would have Mark as a certain Higumen of Tarsus responding in
*Opuscula* xi and iv respectively to suspicions of Chalcedonian and Messalian sympathies
raised by Severus in 515–18. Cf. Hesse's sceptical reply, 'Was Mark the Monk a Sixth-
Century Higumen near Tarsus?'

## 5.2 The Fall and its Consequences

The Fall provides a natural starting-point for our examination of the relations obtaining between Mark and Macarius. Mark's account distinguishes three things experienced by Adam: 'Suggestion (προσβολή), according to the economy; transgression, according to his own lack of faith; and death, according to the just judgement of God' (IV 1025C).

Susceptibility to demonic suggestion is part and parcel of the human condition (IV 1013C). Transgression is, and has always been, 'a matter of choice, and not of necessity' (προαιρετικὴ καὶ οὐκ ἀναγκαστική) (IV 1025D). We cannot, therefore, have inherited the actual transgression of Adam. If we had, we would be transgressors 'according to the necessity of transmission' (κατὰ τὴν ἐκ διαδοχῆς ἀνάγκην) and consequently not liable to blame. What we have inherited is death, 'which is alienation from God'. The death of Adam, his alienation from God, has also alienated us from God (IV 1017CD).

Death is first and foremost separation from God. The physical process of decay is but a corollary of this separation. Kallistos Ware has lucidly indicated how Mark's understanding of death embraces not just physical mortality but also spiritual infirmity and even an element of guilt.[7] These wider implications of death are most fully developed outside the treatise *On Baptism*. Mark explains that, while the act of Adam's transgression was his alone, it has nevertheless placed all humanity 'under sin', in, that is, a state of sin: 'all are born under the sin of the transgression' (III 980C). He expands: 'No one was exempted from the accusation (ἔγκλημα), because the root of our nature—I mean the first man—was subject to it' (XI.31 (18)).[8]

Because of the natural solidarity of humanity in Adam, all are subject to the consequences of the Fall. Mark goes on to chronicle the steady degeneration of humankind to the point where its involvement with sin became an 'inextricable bond' (ἄλυτος δεσμός) (XI.31–2 (18)). Elsewhere, he writes that we became 'captives' and 'dominated by the enemy (ὑπὸ τοῦ ἐχθροῦ κυριευόμενοι)

---

[7] Introduction to Zirnheld (tr.), *Marc le Moine*, xvi–xxi.
[8] For the solidarity of man in Adam, see also IV. 10 (1013C).

through the operations of the passions'.[9] He calls this state one of 'grievous captivity' (χαλεπὴ αἰχμαλωσία), in which we were 'ruled over by invisible and bitter death' (βασιλευόμενοι ὑπὸ τοῦ ἀοράτου καὶ πικροῦ θανάτου) (v 1041D). Even in *Opusculum* iv, generally very restrained on the consequences of the Fall, Mark allows that man's lapsarian condition was one of 'servitude' or 'slavery' (δουλεία) (iv 988c).

Macarius gives more consideration than Mark to the question of in what exactly the act of transgression consisted. He holds that the commandment was essentially a sign of Adam's creaturely status, a warning to him not to consider himself a god. It was this warning that Adam failed to respect (i 2.3.3).[10] There was no compulsion in this: the opposing power always operates by persuasion, not necessity (προτρεπτική ἐστιν, οὐκ ἀναγκαστική) (i 8.4.3).[11] Adam chose to listen to the word of the evil one, and so fell (i 2.3.4). Because of his disobedience, Adam's soul died, being separated from the life of God (i 28.1.3). The prince of darkness captured his soul, surrounding it with the power of darkness. Because the soul was thus subjected, the body became subject to physical death (i 28.1.4). Adam's posterity have inherited not only physical mortality but also Adam's inner subjection to evil:

Just as Adam, having transgressed, received into himself the leaven of evil passions, so also those begotten by him, the whole race of Adam

---

[9] Cf. Proposition 1 of the list of John of Damascus (J 1): '[They say] that Satan personally co-dwells in a human being and rules (κυριεύει) him in every way.' Macarius avoids the verb κυριεύω in this context, but is happy to use βασιλεύω (iii 8.3.1, cited below). Paul uses both of sin in Romans 6: 12, 14.

[10] Cf. Dörries, *Die Theologie*, 42–3. Dörries holds that this exegesis of the nature of the transgression strikingly anticipates much modern exegesis. Mark does not go into any detail as to the precise nature of the act by which Adam fell. Macarius also gives more attention than Mark to the state of Adam in paradise, demonstrating an understanding of original righteousness—Adam is seen 'rejoicing in the contemplation of divine good things'—coupled with a sense of Adam's scope for growth 'towards a greater glory' (i 2.3.6, 12). It is a pity that Macarius is not included in Williams's *Ideas of the Fall* in that he defies the overly schematic categorizations with which Williams works. For a fuller and more recent analysis of the doctrines of the Fall, see Gross, *Geschichte des Erbsündendogmas*, esp. ii. 158–77, in which he discusses the Fall in Mark, Diadochus, and Macarius.

[11] Cf. Mark iv.17 (1025D), cited above. This kind of terminology is not unusual: Cyril of Jerusalem, for example, writes that the devil can suggest sin, τὸ δὲ καὶ ἀναγκάσαι παρὰ προαίρεσιν οὐκ ἔχει τὴν ἐξουσίαν (*Catecheses ad illuminandos* iv.21: PG 33 481B). The formulation of the idea in Mark and Macarius is, nonetheless, remarkably close.

have, *by participation* (κατὰ μετοχήν), shared in this leaven. (II 24.2, emphasis mine)

You are the son of him who transgressed the commandment, and because you are his son, the gross darkness, the spider's web, the disobedience and the [flaming] sword are necessarily fixed in you as in all his sons. (III 21.3.3)[12]

When [Adam] transgressed the commandment of God, he fell under the sentence (ὑπὸ τὴν ἀπόφασιν γέγονεν). Ruled over (βασιλευθείς) by the evil one, his desires became as savage [as those of his ruler], and all the race born of him (πᾶν τὸ ἐξ αὐτοῦ γένος) found itself ruled over [by the evil one], in savagery and isolation. (III 8.3.1)

From the transgression of Adam the whole human race has received into its nature, into its soul and body, a bitter poison of death (φάρμακον πικρὸν θανάτου), darkness, and sin. (III 18.1.3)[13]

Like Mark, Macarius holds that because of its natural solidarity in Adam, all humanity bears the consequences, both physical and spiritual, of Adam's transgression.[14] The spiritual inheritance of the Fall is, for Macarius, indwelling sin, the 'evil inheritance of the passions' (I 29.2.8), the 'ancient empassioned holding' that has deeply wounded every soul (I 25.1.6). The Fall is a trans-historical event, a reality to each and every soul (I 2.3.13).[15]

Macarius anticipates Mark in using the legal term ἔγκλημα, albeit in the plural, for the charge or accusation to which man has become subject due to Adam's transgression. This is an unusual term to use in the context of the Fall; I am not aware of any writer who uses the term in this context. Macarius writes that the Lord cancels the 'legal right arising from the disobedience'

---

[12] The spider's web appears to be either a metaphor for the fragility of human existence or, and this would perhaps fit better with the context, an allusion to the webs of deceit woven by evil within the soul. Desprez has a useful note on this metaphor in his edition of the text.

[13] This recalls Gregory of Nyssa's designation of evil as a δηλητήριον (*Or. cat.* 37: GNO 3 (4), p. 93). Williams, *Ideas of the Fall*, 278, calls this 'a momentary emergence of the characteristically "African" tendency to conceive the results of the Fall as involving a positive *depravatio*, and not a mere *deprivatio*'. In Macarius we have more than a momentary emergence of what Williams calls the 'African' tendency.

[14] Mark's argument that we cannot be transgressors 'according to the necessity of transmission' could, on a superficial reading, be taken as a criticism of Macarius' view that we are 'necessarily' sons of the transgressor, and therefore subject to the consequences of his transgression. Taken as a whole, however, Mark's account agrees that we do indeed inherit the consequences of the transgression simply by virtue of being human.

[15] For the re-enactment of the Fall within each and every soul, see below, Ch. 5.6.

(τὸ δικαίωμα τῆς παρακοῆς) held by the devil over us by taking upon himself the 'charges' (τὰ ἐγκλήματα) against us (I 37.6).

Macarius also anticipates Mark in his descriptions of man's fallen state as one of captivity and enslavement. In addition to the citations already given, Macarius declares that man has fallen into a state of 'shameful slavery and dreadful captivity' (αἰσχρᾶς δουλείας καὶ δεινῆς αἰχμαλωσίας) (I 61.1.8). He is 'in captivity and bitter slavery and is bound in the bonds of sin' (ὑπὸ τὴν αἰχμαλωσίαν καὶ τὴν δουλείαν τὴν πικρὰν καὶ ἔτι δέδεται ἐν τοῖς δεσμοῖς τῆς ἁμαρτίας) (I 61.2.3). He must separate himself 'from the dreadful companionship and grievous habit of sin' (ἐκ τῆς δεινῆς συντροφίας καὶ χαλεπῆς συνηθείας τῆς ἁμαρτίας) (III 21.3.3).[16]

The essentials of our authors' understanding of the consequences of the Fall are the same. They share a sombre estimation of the consequences of the Fall, and may be said to agree with the statement of Gregory of Nyssa that 'human nature is weak with regard to the doing of good, in that it was once and for all hamstrung by wickedness'.[17] In both Macarius and Mark, inherited death is seen primarily as a spiritual reality; physical death is an epiphenomenon, attendant upon the death of the soul. The effects of the Fall extend to all humanity by virtue of the solidarity of humanity in Adam. Both describe the state of fallen man as one of 'captivity', using substantially the same distinctive vocabulary. Both speak of the handing down of the ἔγκλημα incurred at the Fall—a term which, atypically for the Eastern Christian tradition, implies an element of inherited guilt. The only tangible difference is Mark's refusal to accept the theory of inherited indwelling sin, Macarius' 'veil of the passions'. We shall discuss the reasons for this below. The sombreness of our two authors with respect to the Fall must, of course, be seen within the

---

[16] Αἰχμαλωσία, used by both Macarius and Mark, is not a common term for the captivity consequent upon the Fall. It does, however, crop up in Clement of Alexandria (Paed. 1.8.65.3: GCS 12, p. 128): τῆς τοῦ ἀντικειμένου αἰχμαλωσίας. Clement also speaks of man being 'bound' by sins (Prot. XI.111.1: GCS 12, p. 78). This passage indicates an implicit understanding of the solidarity of humanity in Adam, an understanding shared by Irenaeus, see Williams, Ideas of the Fall, 202–3. Overall, however, Clement's estimation of the gravity of the Fall is far less sombre than that of either Macarius or Mark. Macarius, in particular, has a sense of the severity of the wound inflicted by the Fall that is quite as acute as that of Augustine (as Gross, Geschichte des Erbsündendogmas, 176–7).

[17] De oratione dominica 4 (GNO 7 (2), p. 47).

context of their teaching on redemption—a gift that is conveyed to humanity primarily by means of the sacrament of baptism.

## 5.3 Baptism

Mark stresses baptism more than any previous ascetic writer. Evagrius, for example, barely mentions the sacrament. Babai the Great tells us that Mark wrote the treatise *On Baptism* (*Op.* IV) specifically against the Messalians.[18] Henry Chadwick has nuanced the question by suggesting that Mark is in fact defending himself against a charge of Messalianism, hence the intensity of his rebuttal; Mark, it might be said, protests too much.[19] Peterson, working on the limited Macarian material in Migne, followed Kmosko in concluding that Mark was directly attacking Macarius in *Opusculum* IV.[20] Kallistos Ware has drawn attention to the far richer baptismal teaching of Macarius to be found in Collections I and III. He concludes with the suggestion that the baptismal teaching of Mark does not so much refute as complement that of Macarius.[21] Othmar Hesse, who dedicated the bulk of his doctoral dissertation to the issue of baptism, follows Peterson in arguing that, in this area, Mark is consciously opposing the teaching of Macarius—notwithstanding Hesse's fuller knowledge of the Macarian corpus.[22] More recently de Durand has demurred from Hesse's thesis regarding the target of *Op.* IV.[23]

It may help our appreciation of the nature of Mark's baptismal theology if we begin by looking at the treatment of baptism found outside his treatise *On Baptism*. *Opusculum* II, *On Those who Think that they are Justified by their Works*, contains what is manifestly a critique of the Messalians: 'Some say that: "we are unable to do good unless we consciously (ἐναργῶς) receive the grace of the Spirit." Those who are always by choice involved in pleasures refrain from

---

[18] *Commentary on the Kephalia Gnostika of Evagrius* (III.85), ed. Frankenberg, *Euagrius Ponticus*, p. 253.

[19] 'The Identity and Date of Mark the Monk'.

[20] 'Die Schrift des Eremiten Markus über die Taufe und die Messalianer'. Cf. Kmosko, *Liber graduum*, xcv: 'opusculum De baptismo placitis Macarii e diametro oppositum est'.

[21] 'The Sacrament of Baptism and the Ascetic Life in the Teaching of Mark the Monk'.

[22] 'Markos Eremites und Symeon von Mesopotamien'. See also Dörries, *Symeon von Mesopotamien*, 444–7, and *Die Theologie*, 137 n. 20.

[23] De Durand, *Marc le Moine: Traités*, i. 275–87.

doing what lies within their power on the grounds that they lack help (II.55 937C).' This comes as a riposte to the deterministic and patently Messalian claim that it is impossible to do good without the active and felt presence of grace. Macarius had also pinpointed this aspect of the Messalian tendency in very similar terms. Speaking of those unable to put up with the necessary trials of the spiritual life, he observes: 'The resolutions (προαιρέσεις) of such as these are as follows: "If I do not straight away receive the grace of the Spirit, I shall leave, it is impossible for me to stand fast, I cannot endure for long; if I do receive it, then I shall remain"' (III 17.1.1).[24] Macarius goes on to emphasize the necessity of trials, the needfulness of disinterested service, and the proper attitude to take upon the reception of grace, that is, one of thanksgiving. A man such as the one described above will never be able to survive tribulation, even if he does receive grace.

Mark counters the Messalian misconception of grace with a distinction between hidden and revealed grace:

Grace has been given secretly (μυστικῶς) to those who have been baptised in Christ; it becomes active (ἐνεργεῖ) to the degree that they put the commandments into practice. It never ceases to help us hiddenly (κρυφίως); but it depends on us (ἐφ᾿ ἡμῖν ἐστι) to do or not to do good, so far as we are able. (II.56 937D)

Mark adds that baptismal grace is a 'talent' that must be worked with if we are to 'enter consciously (ἐναργῶς) into the joy of the Lord' (ibid.).[25] In both his use of the image of the talent and his distinction between hidden and revealed grace, Mark is, as we shall see, drawing upon Macarius. Elsewhere, Mark stresses the fact that baptism is the single foundation of repentance (III 976D). Necessarily, therefore, post-baptismal repentance must be allowed (III 977A). In his *Discussion of the Intellect with its Own Soul*, Mark speaks of the revelation of the hidden grace imparted at baptism (VIII 1108D). *Opuscula* V, VII, and IX do not specifically deal with baptismal grace. *Opusculum* XI contains several scattered references to baptism and, particularly, to the baptismal creed known by Mark. The references in *Opuscula* II and VIII clearly presuppose—or anticipate—the teaching on hidden and revealed grace contained in *Opusculum* IV. The fact that baptismal grace is

---

[24] Cf. also TV h.10.1.     [25] Some MSS have ἐνεργῶς (actively).

not discussed in *Opusculum* x, *On Melchizedek*, is not surprising, given the subject matter. The same can be said of *Opusculum* vii, *Controversy with an Advocate*: the question simply did not come up in the debate itself, or the discussion that followed. The total absence of the theme in *Opusculum* v, *To Nicholas*, is indeed odd, especially given the more general nature of this letter.[26] We should not, however, rule out the possibility that Mark was simply taking baptism for granted in his letter to a familiar protégé. On balance, it can be said that Mark's baptismal teaching does run throughout his works, and not just in the polemical treatise *On Baptism*.

Mark begins his *On Baptism* by setting himself against the proposition that 'the ancient sin (τὴν παλαιὰν ἁμαρτίαν) is removed by ascetic effort (ἐξ ἀγώνων)'. This is presented as the position of those who find in themselves the same 'operation of sin' (τὴν αὐτὴν ἐνέργειαν τῆς ἁμαρτίας) after baptism (IV 985A).[27] Mark is concerned to refute the claim associated with the Messalians that baptism is at best neutral, and that perfection comes only through assiduous prayer and the sensible advent of the Holy Spirit.[28] Mark again insists that the grace of baptism is perfect and complete (IV 985C), albeit conferred 'secretly' (μυστικῶς) (IV 988C) and 'imperceptibly' (λεληθότως) (IV 992D). The purpose of the Christian life is therefore the discovery of that which we already have: 'the perfection which has been given us' (τὴν δεδομένην ἡμῖν τελειότητα) (IV 988A). The purification worked secretly at baptism is 'found to be active (ἐνεργῶς) through the practice of the commandments' (IV 988C). It is absolutely necessary that we strive for the revelation of this grace: 'If we do not put the commandments of God into practice, the grace that has been given us will not be revealed (ἀποκαλύπτεται)' (IV 1008B).

Mark expands his defence of baptism by asserting that baptism dissolves the state of sin in which man has languished since the Fall: 'If, having been baptised, we have not been freed from ancestral sin, it is clear that we would not even be able to practise the works of freedom. If we are able to do these, it is clear that we

---

[26] De Durand, 'Études sur Marc le Moine I: L'Épître à Nicholas', discerns many such oddities in this work, using them as an argument against its authenticity. See also the discussion of *Opusculum* v below, Ch. 5.8.

[27] On post-baptismal sin, see below, Ch. 5.3.

[28] The charges against the Messalians on this issue are collected together by Columba Stewart in his handy arrangement of the anti-Messalian lists, '*Working the Earth of the Heart*', 246–9.

have hiddenly been freed from the servitude of sin' (IV 988CD). No 'remnant' (ἐγκατάλειμμα) of the sin of Adam disposes us to sin after baptism (IV 992C). Through baptism, man is restored to paradise: 'By the grace of God you have become a new Adam [...]. The Lord came for our sakes and died for us; he freed us from ancestral death; he cleanses and renews through baptism; he sets us in the paradise of the Church [...]' (IV 1025AB).[29] In other words, the situation of the baptized soul is that of Adam: the slate is wiped clean. Such an insistence on the complete effacement of all moral and spiritual effects of the Fall is unusual. Gregory of Nyssa had held that the waters of baptism bring about 'not a complete effacement but a certain break in the continuity of evil'.[30] Even Diadochus, for all his stress on the power of baptism, allows for the continuing 'duality of will', the fractured psyche inherited from Adam (*GC* 78). Furthermore, according to Mark, baptism does not only convey liberation from the non-physical effects of original sin, it also confers the indwelling of Christ (IV 1005B), that is, the indwelling of the Holy Trinity (IV 1008D–1009A).

Macarius' teaching on baptism developed on two fronts: against nascent Messalian anti-sacramentalism and against the proposition that baptism confers immutability in the good.[31] The latter proposition crops up explicitly only in the Arabic Collection TV, but is implicit throughout Macarius' work. Macarius reports certain 'false brethren' as saying:

'He who has obtained the grace of God remains forever immutable and has no possibility of changing.' They base themselves for this assertion on the witness of the Apostle who said: 'For as many of you as have been baptized into Christ, have put on Christ (Gal. 3: 27).' They assert that, because they have put on Christ, they cannot thereafter change. (TV h.10.5)

Hesse wrongly supposes this group to be 'kirchliche Mönche' whose position Macarius has misrepresented.[32] Such a determin-istic view of baptism, which Macarius rightly condemns, would certainly not be representative of traditional Church teaching.

---

[29] On paradise, see below (Ch. 5.6).    [30] *Or. cat.* 35 (GNO 3 (4), p. 89).

[31] The best exposition of Macarius' baptismal teaching is Desprez, 'Le Baptême chez le Pseudo-Macaire'.

[32] Hesse, 'Markos Eremites', 57.

Even Mark, for all his exaltation of baptism, would not have gone so far—on the contrary, he stresses post-baptismal freedom: '[We do not pretend that] every man who has been baptized cannot thereafter change' (IV 1004B). It does not seem to me necessary to regard the teaching of these 'false brethren' to whom Macarius refers as a caricature of traditional Church teaching on baptism. It is more plausible, and more straightforward, to take the passage as a critique of a tendency to see baptismal grace as automatic and irresistible. Mark follows Macarius in rejecting such a deterministic approach.

Notwithstanding the paucity of references to sacramental baptism in Collection II, Macarius develops in the other main collections an unambiguous critique of the Messalian disregard for baptism and conflation of the sensation of grace with the presence thereof. He makes the fundamental assertion that the Holy Spirit is present in 'all the mystagogy of holy baptism' (1 52.1.5). In order to explain how he can hold baptism to be 'true and worthy of faith', and yet hope to receive still more from heaven, Macarius develops in Logos 1 43 a crucial distinction between hidden and revealed grace, one that was to prove central to Mark's baptismal theology. In baptism, writes Macarius, 'we receive the beginning (ἀρχή) of the real existence (ὑπόστασις) of the Spirit and of our salvation'.[33] Initially this 'participation in the Spirit' is often received 'in a very subtle manner' (ἀπὸ πολλῆς λεπτότητος), so subtly that one can be said to be as if 'unaware of its activity' (ὡς ἀγνοεῖν τὴν ἐνέργειαν). This beginning must be developed through progress in the virtues 'until it is perceived and revealed' (ἕως αἰσθήσεως καὶ ἀποκαλύψεως), until the 'complete removal of the veil of darkness and the perfect acquisition of the Spirit of adoption, the Paraclete' (1 43.2). Macarius concludes this discussion in no uncertain terms: 'Thus baptism is for us true and sure and in it we receive the life of the Spirit; if we persevere and make progress in all the virtues, with effort and struggle, then this life will grow and manifest itself in us, perfecting us by its own grace' (1 43.6). Macarius' understanding of the divine indwelling conferred at baptism differs from that of Mark only in

---

[33] Cf. Hebrews 3: 14. Desprez ('Le Baptême', 144–5) shows that this application of this verse is original to Macarius, who takes it to be equivalent to the seal of the Spirit, the 'pledge of our inheritance', of Ephesians 1: 14.

its somewhat more dynamic character, in its greater insistence on the progressive character of the revelation of the inward presence of the Spirit.

Macarius also anticipates Mark in holding that the indwelling of the Spirit necessarily entails the indwelling of the Trinity:

Speaking of [the inner communion of the Spirit], St Paul says: 'The grace of our Lord Jesus Christ, the love of God the Father, and the communion of the Holy Spirit' and so on [2 Cor. 13: 14]. Consider the words carefully, and you will find that the holy and venerable Trinity dwells in the purified man, through divine assistance and the man's own excellent conduct. I say indwelling not as it is in itself—for the Trinity is uncontainable (ἀχώρητος) by any created thing—but according to the capacity (χωρητικόν) and receptivity of the man in whom it has been well-pleased. (I 52.2.5-6)

Macarius' explanation of how exactly God can be said to dwell in us is also taken up by Mark. Questioned on his statement that the Spirit dwells perfectly in us after baptism, whereas Paul tells us we have but the 'first fruits' of the Spirit, Mark argues:

He spoke of the 'first fruits' (ἀπαρχή) not as if to suggest a part of the whole, or some sort of fraction of the Spirit—for the Spirit cannot be fractioned or changed—but in a way which manifests our capacity (χωρητικόν), which cannot contain (χωρῆσαι) all the operation of the Spirit, unless it be by means of the perfect commandment, which is death. (IV 1009D–1012A)[34]

Logos I 25 further develops Macarius' theme of the progressive revelation of baptismal grace, beginning with the question of why some receive the grace of baptism in a very subtle manner, others more actively (ἐνεργῶς) (I 25.2.3). Macarius explains:

The grace already laid down (πρόκειται) at baptism wishes to visit every soul richly and desires that the perfection of the divine power be given speedily—but participation in grace comes about according to the varying measure of faith and piety of each. [The grace of baptism] grants forgiveness of sins to all equally, but grants the capacity to receive the

---

[34] The reference to baptism as the 'first fruits' of the Spirit (cf. Rom. 8: 23) ties in with the image of the talent, to which we return below. Macarius takes the 'first fruits' of the Spirit to be equivalent to the Pauline 'pledge of the Spirit' (2 Cor. 1: 22; 5: 5) and thus, implicitly, to baptismal grace (*EM* 8.4; I 52.1.4). Mark's reference should also be compared with Macarius' description of baptism as 'the beginning (ἀρχή) of the life of the Spirit' (I 43.2), cited above.

Spirit according to the measure of faith, waiting for and encouraging all men to come, through progress in the virtues and an excellent manner of life [ . . . ], to perfect liberation from the passions and the complete and active indwelling (ἐνεργὴς ἐνοίκησις) of the Holy Spirit.   (I 25.2.4–5)

Thus the Christian life is the active realization of what we already have. We must pray that Christ who is in us 'hiddenly' (κρυπτῶς) be revealed 'manifestly' (ἐμφανῶς) (I 38.1.3). Macarius clearly does not equate the presence of grace with the manifestation thereof—the equation Hausherr characterizes, in a burst of over-simplification, as the fundamental error of Messalianism.[35] The following passage, while not concerned with specifically baptismal grace, makes this plain:

Grace is with many imperceptibly (λεληθότως) and in many ways, and yet they do not hear the word. It is there in the very heart and intellect, guiding and shepherding, but they do not know it. But in time, when they come to knowledge, then grace itself reminds them, saying that 'at that time, in that event, I helped you and ordered things according to [God's] dispensation for you; likewise I helped you hiddenly (κρυπτῶς) on many other occasions'.   (I 34.5)[36]

As a further illustration of his teaching on baptismal grace, Macarius describes baptism as a 'pledge' and 'talent': 'In possessing the pledge (ἀρραβών) of baptism you possess the talent in its completeness (τέλειον), but if you fail to work with it, you yourself will remain incomplete (ἀτελής), and not only that, but you will be deprived of it' (III 28.3.3).[37] Here Macarius is following the parable of the talents to its conclusion: what is given can be taken away. Mark agrees that one will be incomplete if one does not work with the talent, and indeed that grace will not be revealed if one does not work with it. He would not, however, have accepted that baptismal grace can ever be entirely withdrawn.[38] Macarius' *Great Letter* expands upon the theme of the talent:

---

[35] 'L'Erreur fondamentale et la logique du Messalianisme'.

[36] Like Mark (II.56 937D), cited above, Macarius holds that grace never ceases to help us in a hidden way.

[37] Note the description of baptismal grace as 'perfect' or 'complete'—exactly as in Mark.

[38] The deprivation of grace of which Macarius speaks should not be taken in an absolute sense. Elsewhere he suggests that grace is 'rooted in man like a substance (ὡς μία οὐσία)' (II 8.2), that the lamp of grace 'always shines within' (II 8.5), and that 'the net of grace is spread out upon all' (II 15.52). It seems that what he is saying is that while grace will never

The faithful have received the pledge (ἀρραβών) of the ineffable beneficence [of the Holy Spirit] by holy baptism in the thrice-blessed name, the great and immaculate mystery entrusted to us for the growth and development of the perfect inheritance and the multiplication of the talent.[39] For the divine and comforting Spirit, given to the apostles and through them administered to the single true Church of God, is present from the hour of baptism differently and in many ways according to the proportion of faith [cf. Rom. 12: 6] of each of those who approach baptism out of a sincere faith; each receives his pound (μνᾶ), as the Gospel says [cf. Luke 19: 13–25], for its multiplication, cultivation (ἐπεργασία), and growth.  (*EM* 2.3)

In addition to borrowing the image of the talent, Mark also takes up Macarius' distinctive use of the Pauline phrase 'according to the proportion of faith' in the context of baptism. As Mark puts it (IV 1001D): 'the remission of sins and the gift of the Spirit are given through baptism according to the proportion of faith'.[40]

The principle that baptism restores man to the position of Adam is also anticipated by Macarius: 'Through the coming of Christ, mankind reaches, through the power of baptism, the first measure of Adam, having become the master of demons and passions, the "last enemy which is death" laid "under the feet" of Adam [cf. 1 Cor. 15: 26–7]' (III 1.2.1).[41] This particular passage ought to be read in a dynamic sense, that is, as indicating that through the manifestation of baptismal grace, through the power inherent in baptism, man regains the stature of Adam. It is clear

cease to be with us hiddenly, we can—and indeed must from time to time—be deprived of the experience of it. He makes this clear in 11 40.7 in which he insists that the grace of the Spirit is in us even when it appears to us to retire. Thus Macarius' teaching is not, in fact, so very distant from that of Mark. What Mark has done is to remove the ambiguity in Macarius' teaching on this point.

[39] Basil implicitly compares baptism to the Gospel talent in *On Baptism* 11.1 (PG 31 1581C), speaking of our need to cultivate the grace given us in the hope of hearing the praise addressed to the faithful servant of Matthew 25: 21. This is noted by Desprez, 'Le Baptême', 135 n. 62. Macarius may have drawn upon Basil here, but has made the analogy far more explicit.

[40] Desprez comments ('Le Baptême', 135 n. 63a), following a detailed survey, that: 'Macaire semble donc original quand il entend Rom. 12: 6 de l'habillation à la grâce baptismale par le moyen de la foi. Or il est piquant que cette exégèse se retrouve dans le *De fide orthodoxa* de Saint Jean Damascène—dont le *De haeresibus* nous transmet précisément la liste de propositions macariennes condamnées. Jean écrit en effet: "La rémission des péchés est donnée pareillement à tous par le baptême, mais la grâce de l'Esprit en proportion (κατὰ τὴν ἀναλογίαν) de la foi et de la purification préalable" (*De fide orthodoxa* 82: PTS 12, p. 184).' This exegesis is most likely to have come to John not directly from Macarius, but via Mark.

[41] Cf. Mark, IV 1025AB, cited above.

from the teaching outlined above that the 'veil of the passions', the inheritance of the Fall, is not immediately removed by baptism but rather by the revelation of the grace hiddenly conferred by baptism.

It will be obvious that there are many points of contact, as well as many differences, between Macarius' teaching and that of Mark. These are so palpable as to warrant us to speak of Mark's work as a kind of dialogue with Macarius. Mark's basic schema is that of Macarius: baptismal grace is itself perfect but is initially conferred hiddenly and imperceptibly (μυστικῶς/κρυπτῶς/λεληθότως in Mark; ἀπὸ πολλῆς λεπτότητος/ὡς ἀγνοεῖν τὴν ἐνέργειαν/κρυπτῶς/λεληθότως in Macarius); it must be made manifest and 'active' through the cultivation of the virtues. Mark freely uses Macarius' identification of baptismal grace with the Gospel talent to illustrate the need to realize the hidden gift entrusted to every baptized Christian. Mark has developed, clarified, and in some senses simplified Macarius' defence of baptism and elucidation of the workings of grace. He has followed Macarius in attacking both a deterministic and a minimizing (Messalian) approach to baptismal grace. Mark's teaching on baptism is, *pace* Kmosko, Peterson, and Hesse, fundamentally that of Macarius. Mark has brought out the profoundly anti-Messalian character of Macarius' teaching on baptism. Where Mark differs from Macarius—which he does as a thoughtful disciple rather than as an opponent—is on the question of the removal of original sin. Mark insists that no non-physical effect of the sin of Adam remains with the baptized Christian. Macarius teaches that while sins are forgiven in baptism, the complete removal of the veil of the passions inherited from the Fall requires the active manifestation of the 'life' of the Spirit within us. The bone of contention is, thus, a matter of precisely when the effects of original sin are entirely removed: at baptism or, through the power inherent in baptism, later. We shall see in the following section which of the two answers is the more consistent and satisfactory in explaining the troubling question of post-baptismal sin.

We may also note, by way of a postscript to this section, that neither Mark nor Macarius expands upon the baptismal rite itself. The only aspect of the rite that draws either author is the confession of faith, used by each to underscore the orthodoxy of a theological position: faith in the Trinity in Macarius (*EM* 1.3);

Christology in Mark (XI.15–16 (9)). Moreover, neither makes any mention of chrismation in terms of a distinct post-baptismal rite of union especially associated with the gift of the Holy Spirit. In each it is clear that the gift of the Spirit is conferred at baptism (Macarius, *EM* 2.3; Mark, *Op.* IV 1001D). Our authors may well be including a post-baptismal unction within the designation 'baptism'. The point is that neither appear to know of the association of such a rite with the gift of the Spirit. Vincent Desprez, pointing to the fact that the rite of chrismation is first mentioned by Cyril of Jerusalem and the *Apostolic Constitutions* (Antioch AD 380), but still unknown to Theodore of Mopsuestia, suggests that the absence of this additional rite confirms his residence in Syria or Asia Minor around the year 400.[42] This raises the question of whether the similar absence in Mark could be used to date and locate that elusive figure. It must be admitted, however, that any conclusions reached on this basis, as in any argument from silence, would be extremely fragile and, on balance, unsustainable.

## 5.4  The Post-Baptismal Struggle

### 5.4.1  Grace and Human Freedom

As we have seen, both Mark and Macarius hold that while baptismal grace is in itself perfect, it must be made manifest through the practice of the virtues. This, of course, raises the question of the exact nature of man's contribution to his own salvation. Here Mark again follows the teaching of Macarius. Macarius had argued that the virtues are, strictly speaking, not our work but that of God in and through us: 'How can someone pray', he asks, 'without having been moved by the Spirit?'. He continues:

Thus the virtuous soul (ἡ ἐνάρετος ψυχή) is built into (προσοικοδομεῖται) the Church not by virtue of what it has done but by virtue of what it has desired (οὐχ ὅτι ἐποίησεν ἀλλ' ὅτι ἐπόθησεν). For it is not his own activity that saves man, but God who has granted the capacity (τὴν δύναμιν). Even if someone bears the stigmata of the Lord, he must not be conceited in this, no matter what his actions have been; all he has done, in fact, is to love and to apply himself to action.   (II 37.9)

---

[42] Desprez, 'Le Baptême', 152.

Man is called to give over his will to God. Without this offering God will do nothing. If we do offer up our will, the grace of God does the rest, even condescending to attribute the whole work to us:

We have previously said that man possesses the ability to apply himself (τὴν ἐπιτήδευσιν) by nature, and it is this that God exacts. Scripture therefore prescribes man to first reflect and, having reflected, to love and to apply himself voluntarily. The energizing of the intellect, the endurance of the labour and the completion of the work is granted by the grace of the Lord to him who has willed and believed. (II 37.10)

Macarius concludes with the rhetorical question: 'How is the will to be manifested, if not by voluntary labour?' (ibid.).

Mark follows this teaching carefully. He exhorts the baptized Christian: 'Give only your labour—the capacity (τὴν δύναμιν) for which you have received—and prepare yourself for the manifestation of him who dwells in you' (IV 1005B). He well appreciates the limits of our contribution: 'Let none of those who practise the virtues suppose that he has done any good thing through his own capacity alone' (IV 1005C). Similarly:

One must not pretend to cut off (ἐκκόπτειν)[43] the sin of Adam—or even our own post-baptismal sins—through struggles (δι' ἀγώνων)[44] but only through Christ. [ . . . ] It depends on us (ἐφ' ἡμῖν ἐστι) only to please him in the virtues, whereas to put them into practice, or to cut off sins, is impossible without God. (IV 1005D–1008A)

Mark insists that it is baptismal grace itself that gives us the capacity to realize the hidden gift of baptism (IV 1004BC, 1005B). This understanding is implicit in Macarius' teaching on grace; it is the import of the 'power of baptism' by which man regains the stature of Adam (III 1.2.1, cited above). Mark tends to make the connection with specifically baptismal grace rather more explicit than does Macarius.

Thus it is the exercise of man's free will that is required of him. Thereafter all the good he does is, in fact, the work of God in him. The grace conferred at baptism is not, therefore, irresistible or automatic. Macarius speaks of the talent of baptismal grace being

---

[43] Cf. the Messalian claim reported by Theodoret, *Haer. fab. comp.* IV.11 (PG 83 429B): baptism 'does not cut off the root of sin' (τὴν δὲ ῥίζαν οὐκ ἐκκόπτει τῆς ἁμαρτίας).

[44] Mark opens *Op.* IV with an attack on those who claim that the ancient sin is cleansed 'through struggles' (ἐξ ἀγώνων) (985A). He does, however, allow the need for a 'ceaseless struggle' (ἀδιάλειπτον ἀγῶνα) (V 1029B).

taken away from one who fails to work with it (III 28.3.3); Mark, more cautiously, refers to the 'profanation' of that grace by one who fails to perform the commandments (III 981CD; cf. IV 1004C) and asserts, as we have seen, that without human effort grace will not be made manifest. This understanding of the importance of human free will lies behind the following observations: 'It is in the will of man whether to turn to good or to evil' (ἐν τῷ θελήματι τοῦ ἀνθρώπου ἦ τὸ τραπῆναι αὐτὸν ἐπὶ τὸ ἀγαθὸν ἢ τὸ κακόν) (Macarius, II 15.40); '[Man] has the authority to incline to whichever way he wills: whether to good or to evil' (ἐξουσίαν ἔχοντας ῥέπειν ἐφ' ὃ ἂν θέλωμεν, ἤτοι ἀγαθὸν ἤτοι κακόν) (Mark, IV 989A). Macarius also uses the verb ῥέπω (incline/turn/tend) in this context: trials are allowed to test man's faculty of self-determination, to see 'which way he inclines' (ποῦ ῥέπει) (II 27.9). Similarly, 'You have self-determination, to incline to whichever way you wish' (σὺ ἔχεις τὸ αὐτεξούσιον, ῥέψαι ὅπου βούλει) (II 27.10). The reality of man's free will recognized by our authors allows them to speak of the work of salvation as one of co-operation (συνεργία) (Macarius, I 25.1.12; Mark, V 1049B).

Mark's teaching on the complex relationship between divine grace and human freedom is very much that of Macarius. While both are certainly expressing a shared tradition, the similarity of that expression is such that we can legitimately posit a definite connection here. To appreciate precisely how human free will is to be offered to God in practice, we must first look at the power of the enemy.

### 5.4.2   The Power of Evil

The opening of the treatise *On Baptism* describes the argument of those who would deny the power of baptism because of their discovery in themselves of the 'same activity of sin' after baptism (IV 985A). Such a position squares very well with the reported Messalian position allowing to baptism, at best, a kind of razor action—unable to cut off the roots of sins.[45] It also looks very like a criticism of Macarius' argument against a simplistic view of the effects of baptism:

If you say that through the coming of Christ sin has been condemned and that, after baptism, evil no longer has any hold in the heart to spread

---

[45] Theodoret, *Haer. fab. comp.* IV.11 (429B).

thoughts, do you not know that from the coming of the Lord until now all those who have been baptized have sometimes had evil thoughts? [...] Do we not find that many sins come about after baptism and that many sin? The robber does, therefore, have a hold [in us], even after baptism, to come in and do what he wishes. (II 15.14)

Macarius' understanding is, as we have seen, that baptism does not immediately expel indwelling sin—the 'veil of the passions' inherited from Adam. Mark, on the other hand, is unwilling to allow any remnant of the sin of Adam after baptism, particularly any notion of the persistence of indwelling sin. Mark's denial that sin has any hold within after baptism leads him into some exegetical difficulties. Macarius had used Matthew 15: 19 to illustrate the fact that evil thoughts do come from within, from the heart (II 15.13). Mark counters that the dominical saying cannot apply to a believing heart, but to a heart full of vainglory (IV 1000D). He also shows himself to be in difficulty when faced with Romans 7: 23: the law of sin perceived by St Paul in his members and standing in opposition to the law of the intellect. Again, Macarius had used this as a validation of his theory of indwelling sin (I 40.3.7; II 27.2; III 16.3.4). Mark argues that in the whole passage Paul is speaking not in his own baptized person but in the person of an unbaptized Jew. It is obvious why Mark should have felt so uneasy with this passage. It provides striking testimony to the almost compelling power of indwelling sin—a power felt keenly by a Macarius or an Augustine.[46] Mark avoids accepting the testimony of Romans chiefly because of what he saw as an implied obviation of personal responsibility for sin, of which more below.

Given Mark's unease concerning the possible implications of the doctrine of indwelling sin, it is striking to find him freely drawing upon the rich stock of Macarian descriptions of the nature and power of the inner workings of evil:

Just as some snakes lurk (φωλεύοντες) in forest glades and others in houses, so there are passions that take shape in our thoughts and others that express themselves in actions. (1.179 928A)[47]

---

[46] Hesse justly remarks that 'Es ist völlig abwegig zu denken, Markos habe die "mens Augustini" gehabt. Der Sünden- und Gnadenlehre Augustins kongenial, ohne jedoch von ihr abhängig zu sein, ist vielmehr die Sünden- und Geistlehre Symeons.' 'Markos Eremites', 96.

[47] Cf. Macarius, I 3.3.5: the soul after the Fall as a den of snakes, swarming like fishes. Similarly, we must penetrate the chambers and storehouses of the soul and kill the

[...] the evils welling up from within the heart (τῶν ἔνδοθεν τῆς καρδίας βρυόντων κακῶν). (v 1029B)[48]

[...] the hidden inner swarm (ἐσμός) of passions, energized by evil spirits. (v 1036A)[49]

[...] muddied (βορβορούμενοι) by the operations of the passions. (v 1033C)[50]

[...] the deeper and more inward passions of the soul, more difficult to discover and correct, covering and darkening (καλύπτοντα καὶ σκοτίζοντα) the soul with a terrible interference. (v 1045BC)[51]

[...] laziness, which weaves in the soul a dark garment and veil of black clouds (τὸ σκοτεινὸν τοῦ μελανοῦ νέφους ἔνδυμα καὶ κάλυμμα). (v 1049A)[52]

[...] the intellect is blinded (ἐκτυφλοῦται) by these three passions: I mean avarice, vainglory and pleasure. (I.104 917C)[53]

[the intellect] will be darkened (σκοτισθήσεται) [...] if the soul is befogged (ὁμιχλώδης) [...]. (II.140 952C)[54]

murderous snake that is lurking (φωλεύοντα) there (II 17.15). Macarius' imagery is, as always, a good deal more graphic than that of Mark. The Messalians, according to the anti-Messalian lists, took this kind of imagery literally, see T 3 and J 24: demons exiting as visible smoke or snakes or some other wild beast. See also J 12: the soul without conscious experience of Christ as a den of serpents and venomous beasts.

[48] Cf. Macarius, I 61.1.7: the welling-up (using βρύω) of a muddy spring of lawlessness from within the fallen soul. Also I 6.3.2, 7.9.3, 12.2.1 (the spring of evil and impure thoughts), 14.35, 29.2.7, 33.1.6 (the welling-up of many impure thoughts in the heart). Note that the good is also described as a spring welling up from within, for example I 34.7. It is surprising to find Mark using this kind of language given the implication it bears of indwelling sin. The context suggests that all are subject to this 'welling-up' of evils from the heart, Mark is simply discussing how we are to cope with this situation. Elsewhere, as we have seen, he argues that the Lord's saying that evil thoughts come from the heart of man (Matt. 15: 18) cannot possibly refer to a believing heart (IV 1000D). The two passages are not easily reconcilable.

[49] Cf. Macarius, I 11.3.4: 'the swarm of evils encircling the soul'. See also the 'swarm of evils' in Mark XI.32 (18).

[50] Cf. Macarius, I 61.1.7 (noted above); III 25.4.3 and 25.5.2: fallen man 'muddied'; and II 4.5: the 'mud of pleasures'.

[51] Note the 'veiling' imagery, so common in Macarius, for example the 'veil of hidden inner passions' (I 25.1.7) and the 'veil of darkness' (II 42.3).

[52] While Macarius' clothing imagery is almost always to do with garments of light, he does speak of the prince of darkness 'enveloping and clothing the soul in the power of darkness' (II 2.1). Cf. also II 32.4: the 'garments of darkness'. Note again Mark's use of the Macarian 'veil' motif.

[53] 1.103 in Migne's numbering. Cf. Macarius, I 6.3.5: the darkening and blinding of the intellect. Similarly I 35.4: the soul blinded by sin. Evagrius too speaks of the darkening of the intellect, *Praktikos* 74 (p. 662).

[54] For the darkening of the intellect, see I 6.3.5 (noted above) and II 26.1. Macarius describes the opposing power as 'befogging' (ὁμιχλώδης) in I 6.3.5 and I 7.11.1.

[sin is] is darkness and fog for the soul (σκότος καὶ ὁμίχλη ψυχῆς). (II.211 964B).[55]

[...] through pleasure-seeking and vainglory the soul has been darkened and has fallen into the abyss of ignorance (εἰς τὸν βυθὸν τῆς ἀγνοίας). (IV 1020D)[56]

[anger] devastates and confuses and darkens (σκοτίζοντος) the whole soul [...]. It becomes a house for the evil one in the soul. (V 1041AB)[57]

[...] obscure and dark passions (δυσφανῆ καὶ σκοτεινὰ πάθη). (VII 1089B)[58]

[...] every evil lurking (ἐμφωλευούσης) in us [...] hidden evil (τὴν ἐγκεκρυμμένην κακίαν). (VII 1096A)[59]

It will be noted that many, but by no means all, of these references come from *Opusculum* V, *To Nicholas*. We shall return to this question within our discussion of the authenticity of that work below (Ch. 5.8). Mark's willingness to use certain of the more graphic Macarian motifs describing the action of evil within need not, however, necessarily contradict his very fundamental point that even if we do sense this activity within after baptism, this is solely our responsibility and in no way implies the deficiency of baptism. To this question of personal responsibility we may now turn.

### 5.4.3 The Process of Temptation

Mark's affirmation of our personal responsibility for sin is founded upon his estimation of the sovereignty of human free will regained at baptism: 'After baptism neither God nor Satan forces the will with violence' (τὸ γὰρ θέλημα μετὰ τὸ βάπτισμα οὔτε θεὸς οὔτε σατανᾶς βιάζεται) (IV 988B).[60]

[55] Macarius routinely uses 'darkness' and 'fog' as metaphors for sin, see for example I 16.1.11; II 9.11; III 1.3.3.

[56] Cf. Macarius, I 3.5.6–8: man's fall into and rescue from the 'abyss of unknowing' (τὸν βυθὸν τῆς ἀγνωσίας). Also III 25.4.2: the soul's fall 'into the abyss of evil passions' (εἰς βυθὸν παθῶν κακίας).

[57] This need not imply a Macarian understanding of indwelling evil. In this instance it is our sin (of anger) that allows evil to take up its abode in us.

[58] Note that the parallel Migne numbering appears to have dropped out of de Durand's edition at this point. The citation can be found on p. 64 (line 16) of that edition. Cf. Macarius, II 9.11: 'the passions of darkness'.

[59] For lurking, see above, n. 47. For another instance of lurking in Mark, see V 1045C. Cf. also Macarius, I 40.1.5: τὰ ἐναποκεκρυμμένα ἐν ἡμῖν πάθη.

[60] Similarly, he declares that man's faculty of self-determination is 'not liable to compulsion' (ἀβίαστος) after baptism (IV 989B).

This is an estimation he shares with, and may have derived from, Macarius. Noting man's capacity to either cultivate or separate himself from baptismal grace, Macarius concludes: 'From this we may recognize the fact that, after the advent of the Spirit at baptism according to the proportion of faith (cf. Rom. 12: 6), God does not remove from man the authority of his free will' (TV h.10.7).[61]

This principle is in no way abnegated by, indeed it requires, the persistence of demonic suggestion. Mark points out that immunity to suggestion is the property of immutable nature alone. Our nature, fallen or unfallen, is mutable and therefore susceptible. Adam was 'susceptible to the suggestion of Satan' (δεκτικὸς ἦν τῆς τοῦ σατανᾶ προσβολῆς); so also are we, being of one nature with him. It was by no necessity of nature that Adam transgressed. Like him we have the authority to cede or not to cede to suggestion (IV 1013C). Suggestion is permitted in order to test 'the inclination of the inward disposition of man' (τὸ ἐνδιάθετον ποῦ ῥέπει) (IV 1016B). Simple suggestion (ἡ μονολόγιστος προσβολή) is a matter of necessity (ἀναγκαστική) (IV 1017A). Even when the intellect, through negligence, becomes receptive to such suggestion, Satan has no power to move the thoughts (IV 1016B). Simple suggestion is image-free; but as soon as it is accompanied by images it constitutes a thought, and already involves an element of assent, and hence of guilt (I.141–2 921D–924A). Such thoughts may be accompanied by what Mark calls a 'momentary disturbance' (παραρριπισμός) (V 1040B). He goes on to speak of 'converse' (ὁμιλία) with the thoughts, pointing out that this is clearly a matter of choice (προαιρετική) and already far from innocent (IV 1017B). Such 'converse' with an evil thought potentially leads on to 'coupling' (συνδυασμός) (IV 997C) and 'assent' (συγκατάθεσις) (IV 1021C).[62]

---

[61] In this eloquent treatise Macarius is attacking a deterministic view of grace. He also argues: 'But because many consecrate themselves exclusively to the good, separate themselves from evil, and obtain eternal salvation, we can recognise from what has been said that because of free will, it is neither the will of God nor the will of Satan that act, but the will of man, which no one can obstruct' (TV h.10.4). On Macarius' interpretation of Rom. 12: 6, see above, Ch. 5.3. Cf. also, without specific reference to baptism, I 2.9.2: 'neither the Lord nor Satan lay hold of man by force' (βίᾳ γὰρ οὐ λαμβάνει αὐτὸν οὔτε ὁ κύριος, οὔτε ὁ σατανᾶς) and TV h.10.8: 'The will of man is never forced or constrained.'

[62] On the process of temptation in Mark see Kallistos Ware, Introduction to Zirnheld (tr.), *Marc le Moine*, xxviii–xxxiii.

Mark's analysis is broadly in agreement with that of Macarius, albeit rather more precise. Macarius allows that, following the Incarnation and the gift of baptism, Satan is stronger than man in one respect alone: 'in the suggestion of thoughts' (εἰς τὸ ὑποβάλλειν τοὺς διαλογισμούς) (I 6.1). The demons have no power to enter into men. They are able only to 'bring forward' (παραδείκνυμι) the pleasures in order, if they are able, to move the faculty of self-determination into evil desire. If man chooses to follow these thoughts, then, and only then, do the demons have a hold over him (I 38.1.1).[63] Human nature is 'susceptible to (δεκτική) both good and evil, to divine grace and the opposing power, but it is not thereby subjected to necessity (ἀλλ᾽ οὐκ ἀναγκαστική)' (II 15.25; cf. also I 34.4). Both grace and sin 'operate by persuasion not compulsion' (προτρεπτικαί εἰσιν [...] οὐκ ἀναγκαστικαί) (II 27.22). Temptation is allowed for good reason, for education and training (I 8.3.4), and so that Christian souls might demonstrate their love for God (I 55.1.1).[64]

Macarius speaks of 'holding converse' (ὁμιλέω) with evil (III 12.2.1) and of 'becoming friendly' (φιλιάζω) with it (II 27.2)— both having the same import as Mark's ὁμιλία. Macarius advises those faced with indwelling sin not to assent to it in their thoughts, neither to take pleasure in it, nor to obey it (οὐ συμφωνοῦσιν ἐν τοῖς λογισμοῖς οὔτε συνήδονται ἢ ὑπακούουσιν) (II 27.2). Thus we have in Macarius a rough equivalent of the process of converse, coupling, and assent which we find in Mark. Macarius also speaks, using the same vocabulary as Mark, of the need for man to avoid 'coupling with' (συνδυάζων) (II 41.2), or for the soul to refrain from 'agreeing with and communing with' (συναινοῦσα καὶ κοινωνοῦσα), the evil one (I 34.2.7). He does not use the terms παραρριπισμός or συγκατάθεσις.[65]

---

[63] Macarius adopts a very minimizing approach here, not entirely consistent with his frequent references to persistent indwelling evil. He is not, of course, in any sense a systematic theologian and makes no virtue of consistency. His teaching developed on several fronts, often very much on an *ad hoc* basis. In this passage he is reacting to a spiritual pessimism that would exaggerate the power of evil, whereas in his evocations of indwelling sin, he is attacking a facile optimism that would deem the initial advent of grace to mark the end of the spiritual struggle.

[64] Macarius' insistence on the need to withstand trials is also echoed by Mark (III 976B, 980A).

[65] Παραρριπισμός is an uncommon term; it is not in LS, Lampe, or the TLG. Mark may even have coined the term. Συγκατάθεσις is a Stoic term and far more widespread. Origen,

Macarius does use the term 'suggestion' (προσβολή), but does so in a way which Mark was to find unacceptable: 'Each of us wishes to shut out suggestion, but is unable to do so. Why is this the case if not, as the Apostle said, because of indwelling sin, which is the root of the passions and the holding (νομή) of the demons?' (1 38.1.2). Indwelling sin is, according to Macarius, 'the evil inheritance of the passions given to all humanity from the transgression of Adam' (1 29.2.8). It is not, as we have seen, entirely and immediately removed by baptism. Macarius goes on to insist that the 'passions of dishonour' (Rom. 1: 26) are not natural to us (1 40.1.2–3). They are 'not ours, but another's (μὴ ἡμέτερα [...] ἀλλὰ ἀλλότρια)' (1 40.1.5). They are 'accidental' (συμβεβηκόσι) to us (1 40.1.10).

While Mark fully shared Macarius' deeply traditional grasp of the innate integrity of human nature, he evidently felt the insistence on the otherness of the passions and of their derivation from the ongoing inheritance of original sin to be dangerously suggestive of a denial of personal responsibility. Personal responsibility is a key theme of Mark's *œuvre*. Mark, as we have seen, is careful to distinguish between 'suggestion' and 'thoughts'. All Satan is able to do is to present evil things simply as the thoughts form. The direction of the thoughts is solely our concern. Either we like what is proposed, or we recoil in disgust (IV 1016BC). Mark is, however, well aware that suggestions do not necessarily disappear with the first motion of disgust. Mark ascribes solely to us the real cause of the force exerted on us by certain thoughts: 'There are two causes of the activity of evil and both come from us; one acts according to the proportion of our neglect of the commandments, the other dominates us inexorably because of evil works committed after baptism' (IV 992C). We are indeed dominated by sin 'even when

---

for example, had used it to specify the moment at which one can be said to sin (*On 1 Corinthians: JTS* 9, p. 355 l. 59). Evagrius defines the sin of the monk as 'assent (συγκατάθεσις) to the forbidden pleasure proposed by the thought', having previously defined the thought as 'that which rises from the passionate part of the soul and darkens the intellect' (*Praktikos* 74–5, p. 662). Note that Mark would not have accepted this definition of an evil thought—like Macarius, Evagrius does not distinguish between 'thought' and 'suggestion' and allows to the demons the ability to introduce thoughts accompanied by images. See, for example, *Thoughts* 2 (p. 184): 'All demonic images introduce into the soul representations of sensible objects: impressed with which the intellect carries in itself the forms of these objects.' Mark's analysis of temptation is more developed than that of Evagrius and owes no substantial debt to it.

we do not wish it' (καὶ μὴ θέλοντες) (ibid.), but this is always ultimately our responsibility and not that of either Adam or Satan (VIII 1104AB). We should not ascribe the thought that precedes an evil action to 'foreign activity' (ἐνέργειαν [...] ἀλλοτρίαν) (IV 997C). Similarly, we should not pride ourselves as if we were warring against 'foreign evils' (ἀλλοτρίοις κακοῖς) (IV 1024B). It is not as if we were innocently dominated by thoughts (IV 1021D). Even those thoughts which take hold of the intellect 'with violence' (βίᾳ) are rooted in our post-baptismal sin or voluntary retention of some 'seed of evil' (IV 997C). Particularly dangerous is 'predisposition' (πρόληψις), which Mark defines as: 'the involuntary remembrance of previous sins which the struggler stops from developing into passion, while the victor forbids even the suggestion' (1.140 921D).[66] Mark returns to the theme of personal responsibility frequently.[67] Always the point is the same: we are exercised by sin 'because of our own fault' (καθ᾿ ἡμετέραν αἰτίαν) (IV 1000B).

The emphasis placed by Mark upon personal responsibility for all but simple image-free (and guiltless) suggestion does appear to be a criticism of Macarius. Macarius had not distinguished between suggestions and thoughts. He regards evil thoughts or suggestions as the product of indwelling sin and as inevitable so long as we fall short of perfection. The difference is therefore primarily a matter of exactly when the element of responsibility (and therefore of guilt) begins. When Mark criticizes Macarius on the 'otherness' of the passions he does so not on the level of nature but on that of will. For Mark, the passions are ours because they result from our acquiescence in suggestion. For Macarius they are a foreign intrusion into our nature stemming from the Fall. The very fact of their existence after baptism is therefore a sign of continuing imperfection rather than of personal responsibility. Macarius is, however, in no doubt as to our responsibility to do all we can to remove this imperfection:

---

[66] Πρόληψις is a Stoic term. Macarius also allows for such 'predisposition'. He writes, for example, of the 'inveterate predisposition (τὴν πολλὴν πρόληψιν) that arises from habituation to evils' (1 22.2.1). Similarly, following the Fall: '[the passions became] established in us as if part of our nature through habit and an inveterate predisposition (συνήθεια καὶ προλήψει πολλῇ)' (11 4.8). Πρόληψις in Macarius does not have precisely the same technical sense as it does in Mark. In Macarius it means simply the inveterate habit of sin that disposes one to sin all the more.

[67] See, for example, IV 1012D, 1016A, 1020B, 1021D–1024D.

Let no one say, 'It is impossible for me to love, think of, or believe in the only Good because I am under the servitude and bonds of sin.' The capacity to perform the works of life perfectly and to extricate and free yourself from the sin that dwells in you is not in your power [...]. But to think of, believe in, love or seek out the Lord, that is in your power and you are capable of not agreeing with (συνήδεσθαι) or collaborating with (συνεργάζεσθαι) indwelling sin. Make yourself the grounds (πρόφασις) on which you are deemed worthy of life by seeking out the Lord, by thinking of him, by loving and awaiting him, and he will grant the strength and the deliverance. For it is this only that he expects from you. (III 26.3.1)

Similarly, he insists that while we are all faced with indwelling sin, it is up to us to indulge it, or to fight against it (II 27.2).

Notwithstanding Macarius' strident attacks on any form of resignation before the fact of indwelling sin, Mark evidently felt the need to stress that the presence of the passions within us after baptism results from our own post-baptismal sin. Mark's theory of temptation is the natural corollary of his doctrine of the total evacuation of evil effected by baptism. He has firmly closed the door to the potential obviation of personal responsibility he appears to have perceived in Macarius' theory of persistent indwelling evil.

### 5.4.4 Spiritual Warfare

While Mark is trenchant in his insistence that evil has no hold on or in us after baptism beyond that which we ourselves accord it, he is under no illusion as to the severity of the spiritual struggle. He calls this struggle 'spiritual-intellectual warfare' (νοερὸς πόλεμος) (x 1132A),[68] a designation that recalls the essentially militant Christianity preached by Macarius, summed up in the call to 'invisible warfare' (ἀόρατος πόλεμος) (I 19.1.4). Mark also likens the spiritual life to the crossing of the sea (II.27 936A), a commonplace image used rather more graphically by Macarius.[69]

---

[68] Cf. II.148 955B: 'spiritual-intellectual combat (τὴν νοητὴν πάλην); II.136 949D: 'our combat against the spirits of evil' (τὴν πάλην ἡμῶν πρὸς τὰ πνευματικὰ τῆς πονηρίας) and V 1029B: 'ceaseless struggle' (ἀδιάλειπτον ἀγῶνα). Cf. also Evagrius, *Praktikos* 34 (p. 578): 'immaterial warfare is more severe than the material' (τοῦ γὰρ ἐνύλου πολέμου ὁ ἄϋλος χαλεπώτερος).

[69] See II 53.12, 28.2, 38.4.

Mark speaks of the necessity and utility of bearing trials in very similar terms to Macarius. Mark defines the cross of Matthew 16: 24 as τὴν τῶν ἐπερχομένων θλίψεων ὑπομονήν ('the endurance of the afflictions that come upon us') (III 976A). This unmistakably recalls Macarius' definition of the cross of Matthew 16: 24 as readiness πάντα ὑπομένειν [...] ἐπερχόμενον πειρασμόν ('to endure every trial that comes upon us') (I 55.1.2).[70] Mark regards the 'bearing of the afflictions that come upon us' as one of three general virtues that englobe all the commandments and that are woven in with the work of repentance (III 976B). Macarius had also taught that 'the endurance of those things which come upon us' constitutes one of the three complex virtues that bring about purity (I 39.1.1).[71] Trials are allowed by God (Mark, II.8 932A; Macarius, I 55.2.1–2). They are to be welcomed with thanksgiving (Mark, II.187 960B; Macarius, II 53.1). They test the will (Mark, II.191 960C; Macarius, II 9.1), and show forth our love for God (Mark, I.65 913B; Macarius, I 55.1.6). Trials are an essentially small labour (Mark, II.175 957B; Macarius, II 49.4), particularly when weighed against the good things to come (Mark, II.156 953D; Macarius, II 49.4).

To express the severity of the struggle Mark uses the language of violence, language ultimately based on Matthew 11: 12. Mark uses this language to explain to his interlocutor why it is that we do not know 'the atmosphere of freedom' (τὸν ἀέρα τῆς ἐλευθερίας) if we have indeed been freed by baptism (IV 989AB).[72] As we would expect, he makes the whole question one of will. The will is itself

---

[70] See also Hesse, 'Markos Eremites', 15–20.

[71] The other general virtues differ: Mark has ceaseless prayer and the purification of the thoughts; Macarius has love of every kind and *encrateia*. Elsewhere Macarius speaks of five all-encompassing virtues: prayer, *encrateia*, mercy, poverty, and long-suffering (II 37.8). Origen had spoken of 'all-encompassing virtue' (ἡ περιεκτικὴ ἀρετή) in the singular (*Contra Celsum* v.39: GCS 3, p. 43).

[72] Here I depart from de Durand who favours ἔργα (works) over ἀέρα (atmosphere/air), despite the latter having the more ancient witness. Mark's interlocutor claims that this 'atmosphere of freedom' is known by 'the strugglers' (οἱ ἀγωνιζόμενοι) (ibid.). Macarius had spoken of 'the divine atmosphere' (τὸν ἀέρα τὸν θεϊκόν) into which the inner man is raised (I 18.4.12). Similarly man attains the 'atmosphere of the divinity' with the wings of the Spirit (III 4.2.2; II 52.6). Macarius certainly puts a great emphasis on freedom (understood primarily as freedom from the passions) and the difficulty of attaining it (II 8.5; I 4.11.4) but does not speak in so many words of the 'atmosphere of freedom'. Dörries notes that Mark is not attacking Macarius here, despite the coincidence of language, and that what he has in view is rather a misappropriation of Macarius on the part of a pneumatic

'not liable to compulsion' (ἀβίαστος). The violence enjoined by
Matthew 11: 12 is the violence exercised by the will, 'so that each of
us should force himself with violence (βιάζομαι) after baptism so as
to not turn towards evil but to remain turned towards the good (εἰς
τὸ ἀγαθόν)' (IV 989B). Similarly, 'He who forces himself with
violence until death and holds on to repentance will be saved
through violence (διὰ τὴν βίαν) even if he has erred in some way'
(III 984A). This kind of language is extremely common in Macarius; his Homily 11 19, for example, is taken up entirely with the
theme of evangelical violence. The emphasis here is subtly different from that in Mark. For Macarius, we must force ourselves
'towards the good' (εἰς τὸ ἀγαθόν) (11 19.3), rather than force
ourselves to remain so turned.[73] Moreover, for Macarius, the
stage at which we must do ourselves violence is the initial period
of struggle. It is enjoined because of indwelling sin. Such violence
can of itself produce nothing beyond natural effects, but seeing the
free will exercised in these efforts, the Lord will come and accomplish in us that which we could not accomplish even with violence
(11 19.6). Mark does not take this schema on board, saving the
element pertaining to the will, chiefly because of its dependence
on the doctrine of continued indwelling sin. What he appears to be
doing in response to his interlocutor is to salvage the Macarian
language of violence, which he recognizes as being of great moral
value, while disregarding the suspect baggage of the doctrine of
indwelling sin.

## 5.4.5   Prayer

Mark inherits from Macarius an insistence on the primacy of
prayer coupled with a firm conviction of the interconnectedness
of the virtues. This is a coupling developed by Macarius in
reaction to the exclusive stress on prayer characteristic of the
Messalian tendency. Mark sums up his teaching on this point as
follows: 'Prayer is called virtue, and indeed is the mother of the
virtues: for it gives birth to them through its conjunction

---

monasticism evincing precisely the same combination of spiritual pretension and naivety
against which Macarius himself had warned. *Die Theologie*, 143 n. 52.

[73] But note *EM* 1.1, which speaks of the soul as 'having a natural inclination towards
good things' (κατὰ φύσιν τὴν ἐπὶ τὰ καλὰ ῥοπὴν ἐχούσης).

(συνάφεια) with Christ' (11.33 936B). He goes on to add that, 'No single virtue by itself opens the door of our nature to us; they must all be linked together in the correct sequence (ἀκολούθως ἐξήρτηνται)' (11.38 936C). Macarius, for his part, had declared:

> Perseverance in prayer is the head of every good endeavour and chief of all upright works, through which we are able to acquire by daily supplication of God the rest of the virtues. It is from this that those who are worthy acquire [...] the conjunction (συνάφεια) of the disposition of the intellect with the Lord in ineffable love. (*EM* 8.3)

Elsewhere he teaches that: 'The virtues are bound to and depend upon each other; like some sacred chain one is linked to the other (μία ἀπὸ τῆς μίας ἀπήρτηνται) [...]' (*EM* 8.1). Thus in both Macarius and Mark prayer is not only the chief virtue, but also the virtue that ushers in the other virtues. At the same time prayer depends upon the other virtues; as Macarius puts it, 'Without the other members of virtue, it is dead' (11 53.3).[74] The theme of the primacy of prayer amongst the virtues is also found in, amongst others, Cassian, the *Apophthegmata*, Gregory of Nyssa, and Pseudo-Chrysostom.[75] Prayer as the 'mother' of the virtues is an image first used by Nilus.[76] Evagrius tends to treat prayer as being above the virtues.[77] The theme of interconnectedness of the virtues is Stoic in its roots.[78] It also is found in Gregory of Nyssa.[79] Given that Mark stands in a far more direct relationship with Macarius than with Gregory it is more plausible to suggest that Mark draws his coupling of the themes of primacy and of interconnectedness from Macarius rather than Gregory. It also stands, incidentally, as another example of the close relationship obtaining between Gregory and Macarius.

---

[74] See also 1 7.18.1: Christians should occupy their intellect not with prayer alone but with all the virtues.

[75] Cassian, *Conf.* IX.2 (SC 54, p. 40): 'Just as the crown of the building of all virtues is perfection in prayer, so unless everything has been united and compacted by this as its crown, it cannot possibly continue strong and stable.' *AP* (Alph.) Agathon 9 (PG 65 112BC): 'There is no labour greater than that of prayer to God.' Gregory of Nyssa, *De oratione dominica* (GNO 7 (2), pp. 8–9): 'There is no more precious activity than prayer.' (Ps-) Chrysostom, *De precatione* 11 (PG 50 779)): 'Prayer is the head (κεφάλαιον) of all good things.'

[76] Nilus, *Ep.* 3.90 (PG 79 428C): 'prayer is the mother of all the virtues'.

[77] Evagrius, *OP* 150 (PG 79 1200A): 'prayer is more divine than all the virtues'.

[78] See Zeller, *Stoics, Epicureans and Sceptics*, 244–51. A good example is Plutarch, *Sto. rep.* 27.1 (cited by Zeller on p. 247).

[79] Gregory of Nyssa, *De virginitate* 15 (GNO 8 (1), p. 311).

As regards the actual practice of prayer, Mark puts the emphasis on inner disposition: 'We call prayer not only that which is indicated by bodily posture [lit. through the flesh] but that which is offered to God through undistracted thought (δι' ἐννοίας ἀπερισπάστου)' (VII 1076c). This is in itself a commonplace, appreciated by both Evagrius and Macarius:

Do not pray only with outward forms and gestures, but with reverence and awe try to make your intellect aware of spiritual prayer. (Evagrius, *OP* 28 1173A)

We should not pray according to bodily habits, whether of cries, or of a custom of silence, or of the bending of the knees, but soberly (νηφαλέως), being attentive to the intellect and waiting for God [ ... ]. (Macarius, II 33.1; cf. also I 29.1.3)

It is clear from the reference to 'cries' in the passage cited above that Macarius is here attempting a kind of compromise with Messalian habits of prayer. He goes on to allow whatever bodily habit suits, so long as the intellect is firmly rooted in God, while elsewhere he appears to rule out cries altogether (II 6.1). This kind of reform does not appear to be on Mark's agenda. It is a further example of the narrowness of his critique of the Messalians.

Mark's reference to 'undistracted' prayer is typical. Elsewhere he writes, 'When the intelligence cries aloud undistractedly (ἀπερισπάστως), the Lord hears it' (II.31 936B); that 'The intellect that prays undistractedly (ἀπερισπάστως) afflicts the heart' (II.32 936B); and that the Lord leads us 'to the habit (ἕξις) of sacred virtue, that is to say, of undistracted prayer (τῆς ἀπερισπάστου προσευχῆς)' (VII 1076D). Similarly: 'Unroving (ἄρρεμβος) prayer is a sign of the love of God in him who perseveres. Neglect of it and wandering (ρεμβασμός) are proof of the love of pleasure' (II.90 944B). Equally: 'It is one thing to entreat God with an unroving mind (ἀρρέμβῳ διανοίᾳ); it is another to be present in body but to wander with the mind' (VII 1077A). Finally, undistracted prayer entails 'the unwavering state of the intellect' (τὸ ἀμετεώριστον τοῦ νοός) (VII 1076D).

All of these elements are to be found in Macarius. The prayer taught and granted by the Spirit is 'undistracted, unwandering' (ἀπερίσπαστον, ἀρέμβαστον) (I 29.1.11). These adjectives—more or less synonymous in Macarius as in Mark—are common epithets for pure prayer in the Macarian corpus. Moreover, the terms

ῥεμβασμός (wandering) and ῥέμβομαι/ῥεμβάζω (to wander) are
also standard in Macarius, being used to indicate the wandering of
the thoughts and the intellect as, for example, in the following:
'And the soul turns itself from wanderings (ῥεμβασμοί), guarding
its heart so that its thoughts might not wander (ῥέμβομαι) over the
world' (II 4.4). Lastly, Macarius speaks of the rational nature of the
soul as being in an 'unwavering state' (ἀμετεώριστος) (I 39.1.3).
The exact term ἄρρεμβος in the context of prayer is most unusual;
the only examples I can trace are in Mark and in Nilus.[80] It will
have been noted that Mark prefers this term to the Macarian
ἀρέμβαστος. Ῥεμβασμός is a more common term, also cropping
up in the context of distraction of mind in Evagrius, Nilus, and the
*Historia monachorum*.[81] There are also examples of prayer that is
ἀπερίσπαστος in Clement of Alexandria, Basil, and Gregory
Nazianzen.[82] Evagrius uses the adverb ἀπερισπάστως of prayer
on several occasions. In the *Praktikos* 63 (p. 646) and 69 (p. 654),
and in *On Prayer* 17 (1172A), it appears to be a stage on the road to
impassibility, not, as in Macarius, as equivalent to 'pure prayer'.
*On Prayer* 35 in the *Philokalia* version has it, however, that: 'undistracted prayer is the highest intellection of the intellect'.[83] Mark's
usage fits with this last observation, also the standard usage of
Macarius, rather than with the former Evagrian examples. Lastly
the need for the mind to be ἀμετεώριστος in prayer is found also in
Basil.[84] To sum up, Mark's descriptive vocabulary of prayer has
many forebears, amongst whom Macarius can certainly be
counted.

On a more profound level, we must also consider exactly what
Mark means by undistracted prayer. Does he follow Evagrius in
treating prayer as a process of stripping by which the intellect is
revealed as naked and able to truly contemplate its Creator, or is
his teaching founded in the richer earth of the Macarian prayer of
the heart?

---

[80] Nilus, *Ep.* 3.148 (PG 79 452D): προσευχῆς νηφούσης καὶ ἀρέμβου.
[81] Evagrius, *Ad monachos* (Add.) 2 (p. 201): Ῥεμβασμὸς ἐπιθυμίας μεταλλεύει νοῦν ἄκακον;
Nilus, *De voluntaria paupertate* 61 (PG 79 1052A); *HM* 1.23 (p. 17).
[82] Clement, *Strom.* 7.7.43.5 (GCS 17, p. 32); Basil, *Longer Rules* 8.3 (PG 31 940B) and *Ep.*
207 (Courtonne, vol. ii, p. 185); Gregory Nazianzen, *Or.* 19.7 (PG 35 1052A).
[83] *Philokalia*, 3rd edn., i. 180 (not in PG).
[84] *Shorter Rules* 201 (PG 31 1216BC). See also the unwavering hearts praised in *Ep.* 207
(Courtonne, vol. ii, p. 186).

Mark does, on one occasion, use the Evagrian phrase 'naked
intellect' (IV 1017A). He does not, however, develop the concomitant teaching on non-iconic prayer. He speaks of the cleansing of
the thoughts, not of their eradication (III 981B). This is precisely
what we find in Macarius.[85] Similarly, Mark speaks of the need to
'transcend sensory things' (II.135 949D), again very much in the
Macarian tradition. Where Mark speaks of 'pure prayer', for
example of our attaining the 'fortress of pure prayer' (καθαρᾶς
προσευχῆς ὀχυρὸν τόπον) (II.162 956B), he does so in the Macarian
sense of undistracted prayer rather than the Evagrian sense of
strictly non-iconic prayer. Furthermore, the constant remembrance (μνήμη) of God recommended by Mark is certainly iconic.
In *To Nicholas* he prescribes an uninterrupted meditation (μελέτη)
on the bounties of God accorded to the said young man (V 1029C–
1032C). A later passage in the same letter advises the detailed
recollection of Christ's earthly life and Passion (V 1041D–1045B).

Where Mark sets himself most clearly in the Macarian tradition
is in his treatment of the prayer of the heart. He holds, for
example, that the devil redoubles his efforts when he sees that
the intellect prays 'from the heart' (ἐκ καρδίας) (II.81 941B) and
recommends the Christian to 'abide in his heart' (IV 1005D).
Elsewhere, Mark gives a vivid description of the proper work of
the intellect in the heart:

> The intellect has the authority to watch over the heart and to guard it
> with all vigilance, through prayer essaying to enter into its most inward
> and undisturbed chambers (τὰ ἐνδότερα καὶ ἀνενόχλητα ταμιεῖα), where
> no winds of evil thoughts violently (βιαίως) push both soul and body onto
> the precipices of voluptuousness (τοὺς κρημνοὺς τῆς ἡδυπαθείας) and
> throw them into the bitumous pits (φρέατα ἀσφάλτου), and where there
> is no wide and spacious road strewn with words and forms of worldly
> wisdom [ . . . ]. The pure innermost chambers of the soul and the house
> of Christ receive the naked intellect which bears nothing of this world.
> (IV 1016D–1017A)

This passage, besides the basic theme of the prayer of the intellect
in the heart, is full of Macarian allusions. The chambers of the
heart, the violence of evil winds, and the precipices all hark back to
Macarius.[86] Similarly, Macarius had also charged the intellect

---

[85] See also the discussions of prayer in Chs. 4 and 6.7.

[86] For the chambers of the heart, see II 17.15, 41.1. For the winds, see II 43.9: the power
of the enemy shakes the thought like the winds (cf. Anthony, *Ep.* 4.3 (p. 210): the friendship

with watching over the heart (I 25.1.17) and with bringing forth fruit from the earth of the heart (I 18.6.12). For Mark, as for Macarius, prayer is primarily an activity of the intellect in and through the heart.

Mark says very little about the actual practice of prayer. The importance he attaches to the inner, undistracted, state of the mind, as opposed to mere bodily practices, may be taken to imply a doctrine of implicit, unspoken, prayer, but Mark, unlike Macarius, never quite spells this out.[87] Mark does not take the opportunity to attack the Messalians on this point. He does teach that the remembrance of God should be continual (V 1045AB, 1029CD, 1032C). In the same vein he interprets I Thessalonians 5: 17 to be indicative of undistracted prayer, conducted by the unwavering intellect (VII 1076D). Ceaseless prayer is one of the three virtues which englobe all the commandments and which constitute the work of repentance (III 976AB). Apart from a single passing reference to 'intense prayer' (V 1029A), this is virtually all Mark tells us about prayer. Prayer is the chief virtue but should not be divorced from the other virtues; it should be pure and undistracted; it is the work of the intellect in and through the heart; and finally, it should be ceaseless. While Mark's is not a rich teaching on prayer, it should be clear from this section that he is working in this respect broadly within the Macarian tradition.

### 5.4.6 The Inner Liturgy

Closely bound up with Mark's understanding of prayer is his teaching on the offering up of the thoughts to God, a teaching he developed within the tradition of the inner liturgy.[88] In a powerful piece of deeply Pauline typology Mark offers an interpretation of that which was accomplished under the Law (IV 993A–996D). All the mysteries enunciated in the Old Testament

---

of the body moved by 'alien winds'). In II 4.3 Macarius speaks of the disordered desires and pleasures as the 'precipices' ($\kappa\rho\eta\mu\nuo\acute{\iota}$) of life. See also Peterson, 'Die Schrift des Eremiten Markus über die Taufe und die Messalianer', 285–6.

[87] For implicit prayer in Origen and Basil, see Kallistos Ware, Introduction to Zirnheld (tr.), *Marc le Moine*, xxxvii.

[88] The best introduction to the theme of the inner Liturgy is van Parys, 'La Liturgie du coeur selon S Grégoire le Sinaïte'. The theme is deeply scriptural: Psalm 50(51): 17 and Romans 12: 1 have the human person as a sacrifice to God, similarly 4 Maccabees 17: 20–2: martyrdom as a propitiatory sacrifice.

have come about hiddenly in us at baptism and are to be experienced through the practice of the commandments.[89] In a paren-
thesis, Mark attacks an interlocutor who apparently implies that
these mysteries come about solely by our own efforts. We are to
offer to Christ the High Priest 'the thoughts of our nature' after
having traversed the road of the commandments. This road is a
dangerous one, requiring much prayer and steadfast hope. Only a
few reach the city and are offered in sacrifice. Warming to the
theme, Mark continues:

> The city is luminous and steadfast discernment in Christ [ . . . ].[90] The
> temple is the God-created sacred enclosure (θεόκτιστον τέμενος) of the
> soul and body; the altar is the foundation of hope in this temple, on
> which the first-born thought (πρωτογενὴς λογισμός) of every happening
> is offered up in sacrifice by the intellect like a first-born animal, as
> propitiation for the one who offers it up, so long as it is brought up
> stainless. And that temple has a more inward part, beyond the veil,
> and which Christ Jesus entered before us as a forerunner; and where
> he dwells in us [ . . . ]. This is the most inward, hidden, and pure space
> of the heart (τὸ ἐνδότατον καὶ ἀπόκρυφον καὶ εἰλικρινὲς χώρημα τῆς
> καρδίας). (IV 996BC)

This inner space may be opened only under the action of God and
of universal, rational, and intellectual hope; only then can the
indwelling Lord be known with certainty. In this opened inner
space the heavenly High Priest receives the first-born thoughts of
the intellect (τοὺς πρωτοτόκους τοῦ νοῦ λογισμούς) and consumes
these with the divine fire (IV 996C).

Mark returns to the theme later in the same treatise. In a
passage affirming that God is the source of all our good actions,
he writes:

> Each most royal [or ruling: βασιλικώτατος][91] intellect first of all takes
> from the hidden temple of the heart (ἀπὸ τοῦ κρυπτοῦ τῆς καρδίας ναοῦ)

---

[89] Cf. Macarius' typology in Logos 1 24: virtually all the events of the Old Testament are types of the experience of the soul.

[90] Macarius, like Origen before him (*Commentary on Lamentations* fr. 8: GCS 6, p. 238), tends to interpret Old Testament references to Jerusalem as figuring the soul (e.g. 1 24.9). Similarly Gregory of Nyssa, *Cant.* 15 (GNO 6, pp. 444–5).

[91] Macarius similarly speaks of the four 'very royal [or ruling] faculties of the soul' (οἱ βασιλικώτεροι λογισμοὶ τῆς ψυχῆς): the will, the conscience, the intellect, and the loving power (11 1.3). The use of the comparative and superlative of βασιλικός (royal/ruling) in this context is very unusual (Lampe, LS, and the TLG give no other examples). In Macarius it is used as an equivalent of the 'leading faculties' of the soul (οἱ ἡγεμονικοὶ λογισμοί) (ibid.).

the good dispositions brought about by the indwelling Christ. It then leads them to the city of virtue (τὴν ἐνάρετον πολιτείαν) which is called Jerusalem and offers them by means of its good thoughts to Christ who has given them in the first place. (IV 1008B).

When asked to explain his placing of the heavenly Jerusalem in the heart, Mark replies that while not only Jerusalem but all the good things of the resurrection are indeed from above, yet: 'The pledges and the first-fruits (οἱ ἀρραβῶνες καὶ αἱ ἀπαρχαί) of these good things are active spiritually in the hearts of those who believe firmly as from now (ἀπὸ τοῦ νῦν) so that being filled with certitude (πληροφορηθέντες) about the things to come we might despise the things of the present' (IV 1009B).[92]

This conjunction of the Pauline terms 'pledge' (ἀρραβών) and 'first-fruits' (ἀπαρχή)[93] is also found in Macarius:

What else does the kingdom within signify than the heavenly gladness of the Spirit that has been actively realized in worthy souls? For if the saints do indeed have enjoyment and joy and gladness in the kingdom, then [it follows that] worthy and faithful souls are granted to acquire the pledge and first-fruits (τὸν ἀρραβῶνα καὶ τὴν ἀπαρχήν) of this state here and now (ἐντεῦθεν ἤδη), through the active communion of the Spirit. (*EM* 8.4)

The theme of the inner liturgy is a prominent feature in Macarian spirituality. In the *Great Letter*, Macarius considers the offering of a first-born lamb by Abel, the fruits, but not the first-fruits, offered by Cain, and the first-fruits brought to Melchizedek by Abraham (*EM* 7.10). Asking what higher contemplation the Spirit indicates here, Macarius observes that the inner meaning of these offerings is that:

The first and foremost parts of our whole composite nature—the intellect, the conscience, the disposition, the upright thought, the loving power of the soul—that is to say, the first-fruits (τὴν ἀπαρχήν) of our whole man, must always first of all be offered to God as a holy sacrifice of the heart, all the firstlings and the first of the upright thoughts (τὰ ἀκροθίνια καὶ τὰ πρῶτα τῶν ὀρθῶν λογισμῶν) being wholly dedicated to the remembrance and love of God. (*EM* 7.11)

Mark appears to be using the term as a rough equivalent of the Stoic ἡγεμονικόν (the leading/governing part of the soul).

[92] Chrysostom offers a similar interpretation of Romans 8: 23: the 'first-fruits' (ἀπαρχή) of the Spirit indicate the taste of future things here and now (*In ep. ad Rom.* 14.6: PG 60 531).

[93] Paul speaks of: 'the pledge of the Spirit' (2 Cor. 1: 22; 5: 5); 'the pledge of our inheritance' (Eph. 1: 14); and 'the first-fruits of the Holy Spirit' (Rom. 8: 23).

Elsewhere, Macarius writes of our need to make the body an altar, to place our thoughts on it and call down the fire of the Lord (II 31.5).[94] He speaks in great detail of the immolation of the soul, a sacrifice carried out by Christ the High Priest (II 1.6; III 7.2.1). Macarius frequently uses the biblical theme of man as the temple of God (I 40.1.13 is a good example), and adds to that theme an understanding of the heart as the altar of the Holy Spirit (I 7.18.3, 52.2.3). For Macarius, 'the church of Christ and temple of God and true altar and living sacrifice is the man of God' (I 52.1.1). Similarly: 'the visible temple is a shadow of the temple of the heart' (I 52.2.1).

In early Christian literature, the theme is an ancient and widespread one. The concept of the martyr as sacrifice is very clear in Ignatius of Antioch's *Epistle to the Romans* and in the *Martyrdom of Polycarp*. The *Sentences of Sextus* speak of the pious mind as a temple of God and the pure and stainless heart as the best altar of God.[95] Origen also takes up the theme,[96] as does Evagrius, speaking of the 'intelligible altar' on which we must offer incense acceptable to God.[97] Similarly, he writes that the pure intellect that grasps no sensory thing at the time of prayer is a 'censer'.[98] For Evagrius it is the intellect, not the body or the heart, that is the temple of the Holy Trinity.[99] The theme of the inner liturgy also has a prominent place in the *Liber graduum* which establishes a three-

---

[94] This invocation is strikingly similar to Anthony's injunction: 'Lift up your body in which you are clothed and make it an altar and lay upon it all your thoughts and leave all evil counsels before God, and lift up the hands of your heart to him, that is to the Creator of the mind, and pray to God that he gives you the great invisible fire, that it may descend from above and consume the altar and all upon it, as well as all the priests of Baal, who are the hostile works of the enemy, that they may fear and flee before you as before the prophet Elijah. Then you will see as it were the track of a man over the sea, who will bring you the spiritual rain which is the comfort of the Spirit of Comfort' (*Ep.* 6.72–7, p. 221). The Macarian text is as follows: 'Let us therefore take up this body and make it an altar and lay upon it all our thought (ἐνθύμησις) and pray to the Lord to send from heaven the invisible and great fire and to consume the altar and all upon it. And may all the priests of Baal, which are the hostile powers, be overcome, and then we shall see the spiritual rain like the track of a man.' This is further evidence of a possible connection between the *Letters* of Anthony and the Macarian corpus.

[95] *Sentences of Sextus* 46ab (Chadwick, p. 16).

[96] See, for example, his *Commentary on Lamentations* fr. 49 (GCS 6, p. 257): 'The soul's altar is the rational faculty, through which the passions, put to death, are offered as sacrifice.'

[97] *OP* 147 1197D. Cf. also *KG* v.53 p. 119: the intellect as altar.

[98] *Skemmata* 6, p. 374.

[99] *Skemmata* 34, p. 377.

fold hierarchy of the visible Church, the Church of the heart and the higher or heavenly Church.[100]

In locating the inner liturgy primarily in the heart, Mark shows himself to be more obviously in the Macarian than the Evagrian tradition. The characterization of the offering in terms of the first thoughts also identifies his treatment more closely with that of Macarius.[101] Mark also echoes Macarius in speaking of the consuming of the thoughts by the divine fire and of Christ as the High Priest of the inner liturgy. In Macarius we see very clearly the emergence of the theme of the inner liturgy out of the theology of martyrdom. Macarius' interiorization of this theology is expressed in his powerful descriptions of the sacrifice of the soul and in his call to offer up our first thoughts to God upon the altar of the heart. While Macarius is certainly not the only source of inspiration drawn on by Mark in his own subtle and elegant development of the theme, he should certainly be reckoned a key contributor. We may also note that unlike Macarius—especially in his key treatise Logos 1 52—Mark makes no effort to relate the theme of the inner liturgy to the eucharistic worship of the Church. This is a further illustration of the narrowness of Mark's Messalian critique, and indeed of his distance from the real heat of the Messalian controversy.

### 5.4.7 Apatheia

Mark gives considerably less emphasis to *apatheia* than either Macarius or Evagrius. Indeed he avoids it altogether in his polemical treatise *On Baptism*, doubtless because of the term's association with Messalian declarations of impeccability.[102] Elsewhere, he writes that *hesychia*, joined to the four virtues of patience, humility, keeping vigil, and self-control, is the quickest route to *apatheia* (11.28 936A). He also asserts that the work of repentance, woven in with the three general commandments concerning the purification of the thoughts, ceaseless prayer, and the bearing of tribulation, produces *apatheia* in those who persevere (111 976B). Nowhere

---

[100] Memra 12: PS 3 285–304.

[101] Evagrius does say that the man who always dedicates his first-born thoughts to God has perfect prayer (*OP* 126 1193C), but this is not explicitly related to the theme of the inner liturgy.

[102] In Timothy's list, propositions T 4, 5, 9, 10, 11, 16, and 19. In John's list, propositions J 7 and 18.

does he give a definition of what exactly *apatheia* is, nor of its relation to love or knowledge. What is clear is that *apatheia* is not an inalienable state. One should not say 'How is it possible for a spiritual one to fall?'[103] Such a one, says Mark, can enjoy *apatheia* through prayer, but if he relaxes his efforts then he is necessarily seduced by the passions and dragged downwards violently and against his will (III 977 BCD). This warning is repeated elsewhere (II.70 940D; IV 1004B), in each case without specific mention of *apatheia*. Mark also affirms that the one who is impassible can still be afflicted, if not on his own account then on behalf of his neighbour (II.123 948D). In teaching that *apatheia* never equates to impeccability, Mark follows the teaching of both Evagrius and Macarius.[104] It is evident that while Mark does value the state of *apatheia*, he regards this state as essentially secondary to the real goal of the spiritual life: the manifestation of baptismal grace.

## 5.5   The Revelation of Baptismal Grace

As we have seen, Mark understands the goal of the spiritual struggle to be the manifestation of the perfect gift of grace hiddenly received at baptism. While he holds that this manifestation will never be completed in this life (IV 1005B, 1012A), the way in which he describes the experience of this process of revelation draws deeply on Macarian concepts and terminology. By employing the Macarian distinction between hidden and revealed grace, Mark precludes any confusion of the presence of grace with the sensation thereof. He is, however, entirely at one with Macarius in holding that the revelation of grace must necessarily be felt and experienced.

---

[103] The question clearly implies a Messalian understanding of *apatheia*. Macarius had faced similar questions. In II 15.16: 'Is it possible for a man who has the gift [of the Holy Spirit] to fall?' Similarly II 27.9: 'How is it that some fall after the visitation of grace?' On this theme see also below, Ch. 5.7. The question of *apatheia* is also addressed in Ch. 6.5.

[104] To the question of II 15.16, Macarius replies by emphasizing the ongoing dangers of negligence and carelessness. To that of II 27.9 he points out the persistence of human free will. Evagrius equally refers to those that have acquired *apatheia* and then fallen (*Schol. Eccl.* 46, p. 142). Note that Mark generally follows Macarius and Evagrius in regarding the passions in invariably negative terms. The only exception are the post-lapsarian physical passions of death, fatigue, hunger, and thirst, which Mark regards as morally neutral (V 1044A).

To express the fullness of this felt revelation, Mark uses the Macarian phrase 'in all plenitude and perception' (ἐν πάσῃ πληροφορίᾳ καὶ αἰσθήσει). For example, through forgiveness we will find the grace of baptism no longer present 'imperceptibly' (ἀδήλως) but active 'in all plenitude and perception' (ἐν πάσῃ πληροφορίᾳ καὶ αἰσθήσει) (VIII 1108D). Mark also adds the phrase to a citation of Ephesians 3: 14–17 used to illustrate the efficacious revelation of baptismal grace and the indwelling Christ (IV 1004D). Macarius does not add to this passage of Ephesians in this way, although, as Columba Stewart points out, the phrase does crop up in close proximity to the Ephesians passage in Logos 1 36.3.1–2, a Logos long attributed in the manuscript tradition to Mark.[105] Mark also speaks of our 'becoming fully conscious of' (πληροφορεῖται) previously hidden baptismal grace through the practice of the commandments (II.85 944A). In *To Nicholas*, Mark writes of receiving 'assurance (πληροφορία) by experience' of the utility of moderating one's intake of water (V 1041A). Other uses of the verb involve a sense of certitude (IV 1009B, 1020D, 1024D; V 1040B) or simply of persuasion (VII 1089AD, 1093A, 1100C). Excepting the rhetorical examples from *Opusculum* VII, and perhaps the 'assurance' of V 1041A, Mark's use of πληροφορία and πληροφορέω is broadly Macarian. This is particularly true of the striking use of the phrase ἐν πάσῃ πληροφορίᾳ καὶ αἰσθήσει, a bold move in an anti-Messalian writer who may himself have been suspected of Messalian sympathies.[106]

Mark does not use the term αἴσθησις (perception/sense/sensation) outside the two examples of the Macarian-Messalian phrase discussed above, with the single exception of a mention in his *On Melchizedek* of the need to offer the five senses to God 'spiritually' (νοερῶς) (X 1132A). This is one of the few hints of an understanding of the spiritual senses we find in his works.[107] He does, however, use the term πεῖρα (experience) in relation to the revelation of baptismal grace: 'We have received the aforesaid mysteries at our baptism, but do not know it (ἀγνοοῦμεν).[108]

---

[105] Stewart, '*Working the Earth of the Heart*', 114–15.
[106] As previously noted, the phrase had featured in the anti-Messalian list of John of Damascus (J 7).
[107] See also the spiritual sight of St Paul (II.188 960B) and a reference to the 'eyes of the heart' (I.5 905B).
[108] Cf. Macarius, I 43.2: baptismal grace received so subtly ὡς ἀγνοεῖν τὴν ἐνέργειαν.

When, however, we condemn ourselves for our lack of faith, and
believe sincerely in [Christ] by means of all the commandments,
then we shall receive experience (πεῖρα) of these things, and
confess that the grace of holy baptism is indeed perfect [ . . . ]'
(IV 993C). He also writes of the acquisition of 'the experience of
divine assistance' (πεῖραν θείας ἀντιλήψεως) (1.187 928C); the 'experience' of one's hidden desires furnished by tribulation (II.191
960C); the 'experience' of demonic suggestion (IV 1013C); 'chance
experience' (II.211 964C); and the assurance furnished by experience of the wisdom of moderation (V 1041A). The first two
examples follow closely the Macarian language of experience,
using it to convey the lived reality of the operation of grace in
us. The second pair describe the experience of evil. This is also a
usage found in Macarius, but Mark develops nothing like the
experiential theory of knowledge found in his predecessor. The
latter two examples do not appear to have any connection with
Macarian usage.

Mark's favoured description of the revelation of baptismal grace
comes in terms of the manifestation of the indwelling Trinity. We
should prepare ourselves 'for the manifestation of the indwelling
one' (πρὸς τὴν ἐμφάνειαν τοῦ ἐνοικοῦντος) (IV 1003B). This echoes
the treatment of Macarius who speaks of the perfect revelation of
baptismal grace as 'the completely full and active indwelling of the
Holy Spirit' (ἡ πληρεστάτη τοῦ ἁγίου πνεύματος καὶ ἐνεργὴς
ἐνοίκησις) (I 25.2.5). Mark also follows Macarius in speaking of
the operation of 'active grace' (V 1049D; cf. I 25.1.9) and in
asserting that perfection requires 'active love' (III 981A; cf.
EM 3.13).

It is surprising that Mark gives almost no attention to the
eucharist. He could surely have applied his teaching on the revelation of baptismal grace to the need to actively experience
the grace of the eucharist. Macarius is far more expansive on the
subject, asserting quite unambiguously that the bread and wine of
the eucharist, sanctified by word and by the power of the Spirit,
become the body and blood of Christ (I 26.3); and that those who
receive these with faith become participants of the Holy Spirit
(I 22.1.6–8).[109] Given that the Messalians were accused of

---

[109] For the eucharist in Macarius see especially Desprez, 'L'Eucharistie d'après le
Pseudo-Macaire et son arrière-plan syrien'.

regarding the eucharist as, at best, neutral, it is interesting that Mark should practically ignore the question. Again, Macarius' is shown to be the more thoroughgoing anti-Messalian critique of the two.

To sum up, not only does Mark use the scheme of hidden and revealed grace formulated by Macarius, but he also uses key features of the Macarian vocabulary of spiritual experience to describe the process of revelation. The use of the key phrase ἐν πάσῃ πληροφορίᾳ καὶ αἰσθήσει is a particularly clear sign of Macarian influence in this respect.

## 5.6 Exegesis

Otmar Hesse has made a penetrating study of the exegetical parallels between Mark and Macarius.[110] The most significant of these relate to Matthew 16: 24 (*Op.* III; Logos I 55);[111] the paradise myth of Genesis (*Op.* IV and *Op.* VIII; Logos I 36);[112] Luke 16: 10 (*Op.* VII; Homily II 48); John 15: 5 (*Op.* II; Logos I 38); and the parable of the ten virgins in Matthew 25: 1–13 (*Op.* V; Homily II 4). What follows is my own analysis of the parallels to which he has drawn attention.

As a further illustration of his point that baptism restores us to the position of Adam, Mark remarks that baptism places us 'in the paradise of the Church', a trust we betray by tasting the tree of knowledge of good and evil, that is, by judging others (IV 1025AB). Similarly, Mark points out that while the sin of Adam and Eve was personal to them, yet we, regenerated and placed 'in the paradise of the Church', transgress spiritually by judging others (VIII 1103BC). Macarius had also written of the inner re-enactment of the Fall that takes place in the paradise that is in the heart, albeit with no specific reference to baptism. In contrast to Mark, Macarius takes our eating of the fruit of the tree to mean the remembrance of the things of this perishable life (I 36.1). While the parallel is not in itself very close, it would have been entirely

---

[110] Hesse, 'Markos Eremites', 14–43. See also the overly sceptical discussion of Hesse's claims in de Durand, *Marc le Moine: Traités*, i. 281–5.

[111] Discussed above, Ch. 5.4.4.

[112] See also Hesse's article, 'Vom Paradies der Kirche und vom Paradies im Herzen. Zur Deutung der Paradiesesgeschichte bei Makarios/Symeon und Markos Eremites'.

typical of Mark to take the Macarian theme of the re-enactment of the Fall within the paradise of the heart and give it a more explicit relation to baptism.[113] If he has indeed taken the idea from Macarius, Mark has also substituted the principle of not judging others for the radical disregard for the things of the morrow taught in the Macarian text.[114]

The parallel between the exegesis of Luke 16: 10[115] in our authors is made particularly interesting by the variant readings adopted by our authors of the Gospel text:

ὁ πιστὸς ἐν ἐλαχίστῳ καὶ ἐν πολλῷ πιστός ἐστιν, καὶ ὁ ἐν ἐλαχίστῳ ἄδικος καὶ ἐν πολλῷ ἄδικός ἐστιν. (Luke 16: 10)

ὁ πιστὸς ἐν ὀλίγῳ πιστὸς καὶ ἐν πολλῷ πιστός ἐστι, καὶ ὁ ἐν ὀλίγῳ ἄπιστος καὶ ἐν πολλῷ ἄπιστός ἐστιν. (Macarius, 11 48.1)

ὁ ἐν μικρῷ πιστὸς καὶ ἐν μεγάλῳ πιστός ἐστιν καὶ ὁ ἐν μικρῷ ἄπιστος, καὶ ἐν μεγάλῳ ἄπιστός ἐστιν. (Mark, VII 1077C)

The Marcan text as given here reflects de Durand's rejection of the PG reading ὀλίγῳ / πολλῷ followed by Hesse (based on the unreliable Parisinus graecus 1037 (MS F)) for the better-attested μικρῷ / μεγάλῳ. The PG reading would, of course, certainly strengthen the case for direct reliance on Macarius here, but it must be recognized that it is very much a minority reading. The use of ἄπιστος for the Gospel ἄδικος in both Mark and Macarius is also, in Mark's case, a minority reading—but one that is accepted by de Durand. Aelred Baker suggests that the Macarian variant is ultimately derived from the Syriac *qlyl* (a little, a few: Payne-Smith), as found in the Syriac text of the New Testament.[116] Both μικρῷ and ὀλίγῳ would serve as a retroversion of this term. The Syriac New Testament *sgy* (much, many, great:

---

[113] To back up the possibility of the connection here we should note Hesse's observation that both the Marcan and Macarian discussions of the theme make use of an unusual conflation of Luke 6: 37 and Matthew 6: 14: ἄφετε καὶ ἀφεθήσεται ὑμῖν ('forgive and it will be forgiven unto you') (Mark IV 1025B; Macarius I 36.2.4). The variant appears to go back to Tatian's *Diatessaron*.

[114] See also VII 1077CD, in which Mark allows a limited concern for the cares of this life. If Mark was, as seems most plausible, writing in the years after 431, he may have been motivated by a desire to disassociate himself from the Acemite rejection of all future earthly concerns, particularly given the low standing of the Acemite cause in the years following Alexander the Acemite's expulsion from Constantinople in 426.

[115] 'He who is faithful in a very little is faithful also in much; and he who is dishonest in a very little is dishonest also in much' (RSV).

[116] Baker, 'Syriac and the Scriptural Quotations of Pseudo-Macarius', 143.

Payne-Smith) might be put into Greek as either πολλῷ or μεγάλῳ. Furthermore, while the Syriac New Testament gives ʿol (unjust, unrighteous: Payne-Smith) as an equivalent for ἄδικος, Baker cites three witnesses to the *Diatessaron* that would support the Greek retroversion ἄπιστος. It seems clear that Mark has followed a variant reading of Luke 16: 10 here, one with affinities to the Syriac Bible and Diatessaron, and which he may have picked up from Macarius. While the text given by de Durand does not allow us to be as sure as Hesse has been about a direct connection between Mark and Macarius here, a good case for such a connection can certainly still be made.

The context in which Mark and Macarius use the Gospel quotation does help illumine the problem. Mark writes that the Lord spoke this saying to call us 'to greater faith' (εἰς μείζονα πίστιν) (ibid.); Macarius writes that the Lord spoke this to lead us 'to perfect faith' (εἰς τελείαν πίστιν) (ibid.). Both define the 'small / few things' as 'transitory things' (τῶν προσκαίρων) (Macarius, II 48.2; Mark, VII 1077C) concerning which we should have no care (μέριμνα). They contrast these transitory things to 'eternal good things' (τὰ αἰώνια ἀγαθά) (Macarius, II 48.2; Mark, VII 1077C). Both use Matthew 6: 25 and 6: 33 to illustrate the point (Macarius, II 48.1–3; Mark, VII 1077BC). It seems to me undeniable that Mark is drawing upon Macarian exegesis here. The only slight difference is that Mark pauses to allow a certain amount of concern for the things of today, if not for those of the morrow (VII 1077CD). In sum, it is quite clear that Mark knew and drew upon some version of what we know as Homily II 48.

Both authors explain John 15: 5 as illustrating the need to pray before every act. Mark uses the verb προσεύχομαι, Macarius δέομαι. If we do this we shall be taking the right path, they argue, both using the verb εὐοδέω (Macarius, I 38.2.1; Mark, II.154 953CD). While this is not in itself an outstanding parallel, it is strengthened by the fact that other passages in Mark's *Op.* II demonstrate awareness of the Macarian Logos I 38. Hesse draws attention to two Marcan passages that illustrate this awareness. The first comes from *Op.* II.137, in which Mark begins with a call to enter into the acquisition of the spiritual rest to which Paul refers in Hebrews 4: 11 and to devote oneself to spiritual hope. The Macarian text begins with a discussion of the need to battle with the spirits of evil and so to enter into the kingdom of heaven, the kingdom being 'the Spirit of Christ who loves mankind and who works *apatheia* and faith in the soul' (τὸ φιλάνθρωπον πνεῦμα Χριστοῦ, ἀπάθειαν καὶ πίστιν ἐνέργουν τῇ ψυχῇ) (1 38.2.6–7). The respective texts are as follows:

οὐ λέγομεν δὲ ὅτι ἡ βασιλεία τῶν οὐρανῶν ὧδε τέλος ἔχει, ὡς ἀποκλείοντες τὰ μέλλοντα, ἀλλ' ὅτι ἀπεντεῦθεν ἐστι κοινωνῆσαι τῷ ἁγίῳ πνεύματι καὶ ἐνεργῶς πιστεῦσαι περὶ τῆς αἰωνίου ζωῆς [...].
(Macarius, 1 38.2.8)

ταῦτα δὲ εἰρήκαμεν οὐκ ἀποκλείοντες τὰ μέλλοντα οὔτε ὧδε τὴν καθολικὴν ἀνταπόδοσιν εἶναι ὁρίσαντες· ἀλλ' ὅτι χρὴ πρῶτον ἐν τῇ καρδίᾳ ἐνεργοῦσαν ἔχειν τὴν χάριν τοῦ ἁγίου πνεύματος· καὶ οὕτω κατ' ἀναλογίαν εἰσελθεῖν εἰς τὴν βασιλείαν τῶν οὐρανῶν. τοῦτο φανεροποιῶν ὁ κύριος ἔλεγεν· ἡ βασιλεία τῶν οὐρανῶν ἐντὸς ὑμῶν ἐστι.   (Mark, 11.137 952AB)

Both go on to cite 2 Corinthians 13: 5 in the context of a discussion of the need to recognize the indwelling Christ. The similarities between the two accounts are striking. Hesse also notes the similarities between the distinction between γνῶσις τῶν πραγμάτων and ἐπίγνωσις ἀληθείας made by Mark (11.135 949CD) and that between γνῶσις ψιλή and γνῶσις ἀληθείας made by Macarius (1 38.2.9).[117] Both allow a legitimate function to 'mere knowledge' or 'knowledge of things'. Macarius has it that mere knowledge is acquired (προσγίνεται) through hope in visible things; Mark holds that knowledge of truth is acquired (προσγίνεται) through hope in Christ. Both insist on the need to transcend (using ὑπερβαίνω) earthly (Macarius) or sensible (Mark) things in order to attain knowledge of truth. All this amounts to the certainty that Mark knew Logos 1 38.2.

The last parallel adduced by Hesse concerns the parable of the ten virgins of Matthew 25: 1–13. Macarius observes that the foolish virgins have been made sluggish 'through carelessness and slackness and idleness and ignorance or the supposition of righteousness' (δι' ἀμέλειαν καὶ χαυνότητα καὶ ῥαθυμίαν καὶ ἀγνωσίαν ἢ καὶ οἴησιν δικαιοσύνης) (11 4.6). Mark writes that they have remained unaware of their inner impurity 'through carelessness and ignorance and idleness' (διὰ δὲ ἀμέλειαν καὶ ἄγνοιαν καὶ ῥαθυμίαν) (v 1036A). A little later he also lists the 'supposition of righteous-

---

[117] Mark also speaks of γνῶσις ψιλή in 11.7 932A.

ness' (οἴησις δικαιοσύνης) among their alleged vices (v 1036B).
Macarius continues, 'because of which they were shut out of the
bridal chamber of the kingdom' (διὸ καὶ τοῦ νυμφῶνος τῆς
βασιλείας ἀπεκλείσθησαν); Mark concludes, 'because of which
[. . .] they were shut out of the heavenly bridal chamber' (διόπερ
[. . .] καὶ νυμφῶνος ἐπουρανίου ἀποκλεισθεῖσαι). Hesse sees evidence of an extra-canonical source in our authors' use of 'bridal
chamber' (ὁ νυμφών) for the Gospel text's 'marriage feast' (οἱ
γάμοι) and in the fact that they speak of the foolish virgins being
shut out of the bridal chamber (using ἀποκλείω) rather than the
Gospel's rather simpler 'and the door was shut' (using κλείω).[118]
The Syriac New Testament, as would be expected, supports the
Greek Gospel text rather than the supposed variant used by our
writers. Hesse suggests, relying on Staats,[119] that Mark and
Macarius are drawing on a variant also witnessed by the *Epistula
apostolorum* and a series of Syriac writers.[120] It should, however, be
noted that Macarius uses the same terminology in *EM* 9.11,
whereas Mark does not discuss the ten virgins elsewhere. Equally,
the two interpretations do differ in some respects, for example in
respect of the nature of the oil.[121] Nevertheless the similarities are
such as to indicate that Mark certainly knew Macarius' treatment
of the parable and made use of elements of that treatment in his
own interpretation.

### 5.7 Aspects of the Ascetic Life

Mark's conception of the spiritual life involves a certain, fluid,
distinction between 'beginners' (οἱ ἀρχόμενοι), 'intermediates' (οἱ
μέσοι) and 'the perfect' (οἱ τέλειοι) (III 976C). The latter two
classifications are equivalent to the 'those making progress' (οἱ ἐν
προκοπῇ τυγχάνοντες) and the 'spiritual ones' (οἱ πνευματικοί)
referred to later in the same treatise (III 977B). The term 'spiritual

[118] Hesse, 'Markos Eremites', 41.
[119] Staats, 'Die törichten Jungfrauen von Mt. 25 in gnostischer und antignostischer
Literatur'.
[120] In fact the notion of the heavenly bridal chamber became a key theological concept
in the Syriac tradition.
[121] For Macarius, the oil represents the grace of the Holy Spirit, for Mark it is indicative
of the virtues. De Durand, 'L'Épître à Nicholas', finds the respective interpretations very
different.

ones' is particularly noteworthy given its currency amongst the
Messalians who, we are told, used it to designate the distinct class
of ascetics who had achieved the inalienable state of *apatheia*
accorded by the Holy Spirit.[122] Mark clearly distances himself
from the Messalian position by attacking the implication of the
question 'How is it possible for a spiritual one to fall?' He states in
no uncertain terms that the state of *apatheia* is never inalienable (III
977BC).

Mark's position is very much that of Macarius. Macarius does
not speak in so many words of 'beginners' and 'intermediates'. He
does, however, speak frequently of 'the perfect' and, less often, of
'the spiritual ones'.[123] In Homily II 15.16, Macarius is asked: 'Is it
possible for the man who has received the gift [of grace] to fall?'
The similarity between this question and that dealt with by Mark
above hardly needs to be pointed out. Macarius' straightforward
reply anticipates in certain respects that of Mark: 'If he is negligent, he falls.' Macarius goes on to emphasize the permanence of
the spiritual struggle. Asked whether they are wholly free from
care (using ἀμεριμνέω), he replies that they are indeed subject to
spiritual warfare but remain free from care in so far as they are
experienced in that combat and guided by God (II 15.18). Elsewhere he submits that even the perfect live in fear while in the
flesh (II 26.23) and notes, in a clear rebuttal of the Messalian
supposition of inalienable *apatheia*, that many have gone astray
by assuming that they are free from cares immediately upon the
first visitation of grace (II 10.2–3). It may have been his dismay at

---

[122] Theodoret, *Haer. fab. comp.* IV.II (429C); T 13 and 19.

[123] For 'the perfect', see I 18.5.3: 'the perfect are entirely free from cares'. But note that
the perfect remain exposed to tribulation (II 26.23) and never lose their free will, that is the
possibility of falling (II 27.9). For 'the spiritual ones' see II 14.6, but note the disparaging
comment of III 7.7.2 on those who suppose themselves to be πνευματικοί after acquiring
only a few superficial and bodily virtues. This is a clear attack on Messalian pretension. The
concept of 'the perfect' as a distinct level of monks is discernible in Pachomius, *VP* (first
Greek *Life*) 32: 'If any of the brethren who had not yet attained perfection [wished to see a
relative ... ]'. Similarly the *Historia monachorum* 12 (p. 8): the account is to 'provide a
paradigm and a testimony for the perfect, and to edify and benefit those who are only
beginners in the spiritual life'. See also Cassian, *Conf.* XXI.29 ff. (SC 64, pp. 104 ff.): the
perfect are able to go beyond certain fixed rules. The *Liber graduum*'s firm distinction within
the Christian community at large between the just and the perfect must also be mentioned.
It is an important source for the Messalian conception of the spiritual life. Where the
Messalians departed from traditional distinctions of levels in the monastic life was in their
reification of those distinctions and their supposition that 'spiritual ones' must necessarily
remain such.

the scale of the loss of so many who had begun so well to aberrant forms of asceticism that prompted him to remark that he had 'never yet seen a perfect Christian' (II 8.5). The sense shared by Mark and Macarius of the fragility of the perfected condition in this life prevents them from setting up a separate class of 'spiritual ones' after the manner of the Messalians.

Within the monastic community, Macarius makes, in the *Great Letter*, a distinction between those that pray and those that serve. While he is unambiguous in asserting the superiority of prayer, he also stresses the importance of work and service, writing that they 'both spring from the same good root' (*EM* 11.11). Elsewhere he speaks of those that pray, those that read, and those that work (II 3.1–2). It would be stretching the evidence to extract a teaching of separate classes of monks from this. The members of the monastic community have different tasks, like the members of the body, and all that is done is 'for the common good' (εἰς κοινὴν ὠφέλειαν) (II 3.2).

The question of the proper relationship between prayer and work is also dealt with by Mark in the *Controversy with an Advocate*. The opening remarks of the advocate are very telling in this respect. In addition to asking why the monks object to pursuing cases in the courts, he also wants to know why they abstain from 'sensible works' (αἰσθητῶν ἔργων). He goes on to accuse the monks of an 'unnatural laziness' (VII 1072A). The advocate reproaches Mark and his circle with one of the chief accusations levelled against the Messalians: disdain for manual labour. Indeed, he uses the same term, 'sensible works', as that found in Timothy of Constantinople's list.[124] It does seem plausible that Mark is here being implicitly accused of Messalianism. If this is the case, it would support Chadwick's hypothesis that Mark wrote his *On Baptism* to clear himself from a suspicion of Messalian sympathies—a hypothesis that need not necessarily rely on Mark's having been the Mark of Tarsus indicted by Severus, a figure who Chadwick suggests may be identical with our Mark.[125]

Mark's reply to this charge is very forthright. He asserts that the work of the monk is to seek the Kingdom in prayer. All else will

---

[124] T 13: 'They say that the work of the hands is to be avoided as something repellent. And so they call themselves "spiritual ones", not judging it possible or right for such people to touch sensible work. In this they are rejecting the tradition of the apostles.'

[125] 'The Identity and Date of Mark the Monk'.

follow upon that quest (vii 1072c). Nevertheless, he allows a legitimate concern for the things of each day, observing that it is not possible to neglect the life of the body altogether (vii 1077cd). The monk should neither prefer service to prayer nor avoid service under the pretext of prayer (vii 1077d). Mark admits that a great deal of discretion is required to identify acts of service that may properly be preferred to prayer (vii 1080bc). Mark sums up his attitude to the relation between work and prayer by commenting that the apostles' institution of the diaconate (Acts 6: 2–6) indicates that: 'It is good for those who cannot yet persevere in prayer to devote themselves to service, so as not to lose them both. But for those who are able, it is better not to neglect what is best' (vii 1080d).

Mark's advice echoes that of Macarius: 'Those who are not yet able to give themselves completely to the work of prayer because of their [spiritual] immaturity should ready themselves for the service [ . . . ] of the brethren with faith and reverence and fear of God' (*EM* 10.1). Macarius' advice is repeated several times in the *Great Letter*, with injunctions for those able to persevere in prayer not to look down upon those that serve and for those that serve not to resent those that pray (*EM* 11.2). Macarius uses the same text (Acts 6: 2–6) as Mark to justify this arrangement (*EM* 11.10). It is clear that both regard the work of prayer as infinitely superior to that of service but recognize the utility and indeed necessity of that secondary labour. Both seem to regard service as a kind of noviciate, most suitable for those who are not yet able to persevere in prayer. Both also allow for a distinct, but not separate, group of monks dedicated wholly to prayer. Mark's perspective is somewhat different from that of Macarius. He speaks of minimizing rather than excluding material concerns. He also has less of a grasp of the monastic community as an organic whole than does Macarius. Nevertheless, the very definite echoes of the *Great Letter* in Mark's *Controversy with an Advocate* do strongly suggest that Mark knew some form of that work.

Repentance is a key aspect of Mark's ascetic teaching. He goes so far as to suggest that we should repent not only our own sins, but also those of others, including that of Adam. Thus even the perfect have a debt of repentance right up to death (iii 980a–984b). This is not a teaching developed by Macarius, except in so far as it is included in his doctrine of prayer and intercession for the whole Adam.[126]

Mark singles out the vice of seeking to please men (ἀνθρωπαρέσκεια)—condemned by St Paul in Ephesians 6: 6 and Colossians 3: 22—as especially insidious, given that it can be masked by words and acts of outward piety. It is therefore peculiarly difficult to detect. This provokes a lively discussion with the advocate (VII 1085A–1089A). Mark's sense of the special dangers of this vice may have drawn upon Macarius' treatment of this vice as one of the most violent and hidden passions of the soul (*EM* 3.3). Macarius' first text on the vice is Psalm 52(53): 5, as is Mark's (VII 1088C). Mark goes on to cite Ephesians 6: 6 and Galatians 1: 10, neither of which are adduced by Macarius here, and concludes with Luke 6: 26 and a paraphrase of Matthew 6: 1, both of which are also brought forward by Macarius.

Closely related to this vice of seeking to please men is the theme of inward asceticism. Mark makes a great deal of this theme in his *To Nicholas*.[127] The emphasis in that epistle is very much on authentic, inward, monasticism. Mark has gone to live with the 'true athletes and workers of Christ' (V 1029B). He seems filled with a desire for true Christianity (V 1033AB) and is acutely conscious of the dangers of merely outward asceticism. In a nice play on words he remarks: 'Other people regard us as saints (ἅγιοι), but in reality we are still savages (ἄγριοι)' (V 1033B). Inside, he continues, we are 'stained with thoughts of fornication and muddied by the operations of the passions' (V 1033BC). Our *ascesis* is merely in appearance, says Mark, we content ourselves with only exterior practices (τῶν ἔξωθεν ἐπιτηδευμάτων) (V 1033C). This kind of teaching is very like that of Macarius, who stresses the insufficiency of 'outward forms and practices' (τοῖς ἐξωτέροις σχήμασι καὶ ἤθεσιν) (*EM* 13.6) and derides those who 'consider themselves to be in good [spiritual] health—that is to say "spiritual ones"—because of a few superficial and bodily virtues (διά τινας ἐπιπολαίους καὶ σωματικὰς ἀρετάς), while inside they are held fast by fearful hidden passions' (III 7.7.2). He also warns: 'There are some who have desisted from outward unchastity, fraud, and similar iniquities and who on this account regard themselves as saints, when in

---

[126] Homily 11 18.8 is a good example of such 'universal' prayer.
[127] Cf. Hesse's discussion of the theme, 'Markos Eremites', 138–9.

fact these persons inexperienced in the truth are far from being saints. For evil frequently dwells in the intellect of such people, thriving there and creeping around' (1 16.3.4). This is a warning Mark evidently took to heart.


## 5.8   *Op.* v: *To Nicholas*

Mark's epistle *To Nicholas* has proved very popular. It is one of the three works of his included in the *Philokalia*. There have, however, been serious doubts raised recently as to its authenticity, most notably by de Durand.[128] Hesse had noted certain 'difficulties' with the piece: it is absent from the Syriac Mark and lacks certain distinctive Marcan themes—baptism being the most obvious example. He nevertheless cautiously concluded that it was indeed the work of the real Mark.[129] De Durand, citing what he saw as a patent dissimilitude of style and thoughts, found himself unable to accept the authenticity of the work. In what follows, I present a brief discussion of the Macarian element in *To Nicholas* and of the place of that work within the Marcan corpus.

The fact that the work is a letter to a disciple—the only epistle in the Marcan corpus—must always be borne in mind. The letter is predominately moral in tone and has very little dogmatic content. This helps to explain why Mark makes no comment on Nicholas' apparent use of Romans 7: 23 to illustrate his sense of the power of the inner workings of evil (v 1029A), notwithstanding the interpretation of that passage Mark offers in his *On Baptism* (IV 992D–993A). He may have taken for granted a sense of the power of baptism on Nicholas' part, a supposition he could not make of his interlocutor in the polemic work *On Baptism*. Alternatively, Mark may have written this letter before reflecting deeply on the subject of baptism: we must not exclude the possibility of evolution in Mark's thought. Certainly Mark's sojourn amongst the 'true workers and athletes of Christ',[130] in an unnamed desert (v 1029B) seems to

---

[128] 'L'Épître à Nicholas'. This should now be complemented by de Durand's introduction to the piece in his edition of the text: *Marc le Moine: Traités*, ii. 97–104.

[129] Hesse, 'Markos Eremites', 152. See also his 'Markus Eremita in der syrischen Literatur'. The *Letter* was known to Photius (*Bibliotheca* 200: Henry, vol. iii, p. 99). Its MSS witnesses are as good as those of *Opuscula* III, IV, and VIII. The chief difficulties are to do with the content of the *Letter*.

have fired him with an acute sense of the power of evil within, a sense which is not, as we have seen, absent in his other works. Thus he calls for a 'ceaseless struggle' (ἀδιάλειπτον ἀγῶνα) (v 1029B)[131] against 'the opposing powers' (τὰς ἀντικειμένας ἐνεργείας) (v 1029C)—very much in the spirit of the militant Christianity preached by Macarius.[132] Similarly, Mark, like Macarius, speaks of 'true Christianity': 'No one can become a true Christian unless he has given himself up completely to the Cross in a spirit of humility and self-denial, and makes himself lower than all, letting himself be trampled underfoot and despised, ill-treated, derided, and mocked, bearing all things with joy for the Lord's sake' (v 1033AB).[133] The designation of ignorance as the cause of evils (v 1032B) essentially repeats Macarius *EM* 1.1. The practice of remembering the bounties of God recommended by Mark (v 1029C–1032C) is clearly directed at Nicholas' own circumstances. We should not therefore be surprised that it is not closely paralleled in the remainder of the Marcan corpus, or indeed in Macarius. Mark's attacks on merely outward piety (v 1033B–1036C) share, as I have shown, certain features with those of Macarius. They are not, as we have seen, confined to *Op.* v. We have also seen that the exegesis of the parable of the wise and foolish virgins has substantial similarities with that of Macarius. Mark mentions the inner liturgy (v 1036CD), a theme we have found elsewhere in his works. He speaks of the 'wound of love' (v 1037B), the only time he uses this ancient motif, much beloved of Macarius, in his extant works.[134] He uses πληροφορέω

---

[130] Cf. the 'real monks' (οἱ ὄντως μοναχοί) of VII 1089D (the column number in PG is missing in de Durand. The phrase in question appears on p. 66 of de Durand's edition).

[131] For ἀγών in Macarius see II 3.3 (line 44) and notes. The fact that Mark denies that the ancient sin is cleansed ἐξ ἀγώνων (IV 985A) would not preclude him preaching the need for a 'ceaseless struggle'.

[132] This is a common term for enemy spirits often used by Macarius, e.g. II 31.5.

[133] Cf. *EM* 5.2: the daily bearing of the Cross 'with joy and gladness'. The theme of 'true Christianity' is central to Macarius, see especially III 25.6.2: 'All the heresies are satisfied with empty words, an assumption of right thinking, and a vain supposition of righteousness; but the true children of the Church of Christ are revealed in works of truth and faith and by an operation of the divine Spirit settling upon the soul and covering it with its shadow; grace produces [in such a soul] worthy fruits with power, sensation, and plenitude, and effects in the inner man of the heart a renewal of the intellect, a transformation and a new and novel creation. Such is true Christianity, [the teaching] of all the holy Scriptures [transmitted] in truth by the exact apostolic tradition.'

in a distinctly Macarian way (v 1040B), as he does elsewhere. His description of the Fall as a 'grievous captivity' (v 1041D), using very similar terminology to Macarius, is also paralleled elsewhere in his writings. His description of the double movement of the Incarnation: 'becoming what we are in order that we might become what he is' (γενόμενος ὅ ἐσμεν ἵνα γένωμεθα ὅ ἐστιν) (v 1044A), is precisely that found in Macarius and accords perfectly with the Marcan corpus as a whole.[135] Mark's description of the battle against the three giants of ignorance, forgetfulness, and laziness is Macarian in its anthropology—the intellect is to descend 'into the depths of the heart' (εἰς τὰ τῆς καρδίας βάθη) to do battle with these giants (v 1049B). This anthropology is that of the Marcan corpus as a whole. Macarius had, however, plainly rejected the depiction of sin as a 'giant', taking it to imply the superiority of sin over the soul (II 27.22). The imagery may, in fact, come from Evagrius, who interprets the 'assembly of the giants' of Proverbs 21: 16 (LXX) as denoting malice and ignorance.[136] *To Nicholas* also contains teaching on divine–human co-operation (συνέργεια) (v 1040D, 1041A, 1049B, 1049D) that is very much that which we find in Macarius and indeed in the remainder of the Marcan corpus (e.g. II.88 944A). The work ends with the theme of the establishment of 'active grace' in the soul, a process that might be taken to imply the teaching on 'hidden grace' developed in Mark's various treatments of baptism.

*To Nicholas* is certainly a work that has drawn upon Macarius. It is not, however, isolated within the Marcan corpus in doing so. The Macarian elements taken up in *To Nicholas* are, moreover, perfectly in accord with the teaching of the Marcan corpus as a whole, even when not explicitly paralleled elsewhere. This is broadly to agree with the conclusion of Hesse, who sees 'a far-reaching and substantial agreement' between *To Nicholas* and Macarius, in particular his *Great Letter.*[137] Notwithstanding the 'astounding' lack of any mention of baptism, Hesse concludes that the work is that of Mark. He adds that it is quite conceivable

---

[134] It derives ultimately from the Song of Songs. For examples in Macarius, see I 40.2.3; II 5.6 (p. 50), 5.9, 10.1, 10.2, 28.5; III 7.5.1.
[135] See Macarius, I 3.4.2: γενόμενος ὅ ἐσμεν κατ᾽ οἰκονομίαν, ἵνα γένωμεθα ἡμεῖς ὅ ἐστιν. This in turn appears indebted to Irenaeus, *AH* v (Preface) (SC 153, p. 15): γεγονότι τοῦτο ὅπερ ἐσμὲν ἡμεῖς, ἵνα ἡμᾶς καταρτίσῃ ἐκεῖνο ὅπερ ἐστίν.
[136] *Schol. Prov.* 226, p. 320.                    [137] 'Markos Eremites', 139.

that the author of *Op.* v is a disciple or close ally of Macarius-Symeon.[138] On the basis of the text in isolation, Hesse observes that the author could almost be Macarius-Symeon himself. De Durand's analysis is quite different. He sees only superficial analogues between this work and that of Macarius, and concludes that these do not diminish the distance between:

le moralisme un peu étriqué du Pseudo-Marc et la mysticisme plein d'élan, de pittoresque et de pathétique qui coule à pleins bords dans le corpus Macarien. [...] A tout prendre, le Marc véritable serait sans doute plus proche des textes pseudo-macariens, même s'il a polémiqué à mots couverts contre certains tenants de cette spiritualité.[139]

Hesse has perhaps overestimated the depth of the undoubted parallels that exist between *Op.* v and the Macarian writings. There is a far more serious and interesting engagement with Macarius in Mark's *Op.* iv. De Durand is right to point out the distance between the unexpansive *Op.* v and the flights of the Macarian imagination, although it must be recognized that the entire Marcan corpus comes over as distinctly pedestrian when set against Macarius. *Op.* v is no exception. I would also argue that de Durand has given insufficient weight to the influence of the fact that it is a letter, written to a specific disciple and much inspired by the 'true workers and athletes' amongst whom Mark was staying at the time. Moreover, he does not make sufficient allowance for development in Mark's teaching. While the authenticity of *Op.* v does not significantly affect the arguments presented in this chapter and with all due deference to Marcan scholars, I would suggest the work is indeed that of Mark. It is easy to see how a work such as this might provoke an accusation of Messalianism, to which Mark would reply with his *On Baptism*, but such a scenario remains purely conjectural.

## 5.9 Christology

Given that many of the debates concerning Mark's date and location have revolved around his Christology, it may be helpful

---

[138] 'Markos Eremites', 141.    [139] 'L'Épître à Nicholas', 277–8.

to conclude this chapter with a brief discussion of his teaching on
the person of Christ in comparison with that of Macarius.

Mark's standpoint is resolutely Alexandrine. The Word made
man is, according to the apostolic preaching, 'one and not two,
even if conceptually he is of two [elements], indivisibly united' (ἕνα
καὶ οὐ δύο, κἂν ἐκ δύο νοοῖτο ἡνωμένον ἀδιαρέτως) (VII 1100D).[140]
This standpoint runs right through his two major works devoted to
Christology: *Op.* x *On Melchizedek* and *Op.* XI, traditionally known
as *Against the Nestorians*.[141] In both these works, Mark writes of the
hypostatic union. In *Op.* x Mark writes that the holy body of the
Lord has been hypostatically (ὑποστατικῶς) united to the Word
(x 1124B);[142] in *Op.* XI he speaks of the hypostatic union eight times
(13 (8), 17 (10), 21 (13), 26 (15) (×2), 30 (16), 34 (20), 42 (23)), always to
refute those who would divide the Word and the flesh (flesh, of
course, in the Johannine rather than Pauline sense). The whole
thrust of Mark's argument is against those who would find two
subjects in Christ. Christ, he insists, is 'indivisible' (ἀδιαίρετος)
(7 (5)) and 'inseparable' (ἀχώριστος) (17 (10)). Mark writes that
Jesus Christ is the name 'of the indivisible conjunction' (τῆς
ἀδιαιρέτου συναφείας) (21 (12)).[143] Mark will also speak of the
uniting of the Word with the 'Lord's man' (ὁ κυριακὸς ἄνθρωπος)
(20 (12)), an expression he also uses in *Op.* v (1045A), and one which
had been criticized by Gregory Nazianzen as used by the Apol-
linarians.[144] Mark's Creed certainly included a confession that the
Logos took a human soul in becoming incarnate (16 (9)). This
article doubtless developed out of the Apollinarian controversy.

---

[140] MS C (Coislinianus 123) has 'corrected' this to ἐν δύο.

[141] The full title is, 'Against those who say that the flesh of the Lord is not united to the
Word, but that it is merely worn like a garment, and that, for this reason, there is a
difference between him who carries and that which is carried'. Sabaiticus 366 (thirteenth
century, and the basis of the Papadopoulos-Kerameus and Kunze editions) has 'that is to
say, against the Nestorians'. The more ancient and reliable Cryptoferratensis B a 19 (AD
965, and the basis of the Rocchi edition) does not have this gloss. The title 'On the
Hypostatic Union' has been suggested by Gribomont, in 'Encore Marc l'Ermite: l'union
selon l'hypostase', on the basis of the content of the treatise.

[142] To illustrate what he means by hypostatic union, Mark uses the somewhat unfortu-
nate analogy of the passage of a swollen river into the sea (x 1124c). In XI. 26 (15) he uses the
more familiar image of gold in the fire.

[143] Note that Cyril of Alexandria had rejected the term συνάφεια as weak in meaning
and dangerous in implication. See his *Quod unus sit Christus* (SC 97, pp. 363–4).

[144] *Ep.* 101.12 (SC 208, p. 40).

The fact that this is the only mention of the human soul *per se* in *Op.* XI makes it unlikely that Mark is here attacking an Origenist Christology: surely, if he were making such an attack, he would at least mention the chief article of such a Christology, that is, the pre-existence of the human soul of Christ. Indeed, in the same passage he is happy to speak of the soul as the *instrument* of the union—a feature of his Christology that has decidedly Origenist overtones. The very last section of the *Op.* XI makes a striking turnaround. The emphasis is shifted onto the unconfused character of the union. Each nature makes its own that which pertains to the other for our sakes, but does so in a union which is 'unconfused' (ἀσύγχυτος), so that 'Christ who issues from both [natures]' (ὁ ἐξ ἀμφοῖν Χριστός) might become the mediator between God and man (51–2 (30)).

My own position on the dating and target of this work is as follows. The use of the phrase 'hypostatic union' with little explanation does, as Kallistos Ware points out, imply a date post-Ephesus (431).[145] The fact that Mark uses three out of four of the Chalcedonian alpha privatives suggests to me that he was also writing after Chalcedon, although it must also be borne in mind that all these have a pre-Chalcedonian pedigree. The emphasis he gives to the ἐκ δύο over the ἐν δύο formula might suggest that he was of the party that did not accept Chalcedon, but that was certainly willing to build bridges with the Chalcedonian side. It is, as we have said, odd that such a resolutely Cyrilline writer should never mention the title 'Theotokos': was he perhaps trying to avoid what he may have seen as a shibboleth, to direct attention away from slogans to the central argument on the unity of Christ? Or is it that he was simply operating in a context in which both sides of the debate, Chalcedonian and non-Chalcedonian, accepted the term without question? He may, perhaps, be associated with the imperial policy encapsulated in the *Henotikon* of Zeno (482), an attempt to impose unity by sidelining, but not rejecting, Chalcedonian theology. Mark's use of the phrase 'one and not two' (ἕνα καὶ οὐ δύο), also found in the *Henotikon*, may be taken as a further support of this suggestion. We should also note his studied avoidance of the term φύσις, either in the singular or in the plural—again something that

---

[145] Introduction to Zirnheld (tr.), *Marc le Moine*, xiii.

would make very good sense in the context of the *Henotikon*. In sum, while much remains open to discussion, there are good grounds for placing this treatise in the latter half of the fifth century and for seeing it as the work of a writer of the Alexandrine tradition prepared to integrate Chalcedon within his own deeply Cyrilline framework. In this respect he may even be seen as a forerunner of sixth-century 'Neo-Chalcedonianism'.

Macarius' Christology is a much neglected area of his thought. He is very much in the Alexandrine tradition later shared by Mark. In Homily II 52.6, he insists in no uncertain terms on the reality of the union between the divine and human in Christ, using an image pioneered by Origen: 'Just as the body of the Lord, mixed with the divinity, is God, so iron in the fire becomes fire.' Going further, Macarius writes, 'The flesh with the soul and the divinity became *one thing*, even though they are two' (ἡ γὰρ σὰρξ σὺν τῇ ψυχῇ καὶ ἡ θεότης ἕν τι γεγόνασι κἂν δύο εἰσίν) (I 10.4.5).[146] He goes on in a remarkable piece of poetic theology to observe:

As wool dyed in purple results in one beautiful form (εἶδος), even though it comes from two (ἐκ δύο) natures and hypostases—and it is no longer possible for the wool to be separated from the dye, nor the dye from the wool—so the flesh with the soul united to the divinity results in one thing, that is to say one hypostasis: the heavenly God worshipped with the flesh.   (I 10.4.6)

Note that Macarius, like Mark, speaks rather of the (ensouled) flesh than of the human 'nature' of Christ. Also like Mark, Macarius certainly prefers the ἐκ δύο formula to the ἐν δύο, although it must be remembered that the latter formula would have been quite unparalleled in the fourth-century Greek East. Macarius' κἂν δύο εἰσίν looks very like Mark's κἂν ἐκ δύο νοοῖτο. Furthermore we note in Macarius an embryonic doctrine of the hypostatic union. While many of these features may simply be the result of a shared Christological tradition, and while Macarius' Christology is necessarily less developed than that of Mark, it is worth noting that their respective teachings on the person of Christ demonstrate a deep affinity.

---

[146] Note the mention of the human soul: Macarius inherited from the Cappadocians an antipathy towards Apollinarian Christology.

## 5.10 Conclusion

Mark's work certainly stands in close relation to that of Macarius. His doctrine of the Fall relies in certain key respects on that of Macarius. His teaching on the interaction between divine grace and human freedom is also indebted to that of Macarius. His descriptions of the power of evil employ Macarian language and imagery. His understanding of the relations between prayer and virtue and prayer and work are, again, Macarian. Similarly, his prayer is far more the undistracted prayer of the intellect in and through the heart of Macarius than the non-iconic prayer of the naked intellect of Evagrius. Macarius must also be accounted an important contributor to Mark's treatment of the theme of the inner liturgy. The exegetical parallels examined in this chapter have provided some very concrete examples of Mark's acquaintance with the Macarian corpus. The Macarian element in *To Nicholas* is patent. The question of its authenticity does not significantly affect the conclusions of this chapter. Lastly, both authors clearly work within a shared Christological tradition.

Mark was, however, by no means a passive recipient of Macarius' teaching. Most notably, he enters into a profound dialogue with Macarius on the question of baptism, rejecting the doctrine of indwelling sin and resolutely propounding the total evacuation of evil effected by baptism. All Mark's major differences with Macarius, particularly on temptation and personal responsibility, are related to this question. Mark nevertheless follows Macarius in opposing both a deterministic and a minimizing understanding of baptismal grace, opposing the one by asserting the sovereignty of human free will, and the other by means of the distinction between hidden and revealed grace. The fact that Mark's teaching on baptism relies so heavily on that of Macarius indicates that where Mark does criticize Macarius, he does so within the Macarian tradition, as a thoughtful disciple, and not as an outside antagonist. What he has done, essentially, is to refine and tighten up the Macarian critique of the Messalian rejection of baptism by excluding any potential suggestion of the insufficiency of baptism.

There are also other aspects of Macarian teaching not taken up by Mark. He does not use the theme of the two souls, ecstasy, nuptial imagery, or mixing language. All of these might have been dealt with had Mark been attacking Macarius as a Messalian. Mark is also curiously limited in his anti-Messalianism. He does not deal with Messalian disregard for the eucharist or for the ecclesiastical structures of the Church, nor does he engage them on the question of dreams and visions. The only points on which he does engage them are on baptism and, to a much lesser extent, *apatheia* and prayer. In each of these areas he relies greatly on the far more thoroughgoing critique of the Messalian tendency developed by Macarius.

Mark certainly belongs within the Macarian spiritual tradition. It is clear that he was familiar with a collection of the Macarian writings and was deeply influenced by them. This influence was, however, never mechanical or automatic: on a number of points Mark enters into a very constructive dialogue with Macarius. In the final analysis it must be acknowledged that Mark always keeps at a certain distance from his sources—and this applies equally to his, less significant, Evagrian inheritance. It may also be said that Mark is neither as original and engaging as Macarius, nor as limpid and systematic as Evagrius. A more profound integration of the Evagrian and Macarian traditions would have to await the work of Diadochus of Photice.

# 6

## Diadochus of Photice

### 6.1 Introduction

We know very little about the life of Diadochus, sometime bishop of Photice in northern Epirus.[1] Photius lists him amongst the defenders of the two natures at the time of the Council of Chalcedon.[2] Since the bishop of Photice at the Council of Chalcedon itself was named John, we can assume that Diadochus took up his see after 451. He signed the letter sent by the bishops of Old Epirus to Emperor Leo I following the assassination of Proterius of Alexandria in 457.[3] He had died by 486, the date of the *History of the Vandal Persecution* of Victor of Vita, which describes the 'blessed Diadochus' as 'great and worthy to be celebrated with every type of praise, for many of his writings like bright stars illustrate the catholic faith'.[4] Marrou has suggested that Diadochus may have been carried off to Carthage following a Vandal raid on Epirus between 467 and 474.[5] The *Gnostic Chapters*, his most important work, are addressed to certain 'brethren' (*GC* 1) and refer to those who practise *encrateia* both in coenobia and in cities, and to anchorites (*GC* 53), indicating that Diadochus wrote that work as a monk and for monks.[6] The Christological concerns of his *Sermon on the Ascension* are perhaps more suggestive of the work of a bishop.

---

[1] On Diadochus in general, see the invaluable introduction of des Places to his *Diadoque de Photicé: Oeuvres spirituelles* (SC 5 ter); Kallistos Ware, 'The Jesus Prayer in St Diadochus of Photice' and 'Diadochus von Photice'; Vincenzo Messana, 'San Diadocho di Fotica'. A further edition of the text may also be mentioned: Rutherford (ed. and tr.), *One Hundred Practical Texts of Perception and Spiritual Discernment from Diadochos of Photike: Text, Translation and Commentary*. This last appeared too late for me to make use of.

[2] *Bibliotheca* 231 (Henry, vol. v, p. 65). Diadochus' Christology, expressed in his *Sermon on the Ascension* 4–6, justifies this claim.

[3] Schwartz, *ACO* II.5, p. 95

[4] CSEL 7, p. 2.

[5] 'Diadoque de Photiké et Victor de Vita'. Des Places takes this as a possible explanation of Julian Pomerius' (fifth century) knowledge of Diadochus' works: *Diadoque de Photicé*, 10.

[6] His other works are the *Sermon on the Ascension* and *Vision*. The *Catechesis* appears to be a much later work, possibly of St Symeon the New Theologian.

Diadochus may conceivably have been promoted to the episco-
pate following a spell as superior of a monastic community.

Diadochus' work represents a conscious and creative synthesis
of the spiritual traditions of Evagrius and Macarius. Dörr and des
Places have stressed particularly the Evagrian element, and have
presented Diadochus primarily as an anti-Messalian author.[7] Dörries has, more recently, argued that the influence of Macarius is, in
fact, far more significant than that of Evagrius and that Diadochus
can therefore be seen as a disciple, even a direct disciple, of
Macarius, thus a representative of a 'moderate' or 'reformed'
Messalianism.[8]

## 6.2   The Language of Sense (Αἴσθησις)

The Macarian legacy in the work of Diadochus is at its most
palpable in the language of sense found throughout the *Gnostic
Chapters*.[9] This gives the spiritual teaching of the *Chapters*
a profoundly affective tone that is precisely in the manner of
Macarius.[10]

Diadochus' use of the language of sense should be approached
against the background of the doctrine of the spiritual senses.

---

[7] Dörr, *Diadochus von Photike und die Messalianer*; des Places, *Diadoque de Photicé*.

[8] Dörries, 'Diadochus und Symeon: Das Verhältnis der κεφάλαια γνωστικά zum
Messalianismus'. But see Desprez, 'Pseudo-Macaire', 39: 'Diadoque doit cependant être
plus éloigné de Macaire et surtout du mouvement messalien que ne le pense Dörries; car
Diadoque ne réfute chez ses adversaires que la cohabitation du péché et de la grâce qui est
déjà chez Macaire une note antimessalienne.' The question of coexistence will be discussed
in detail below. Fr Desprez has developed his thinking on the relation between Diadochus
and Macarius in an as yet unpublished article entitled 'Diadoque de Photicé et le Pseudo-
Macaire: Du débat vers un bilan?' He has been kind enough to let me see this very helpful
work.

[9] On αἴσθησις / αἰσθάνομαι in Macarius see the indispensable discussion of Stewart,
'*Working the Earth of the Heart*', 116–38. This includes a short discussion of αἴσθησις in
Diadochus and Mark, 137–8. On the spiritual sense in Diadochus see Horn, 'Sens de
l'esprit d'après Diadoque de Photicé' and des Places, *Diadoque de Photicé*, §§37–8. Rahner's
seminal article, 'Le Début d'une doctrine des cinq sens spirituels chez Origène', also
discusses Macarius, Evagrius, and Diadochus. See also Fraigneau-Julien, 'Les Sens spirituels et la vision de Dieu selon Syméon le Nouveau théologien' and Canévet, 'Sens
spirituel'.

[10] Some care needs to be taken with the term 'affective'. In modern usage it can very
often indicate the merely emotional as opposed to the rational or intellectual. In using it
here I am attempting to convey the essentially holistic nature of our authors' anthropology:
one in which the senses and emotions are equally integral to the human person as are the
reason and intellect.

Origen is generally credited with having pioneered this doctrine. He had taught that there is within man 'a certain generic divine sense', quoting the traditional Alexandrine reading of Proverbs 2: 5, 'You shall find a divine sense.'[11] This divine sense operates in five modes, analogous to the five physical senses: a sight to see metaphysical realities such as the cherubim and seraphim, a hearing to hear that which has no objective existence in the air, a taste which is nourished by the living bread, a smell which smells spiritual things, and a sense of touch such as that which the Apostle John spoke of (1 John 1: 1).[12] These modes are the 'divine' or 'spiritual senses'.

Evagrius also takes up this doctrine, speaking, in his own *Gnostic Chapters*, of the intellect's need for a 'spiritual sense' in order to distinguish spiritual things.[13] He defines this 'spiritual sense' as 'the impassibility of the rational soul, produced by the grace of God'.[14] He also speaks of the five spiritual senses of the intellect: 'Sight shows it intelligible objects nakedly; with the hearing it receives the *logoi* concerning these objects; the sense of smell delights in the scent which is foreign to all dissimulation; the mouth receives the taste of these things, and by means of touch it is made steadfast, grasping the exact manifestation of things.'[15] The doctrine of the spiritual senses is also evident in his *Advice to a Virgin*: 'Virgin eyes will see the Lord.| The ears of virgins will hear the Lord.| The mouth of virgins will kiss the Bridegroom.| The nose of virgins is drawn by the scent of his ointments [cf. S. of S. 1: 3].|

---

[11] This is a reading also known to Clement. The LXX has 'knowledge of God' (ἐπίγνωσιν Θεοῦ).

[12] *Contra Celsum* 1.48 (GCS 2, p. 98). In *De Principiis* 1.1.9 (GCS 22, p. 27) Origen asserts, again referring to Proverbs 2: 5, that Solomon 'knew that there exist in us two sorts of sense, one mortal, corruptible, and human, the other immortal and intellectual, the sense he calls "divine"'. To see with the 'eyes of the heart' (cf. Eph. 1: 18), for example, is 'virtute intelligente aliquid intellectuale conicere'. It is the 'divine sense' that sees God, the sight not of the eyes but of the 'pure heart' (cf. Matt. 5: 8), that is to say, of the intellect. Origen developed his understanding of the spiritual senses to explain the sensory language of Scripture in response both to the Gnostics and to pagan critics such as Celsus. His is an essentially spiritualizing approach, one which transposes the language of the bodily senses to the faculties of the soul. It is not primarily for Origen a question of how to express the variety or immediacy of the experience of God, but rather one of exegesis and apology. The sense of variety is essentially a secondary effect of his teaching. Origen's commentaries on Scripture naturally return to the theme frequently. See, for example, *Commentary on the Song of Songs* 1.4.10–19 (GCS 33, pp. 104–5); *Commentary on Luke* fr. 57 (GCS 49, pp. 308–9); *Commentary on John* 10.40 (GCS 10, p. 218).

[13] *KG* 1.33 (p. 33).      [14] *KG* 1.37 (p. 35).      [15] *KG* 11.35 (p. 75).

Virgin hands will touch the Lord.'[16] The spiritual senses are, in
Evagrius, the faculties by which the contemplative intellect grasps
the true nature of things and ascends towards theology. In the
realm of theology it seems that the senses, spiritual or otherwise,
are to be left behind: 'Blessed is the intellect that has acquired
complete freedom from senses (ἀναισθησία) during prayer.'[17]

Macarius teaches that the soul has five 'senses' or 'faculties'
(I 49.2.3). These he lists, in a very different way than Origen and
Evagrius, as understanding, knowledge, discernment, patience,
and mercy.[18] Elsewhere he implies an understanding of the spiritual senses more in line with that of Origen and his epigones. The
Fall, claims Macarius, has caused us to lose the 'intellectual and
deathless senses' (I 58.3.3).[19] It has 'blinded the eyes of the soul'
(I 35.3). The soul's return to health is consistently spoken of in
terms of the restoration of the spiritual senses, the reopening of the
eyes of the soul and the acquisition of the taste of grace.[20] We may
now turn to the language of sense in Diadochus.

---

[16] *Advice to a Virgin* 55 (p. 151).

[17] *OP* 120 1193B. Macarius regards ἀναισθησία as a negative quality (I 31.3.7), as one
would expect in an author who looked for an experience of God ἐν πάσῃ αἰσθήσει καὶ
πληροφορίᾳ. Maximus also treats it as a negative quality (*QT* 62, p. 129.209).

[18] In Greek: σύνεσις, γνῶσις, διάκρισις, ὑπομονή, ἔλεος. Macarius draws an analogy
between the five senses of the soul operating as they should and the five wise virgins. The
parallel text in II 4.7 omits the list of these senses. Macarius' list includes moral virtues as
well as aspects of the operation of the intellect. Discernment, as we shall see, is an activity of
the intellectual sense of the soul. There is a connection between Macarius' exegesis of
Matthew 25 and that of the second-century *Epistula apostolorum*, which speaks, without
reference to the spiritual senses, of the five wise virgins as representing knowledge, insight,
obedience, patience, and mercy. See Staats, *Gregor von Nyssa*, 95 n. 9a (cited in Stewart,
'*Working the Earth of the Heart*', 124) and Hornschuh, *Studien zur Epistula Apostolorum*, 21 ff.
Stewart also mentions Origen's exegesis of the five wise virgins in terms of the spiritual
senses, with a list quite different to that of Macarius (*Comm. ser. in Mt.* 63–4: GCS 38,
pp. 148–51).

[19] Note that he uses αἰσθητήριον rather than αἴσθησις here. Macarius usually uses the
former term in preference to the latter for the physical senses. In his choice of vocabulary,
he seems to be emphasizing the correspondence between the physical and the spiritual
senses. Macarius also connects the doctrine of the spiritual senses to his theme of the
'second soul', which is the work of the Spirit in us. In I 63.1.2 he writes, 'There are other
ears and other eyes and other cries and another mind and another soul, which is that very
divine and heavenly Spirit which hears and cries and prays and knows and does the will of
God in truth.' Rom. 8: 26 is clearly in the background here.

[20] The Lord re-establishes the 'intellectual senses' of the soul (I 58.3.3). At Pentecost, the
Spirit uncovered the 'eyes of the heart' of the apostles (I 63.1.5). The Lord came so as to
allow the soul to see him 'with its intellectual eyes' (I 28.1.4). References to the 'eyes of
heart', 'eyes of the soul' and 'intellectual eyes', or 'eyes of the intellect', are commonplace in
the Macarian writings. For the taste of grace, see the discussion below.

Diadochus habitually speaks of αἴσθησις in the singular.[21] The natural sense of the soul is single, but has been split by the Fall. The purpose of the ascetic life is to reunite the split disposition of the soul, now torn between heavenly and earthly aspirations. This reunion is to be effected by the Holy Spirit (*GC* 25, 29). The inner sense is described as 'intellectual sense' (αἴσθησις νοερά) (*GC* 1, 7); 'sense of the intellect' (αἴσθησις νοός / τοῦ νοῦ) (*GC* 24, 30, 61, 76, 77, 79, 83); 'sense of the soul' (αἴσθησις τῆς ψυχῆς) (*GC* (12), 14, 25, 29), and 'sense of the heart' (αἴσθησις τῆς καρδίας) (*GC* 14, 16, 23). He also speaks of the 'sense of the spirit' or 'spiritual sense' (*GC* 15 (×2)), 'sense' (Defn. 8, p. 84.16; *GC* 9) and 'immaterial sense' (*GC* 24). The variations in Diadochus' descriptions of the inner or spiritual sense should not be taken to imply the existence of different inner senses pertaining to the different constituent elements of man. The distinction is rather one of level. The sense of the intellect or the intellectual sense is the purest sense of our soul, and hence our surest guide in the spiritual life. When restored to its full vigour it communicates the joy it experiences from sensing the divine goodness to the body (*GC* 25). This unifying experience is shared by the whole person—even down to the 'very sense of the bones' (*GC* 14). The spiritual sense is one whether related to the intellect, the soul, the heart, or even, by virtue of the overflowing of spiritual sensation, the body. In each case the term αἴσθησις designates the same reality, that faculty in man capable of perceiving and experiencing the divine.

Where the connection between Diadochus and Macarius is most evident is in the use of the concept of the intellectual sense, the αἴσθησις νοερά, and its equivalent the sense of the intellect, the αἴσθησις νοός / τοῦ νοῦ. The term αἴσθησις νοερά appears to have been coined by Macarius. He uses it to denote the faculty in man capable of spiritual discernment (1 2.10.5) and speaks of our advancing in intellectual sense through gentleness (1 39.1.6). Diadochus also uses the term on two occasions. The intellectual

---

[21] Dörries claims that Diadochus' understanding of just one spiritual sense represents one of the two significant departures he makes from Macarius' teaching, 'Diadochus und Symeon', 412. I argue below that Diadochus' use of the Macarian designation αἴσθησις νοερά to describe this single spiritual sense suggests that Diadochus' understanding is not so different from that of Macarius. It should also be remembered that Origen in the passage from the *Contra Celsum* mentioned above speaks of the five-fold operation of a single divine sense, a teaching faithfully followed by Evagrius.

sense is that faculty by which the soul seeks the invisible (*GC* 1), a faculty which spiritual discourse fully satisfies (using πληροφορέω) (*GC* 7). Like Macarius, he connects the sense of the intellect with the faculty of discernment and uses the analogy of the physical sense of taste to illustrate the operation of that faculty (*GC* 30; cf. Macarius, I 2.10.5).

The mention of taste is important. Diadochus, as we have seen, prefers to speak of the spiritual sense, not senses. Origen and Evagrius had spoken of five spiritual senses, each spiritual sense corresponding to a physical sense. Macarius, while he does speak of the 'five senses of the soul', concentrates his attention on sight and taste. Diadochus also homes in on sight and taste. He defines patience as the perseverance required 'in order to see the invisible as visible with the eyes of the mind (τοῖς τῆς διανοίας ὀφθαλμοῖς) (Defn. 3, p. 84.6–7). This recalls Macarius' reference to the search, by those whose eyes of the mind are illumined, for the invisible object of their hope (II 25.1; cf. Eph. 1: 18). Diadochus also describes the 'eye (ὄμμα) of the soul' as being veiled by the body (*GC* 71).[22] Diadochus' language of taste is thoroughgoing and remarkable. The inner sense tastes the sweetness (*GC* 44, 63, 90), goodness (*GC* 24, 33, 89), and grace (*GC* 30, 36) of God. It is also possible for the theologian to 'taste' the experience of spiritual knowledge (*GC* 72). This language of taste is a stock in trade of the Macarian writings. When Diadochus evokes the tasting of the sweetness of the Lord, the similarities with Macarius are especially tangible.[23]

Αἴσθησις is also used in the *Gnostic Chapters* to denote the sensation or experience of grace. God's action upon the soul is experienced ἐν αἰσθήσει πολλῇ (*GC* 16, 69, 89), ἐν αἰσθήσει ἱκανῇ (*GC* 59), ἐν βαθείᾳ αἰσθήσει (*GC* 88 (×2)) or simply ἐν αἰσθήσει (*GC* 85 (p. 144.20), 90). In each case he is speaking of the inward perception–sensation–experience of grace, exactly following the distinctive understanding of αἴσθησις pioneered in the Macarian

---

[22] The phrase 'eye of the soul' is an ancient one. Origen criticizes Celsus for supposing that the Christians had not heard of it (*Contra Celsum* VII.39: GCS 3, pp. 189–90). Evagrius has 'eye of the soul' in *Skemmata* 24 (p. 377) and 'eyes of the soul' in *Schol. Prov.* 216 (p. 312). Macarius also speaks of the soul's eyes in I 63.2.4 and II 28.4.

[23] Taste is perhaps the most immediate of the spiritual senses, the most obviously suggestive of union with the object tasted. For the taste of the sweetness of God in Macarius see, for example, I 5.4.4, 21.11, 33.4.4; II 14.2, 17.2. The most obvious scriptural root for this is Ps. 33(34): 8, 'Taste and see that the Lord is good.'

writings.[24] Exactly as Macarius, he blurs the distinction between sense (a faculty of perception) and sensation (the experience consequent upon perception).[25] Diadochus confirms his debt to Macarius here by his use of the Macarian phrase ἐν πάσῃ αἰσθήσει καὶ πληροφορίᾳ, (*GC* 40, 44, 68, 90 (×2), 94). He also uses the phrase with the two nouns reversed (*GC* 91).[26]

Diadochus uses the verb αἰσθάνομαι frequently and always to denote the inward perception–experience of some aspect of the working of grace (*GC* 15, 17, 23, 25, 30, 36, 79, 99). Macarius has a somewhat wider range of usages for the verb, speaking of our sensing (that is our perceiving and experiencing) not only the workings of grace but also those of evil. Diadochus' usage of the verb, to indicate perception–experience and not simply awareness or sensory perception, is very much in the manner of Macarius.

Diadochus' language of sense is, of all its potential forerunners, most closely related to that of Macarius. Diadochus follows Macarius in breaking down the semantic barriers between sense and sensation, between perception and experience. His teaching on the spiritual senses is, in its treatment of the αἴσθησις νοερά and its focus on sight and taste, clearly built on that of Macarius. Moreover, the doctrine of the spiritual senses as formulated by Origen and Evagrius differs from that of Diadochus and Macarius because of their very different anthropological presuppositions.[27] The latter, in contrast to the former, have a real sense of the

---

[24] To take just two examples, Macarius speaks of receiving the αἴσθησις of the goodness of the Spirit (I 21.11) and of grace (I 31.6.3). In both cases both perception and experience are indicated.

[25] See (again) Stewart, '*Working the Earth of the Heart*', 117 (and discussion following), for the breaking-down of the semantic distinctions between sense and sensation in Macarius.

[26] The anti-Messalian lists condemn the proposition that participation in the Holy Spirit be 'in all sensation and plenitude' (J 7) or 'in all plenitude and energy' (J 17). Theodoret and Timothy do not mention πληροφορία, but do attack the claim that the Holy Spirit is experienced sensibly (Theodoret, *HE* IV.11 (p. 231); T 3). The condemnation of spiritual plenitude belongs, as I have argued above (Ch. 1.3), to the second (partly Macarian) layer of the anti-Messalian lists. The very natural and unapologetic way in which Diadochus uses the metaphor suggests that he was not familiar with the anti-Messalian lists in the form given by John of Damascus. The concept of πληροφορία is also used on its own by Diadochus. He describes the illumination of the Holy Spirit effected ἐν πάσῃ πληροφορίᾳ (*GC* 89). St Paul is said to have spoken ἐκ τῆς αὐτοῦ πληροφορίας (*GC* 90). The conscience is assured (πληροφορηθῇ) of forgiveness in tears (*GC* 100 (p. 162.4–5). Paul's πληροφορία may be his spiritual plenitude or his certitude. Des Places opts for the former in his translation (p. 151). The πληροφορία of *GC* 100 (p. 162.12) designates certitude, in this case a false certitude.

[27] For anthropology see also below, Ch. 6.5.

participation of the body in the experience of the soul. Thus, whereas for Origen and Evagrius the doctrine is essentially an analogy taken from the realm of the senses and transposed to the soul's apprehension of metaphysical realities, for Macarius and Diadochus it is an expression of the unity of the human person.

We shall discuss in the next section the theology of experience Diadochus builds upon the kind of affective language we have discussed above. The question of the relation between the sensation of grace and the presence thereof will be discussed below (Ch. 6.5).

## 6.3 The Language of Experience (Πεῖρα)

Macarius always uses the term πεῖρα to designate the actual experience of some metaphysical reality. This pattern of usage, as Columba Stewart has ably demonstrated, is unparalleled in any other previous writer.[28] The lived experience of sin and grace lies at the heart of Macarius' spiritual teaching. It is the primary criterion of his epistemology. Diadochus follows Macarius in three main areas: (i) the association of πεῖρα and αἴσθησις; (ii) the recognition of the organic relation between πεῖρα and knowledge; (iii) the necessity of πεῖρα to make progress in the spiritual life.

The kind of affective language discussed in the last section is given coherence by both our authors within a theology of experience. At its most basic level this process is indicated by the connection of the terms πεῖρα and αἴσθησις. Hence Diadochus writes of the incapacity of worldly wisdom to produce any benefit πείρᾳ αἰσθήσεως (*GC* 11).[29] One finds the same conjunction in Macarius: knowledge of the mysteries of the Holy Spirit comes about πείρᾳ καὶ αἰσθήσει (I 50.2.1).[30] The distinction between the constructions is slight: Diadochus speaks of a sensed experience, while Macarius uses the terms virtually as synonyms. The association of terms is not especially significant of itself, rather it serves

---

[28] Stewart, '*Working the Earth of the Heart*', 139–54. As with αἴσθησις and πληροφορία, Stewart emphasizes the very particular and distinctive use made by Macarius of existing Greek terms. See also Miquel, *Le Vocabulaire de l'expérience spirituelle dans la tradition patristique grecque du IVe au XIVe siècle*, 83–105 (Macarius) and 109–12 (Diadochus).

[29] See also *GC* 32 and 33: ἡ πεῖρα τῆς αἰσθήσεως (referring to the sense of the intellect).

[30] See also I 15.1.1–2, 49.2.14, for similar examples.

as a pointer towards the central feature of the affective tradition represented by our authors, that is its experiential epistemology.

Both authors insist on the absolute necessity of direct experience of God's grace if one is to offer spiritual instruction. As Diadochus puts it in *GC* 7:

Spiritual discourse (ὁ πνευματικὸς λόγος) fully satisfies the intellectual sense (τὴν νοερὰν αἴσθησιν πληροφορεῖ), because it comes from God through the operation of love. [...] So it is right always to wait, with a faith energized by love, for the illumination [which enables us] to speak. For nothing is so destitute as a mind that is philosophizing about the things of God when it is without him.

Only the discourse of the illumined is capable of granting us sensed experience. The discourse deriving from the wisdom of the world is capable only of producing self-esteem (*GC* 11). Virtually all this advice is paralleled in Macarius. Only those who give spiritual advice (ὁ πνευματικὸς λόγος) from their own spiritual treasury, from their own communion with the Spirit, are able to bring joy to their audience and to communicate the word of God in all its power and truth. Those who attempt to instruct merely from what they have heard from spiritual men or read in the Bible are quite unable to procure any real benefit for those who listen (II 18.5). Similarly, those who offer spiritual advice (λόγοι πνευματικοί) without knowledge and experience are like someone with a raging thirst in the midst of the desert who pictures a spring and imagines himself drinking, or like someone who describes honey without ever having tasted its sweetness.[31] Spiritual realities are known not in mere words but come about by the operation of the Holy Spirit in the intellect. Only thus can they be spoken about (I 16.3.1–3). Worldly wisdom is incapable of granting us to know the things of the Spirit ἐν πείρᾳ γνώσεως. Only the visit and operation of the Holy Spirit can provide experiential knowledge, in comparison with which the wisdom of the world is 'uncertain and insubstantial' (ἀφανὴς καὶ ἀνυπόστατος) (I 18.4.13).

Diadochus also points out that it is impossible for anyone to offer instruction while the light of the Holy Spirit is shining richly upon him: 'At such a time the soul is drunk with the love of God and, with voice silent, delights in his glory.' One must watch for a

---

[31] John Climacus borrows the illustration of honey in this context, *Ladder of Divine Ascent*, Step 25 (PG 88 1140c).

middle point at which it is possible and appropriate to speak
(*GC* 8).[32] Macarius writes, speaking of himself in the third person,
of the highest states of mystical experience in which a man 'no
longer possessed himself but became like a fool and a barbarian to
this world'. Such states are not permanent precisely so as to allow
such men to give instruction:

> If the man always had these marvels which he was shown and which he
> experienced, he would be incapable of fulfilling the ministry of the word
> [...]. This is why the perfect measure was not accorded him, so that he
> might apply himself to the care of the brethren and the ministry of the
> word. (II 8.3–4)

Diadochus sees an intimate relation between knowledge and
experience. Spiritual knowledge unites man to God 'by experience' (*GC* 9). The theologian, if he humbles himself, may taste, like
the gnostic, 'the experience of spiritual knowledge' (*GC* 72).[33] Only
such knowledge is capable of operating in πείρᾳ αἰσθήσεως
(*GC* 11).[34] This is precisely the association we find expressed with
all his customary vigour by Macarius.[35] The mysteries of God are
known only by experience (I 10.3.3); knowledge is received διὰ
πείρας (I 58.2.5). Knowledge of the heavenly mysteries of the Spirit
is acquired πείρᾳ καὶ αἰσθήσει (I 50.2.1). In teaching the organic
and essential relationship between knowledge and experience,

[32] The only reference to (spiritual) drunkenness in the Diadochan corpus. This ancient
metaphor is given great prominence by Macarius: 'drunk with love' (III 22.3.3); 'sober and
spiritual drunkenness' (I 63.4.6); 'drunk in the Godhead' (II 15.40), and many other
instances. Plotinus also uses the idea (*Enneads* 5.8.10, alluding to Plato, *Symposium* 203b).
Origen and Evagrius tend to be wary of the motif, presumably because of its connotations
of irrationality.

[33] In both *GC* 9 and 72 Diadochus makes a distinction between knowledge (the property
of the gnostic) and wisdom (the property of the theologian). This distinction is not Evagrian:
Diadochus' gnostic is not necessarily a theologian in the making. For Diadochus, knowledge is primarily an inner experience, wisdom the outward expression of the contemplation of God (theology). Diadochus here combines elements from Evagrius and Macarius,
developing an understanding that is very much his own.

[34] Rahner notes: 'For Diadochus, αἴσθησις is more or less an experiential knowledge of
the indwelling of God in the purified soul, the knowledge of its good relations with God, the
perception of divine consolation which penetrates the entire person. Αἴσθησις virtually
becomes the synonym of the word πληροφορία to which it is so often yoked', in, 'Le Début',
142, as cited in Stewart, '*Working the Earth of the Heart*', 129–30.

[35] There are elements of this association in Origen, see Stewart, '*Working the Earth of the
Heart*', 145. Origen is, however, speaking only of experience in the sense of the accumulation
of practical information rather than as actual contact with some metaphysical reality.

Diadochus reveals himself to be a disciple of the experiential epistemology pioneered by Macarius.

Experience is thus the guiding principle of the spiritual teaching of our two authors. The initial experience of grace becomes, for Diadochus, a source of strength for the intellect when passing through the stage of self-reproach and unable to attain faith ἐν αἰσθήσει τῆς καρδίας. When purified through attentiveness, 'then with a fuller experience of God we shall attain what we desire' (*GC* 23). Experience of spiritual warfare gives the intellect greater confidence in itself (*GC* 32). Such warfare is permitted so that we might advance εἰς τὴν πνευματικὴν πεῖραν (*GC* 85). It is necessary for us to have the experience of abandonment by God (*GC* 87). Experience of God's love wipes out anger and self-love (*GC* 91). There is a certain distinction to be made here between πεῖρα as the actual experience of a given metaphysical reality and πεῖρα as the educative consequence of that experience. The former is the more common usage in Diadochus, yet the latter, as seen in *GC* 85 above, will be seen in the next section to be central to Diadochus' understanding of discernment.

Macarius has the same pattern of usage. Πεῖρα usually desig-nates actual experience, as is the case in all the Macarian examples of experiential language quoted in this section thus far. He also sees an intimate connection between faith and experience: 'If we re-ceive experience of the good things to come, then we will acquire a sure faith: for sure faith comes about through experience' (1 39.1.8; cf. Diadochus, *GC* 23.). The following text is a particularly good example of the centrality of experience in the Macarian vision:

> The blessed Apostle Paul, the architect of the Church, forever anxious for the truth and not wishing that those who hear the word should be impeded by ignorance, indicated with great exactitude and clarity the goal of the truth and made known the perfect mystery of Christianity in every believing soul, this being to receive through a divine operation the experience of the effulgence of the heavenly light in holy souls in the revelation and power of the Spirit. (1 58.1.1)

The direct experience of God is for Macarius *the* defining charac-teristic of the Christian revelation. It is a taste that renders the soul ever more desirous of God without ever provoking satiety (1 16.3.3). We shall look at the educative function of experience in the next section.

Diadochus follows Macarius in treating lived experience as the defining feature of the Christian life and the only sure foundation of faith and knowledge. It is clear that πεῖρα underpins his whole teaching, a feature that places him squarely within the Macarian tradition.

## 6.4 Discernment, Dreams, and Visions

The affective–experiential tradition examined in the preceding sections lies behind the theory of discernment taught by our two authors. This connection is made clear by Diadochus' definition of the sense of the intellect as an exact taste of things discerned (Αἴσθησίς ἐστι νοὸς γεῦσις ἀκριβὴς τῶν διακρινομένων) (*GC* 30).[36] This definition is a faithful restatement of Macarius' association of the intellectual sense with the faculty of discernment: the discerning soul knows the difference between the effects of sin and those of grace ἐκ τῆς νοερᾶς αἰσθήσεως (I 2.10.5.). Diadochus proceeds to illustrate his theme with an analogy taken from the realm of sense:

> Just as, when we are healthy, we distinguish unfailingly between good and bad food by our physical sense of taste, and desire the good, so in the same way our intellect, when it begins to act in full health and with great detachment, is able to sense the divine consolation richly and is never again led astray by the enemy. Just as the body is infallible in its sense experience when tasting the delectable things of the earth, so also the intellect, when it triumphs over the thoughts of the flesh, is able to taste unerringly the consolation of the Holy Spirit.   (*GC* 30)

This mirrors, in a somewhat more restrained way, the teaching of Macarius. Macarius teaches that the soul must taste both the bitterness of sin and the sweetness of grace in order to become 'more perceptive and vigilant' (αἰσθητικωτέρα καὶ νηπτικωτέρα) by virtue of this experience, and thus flee evil and attach itself entirely to the Lord. Such a soul possesses perfect knowledge of good and evil πείρᾳ καὶ ἐνεργείᾳ καὶ αἰσθήσει (III 12.2.1–4). Macarius also uses the analogy of the physical sense of taste to describe the experiential basis of discernment: just as the tongue or palate knows by taste the difference between a lettuce and a bitter herb, or between wine and vinegar, so the soul from the intellec-

---

[36] Cf. 'exact discernment' in Macarius (II 4.1).

tual sense knows the difference between the *charismata* of the Spirit and the illusions of Satan (1 2.10.5). Diadochus tones down Macarius' approach, removing all implication of the coexistence of sin and grace,[37] but the basic elements of his treatment, the intellectual sense as the faculty of discernment, the language of taste, and the analogy of the physical sense of taste, are clearly Macarian. This connection may be further explored in Diadochus' teaching on dreams and visions.[38]

Diadochus holds that there are essentially three types of dreams: dreams from God, dreams from Satan, and dreams which are simply the reflection of our thoughts (*GC* 37–8). He takes dreams to be unerring criteria of the health of the soul. The dreams which appear to the soul through the love of God

> do not change from one shape to another; they do not terrify the sense, laugh or suddenly become doom-ridden. But with great gentleness (ἐπιείκεια) they approach the soul, filling it with spiritual delight. As a result, even after the body has woken, the soul yearns for the joy (χαρά) of the dream. Demonic fantasies, however, are quite the opposite: they do not keep the same shape or maintain a constant form for long. [ . . . ] They shout and threaten, often appearing in the form of soldiers and sometimes deafening the soul with their cries (κραυγή). From this the intellect, when it is pure, recognizes them for what they are and awakens the body. (*GC* 37)

Dreams from God bring joy and delight; those from demons bring only trouble and disruption. In other words they are distinguished by their effects. This is something Macarius had made very plain. When asked about the distinction between good and bad dreams, he emphasizes the discretion needed to differentiate between the illusions of Satan and the gifts of the Spirit (1 5.4). The origin of a vision—whether in sleep or otherwise—is betrayed by its effect. Even when Satan transforms himself into an angel of light (as in

---

[37] Contrasting in *GC* 33 the sweetness and joy brought by the Spirit with the 'dank and debilitating sweetness' and 'counterfeit joy' brought by the devil, Diadochus adds: 'It is impossible for someone to taste the divine goodness in the [inner] sense, or to experience the bitterness of the demons perceptibly, unless he first knows for certain that grace dwells in the depths of the intellect, while the evil spirits cluster around the members of the heart.' For the theme of coexistence, see below, Ch. 6.5–6.

[38] Dörries presents Diadochus' attitude to dreams as one of the principal elements linking him to Macarius, 'Diadochus und Symeon', 354–61. He certainly has a point, but rather overstates the case, not making sufficient allowance for the other possible sources of Diadochus' theory of dreams—particularly Evagrius, for whom see below.

2 Cor. 11: 14), he is unable to produce any good effect. The visions
produced by Satan are distasteful and confused (ἀηδῆ καὶ
τεταραγμένα). They procure no longing (πόθος) for God, joy
(χαρά), or any other good thing and weigh down the soul and
body rather than lightening them. In contrast, the soul is embold-
ened by (θαρρεῖ) and takes delight in visions from God (1 5.4.4).
Demonic dreams cannot procure meekness (πραότης), gentleness
(ἐπιείκεια), humility, joy (χαρά), peace, the settled condition of the
thoughts (κατάστασις λογισμῶν), hatred of the world, spiritual rest
in God, desire of heavenly good things (ἐπιθυμία τῶν οὐρανίων
ἀγαθῶν), the cessation of the pleasures and passions, or any of the
works of grace (1 2.10.4).

Diadochus explains that what he has taught concerning dreams
is that which he heard παρὰ τῶν ἐν πείρᾳ γεγονότων (GC 38).
Macarius, on the strength of the teaching outlined above, is
certainly one of those 'persons of experience' to whom Diadochus
is referring. There is, however, also a definite connection between
both accounts and that given in the *Life of Anthony* (35–6):

The vision of the holy ones [i.e. the angels] is not confused
(τεταραγμένη). [ . . . ] It comes about quietly and meekly (πράως) so that
joy (χαρά), happiness, and courage (θάρσος) are straightaway produced in
the soul. [ . . . ] The thoughts of the soul remain undisturbed and unagi-
tated (ἀτάραχοι καὶ ἀκύμαντοι). [ . . . ] A desire for divine and future
things (πόθος τῶν θείων καὶ τῶν μελλόντων) enters it [ . . . ]. On the
other hand, the invasion and apparition of evil spirits comes about
with crashing and noise and cries (κραυγή) such as rough youths or
brigands might produce. From these there follows cowardice of soul,
disturbance and disorder of thoughts (τάραχος καὶ ἀταξία λογισμῶν),
discouragement, hatred towards the ascetics, accidie, sadness, remembrance of family and friends, and fear of death. (VA 35–6)

The nature of a vision is, continues Anthony, known by its effects.
The joy and settled condition (κατάστασις) of the soul indicate the
presence of sanctity; din and disturbance indicate the opposite
(VA 36.4–5).

Macarius' account clearly draws on that of Anthony in respect
of the joy, boldness, settled condition of the thoughts, and desire
for the good things to come produced by good dreams or visions
and the confusion produced by their opposite. The gentleness with
which good dreams approach the soul in Diadochus connects his
account with that of Macarius. The joy of good dreams or visions

is a feature of the teachings of both Macarius and Anthony. The cries Diadochus associates with bad dreams recall Anthony's analysis. Thus Macarius appears to have drawn on Anthony, Diadochus on both Anthony and Macarius.

Evagrius is certainly another source for Diadochus' teaching on dreams.[39] Evagrius treats dreams principally as indicators of the health of the soul. He allows for three types of dreams: demonic dreams that arouse the memory by means of the passions; good dreams caused either by ourselves or by the angels in which we meet the saints; and dreams which are simply the replay of sense impressions.[40] Diadochus, as we have seen, takes this distinction on board, without, however, allowing that we can produce good dreams ourselves. In the *Praktikos* Evagrius describes the kind of pleasurable dreams that result from demonic action upon the *epithumia* and the frightful dreams—of being pursued by armed men, venomous beasts, and the like—caused by the stirring up of the *thumos*.[41] This relation of dreams to the desiring and irascible parts of the soul respectively is not something Diadochus picks up on.[42] The 'armed men' may be compared with the 'soldiers' of Diadochus' account, but this is likely to have been a commonplace. He goes on to assert that those who have attained *apatheia* are no longer disturbed by demonic fantasies in sleep.[43] He does not discuss the discernment of the provenance of these dreams from their effects.

Dreams and visions became an increasingly contentious area of debate with the rise of the Messalian tendency.[44] Macarius'

---

[39] On Evagrius' teaching on dreams see especially Refoulé, 'Rêves et vie spirituelle'.

[40] *Thoughts* 4 (pp. 162–4). Gregory of Nyssa had also made the point that many dreams are simply reruns of sense experiences, *De hominis opificio* 13 (PG 44 171B). On the provenance of dreams see also Homer, *Odyssey* 19.560–9: dreams that enter through the gate of ivory cheat us; those that enter through the gate of horn truly predict the future.

[41] *Praktikos* 55 (pp. 624–6).

[42] Diadochus nowhere makes use of Evagrius' tripartite conception of the soul. He stresses rather the soul's simplicity. The intellect is, for Diadochus, not so much the highest as the deepest part of the soul.

[43] In *Praktikos* 64, Evagrius suggests that to remain calm in the face of the visions of sleep is a proof of impassibility. In other words, one cannot hope to be entirely free of negative dreams; what matters is rather one's reaction to them. The dreams of Clement's gnostic are, by way of contrast, always holy (*Strom.* VII.12.77.3 and 12.78.5: GCS 17, pp. 55 and 56).

[44] The Messalians were accused of seeking bodily visions of God and of holding all dreams to be prophecies. On visions, see Theodoret, *HE* IV.11 (p. 231), *Haer. fab. comp.* IV.11 (429D); T 10, 5; J 18. On dreams, see Theodoret, *HE* IV.11 (p. 229); T 14. The *Apophthegmata* are cautious on the subject of dreams and visions, but fully accept the possibility that they

response was to develop the kind of teaching outlined in Anthony above into an 'energetic' theory of discernment: 'Do you see that it is all a question of operation (ἐνέργεια), and that the intellect is able to discern from operation which visions are from Satan and which from grace?' (I 5.3.4).[45] Diadochus certainly draws upon this theme of discernment by effect and warns, with a healthy scepticism: 'We should never entirely trust anything that appears to us in our dreams. For dreams are for the most part nothing more than images reflecting our wandering thoughts, or else, as I have said, the mockeries of demons.' One can never be quite sure that one is not suffering from some unnoticed beguilement and has therefore lost the track of accurate discernment (*GC* 38). Light sleep is a particularly dangerous time for the soul, the time when it is most susceptible to the illusion of grace. True grace comes to us rather when the body is awake or else on the point of falling asleep (*GC* 32–3). God will not be angry with us, argues Diadochus, if we refuse a genuinely divine vision for fear of delusion. To illustrate this, he uses the example of a master who is not angry at his servant who had refused to admit him at the dead of night for fear of some trick (*GC* 39). This example is very probably inspired by Macarius who had illustrated precisely the same theme with the

may come from God. Abba Poemen counsels that visions and voices witnessed in the spiritual struggle are delusions and should as a rule be ignored (*AP* (Alph.) Poemen 139–40: PG 65 356b–357a). He did, however, recognize that a vision accorded to Abba Zacharias was from God, in contrast to Abba Carion who beat Zacharias upon first hearing of the vision (Zacharias 4 180bc). Visions were evidently part and parcel of the early monastic tradition; see for example, *AP* (Alph.) Daniel 8 (160abc), Theodore of Pherme 25 (193ab), John the Dwarf 14 (208cd), Mark the Egyptian 1 (304abc), Poemen 144 (357b), and Silvanus 2 (408cd). The *Historia monachorum* records several instances of divinely inspired dreams: *HM* I.45 (pp. 26–7) (John of Lycopolis); II.4 (p. 36) (Or); VIII.17, 33–4 (pp. 53, 59–60) (Apollo); x.4 (pp. 76–7) (Patermuthius); and XII.3 (p. 93) (Helle). Only the first example had a prophetic quality, the others concern particular revelations or advice. There was, of course, solid biblical authority for divinely inspired dreams and visions. Origen states (*Contra Celsum* I.48: GCS 2, p. 97): 'All who accept the doctrine of providence are obviously agreed in believing that in dreams many people form images in their minds, some of divine things, others being announcements of future events in life, whether clear or mysterious.' It is noteworthy that neither Macarius, Evagrius, nor Diadochus attributes a prophetic quality to dreams, in contrast to the Messalians.

[45] There is a defensive quality to Macarius' argument here. He finds it necessary to quote biblical examples of dreams brought by grace, stressing in particular Joel 3: 1. If Satan can transform himself into an angel of light, being a mere creature, then God, being infinitely superior, must be able to transform himself into a bright cloud, into the 'sun of righteousness' (Mal. 4: 2), into pure air—granted that in his own nature he is incomprehensible and unapproachable (I 5.4.2–3).

analogy of a man who comes to his wife dressed as a stranger and rejoices when he is repulsed (1 2.10.2).

While Diadochus does allow, as had both Evagrius and Macarius, for the vision of the light of the intellect, he is exceptionally insistent that any physically perceptible or circumscribed vision is necessarily false.[46] This is the central anti-Messalian argument in his works. He writes:

Let no one who hears us speak of the sense of the intellect come to hope that the glory of God will appear to him visibly. We do indeed say that when the soul is pure one senses the divine consolation in an ineffable taste; but no invisible reality appears to it in a visible form [ ... ]. If light or some fiery form should be seen by one of the spiritual strugglers (οἱ ἀγωνιζόμενοι), he should by no means accept such a vision: it is clearly a trick of the enemy. Many have experienced such things and have, in their ignorance, turned away from the way of truth. But we know that so long as we inhabit this corruptible body we are far from God (cf. 2 Cor. 5: 6), that is to say we cannot see visibly either God himself or any of his heavenly wonders.  (*GC* 36)

Any vision that appears ἐν σχήματι is of the enemy: an authentic vision of light is one of total luminosity and not of any shape or form. We should not hope to see any circumscribed vision; our one purpose must rather be to reach the point where we love God ἐν πάσῃ αἰσθήσει καὶ πληροφορίᾳ καρδίας (*GC* 40).[47] In the *Vision*, Diadochus, goes on to explain the various epiphanies of the Bible, teaching that such visions were neither physical nor the result of a change in the divine nature. What the prophets saw, for example, was rather the will—and not the nature—of God, presented to their eyes in a form of glory. Their vision was of the operation (ἐνέργεια) of God's will, not of his nature—such a vision is reserved for the next life (*Vision* 12–13).

There is much in Diadochus' account here that revises the teaching of Macarius. Macarius does refer both to visions (11 8.3) and to God's transforming himself so as to be manifest

---

[46] For the vision of the light of the intellect in Diadochus, see *GC* 40, 59, and 75. In Evagrius see, for example, *Skemmata* 2 (p. 374); *Praktikos* 64 (p. 648); *Gnostikos* 45 (p. 178); *Thoughts* 43 (p. 299). *GC* 40 is clearly a reference to *Praktikos* 64. In Macarius see 1 5.1; 11 7.5–6, 8.3. See also our discussion of this theme above, Ch. 4.

[47] It is a nice irony that an anti-Messalian argument should be crowned by this supposedly Messalian phrase. It is another indication that Diadochus was not aware of the anti-Messalian list as given by John of Damascus.

(1 5.4.2).[48] Where he talks of the vision of light, however, this is certainly uncircumscribed (1 58.2). Moreover, while considerably less clear than Diadochus, he does, on occasion, suggest that the visions brought by grace are not physical. Speaking of the imagery he uses to denote spiritual realities, Macarius stresses that 'the things they denote are ineffable and inexpressible, invisible to the eyes of the body'. Such things are known only 'by the actual experience of the eyes of the soul' (1 63.2.3–4). It is, however, clear that Diadochus is, in his extreme caution on the subject of visions, operating far more obviously in the tradition of Evagrius. Evagrius had counselled: 'Do not long to see angels or powers or Christ sensibly, lest you become utterly mad, taking a wolf as your shepherd and worshipping our enemies, the demons.'[49]

## 6.5  Grace

The most significant revision Diadochus makes of Macarius' teaching is on the subject of the coexistence of sin and grace in the intellect. This is a major theme of the polemic which occupies *GC* 76–89. It must be stressed from the outset that the theme of coexistence is used by Macarius to contradict the Messalian supposition that the advent of grace drives out sin entirely and produces a state of *apatheia* equivalent to impeccability.[50] In emphasizing baptismal grace, Diadochus is certainly attacking Messalian anti-sacramentalism, but on the crucial point of coexistence, he is criticizing not the Messalians but Macarius' own critique of the Messalian understanding of the workings of grace.

Diadochus submits that: 'Some (τινές) have imagined that both grace and sin, that is to say the spirit of truth and the spirit of error,

---

[48] Macarius uses the verb μεταβάλλω here, as in 11 4.11. Cf. Proposition 6 of Timothy's list (T 6): the accusation that the divine nature is transformed (μεταβάλλεται) so as to be mixed with worthy souls.

[49] *OP* 115 (1192D–1193A). See also *OP* 66 (1181A), 72–4 (1181D–1184A), 94 (1188BC), and 114 (1192D). Evagrius' negative attitude to visions and images of any type went against much of the tradition of Egyptian monasticism. This may go some way towards explaining the strength of the anti-Origenist reaction in the course of the Anthropomorphite Controversy.

[50] On the Messalian understanding of *apatheia*, see T 4, 5, 9, 10, 11, 16, and 19; J 7 and 27–8. J 3 charges the Messalians with holding that Satan and the Holy Spirit co-inhabit (συνοικοῦσιν) man, without apparently noting the contradiction with the Messalian position on grace as given elsewhere in that list. This would again suggest that Diadochus had no knowledge of the anti-Messalian lists in the form reported by John of Damascus.

are hidden at the same time in the intellect of the baptized. Consequently, they say one presence (πρόσωπον) urges the intellect to good, the other to the opposite.' From Scripture and the sense of the intellect, Diadochus has learnt that before baptism grace acts from outside, while Satan lurks (ἐμφωλεύει)[51] in the depths of the soul, impeding the free activity of the intellect. After baptism, however, the situation is reversed, grace is within, the demon without. Satan continues to act upon the soul, not as coexisting (συμπαρών) with grace, but working from outside, through the body (*GC* 76). From the instant of baptism, grace occupies the intellect (*GC* 77). It is impossible for the two opposing πρόσωπα to be present in (ἐμπαρεῖναι) the soul, the form imprinted on which is single and simple, given that 'light has nothing in common with darkness' (2 Cor. 6: 14) (*GC* 78). The most telling statement by Diadochus is the following:

Those who say that the two πρόσωπα of grace and sin are present simultaneously in the hearts of the faithful, quote the text of the Evangelist who says: 'And the light shines in the darkness, and the darkness did not grasp it' [John 1: 5]. In this way they try to justify their opinion that the divine radiance is in no way sullied (μολύνεσθαι) by its contact with the devil, no matter how close the divine light in the soul may be to the diabolic darkness. (*GC* 80)

Diadochus goes on to argue that the 'darkness' in question is the wilful darkness of the human heart, not the darkness of Satan. It is a question of human inability to understand the true light, not of Satan's failing to lay hold of that light (ibid.).

Diadochus is certainly criticizing Macarius here. The theory of coexistence is a central theme of the Macarian writings. The following citation gives an idea both of the nature and of the purpose of that theory:

You will certainly say to me: 'What does light have in common with darkness?' [2 Cor. 6: 14] or 'What agreement is there between the temple

---

[51] Cf. Macarius, I 16.3.7: εἴσελθε γάρ, ὦ οὗτος, διὰ τῆς τῶν λογισμῶν ἐπιτάσεως πρὸς τὸν αἰχμάλωτον καὶ δοῦλον τῆς ἁμαρτίας νοῦν καὶ ἰδὲ τὸν κατώτερον τοῦ νοῦ καὶ βαθύτερον τῶν λογισμῶν εἰς τὰ λεγόμενα ταμεῖα τῆς ψυχῆς ἕρποντα καὶ ἐμφωλεύοντα ὄφιν καὶ φονεύοντά σε διὰ τῶν καιριωτάτων τῆς ψυχῆς σου μελῶν. This is a typical Macarian evocation of indwelling sin, directed at anyone who thinks purity is attained through outward asceticism. The verb ἐμφωλεύω is, as we have seen, frequently used by Macarius to denote the presence of evil.

of God and idols?' [2 Cor. 6: 16]. I answer you with the same words: 'What does light have in common with darkness?' How can the divine light be darkened or muddied (θολοῦται)? How can the undefiled and pure be defiled (μιαίνεται)? For it is written: 'And the light shines in the darkness, and the darkness did not grasp it' [John 1: 5].   (II 17.5)

The import of this is clear: 'Nobody of any sense would have the temerity to say, "Grace is in me, therefore I am wholly freed from sin", rather the two πρόσωπα [of sin and grace] are active in the intellect' (II 17.6).[52] Those who have experience and discretion know that this is the case (ibid.).[53] The manipulation of the same scriptural texts (2 Cor. 6: 14; John 1: 5), the description of sin and grace as πρόσωπα and the discussion of the sullying of the divine light (μολύνω in Diadochus; θολόω and μιαίνω in Macarius) make it palpably clear that Diadochus is directly criticizing Macarius on the specific issue of the coexistence of sin and grace. Macarius took up this theme as a graphic illustration of the permanency of struggle in the spiritual life and consequently a useful counter to hasty claims of impeccability made by certain inexperienced monks of his acquaintance. But given that Diadochus drops the idea of the coexistence of sin and grace in the intellect: how does he explain the continuing spiritual struggle of the baptized?

Diadochus' explanation brings us on to his psychology, anthropology, and baptismal theology. Baptism expels the multiform serpent from the chambers (ταμιεῖα)[54] of the intellect. It removes

---

[52] Note that the parallel text in Collection I (1 16.1.10) has 'in the same man' (ἐν τῷ αὐτῷ ἀνθρώπῳ) for 'in the intellect'. On Diadochus' evidence, it may be claimed that Collection II, in this instance at least, preserves the original reading. This is supported by the fact that the MSS of the more primitive Collection IV, one of the main sources for Collection I, give 'in the same intellect'. See the critical apparatus to 1 16.1.10.

[53] There are many references to coexistence in Macarius, see for example 1 18.5.1–2; 11 2.2, 7.2, 16.1 ff., 17.4 ff., 26.18, 40.7, 50.4; 111 12.2.2. The theme is discussed further below, Ch. 6.6.2. The image of the sun shining in muddy places and not being harmed in any way, used by Macarius in 11 7.2, had been used by Origen to deny that Christ was in any way defiled by human birth (*Contra Celsum* VI.73: GCS 3, pp. 142–3). Henry Chadwick in the notes to his translation of the *Contra Celsum*, 387, traces the image further back, to Diogenes the Cynic as reported by Diogenes Laertius (*Lives of the Philosophers* VI.63): 'Someone having reproached him for going into dirty places, his reply was that the sun too visits cesspools without being defiled.' Chadwick also gives examples of the use of this illustration in Eusebius, Macarius Magnes, Synesius, Cyril of Alexandria, Prudentius, Augustine, and Nemesius of Emesa.

[54] For both the serpent and the inner chambers of Macarius, cf. n. 51 above. See also the 'serpent of sin' of 11 15.28.

the stain or filth (ῥύπος) of sin[55] but does not immediately remove the duality of will (τὸ διπλοῦν τῆς θελήσεως) (*GC* 78).[56] This duality is the schism produced in the natural sense of the soul by the Fall (*GC* 29). Ever since the intellect fell into a state of duality with regard to knowledge (τὸ διπλοῦν τῆς γνώσεως), it has produced good and bad thoughts simultaneously, even against its own will (κἂν μὴ θέλῃ). The memory of man has been split as if into a double mentality (εἰς διπλῆν τινα ἔννοιαν). When it tries to think of God, it suddenly remembers what is bad (*GC* 88). Baptism, in other words, removes sin but does not immediately efface the psychological schism resulting from the Fall. This does not mean that two beings (ὑποστάσεις) are fighting one another in the intellect.[57] After baptism, the intellect is inviolable, Satan is able to act only through the body, on the outer parts of the heart which are not yet illumined by grace ἐν βαθείᾳ τινὶ αἰσθήσει (*GC* 88).

To explain the moral struggles of the baptized further, Diadochus, like Mark, draws freely on Macarius' baptismal theology and understanding of the workings of grace. He borrows the Macarian image of baptism as a pledge (ἀρραβών) (*GC* 78; cf. Macarius, III 28.3). For both our authors, grace is essentially 'laid down' at baptism. The purpose of the spiritual life is to bring about the manifestation of that hidden grace. Diadochus writes, in *GC* 77, that from the moment of baptism, grace is hidden in the depths of the intellect, concealing its presence even from the sense of the intellect.[58] When someone begins to love God with full resolve, grace communicates something of its bounty to the soul by means of the sense of the intellect. As one proceeds in the spiritual life, the

[55] Origen, *Homiliae in Lucam* 14 (GCS 49, p. 98), also speaks of the filth (ῥύπος) of sin removed by baptism. For ῥύπος in Macarius, see I 23.2.8 and 18.4.16.

[56] Cf. Augustine in *Retractiones* 1.15.2 (PL 32 609): 'concupiscentiae reatus in baptismate solvitur, sed infirmitas manet'. Vincent Desprez, 'Diadoque de Photicé et le Pseudo-Macaire', adds: 'La démarche de Diadoque représente une étape vers la distinction tridentine entre le péché original, remis par le baptême, et la concupiscence qui demeure chez le baptisé.' Diadochus' account is more nuanced than that of Mark, who, as we have seen, holds that baptism restores man to the position of Adam with the single difference of physical mortality. Diadochus is less sanguine, adopting a median position between Macarius and Mark on this point.

[57] Cf. I 18.5.1: Macarius uses the example of sun and wind to illustrate the theme of coexistence, each of which maintains its own hypostasis notwithstanding its close contact with the other.

[58] This is very much like Mark's thesis that there is after baptism an 'innermost chamber' where Satan cannot penetrate (IV 996C, 1016D–1017A).

gift of grace granted at baptism is steadily revealed: 'For according
to the progression of the soul, the divine Spirit manifests itself to
the intellect.' This is essentially the same scheme we find in
Macarius. In baptism 'we receive the beginning of the life of the
Spirit; if we persevere and progress in all the virtues, in all zeal and
effort, this life grows and is made manifest in us, perfecting us by
its own grace' (I 43.6). This grace is initially received in a very
subtle manner, so subtly as to be imperceptible. A man who has
received such grace is as if ignorant (ὡς ἀγνοεῖν) of its presence
(I 43.2).[59] Neither Macarius nor Diadochus confuses the presence
of grace with the sensation thereof, and thus they avoid Hausherr's
'fundamental error'.

In describing the pedagogy of grace, Diadochus again draws
heavily on Macarius. Like Macarius, he asserts that grace is not
fully revealed at baptism so as to allow man to manifest his own
free inclination towards God. While the start of the spiritual way is
often marked by a deep sensation of illumination, as the soul
progresses grace operates for the most part without its knowledge
(ἀγνώστως) (*GC* 69). Grace conceals its presence and waits to see
whether the soul inclines to the good. If so, it begins to reveal its
presence in an ineffable sensation (ἀρρήτῳ τινὶ αἰσθήσει), and
again waits to see the movements of the soul, allowing
(παραχωροῦσα) the arrows of demons to reach even to the innermost sense of the soul. If such a man continues to make progress,
then 'the fire of God's grace spreads even to the outer senses of the
heart, consciously (πληροφορητικῶς) burning up the tares of the
human earth'.[60] Such a fiery catharsis further restricts the scope of

---

[59] Cf. also the hidden presence of grace in I 34.5–6.

[60] Cf. also the 'earth of the heart' of *GC* 73. This usage is a telling sign of Macarian
influence. The concept of the 'earth of the heart' with its attendant imagery clearly has
scriptural roots, most obviously in the parable of the sower (Matt. 13: 3–23; Mark 4: 3–20;
Luke 8: 4–15). It was evidently a familiar image in the Syriac tradition, being used, for
example, by Ephrem (*Hymns on the Nativity* 8.7: CSCO 186, p. 60). A survey on the TLG
database has, however, revealed just how uncommon it is in the Greek tradition. Clement
of Alexandria speaks of τὴν σκληροκαρδίαν γῆν (*Strom.* IV.26.169.2: GCS 52, p. 323).
Didymus the Blind, again in reference to the parable, declares: Γῆ τοῦ θεοῦ ἡ ἀγαθὴ
καρδία εἴρηται (*Fragmenta in Psalmos* 70: PTS 15, p. 161), an interpretation he returns to
with some frequency (ibid. 525 (PTS 15, p. 364), 875 (PTS 16, p. 164), 1052 (PTS 16, p. 262));
*Commentarii in Zachariam* 2.212 (SC 84, p. 526), 2.336 (pp. 592–4). Lastly, interpreting the 'new
heaven and new earth' of Isaiah 65: 17, Gregory of Nyssa takes the 'new earth' to refer to
τὴν ἀγαθὴν καρδίαν (*De tridui spatio*: GNO 9, p. 279). The exact phrase 'earth of the heart' is,
amongst Greek sources, first attested in Macarius. He makes prolific use of the phrase with

demonic activity. Finally, when the ascetic has acquired all the virtues, 'grace illumines his whole nature with a deeper sensation (βαθυτέρᾳ τινὶ αἰσθήσει), warming him with great love of God'. At this stage the attacks of demons are unable to reach even the body but, at times, God allows (παραχωρεῖ) even such a one to be submitted to the attacks of demons and leaves his intellect unillumined (ἀφώτιστος), so that human free will should not be bound (δεδεμένος) by the bonds of grace, and that we might advance in spiritual experience (*GC* 85).

With the single exception of the theme of coexistence of sin and grace in the intellect, this teaching represents a crystallization of Macarius' understanding of the workings of grace. Grace is initially received only 'in part' (ἀπὸ μέρους) (II 41.2), or, as Diadochus puts it, 'partially' (μερικῶς) (*GC* 88). Sin maintains its hold on much of the soul. This does not indicate any weakness in grace, rather this is permitted so as to try the free choice of man, to see if he will maintain intact the love of God and have no concourse with evil. If man perseveres in the struggle, grace progressively takes hold of the soul until such time as it is invested entirely with heavenly grace (II 41.2). He must advance through ascetic effort to the sensation and revelation of grace (I 43.2). If man were not submitted to trials and temptations and had only the experience of grace he would be a bound entity (δετός) (II 27.21). The purpose of spiritual warfare is to allow man to manifest his free will. This is the standard procedure (ἀκολουθία) of grace (II 9.1). Grace is granted in accordance to the exercise of free will (II 27.22). Diadochus' teaching on the retraction (παραχώρησις) of grace (*GC* 85–7) has exactly the same function as in Macarius: not only to demonstrate free will, but also to allow the soul to progress in discretion and spiritual experience (*GC* 77, 85; cf. III 12.2.2). Diadochus moreover uses the verb ὑποστέλλω to denote the retraction of grace (*GC* 87), again following an established Macarian usage (I 18.5.5; II 26.7, 27.8; III 12.1.4). The affective language used by Diadochus to describe the progressive revelation of grace, and especially the reference to the fire of God burning up the tares of the earth of the human heart (*GC* 85), only serve to underscore his debt to Macarius.

its attendant imagery and must clearly be regarded as the pioneer of this kind of language within the Greek tradition. The following are typical examples: I 5.2.1, 7.1.1, 18.6.2, 18.6.12, 21.3, 27.1.5, 34.9, 54.3.8; II 26.10; III 8.3.3, 25.5.2.

Diadochus nuances his understanding of the effects of baptism by distinguishing two gifts conferred by baptism, one in actuality and the other in potentiality. The first is the renewal of the divine image brought about by the effacing of every defect (ῥυτίς) of sin.[61] The second, the acquisition of the divine likeness, requires our co-operation. When the intellect begins to taste the bounty of the Holy Spirit in a deep sensation, it should realize that grace is beginning, as it were, to paint (ὥσπερ ἐπιζωγραφεῖν) the divine likeness upon the divine image, virtue by virtue, just as artists (ζωγράφοι) gradually add colour to a monochrome sketch. This process is only completed in all plenitude with the advent of the illumination of love, for only love can confer *apatheia* upon the soul (*GC* 89). Diadochus' distinction between the divine image and likeness operates in much the same way as Macarius' concept of the 'second soul', or 'heavenly image'.[62] Macarius had also used an artistic analogy to describe the depiction of the heavenly image in the soul. Christ, the good painter (ζωγράφος), paints (ζωγραφεῖ) a heavenly man in the soul after his own image and out of the substance of his own light (II 30.4). This may have served as a model for Diadochus' own artistic analogy, used to illustrate the acquisition of the divine likeness.

Diadochus' explanation of the moral struggles of the baptized differs significantly from the teaching of Macarius only in respect of the coexistence of sin and grace in the intellect and the related issue of the scope of demonic activity upon the human person. As we have already noted, this represents a criticism of Macarius and not of the Messalians. In all other respects, Diadochus shows himself to be a faithful disciple of Macarius, drawing all the fundamentals of his baptismal theology and his understanding of the pedagogy of grace from his spiritual master.

---

[61] Diadochus holds that we are in the image of God 'by the intellectual movement of the soul' (*GC* 78). Macarius, similarly, associates the image with the 'intellectual essence' of the soul (II 15.22). Diadochus teaches that the image has been stained since the Fall (ibid.). Macarius is not entirely consistent on this point. In II 12.1, he writes that Adam lost both the image and the promise of the heavenly image. In III 26.5.1–2 he is somewhat more reflective, maintaining that the image remains intact following the Fall, albeit veiled and imprisoned by the passions. In the same vein he pictures Christ saying to the devil, 'You have corrupted and blackened my rational and beautiful image and in a shameful way you have insulted my beauteous, wonderful, and intellectual creature with the passions' (I 63.3.10). Diadochus is in accord with the more reflective Macarius: the Fall has brought about not the loss but the staining / blackening of the image.

[62] Cf. Ch. 8.3.3.

## 6.6 The Ascetic Struggle

### 6.6.1 The Expulsion of Evil

While Diadochus, as we have seen, rules out the coexistence of sin and grace in the intellect, he by no means underestimates the gravity of the spiritual struggle required of the baptized. While Satan is expelled from the soul by baptism, he retains a foothold in the Christian, and lurks (ἐμφωλεύει) in the body. From this platform he is able to assault the soul by means of the body, attacking the intellect by enticing the flesh (*GC* 79, 82).[63] Evil spirits lurk like serpents in the depths of the heart of the unbaptized,[64] but when grace is hidden in the intellect, then they move like dark clouds (νεφέλαι ζοφώδεις) across the heart (*GC* 81). Satan, even after baptism, befogs (καπνίζων) the intellect through the humours of the body (*GC* 76). The soul can be covered with a demonic mist (ἀχλύς) and entirely veiled by clouds of sin (ὑπὸ τῶν νεφῶν ὅλη τῆς ἁμαρτίας σκεπάζεται), both of which must be blown away by the Spirit (*GC* 75). Lastly, the intellect can be darkened (ἐσκοτωμένος) by the fearful power of the passions (ὑπὸ τῆς δεινότητος τῶν παθῶν) (*GC* 61).[65] Smoke, clouds, and mist are, as we have seen, standard Macarian metaphors for demonic activity.[66] He likens the advent of grace in the perfect to the dispersal of clouds in summertime (I 18.5.2) or to the lifting of the baleful mist (ἀχλύς) that shackles the intellect (I 18.6.11–12). Smoke (καπνός) is regularly used as a metaphor for indwelling sin (II 26.25, 43.7).[67] Macarius speaks of the blinding of the eyes of the heart in those who are 'under the dark cloud of sin' (ὑπὸ τὴν σκοτεινὴν νεφέλην τῆς ἁμαρτίας) (I 44.2.3). Just as the eye cannot see if the pupil is covered, 'so if some little smoke or misty power (μικρὸς καπνὸς ἢ ὁμιχλώδης δύναμις)

---

[63] In *GC* 82 he relates this teaching to Romans 7: 25: 'How can St Paul say that "with my intellect I serve the law of God, but with the flesh I serve the law of sin"', unless the intellect is completely free to engage in battle with the demons, gladly submitting itself to grace, whereas the body is attracted by the smell of mindless pleasures?' Desprez notes in his 'Diadoque de Photicé': 'Cela suppose une exégèse de l'Épître aux Romains 7 plus littérale, sinon plus exacte, que celle de Macaire, distinguant entre le noûs ou homme intérieur, gagné à la loi de Dieu, et la "chair" (c'est-à-dire le corps pour Diadoque), où réside la "loi du péché".'

[64] Cf. Macarius I 3.3.5: after the Fall the soul is a 'den of serpents swarming like fish'.

[65] Cf. Macarius I 63.4.3: healing ἐκ τῆς δεινῆς παραλύσεως τῶν παθῶν.

[66] See Ch. 5.4.2.

[67] The Messalians were accused of holding that the indwelling demon exits like visible smoke: T 3 and J 24. This can be taken as a simplification and reification of Macarius' imagery, a materialization of a metaphor.

darkens (ἐπισκοτίσῃ) the intellect, it is blinded and sees nothing' (1 6.3.5). While Diadochus rejects the Macarian theory of coexistence in the intellect, he retains much of Macarius' metaphorical repertoire, valuing it, much as Mark had done, for its very graphic demonstration of the severity of the post-baptismal struggle.

Baptism, as we have seen, pushes the struggle outward, from the intellect to the heart. Diadochus follows Macarius in treating the heart as the locus of the spiritual struggle and as the zone of interface between soul and body. Diadochus allows to Satan the possession only of certain 'parts of the heart' (*GC* 81), more specifically the 'outer senses of the heart' (*GC* 85). This is not, in essence, so very different from Macarius' vivid description of the heart as an unfathomable depth comprising many members and capable of containing not only the activity of grace but also that of evil (II 15.32, 43.7). Diadochus does, in fact, appear to allow a certain coexistence of sin and grace within the human person. After baptism, Satan lodges in the body, in the outer senses of the heart while grace dwells in the depths of the inner person, that is, in the intellect. Diadochus does not wish to lose the theory of coexistence altogether, seeing it as a useful illustration of the reality of the inner struggle against sin.

Diadochus' diluted theory of coexistence pertains, as the theory in general in Macarius, to the early stages of the spiritual life. Evil is able to act in the way described above only 'on those who are still infants in their souls' (ἐπὶ τῶν ἔτι νηπιαζόντων τῇ ψυχῇ) (*GC* 79).[68] Evil is steadily pushed outwards by the synergy of divine grace and human effort. Grace reveals itself in the heart, eventually spreading even to the outer senses of the heart, those parts of the heart formerly occupied by Satan. From this point on, evil can attack only the passionate part of the soul by means of the body. Eventually evil even loses its capacity to assault the body. Even those who reach such a level of immunity are occasionally, by divine permission, given over to the activity of demons, as we have noted above, so as to preserve human free will and allow the soul to progress in spiritual experience. This process of gradual expulsion is almost exactly that found in Macarius.

---

[68] Thus Diadochus, in *GC* 82, takes Romans 7: 22–3 to be written from the perspective of those still engaged in the ascetic struggle and Romans 8: 1–2 to be from the viewpoint of those who have attained perfection. Compare Mark's understanding, discussed above (Ch. 5.4.2), of the former as applying to the unbaptized and the latter to the baptized.

Macarius' theory of coexistence was, as we have seen, a reaction to the central claim of the Messalian scheme: that the acquisition of grace indicates the immediate expulsion of sin and the establishment of a state of inalienable *apatheia*. His many references to indwelling sin, the indwelling demon, and the constant insistence on the necessity of invisible warfare, of spiritual struggle, are designed to indicate that grace takes hold 'little by little' (κατὰ μικρόν), and not, as some say, 'to put on [grace] is to put off [sin] (ἐνδῦσαι, ἐκδῦσαι)' (II 15.41).[69] In a masterly reply to a loaded question on the possibility of coexistence, Macarius uses, as is his wont, an analogy from the created world. Just as in springtime the sun is frequently obscured by clouds but is in no way changed or injured by being so covered, and is revealed in all its splendour when the clouds pass, so it is for spiritual infants or 'beginners' (οἱ ἔτι νηπιάζοντες),[70] those who have tasted grace, but have not yet reached the perfect measure. At one time the Holy Spirit acts upon them, and then rests, at another time evil acts upon them, but there is no communion whatsoever between these two forces. Those who have reached the perfect measure preserve rather the image of summer. Just as in summer there are no more clouds or mists (νέφη καὶ ὁμίχλαι), and the sun shines freely, so those that are pure in intellect and in the whole man are forever perfected in light, having no filth (ῥύπος) in the soul (I 18.5.2). Even such as these are, however, from time to time given over to the evil one by divine permission, according to God's dispensation. At such times the devil is able to act only through the outer body (διὰ τῶν ἔξωθεν τὸ σῶμα), for 'within he no longer has any holding (νομή) nor is he able to enter in to injure the soul, because the inner man abides in the Godhead walled around by grace' (I 18.4.15). The forecast for beginners is sunshine with showers; for the perfect, sunshine with the possibility of the occasional downpour.

Diadochus' treatment of the gradual expulsion of evil is, on balance, somewhat more precise and refined than that of Macarius. This distinction can be largely explained by historical circumstances. Macarius' teaching took shape against the backdrop of the emerging Messalian tendency. His response to Messalian claims of instant impeccability was to stress the ongoing nature of the spiritual struggle even after the initial advent of

---

[69] This looks very like a Messalian slogan.     [70] Cf. Diadochus *GC* 79 (cited above).

grace. His baptismal theology was developed as Messalian anti-sacramentalism became more and more apparent. At a distance of some fifty years, Diadochus was able to give a more reflective and concise account of the gradual purification of the human person. He revises Macarius' doctrine on the expulsion of evil only with respect to the inviolability of the intellect. In every other significant aspect, his teaching reflects that of Macarius.

### 6.6.2 The Human Contribution

To explain man's contribution to this process of expulsion, Diadochus begins with certain basic propositions: 'Only God is good by nature, but with the help of the essential Good, man can become good through careful attention to his way of life' (*GC* 2). Similarly:

> Evil does not exist by nature, nor is anyone evil by nature, for God made nothing that was not good. When in the desire of the heart, someone gives form to that which has no existence, then that which he desires begins to exist. We should therefore turn our attention away from the inclination to evil (τῆς ἕξεως τοῦ κακοῦ) by our concentration on the remembrance of God; for the nature of good is stronger than the inclination to evil, because the one is, while the other is not, unless we make it so. (*GC* 3)

Such suppositions form part of the common stock of Christian thought, particularly as developed in response to dualist forms of Gnosticism by writers from Irenaeus onwards. Macarius certainly shared in this anti-dualist tradition. He argues that all intellectual essences—angels, souls, and demons—were created pure and entirely simple (ἀκέραιοι καὶ ἁπλούστατοι). Those who have deviated towards evil have done so from free will (ἐκ τοῦ αὐτεξουσίου). If it were otherwise, we would make an unjust judge of God. There are certain heretics who claim that matter is unoriginate, that it is a 'root' and that this root is a power equal to that of God. To this he replies that the power of God will necessarily have the final victory. Those who say that evil has real existence (that it is ἐνυπόστατος), know nothing. Evil can have no real existence in God, although in us it operates with all its strength (II 16.1).[71]

---

[71] Macarius is by no means the only source for Diadochus here. See, for example, Athanasius, *VA* 22.1: οὐδὲν γὰρ κακὸν ἐποίησεν ὁ θεός. This is very similar to the formulation in Diadochus *GC* 3: κακὸν γάρ τι ὁ θεὸς οὐκ ἐποίησεν. Cf. also Evagrius, *KG* III.59 (p. 123)

On the basis of the first principles outlined above, Diadochus goes on to consider the process of temptation. The heart does produce good and bad thoughts, but it is not by nature (οὐ φύσει) that it brings forth evil ideas. It does so because of the remembrance of evil (lit. 'the not good') that has been established in it as a habit (ἕξις) as a consequence of the primal deception.[72] Most evil thoughts are, however, conceived of as a result of the bitterness of the demons (*GC* 83). Thus far Diadochus is in agreement with Macarius, and indeed with the mainstream tradition as a whole. Macarius holds that evil thoughts are foreign to our nature (I 18.6.11). Much discernment is needed to distinguish pure and natural thoughts from those that are sinful (I 18.4.10, 54.2.7; II 15.25–6).[73] Evil spirits are the root of evil thoughts (I 54.3.1). Indeed, one of the enemy's principal ruses is to persuade the soul that evil thoughts are its own, thereby causing it to despair of salvation (I 60.1.2).

Diadochus is quick to point out that the fact that the heart produces good and bad thoughts does not imply the coexistence of sin and grace in the intellect. Rather, 'the intellect, which possesses a most subtle sense,[74] makes its own the thoughts suggested to it by the demons through the activity of the flesh; and, in a way we do

---

'There is nothing which has been created by God which is evil.' The theory of the non-existence of evil is a commonplace of the Christian Platonist tradition; see, for example, Origen, *De Principiis* 2.9.2 (GCS 22, pp. 165–6) and *Comm. in Joannem* 2.13 (GCS 10, pp. 68–70); Dionysius, *DN* IV.19 ff. (716B ff.). Macarius' account of the fall of the demons is strikingly similar to that of *VA* 22. Both accounts owe much to the theory of the pre-cosmic fall suggested by Origen, but avoid embracing explicitly the attendant theory of the second creation. The Messalians were accused, according to John of Damascus, of holding 'that evil things are so by nature' (ὅτι φύσει τὰ κακά) (J 13). If this were true, it would suggest that Messalianism was in some way connected with Gnostic, and especially Manichaean, dualism. There may indeed have been a Manichaean current within the Messalian tendency. The passages cited from II 16.1 demonstrate that Macarius was keen to eradicate any such current. He certainly allows for a moral dualism, with his emphasis on the coexistence of sin and grace, but rules out any form of ontological dualism. The fact that there is such a sharp opposition between John's proposition and the teaching of Macarius indicates once again that the additional source material for John's list embraced only a very partial collection (or reading) of the Macarian corpus and must also have contained other elements.

[72] Macarius also speaks of sin as a habit (συνήθεια) (III 21.3.3).

[73] In I 25.1.2 Macarius also distinguishes merely physical natural thoughts, thoughts concerned only with the needs of the body (and which can be manipulated by the demons). More usually the distinction is simply between pure / natural thoughts and evil thoughts, as in I 25.11 and the examples given here.

[74] Cf. Macarius II 15.15: 'the subtlety of the intellect'. Cf. also the subtlety of the soul in III 26.7.3–8.1.

not understand, the complicity of the body accentuates this weakness because of the union (σύγκρασις) of the two'.[75] When we indulge (συνήδεσθαι) the thoughts sown in us by demons we make them our own to such an extent that we engrave them in our heart, producing them henceforward as a result of our own mental activity (*GC* 83).[76] This analysis is somewhat more refined than that of Macarius. Macarius shares the understanding of the body as the means by which evil thoughts assault the soul. Evil thoughts trouble the soul by means of the senses of the body—like muddy water channelled into a pure stream (1 25.1.11). It is the task of the governing intellect to stand guard at the gates of the soul, welcoming pure thoughts into the city of the heart and rejecting those that are evil (1 25.1.17). What we do not find in Macarius is any sustained treatment of the way evil thoughts are made our own to such an extent that they are subsequently produced as a result of our own mental activity. He does speak, as we have seen (Ch. 5.4.3), of the soul assenting to, indulging, and coupling with evil thoughts, but these thoughts are the product of indwelling sin welling up continually within us. They are not, nor do they become, our thoughts. Diadochus' account is, in this respect, analogous to that of Mark. Both assert a sense of personal responsibility with regard to the immediate origin of the thoughts that assail humankind, a sense both appear to have found lacking in Macarius.

Notwithstanding his denial of the possibility of coexistence in the intellect, Diadochus is in no doubt about the severe impediment to the activity of the intellect caused by sin. When agitated or oppressed by the passions, 'the intellect cannot hold fast to the remembrance of God however much one forces it (κἂν ὅπως αὐτόν τις βιάζοιτο). Completely darkened by the fearful power of the passions, it becomes completely foreign even to its own sense' (*GC* 61). This kind of language is interesting. It crops up several times in the *Chapters*: the demons capture the soul by violence (βιαίως) through the senses if they find us fainthearted (*GC* 79). Since the

---

[75] Similarly, in the *Vision* (29.21): 'Man has his integrity in composition (σύγκρασις).' Macarius describes the union of soul and body as a σύγκριμα (1 25.1.1). The terms express the fundamentally holistic nature of the shared anthropology of our authors.

[76] Macarius also uses the verb συνήδομαι in this context: we have the capacity to contradict, resist, and not to indulge the thoughts—but to uproot them is the property of God alone (1 59.2.4).

Fall, the intellect has produced, by necessity, both good and bad thoughts, even if it does not will it (κἂν μὴ θέλῃ) (*GC* 88). All this comes with a proviso that there is a distinction between captivity (αἰχμαλωτισμός) and struggle (πάλη). The former signifies a violent abduction (βιαίας ἀπαγωγῆς), the latter a combat of equal forces (ἰσοσθενοῦς τινος ἀγῶνος). Following baptism, our position is one of struggle not, as it had previously been, one of captivity (*GC* 82). Macarius, as previously noted (Ch. 5.2), also uses the language of captivity to describe the state of man following the Fall: the prince of darkness has captured (αἰχμαλωτεύσας) humanity (II 2.1). Man's captors are, at this stage, stronger than him (II 2.2). After the Incarnation and the gift of baptism, however, man regains his liberty and his capacity to subdue evil (III 1.2.1) At this stage, the intellect is of equal strength (ἰσοδύναμος) with evil (I 34.4).[77] Indwelling sin is, however, expelled only gradually, as we have seen, hence we have good and bad thoughts regardless of our own disposition. Macarius does not go so far as to use the language of violence when speaking of demonic attacks on the baptized soul. In this respect he is more cautious than Diadochus. Macarius, as we have seen, reserves the language of violence to describe the force we must exert on ourselves and to convey the seemingly irresistible character of grace.[78]

Diadochus goes on to discuss the violence or force we must exert upon ourselves in the early stages of the spiritual life. We must work on ourselves ἐκ βίας in order to re-acquire the taste of grace 'in all perception and plenitude' (*GC* 90). Beginners must accomplish the commandments 'with a certain violence of will' (βιαίῳ τινὶ θελήματι) (*GC* 93). Macarius very frequently uses this kind of language to describe the early stages of the spiritual life. It is especially clear in Homily 19: 'When somebody approaches the Lord he must first of all force himself (βιάζεσθαι ἑαυτόν) to the good, even if his heart does not want to (καὶ μὴ θελούσης τῆς καρδίας)' (II 19.3). He must force himself to love without having love, pray without having spiritual prayer, and so on. By this process man can produce only limited results. For the commandments to be accomplished without such forcing (ἄνευ βίας) requires the advent of the Spirit—only then is the soul able to produce spiritual fruits (II 19.2),

---

[77] Cf. also II 3.6 (equally balanced) and II 27.22 (equally balanced and equally strong).
[78] See the discussion of the language of violence in Mark, Ch. 5.4.4.

only then does it acquire true prayer (II 19.9).[79] Diadochus picks up on this distinction between the two stages of the spiritual life, the first pertaining to nature and requiring violence, the second marked by the activity of the Spirit. Thus he distinguishes natural love from the love of the Spirit (*GC* 34); psalmody and vocal prayer from the prayer of the heart (*GC* 73); natural warmth from the warmth of the Spirit (*GC* 74); and the humility of our nature from the humility granted by the Spirit (*GC* 95). Also working on these two levels would seem to be Diadochus' distinction between initial and perfecting joy (*GC* 60). The fact that Diadochus integrates his language of violence within the two-stage Macarian schema suggests that this is a clear case of Macarian influence and not simply the product of his independent reflection on the force with which we are enjoined by Scripture to work out our salvation.

### 6.6.3 Other Aspects

Diadochus' understanding of the passions and of *apatheia* is an important aspect of his spiritual inheritance. In *GC* 62, Diadochus argues that while the incensive or irascible part (ὁ θυμός) of the soul is usually the most troublesome and confusing of the passions, there is a place for righteous anger against, for example, sinners or demons. He suggests that the Lord's own indignation indicates that 'a controlled irascible power is a weapon implanted in our nature by our Creator'. The aim is the control of anger, not its extinction. The one who properly controls the human emotions 'is borne by the horses of virtue through the midst of the ranks of demons, driving the four-horsed chariot of self-control in the fear of God'. This very positive analysis of the potential harnessing of the passions anticipates in some respects the treatment of Abba Isaiah, although Diadochus does not go so far as to explicitly distinguish between natural and counter-natural passions.[80] Diadochus' teaching on the harnessing of the *thumos* recalls Evagrius' teaching on the role of the incensive power of the soul in the fight against the demons.[81] Diadochus does not, however, make use of Evagrius' classification of the eight principal vices. Diadochus

---

[79] See also II 26.20–1: Macarius again explains the distinction between natural and spiritual faith, prayer, and love.

[80] See Abba Isaiah, Logos G2, discussed below, Ch. 7.4.

[81] Cf. *Schol. Eccl.* 56 (p. 158); *Praktikos* 42 (p. 596), 86 (p. 676).

singles out presumption (οἴησις) as 'the mother of all evils' (*GC* 81). This appears to owe something to Macarius, who treats presumption as a particularly dangerous vice, placing it at the top of the list of the hidden passions he gives in Logos III 7.7.3. Macarius' focus on presumption is a reproach of Messalian spiritual pretension. He constantly rams home the message that man must never 'suppose (οἴεσθαι) himself to be anything, even if he practises all the works of righteousness' (II 53.3). Diadochus has inherited this anti-Messalian theme.

Diadochus does not follow Evagrius, and indeed much of the Egyptian monastic tradition, in associating particular demons with particular vices. He distinguishes only two types of evil spirits: the more subtle (λεπτότερα) demons that attack the soul and the more material (ὑλωδέστερα) demons that attack the body (*GC* 81). The reference to the 'more subtle' demons certainly recalls Macarius' teaching on the subtle bodies of the demons, but Macarius does not make this kind of two-fold distinction. The distinction may owe something to Evagrius, who speaks of the demons that attack man's rational nature and of those that attack his animal nature.[82]

Diadochus' understanding of *apatheia* involves, as we have seen, not the eradication of the passions, but their channelling and transformation. In *GC* 98, Diadochus explains that *apatheia* does not mean the cessation of spiritual warfare, but to remain undefeated in that warfare, adding: 'For it is not only to stop doing evil that brings purity, but actually to destroy evil by pursuing what is good.' Here he clearly sets himself apart from the Messalian understanding of *apatheia* as bringing about an end to spiritual warfare. In this he shares in Macarius' insistence on the profoundly militant character of the Christian life, a life in which the struggle never ceases and *apatheia* is never inalienable. Evagrius had also pointed out that *apatheia* does not bring about an end to the ascetic struggle.[83] Other aspects of Diadochus' treatment of *apatheia* are clearly indebted to Evagrius. His mention of the 'confines of impassibility' in *GC* 54 is an obvious reference to Evagrius.[84] In *GC* 89, Diadochus treats *apatheia* as the fruit of

---

[82] *Thoughts* 18 (pp. 214–16).

[83] *Schol. Eccl.* 46 (p. 142); *Gnostikos* 37 (p. 158). But cf. *Praktikos* 68 (p. 652): he who has attained *apatheia* has no further need of perseverance.

[84] *Praktikos* 58 (p. 636). The phrase is also used by Maximus, *CC* 1.88 (p. 84).

love. This is also the preferred schema of Macarius (II 45.7). Evagrius, in contrast, speaks of love as the offspring of *apatheia*.[85] All three are, however, united in seeing an intimate and essential connection between *apatheia* and love. The notion of the 'fire of *apatheia*' (*GC* 17) is not found in either Evagrius or Macarius. It is an eloquent statement of the gulf between Diadochus' understanding of *apatheia* and the traditional image of Stoic imperturbability.

Diadochus makes use of some vivid medical imagery to describe the healing of the soul:

Just as wounds received by the body do not react to the medicine applied to them by doctors if they have been neglected and left unattended but do respond to the action of the medicine once they have been cleaned, and are then quickly healed; in the same way the soul cannot sense the fear of God if it is neglected and wholly covered with the leprosy of pleasure-seeking [ ... ].    (*GC* 17)[86]

When the soul begins to be cleansed, only then does it begin to sense the fear of God 'like a medicine' (ibid.). This analogy is very reminiscent of Macarius:

Just as if someone bearing wounds on his body were to rub earth or mud into them and, going to the doctor, ask to be cured, then the doctor would say to him: 'If you want to be cured, first clean away the earth and dirt that covers your wounds so that, once cleaned, they become clear and visible, no longer covered by any filth. Then I, as I understand my art, will heal your suffering members; for while wounds are covered with mud, the medicine of doctors cannot act and it is impossible to be healed.'    (I 25.1.5)

In the same way the soul, wounded with the passions following the Fall, is commanded by the true physician, Christ, to first remove the filth that covers it, that is to say, to cease from indulging the passions in any way. Only then will the wounds of the soul be healed (I 25.1.6–9). This kind of imagery is very common in Macarius. He also speaks of the 'leprosy of the passions' (II 44.4) and the 'heavenly medicine' supplied by Christ (II 26.24).[87]

---

[85] *Praktikos* Prologue §8 (p. 492), 81 (p. 670); *Ad Monachos* 67 (p. 57).

[86] The ὥσπερ ... οὕτως construction, used to express an analogy between the natural and the spiritual realms, is frequent in both our authors. See *GC* 17, 24, 70, 75, 88, and Macarius virtually *passim*.

[87] Macarius uses the theme with great frequency and ingenuity. See also, for example, I 25.2.6–11, 63.3.6–10; III 7.7.1–2. The theme of Christ as physician is, of course, biblical in origin. It is taken up, amongst others, by Ignatius of Antioch (*Ephesians* 7.2: Lightfoot,

Diadochus enters into a dialogue with Macarius on the question of the legitimacy of earthly medicine for monks. Diadochus' position is that:

There is nothing to stop us from calling a doctor in times of illness. Since human experience would eventually lead to the development of the art [of medicine], for this reason remedies have been implanted in nature. Nevertheless, we should not place our hope of healing in doctors, but in our true saviour and physician, Jesus Christ. (*GC* 53)

Diadochus goes on to make a distinction between those who practise self-control in coenobia or in towns, and anchorites. The advice quoted above applies to the former group. Anchorites, who have less scope for self-vaunting in their illnesses and have the desert for consolation, should forbear from earthly medicine (ibid.). Illnesses are a great opportunity; thankful acceptance of the pains of illness brings one close to the 'confines of impassibility' (*GC* 54). Moreover, since the days of bodily persecution are over, illnesses now provide a means whereby the body can be tested (*GC* 94).[88] Macarius had put forward a slightly harsher viewpoint than Diadochus on the use of earthly medicine, in Homily 11 48.4–6. Speaking in answer to a question, Macarius allows that God has providentially implanted remedies in nature so that fallen man might not perish entirely. These remedies, however, apply to men of the world, to those of the outside, and not those who have embraced the monastic life. Use of medicines, for Macarius, is an indication of incomplete faith. Diadochus essentially follows Macarius with regard to anchorites, but allows a gentler rule for coenobites and city-dwelling encratites. Here he is steering a kind of middle course between Macarius and the rather more liberal approach of Basil the Great.[89]

The chapter immediately following the discussion of the medical question also puts us in mind of Macarius. Speaking of the dangers of the senses, Diadochus writes:

pp. 47–8) and Clement of Alexandria (*Paed.* 1.2.6: GCS 12, p. 93). See also Murray, *Symbols*, 199–203.

[88] This is the theme of monasticism as a second or inner martyrdom. Macarius had similarly argued that the present 'sufferings of the body' are analogous to the physical sufferings of the martyrs (1 55.3.1–2). On this theme in general see Malone, *The Monk and the Martyr*.

[89] Basil, *Longer Rules* 55: PG 31 1044B–1052C. Basil states that we should certainly use and cultivate medicinal plants, recognizing them as a gift from God and as a type of the healing of the soul.

One pursuing the spiritual struggle should never be engrossed by finely branched or shady trees, beautifully flowing springs, meadows in flower, elegant houses, or even visits to his family; neither should he recall any public honours he may have been given. He should gratefully make use of the bare necessities, regarding this life as a foreign road, barren of all fleshly affection. For it is only by constraining our mind thus that we can keep to the eternal way.   (*GC* 55)

Macarius had had a similar sentiment:

Just as a traveller hurrying along a long road sees many plants and mountains and animals and birds but is detained by none of them as he hurries towards his lodging place, or as one entering some city and hastening to his own business does not attend to any of the affairs of the city, nor is he distracted, because of the urgency of his purpose; so also the perfect are entirely detached and are not held or impeded by evil [...].   (I 18.5.3)

Such determination is required in order to focus on the inner life of prayer, to which we may now turn.

### 6.7   Prayer and the Language of Mystical Experience

Diadochus' teaching on prayer is surely his greatest achievement. He draws together elements from the preceding tradition and produces a creative synthesis that is original in the truest sense of the word. Particularly notable in Diadochus' teaching is his focus on the Name of Jesus. He refers twice to τὸ κύριε Ἰησοῦ (*GC* 59, 61). In context, this clearly indicates a prayer of some sort, possibly as it stands, that is, 'O Lord Jesus'.[90] This prayer is to be constant (*GC* 61).[91] It is a task intended to satisfy the intellect's imperative need for activity (*GC* 59). He writes:

He who wishes to purify his heart should keep it constantly enflamed through the remembrance of the Lord Jesus, making this his sole study and ceaseless task. Those who wish to rid themselves of their own corruption cannot pray merely from time to time, but must rather give

---

[90] On prayer in Diadochus, see especially Kallistos Ware, 'The Jesus Prayer in St Diadochus of Photice'.

[91] Diadochus here uses the image of a mother who teaches her child to say father rather than just prattling, to illustrate the soul's repetition, with the help of grace, of the 'O Lord Jesus'. Compare Macarius III 27.1.2: the grace of the Spirit likened to a mother teaching her child to speak.

themselves to prayer at all times, watching over their intellect even when outside places of prayer (τῶν εὐκτηρίων δομῶν). *(GC 97)* Macarius recommends that one should say: ' "I pray you, I pray you, O Lord (δέομαί σου, δέομαί σου, κύριε)." Say this whether you are walking, eating, or drinking and never cease from it' (1 6.3.3). Prayer must be constant, he advises, because the intellect is constantly assaulted by indwelling sin (ibid.). Similarly: 'The Christian should always have the remembrance of God [. . .], so that he might love God not only when he enters the place of prayer (εὐκτήριον), but also have the remembrance of God and love and affection for him whether walking, talking, or eating' (11 43.3). Neither writer sets up any great distinction between the remembrance of God and ceaseless prayer. The latter is simply a particularly efficient means of attaining the former. Both recommend a specific form of words to be repeated in order to focus the mind on the Lord. Both agree that this prayer is to be implicit. Diadochus also follows Macarius in asserting the superiority of silent prayer over prayers said out loud or psalmody *(GC* 73; cf. Macarius, 11 6.1–3).[92]

Diadochus expands upon the 'O Lord Jesus':

Let [the intellect] continually concentrate on these words (τὸ ῥητόν) within its own chambers (ταμιείοις) so intently that is not turned aside to any imagination. Those who meditate unceasingly upon this glorious and holy name in the depths of their heart can sometimes see the light of their own intellect.[93] For when the name is held onto with great care by the mind, then it consumes in an intense sensation all the filth that covers the surface of the soul. *(GC 59)*

This passage is a fine example of the holistic nature of prayer. Prayer, for Diadochus, is the activity of the intellect in and through the heart. It is the activity of the whole human person—precisely as in Macarius. One is not to turn from this prayer towards any imagination or fantasy (φαντασία) (ibid.). Diadochus does not say 'free from images', nor does he speak of the 'naked intellect'; his prayer is not the non-iconic prayer of Evagrius. Diadochus' prohibition on imaginations or fantasies is more in keeping with the undistracted prayer of Macarius, the prayer in which we 'estrange

---

[92] Evagrius had also asserted the superiority of prayer over psalmody, *OP* 85 (PG 79 1185B).
[93] For the vision of the intellect, see Ch. 6.3 above.

ourselves from every earthly thought and turn from every material concept' (1 29.1.4). Moreover, Diadochus' focus on the repetition of the holy name would certainly seem to entail a constant meditation on the person of Christ: something that would not sit easily with Evagrian non-iconic prayer. The effects of prayer are expressed by Diadochus using the affective language of Macarius: again something that distinguishes him from Evagrius.

Diadochus' teaching on prayer is further developed in the importance he assigns to tears. Diadochus advises that at the time of contemplation: 'We should keep the intellect free from any imagination and thereby ensure that with almost every thought we shed tears' (*GC* 68). 'Tears without grief' lie between initial and perfecting joy (*GC* 60).[94] Good dreams can bring about these 'tears without grief' (*GC* 37). Educative παραχώρησις brings tears of thankfulness; the παραχώρησις in which God turns away from the soul should provoke incessant tears (*GC* 87). With spiritual tears, we sow seeds of prayer in the earth of the heart (*GC* 73). Lastly, our conscience is assured of forgiveness 'through tears of love' (*GC* 100). Des Places quotes Hausherr as holding that Diadochus is at the origin of the Byzantine 'theology of tears'. Des Places points out quite rightly that Evagrius anticipated Diadochus here.[95] One should also note Macarius' contribution, summed up in the call: 'Let us purify the heart by the tears of prayer' (1 7.18.8). Continual *penthos* and ceaseless tears lead to the acquisition of a contrite heart (1 8.1.4). This world is one of *penthos* and tears; that to come, one of laughter and joy (III 10.3.3).[96] There is no other method than to shed tears day and night. Tears shed in application and knowledge are a food for the soul (II 25.7–8). We should not be content with our own tears and weeping, for there is another weeping, which is the work of the Spirit in us (1 63.1.1–2). Much of this is, of course, the product of meditation on Scripture. The last reference given from Macarius is based on Romans 8: 26. It stands in close relation to the

---

[94] Some MSS read 'active tears'.

[95] *Diadoque de Photicé*, 106 n. 2. Des Places cites *Praktikos* 57, *OP* 5 (PG 79 1168D), and *OP* 78 (1184C). He might also have mentioned Pachomius in *VP* (first Greek *Life*) 53, 62; *AP* (Alph.), Arsenius 40–2 (PG 65 105B–108B); Gregory of Nazianzus, *Or.* 39.18–19 (SC 358, pp. 189–95) (the baptism of tears).

[96] But cf. 1 33.2.1: tears and joy are said to co-exist in those that intercede for the whole Adam.

'spiritual tears' of *GC* 73, in which Diadochus is again making use of the twofold Macarian schema discussed above (Ch. 6.6.2). Macarius' treatment, like that of Evagrius, demonstrates that the Byzantine 'theology of tears' goes back much further than Hausherr supposed.

Diadochus makes striking use of the language of ecstasy. The definition he gives of knowledge is: 'to lose awareness of oneself through going out to God in ecstasy (ἐν τῷ ἐκστῆναι θεῷ)' (Defn. 5, p. 84.10–11). Such a definition would, surely, have troubled Evagrius or Origen.[97] Macarius regularly speaks of ecstatic experiences (II 7.3, 8.3), but the theme is, of course, both ancient and widespread. In monastic literature, it is referred to with some frequency.[98] Diadochus continues the ecstatic theme in *GC* 14. A man strongly exercised by grace 'is in this life and not in it, for still dwelling in the body he ceaselessly journeys (ἐκδημεῖ) towards God'. There are some similarities in this account, besides the obvious reference to 2 Corinthians 12, to Macarius' descriptions of the activity of the soul, on earth by body, in the heavens by thought (III 18.2.1).[99]

The affective–experiential tradition we have seen throughout the works of Diadochus moves him to express mystical experience in terms of love, fire, and light, often in a manner highly reminiscent of Macarius:

He who loves God in the sense of the heart is known by God. For to the degree that he senses the love of God in his soul, to that extent he enters into the love of God. Such a one remains in a state of intense longing (ἐν ἔρωτί τινι σφοδρῷ) for the illumination of knowledge until he senses the very sense of his bones, no longer knows himself, but is completely transformed by the love of God. [ . . . ] His heart then burns constantly with the fire of love (ἀγάπη) and clings to God with an irresistible desire (ἀνάγκῃ τινὶ πόθου). (*GC* 14)

This kind of language occurs throughout the *Gnostic Chapters*. Perfect love is 'a constant burning and binding of the soul to God through the operation of the Holy Spirit' (*GC* 16). The fear of God burns the soul in the 'fire of *apatheia*' so that it attains

---

[97] Notwithstanding statements such as *Praktikos* 66: 'for knowledge takes the soul up (ἁρπαζούσης) to the heights'. See the fuller discussion of ecstasy below, Ch. 8.10.

[98] In the *Apophthegmata*, see *AP* (Alph.), Anthony 31 (PG 65 85B), John Kolobos 14 (208CD), Poemen 144 (357B), Silvanus 2–3 (408C–409A), Tithoes 6 (428CD).

[99] Cf. also I 28.1.5; II 12.12, 46.4; III 26.4.3, 26.6.2.

perfect love, which is 'complete *apatheia* actuated by the glory of God' (*GC* 17). The shining of the holy and glorious light of the lamp of knowledge within us both shows up and greatly weakens the attacks of the devil (*GC* 28). Theology 'illumines our intellect with a transforming fire' and 'nourishes the intellect with the words of God in the radiance of ineffable light' (*GC* 67). In the 'wind' of the Holy Spirit the contemplative faculty becomes clear, 'beholding the world of light in an atmosphere of light' (*GC* 75). When grace is firmly established within, then we will sense divine longing (πόθος) 'welling up from the depths of the heart' (*GC* 79). 'The fire of God's grace completely burns up the tares of the human earth' (*GC* 85). Lastly Diadochus declares, 'knowledge consists wholly of love' (*GC* 92).

This language of love, fire, and light is in many respects deeply Macarian. It is, however, so very inherent in both authors as to make it difficult, and even counterproductive, to attempt to detect any specific borrowings. This is more than a matter of words. We may, however, mention certain aspects of Macarius' language of mystical experience that illustrate the similarity of his expression with that of Diadochus. Like Diadochus, Macarius closely links ἀγάπη, ἔρως, and πόθος. He speaks of those 'who are inflamed with the heavenly, holy, and pure longing (πόθος) of the Spirit and whose soul is wounded by the desire (ἔρως) of divine love (ἀγάπη) and who burn and are strongly energised by the heavenly longing (πόθος) of Christ' (II 9.9). The soul that truly loves God has a 'measureless and insatiable love (ἀγάπη) for the Lord'. It is 'wounded by the heavenly desire (ἔρως) of the Spirit which, through grace, stirs up in it a perpetual fiery longing (πόθος) for the heavenly Bridegroom' (II 10.4). There is an element of compulsion about this love, as in Diadochus, *GC* 14, the soul is dragged or drawn (ἑλκομένη) daily by spiritual love (ἀγάπη) towards the longing (πόθος) of the heavenly Bridegroom' (I 64.2). Such passages could be multiplied almost *ad infinitum*. Macarius also speaks of the cathartic quality of the divine fire, boiling out the rawness of sin (I 35.8) and destroying the passions (I 50.1.12). The language of light and illumination is, as we have seen, absolutely fundamental to the Macarian vision. Diadochus does not, however, follow Macarius in discussing in any great detail the nature of the divine light. He may have taken Macarius' teaching for granted in this respect. There are no exact Macarian parallels for *apatheia* or theology as 'fire', or for the statement 'knowledge consists wholly of love'. Equally, Diadochus does not use the ancient metaphor of the 'wound of love' so cherished by Macarius. We can, however, affirm that the language of love, fire, and light Diadochus uses to describe mystical experience is very much in the Macarian tradition, albeit so deeply integrated as to preclude the discovery of any very specific borrowings.

## 6.8 Conclusion

Dörries suggests that the unnamed elder of *GC* 13 and 91 may be Macarius-Symeon himself.[100] Diadochus writes: 'I know a man who loves God very greatly, and yet he grieves because he does not love him as much as he would wish. His soul is continually filled with a burning desire that God should be glorified in him and that he himself should be as nothing.' This man, of priestly rank, is a model of humility (*GC* 13). Elsewhere he writes: 'A man who loves the Lord with insatiable resolve once said to me: "Because I desired conscious knowledge of the love of God, God granted this to me in a great sensation of plenitude (ἐν αἰσθήσει πολλῇ καὶ πληροφορίᾳ); and I felt such an energy that my soul longed, with an ineffable joy and love, to leave the body and go to the Lord, and to become unaware of this transient form of life"' (*GC* 91). The second reference in particular is strikingly reminiscent of Macarius. To take this, with Dörries, as evidence of a possible, even a probable, 'persönlicher Schulerschaft', however, raises serious chronological difficulties.[101] One would have to sacrifice the identification of the author of the *Chapters* with Diadochus, Bishop of Photice, if one wanted to establish a personal relationship with Macarius. A man appointed to an episcopal see between 451 and 457 would in all probability have to have been at least seventy at his consecration to have caught the elderly Macarius even in his 'teens. There are, moreover, no grounds in the manuscript tradition to reject the ascription to Diadochus, Bishop of Photice. It is much more probable that Diadochus knew Macarius by his writings, that the works of Macarius were amongst 'the

[100] Dörries, 'Diadochus und Symeon', 377–87.
[101] Dörries, 'Diadochus und Symeon', 390.

contemplations of wise men whose faith is made known through their writings' (*GC* 68), which Diadochus recommends for study. The figure of *GC* 13 and 91 may perhaps be the man who introduced Diadochus to the Macarian tradition, possibly a direct disciple of Macarius.

Diadochus was not, as we have seen, an uncritical reader of Macarius. In particular, he revises the theory of coexistence so as to preserve the integrity of the intellect. This was, as I have argued, not a direct criticism of the Messalians but rather a refinement of Macarius' reaction to the Messalian understanding of grace. Diadochus doubtless felt that Macarius' theory of coexistence was potentially dangerous, and risked undermining the change effected by baptism. Diadochus' solution is to maintain a diluted theory of coexistence whilst insisting on the inviolability of the intellect. Here he is taking a kind of median course between Mark and Macarius, producing perhaps the most satisfactory explanation of the three of the moral struggles of the baptized. The other main point on which he revises Macarius is in his restraint on the subject of dreams and visions. Here he is operating more obviously in the tradition of Evagrius. Diadochus does, however, make full use of Macarius when he comes to the means whereby good and bad dreams and visions are to be distinguished. Again, this may be taken as a tightening up of Macarius' critique of the Messalians. Diadochus' anti-Messalianism, such as it is, is essentially a development and refinement of that worked out by Macarius. Taken as a whole, Diadochus' work is patently in the Macarian tradition. His language of sense and teaching on the spiritual senses is clearly related to that of Macarius. His treatment of the place of experience in the spiritual life and, particularly, his experiential theory of knowledge are certainly built on the work of Macarius. His account of the gradual expulsion of evil is patently Macarian. His baptismal theology develops that of Macarius. He does not confuse the presence of grace with the sensation thereof, but certainly sees the manifestation of grace as necessarily accompanied by sensation—again precisely in the manner of Macarius. The increasing intensity of the manifestation of grace is described with the Macarian vocabulary of πεῖρα, αἴσθησις, and πληροφορία. Diadochus' treatment of prayer draws significant elements from Macarius and is based on a holistic anthropology that is distinctively Macarian. His descriptions of mystical experience in terms of love, fire, and light are strongly reminiscent of Macarius. All this should not obscure the highly creative nature of Diadochus' work. Similarly, it should not detract from Diadochus' use of other early Christian sources, most notably Evagrius, from whom he has important aspects of his teaching on *apatheia*, dreams and visions, and prayer. Nevertheless, for all his greater limpidity and precision, his creativity, and his awareness of other spiritual traditions, it should be acknowledged that Macarius represents the single most important non-biblical source for the teaching of Diadochus.

# 7

# The *Asceticon* of Abba Isaiah

## 7.1 Introduction

The *Asceticon* of Abba Isaiah is a compilation of occasional pieces: homilies, letters, monastic precepts, sayings and other fragments pieced together in the course of the fifth and sixth centuries AD.[1] The manuscript tradition is extremely complex, as witnessed by the sheer diversity of form amongst the Greek, Syriac, Coptic, Ethiopic, Arabic, and Armenian manuscript traditions.[2] The Greek still awaits a critical edition. The Göttingen Project, begun in the early 1960s, has not yet borne fruit.[3] A working text of the Greek *Asceticon* has been prepared by Fr Derwas Chitty, while the most recent edition of the French translation incorporates the extensive researches into the Greek tradition made by René Draguet.[4] Both depend on a wider manuscript base than that used in Augustinos' 1911 edition.[5]

In examining the manuscript tradition of Abba Isaiah one is often reminded of the Macarian textual tradition. Both represent the culmination of a process of organic development, bring together pieces of diverse genres, and lack a truly satisfactory *stemma codicum*.[6] Furthermore, the identity of the authors of both traditions remains hotly debated. Thus the difficulties that beset the study of the *Asceticon* of Abba Isaiah can only be compounded

---

[1] My information on the manuscript tradition of the *Asceticon* is drawn largely from Draguet, *Les Cinq Recensions*, esp. i. 9\*–127\*: 'Introduction au problème Isaïen'.

[2] Ethiopic, ed. Arras (CSCO 238–9); Syriac, ed. Draguet (CSCO 289–90, 293–4) [= Isaiah, S]; Coptic fragments, ed. Guillaumont (Bibliothèque d'études coptes V). For the Arabic tradition see Sauget, 'La Double Recension arabe des Préceptes aux novices de l'abbé Isaïe de Scété'; for the Armenian, Outtier, 'Un Patericon arménien'.

[3] The project had been under the direction of the late Hermann Dörries.

[4] *Abbé Isaïe: Recueil ascétique*, 3rd edn. Chitty's text is held in the library of the House of St Gregory and St Macrina, Oxford. In *The Desert a City*, 74, Chitty explains that this text is a collation of Augustinos' text with the Bodleian MS Cromwell 14.

[5] Augustinos Monachos, *Τοῦ ὁσίου πατρὸς ἡμῶν ἀββᾶ Ἡσαΐου λόγοι κθ'*.

[6] See Draguet, *Les Cinq Recensions*, i. 10\*, citing Dörries, *Die 50 geistlichen Homilien*, xli.

when one attempts to examine its relation to the equally complex Macarian corpus. I cannot pretend to offer in this chapter any conclusive resolution of the textual problems of the two corpora— that would be the stuff of several books (or doctoral theses) and of course necessitate the production of a critical edition of the Greek Isaiah. What I intend to offer in this chapter is a presenta- tion and analysis of the presence of elements drawn from the Macarian tradition as it stands, in that of Isaiah, as it stands. Where applicable, I shall offer observations as to how those elements may enhance our understanding of the respective manu- script traditions.

Until the end of the nineteenth century it had been accepted that the author of the Isaian corpus was the celebrated ascetic of the later fourth and earlier fifth centuries, Isaiah of Scetis, known to us largely through the various collections of the sayings of the Desert Fathers. In 1899 Krüger proposed, in passing, that the corpus was, rather, the work of Isaiah of Gaza, an irenic Heno- physite who died between 488 and 491.[7] This Isaiah has his own *Life* and also appears as a key player in the *Life of Peter the Iberian*. Krüger's thesis rapidly established a new consensus, dissented from only by the monk Augustinos.

More recently, Draguet's work on the Syriac manuscript trad- ition has convinced him that the Isaian corpus is the product of two main redactional layers: the first indeed deriving from Abba Isaiah of Scetis, with the second being introduced between *c*.450 and *c*.500. This second layer is, argues Draguet, palpably distinct from the first not only in terms of the Syriac manuscript tradition, but also in its language and its themes.[8] He does, however, freely admit that the delineation between the two layers is impossible to draw with any exact precision. Draguet offers no firm hypothesis as to the origin of the second layer. He does, however, exclude the possibility that this layer may have been the work of Isaiah of Gaza. The thesis was not accepted by Chitty and given only a

---

[7] See Ahrens and Krüger, *Die Kirchengeschichte des Zacharias Rhetor in deutscher Übersetzung*, 263 n. 13 (= endnotes, pp. 385 f.).

[8] Thus he sums up his argument by saying that between the two layers 's'étend la distance qui sépare le sommaire de l'élaboré, la différence qui distingue une pensée encore simple d'une technicité qui se veut plus savante, en dépendance du type de spiritualité grecque à laquelle le branle fut donné par les Alexandrins.' *Les Cinq Recensions*, i. 37*.

lukewarm reception by Regnault—both very astute judges of the
Isaian corpus.[9]

The debate about the date and authorship of the *Asceticon* is an
intricate one. Much of it centres around the collection of reminiscences known as Logos G30 (=Sv1).[10] The author repeats the
account given to him by 'Abba John' of the departure of Poemen
and Anoub from Scetis 'when the Mazices came there for the first
time and devastated it' (i.e. in 407) (G30.2). Draguet suggests that
the John in question is John Kolobos, the director of the community at Scetis from the death of Paphnutius up to the incursion of
407.[11] This is plausible, but speculative. The reference to the *first*
devastation would put the remark after the second devastation of
*c.*434, although the more primitive Sa recension simply speaks of
the devastation *tout court*. The Paphnutius to whom the author
speaks in G30.3 may be the Paphnutius who directed Scetis in
succession to Macarius of Egypt, preceding John Kolobos and
dying around the turn of the century. Again, this identification is
but speculative. Many of the great figures of Egyptian asceticism,
such as Agathon and Sisoes, are known of only by report (G30.5a,
6a). The warning against anthropomorphism in Logos G6.9
would certainly seem to post-date the outbreak of the Anthropomorphite controversy.[12] We are evidently dealing with an early
fifth-century Egyptian context, but beyond that it is impossible to
be more specific. Those who espouse the ascription to Isaiah of
Gaza point out that this Isaiah is often referred to as 'Isaiah the
Egyptian', and argue that the second- or third-hand reminiscences
of Logos G30 could very plausibly be those of someone who left
Egypt in the first half of the fifth century and died in 489–91.[13]
Draguet, on the other hand, argues that the Isaiah of Logos G30
must have been a mature ascetic by AD 400 and thus could not

---

[9] See Chitty 'Abba Isaiah'; Regnault, 'Isaïe de Scété ou de Gaza' and his introduction
to the French translation (n. 4 above).

[10] G = the common recension of the Greek Isaiah, followed by the number of the Logos
in arabic numerals. S = the common recension of the Syriac Isaiah, followed by the
number of the Logos in roman numerals. In the Greek, Logos G30 is preserved only in
MS ξ (Moscow, Historical Museum 320 = Vladimir 177) (12th cent.).

[11] *Les Cinq Recensions*, ii. 29.

[12] 'He who seeks a representation of God blasphemes God.' This passage is lost in S and ξ.
It is conserved in MSS γ, κ, and β.

[13] See, for example, Guillaumont, 'Une notice syriaque inédite sur la vie de l'Abbé Isaïe'.
Guillaumont argues that the Isaiah of the *Apophthegmata* could quite plausibly be Isaiah of
Gaza.

possibly have died as late as 489–91. He follows Augustinos in using the Isaian section of apophthegms from MS Karakallou 251 to bolster his case, pointing in particular to Apophthegm 8 in which Isaiah has a disciple by the name of Peter at the time when a certain Isaac directed the community at Scetis.[14] Again, it is impossible to be sure of the identity or date of this Isaac and consequently of the Isaiah in question.

Without wishing to rehearse the arguments surrounding the identity of the author at any greater length, it is extremely significant for our purposes that Draguet points out Macarian traits as one of the distinguishing features of the second layer: 'sans entrer à fond dans le sujet, nous avons signalé au passage des traits macariens dans les logoi VII, XI, XXII–XXIII et XXVI'.[15] Regnault comments that Draguet has done so 'sans pouvoir toutefois y reconnaître une influence directe de Macaire ni aucune contamination de ses erreurs messaliennes. Mais cet auteur, qu'on accepte ou non la thèse de M. Dörries l'identifiant à Siméon de Mésopotamie, reste entouré de tant de mystère qu'il est impossible de résoudre pour le moment le problème de ses relations avec Isaïe.'[16]

We are now in a better position to examine this problem, especially given the recent advances in our understanding of the Messalian controversy, and of Macarius' relations with the Messalian tendency, owed in particular to the work of Columba Stewart and Klaus Fitschen. We emphatically do not have to look for 'Messalian contamination' if we are to detect the influence of Macarius. We need not now be so pessimistic as was Regnault, writing in 1971. Chitty's comment, published in the same year, the year of his death, is less proscriptive. He states simply that: 'The relation [of the *Asceticon*] to the "Macarian" homilies, particularly of the long letter to Peter [G25 = SvII] on his approach to the monastic life, awaits further study.'[17] This gives us a good starting-point. If the Macarian traits in the Isaian corpus do indeed prove to be clustered in what Draguet classifies as the second redactional layer, his two-layer thesis will be strengthened.

---

[14] See Draguet, 'Une section "Isaïenne" d'apophtegmes dans le Karakallou 251'. The Isaiah of the *Asceticon* certainly had a disciple named Peter: he is named as the recipient of Logos G25 and as the source of Logos G26.

[15] *Les Cinq Recensions*, i. 82*.

[16] 'Isaïe de Scété ou de Gaza', 2093.

[17] 'Abba Isaiah', 69.

*The Legacy*

## 7.2 Macarian Literature Contained within the Isaian Manuscript Tradition

Both the Greek and the Syriac Isaian collections contain works of Macarius presented under the name of Abba Isaiah. This should not surprise us. The redactors of ascetic literature of our period were far less concerned with accurate ascription than with the quality of the advice given in their material. Macarian literature, as we have noted, is found under many different names—ascribed variously to the two Macarii, Symeon the Stylite, Ephrem, Mark the Monk, Basil of Caesarea, and others. To find pieces of Macarius within the *Asceticon* of Abba Isaiah is therefore quite in keeping with the spirit of the age during which the ascetic collections that have come down to us were compiled. We shall look at the Greek and Syriac traditions in turn.

### 7.2.1 The Greek *Asceticon*

Logos 19 of the Greek *Asceticon* closely parallels Logos 28 of Collection III of the Macarian corpus. Klostermann and Berthold judged Logos 28 to be of questionable pseudo-Macarian authorship, yet nonetheless included it in their edition of Collection III. Desprez has also kept it in his edition, and inclines towards accepting it as an authentic work of our Macarius.[18] Logos 28 is, in fact, well established in the Macarian manuscript tradition. It appears as Epistle 9 of Macarius of Alexandria in the Syriac tradition and in the Arabic tradition as Homily 32.[19] Logos G19 is considerably shorter than the Macarian Logos 28. After an analogy (G19.4) distantly related to III 28.3.1, Logos 19 ends, while Macarius' Logos 28 continues for three additional sections (III 28.3–5). Internal evidence offers no easy solution. Whichever piece has the priority, the other has certainly been reworked to fit in with the other works of the author amongst whose work it is found. Rather than doubting the authenticity of Logos 28, I would argue that its greater length and solid basis in Macarian

---

[18] *Pseudo-Macaire: Oeuvres spirituelles*, 63 and 332.

[19] Epistle 9 is edited in Strothmann, *Die syrische Überlieferung*, i. 247–58. It is not found in the very earliest Syriac MSS, being first attested by MS E (= Vaticanus syriacus 122, fol. 192,6–278,15) (AD 769). Macarius, TV h.32 has been neither edited nor translated because it duplicates material available in the Greek editions.

manuscript traditions indicate its priority over Logos 19.[20] Furthermore, given that the Syriac *Asceticon* includes works of Macarius as works of Isaiah, it is quite reasonable to suppose that a similar process had occurred in the compiling of the Greek *Asceticon*. The piece contains reflections on the action of the Holy Spirit, the destruction of the passions, and the carrying of Christ in the heart, as Mary carried him in the womb.[21] These are all typically Macarian themes that could serve to amplify and enhance the message of the *Asceticon*.

## 7.2.2 The Syriac *Asceticon*

The Syriac collections give great precedence to the works of Macarius. Macarius' Homily 19 of Collection II is placed as Logos I of the Syriac *Asceticon*, while Homily 3 of the same Collection is given as Logos III. This is a development not found in the extant Greek collections of Abba Isaiah. Both Logoi are augmented and retouched by the redactor, yet are very clearly the Macarian Homilies II 19 and 3.[22] We are fortunate in having an early recognition of the Macarian authorship of the first of these by Dadisho Qatraya, the seventh-century monk and scholar of the Church of the East.

Dadisho produced a very learned commentary upon the *Asceticon* of Abba Isaiah in which he presents the work as a unified whole—no easy task—and as in harmony with the best traditions of ascetic literature, by which he understands, principally, the works of Evagrius, Macarius, and Mark.[23] Dadisho is at pains to

[20] Note also that G19.3, discussing the parable of the ten virgins, uses variant νυμφῶν for the Gospel γάμοι. This variant is, as we have seen (Ch. 5.6), also found in Macarius, II 4.6. It is not found in the Asceticon's other treatments of the parable (G16.131, G25.25). Although the text of III 28.2.3 uses the verb, νυμφεύω, rather than the noun, this may nonetheless be taken as a further indicator of the reliance of G19 on III 28.

[21] On this last theme, see Miquel, 'La Naissance de Dieu dans l'âme'. The theme is often encountered in early monastic literature. See, for example, the remarkable saying of Abba Longinus: 'A woman knows she has conceived when she no longer loses any blood. So it is with the soul, it knows it has conceived the Holy Spirit when the passions stop coming out of her. But as long as one is held back in the passions, how dare one believe one is sinless? Give blood, and receive the Spirit' (*AP* (Alph.) Longinus 5 (PG 65 257B)). See also Cronius 1 (248A) and Poemen 205 (Guy, 'Recherches sur la tradition grecque des Apophthegmata Patrum', 31) for the same theme.

[22] See Draguet, *Les Cinq Recensions*, i. 21*. Homily II 19 deals with the need for forceful personal effort; Homily II 3 deals with community life and invisible warfare.

[23] Edited and translated by Draguet, *Commentaire du livre d'Abba Isaïe par Dadisho Qatraya* (CSCO 326–7).

stress the uniformity of their teaching and that of Isaiah. Of Logos I he declares: 'I would, however, inform the reader of this. This discourse formerly formed part of a book of Abba Macarius the Egyptian, the disciple of the blessed Anthony. Macarius had decided to put in writing what he had learnt from the living word of Anthony's mouth for the benefit of the solitaries.'[24] Dadisho goes on to explain that because this homily was attached to another (for which he gives an *incipit* corresponding to Homily 20 of Collection II) and because this discourse was contained 'amongst the letters' of Macarius, its ideas were not readily accessible.[25] In order, therefore, to facilitate the circulation of this Homily, and having retouched it and clarified it, Abba Isaiah, according to Dadisho, placed this Homily at the head of his *Asceticon.*[26]

Dadisho does not appear to be aware of the Macarian authorship of Logos III of the Syriac *Asceticon*, although he does refer the reader to a work of Macarius on a similar theme.[27] The commentary makes fascinating reading, and gives us some idea of the impact of Macarius upon the seventh-century East Syrian tradition. Dadisho's own language is impregnated with Macarian themes and imagery; see for example his description of the pedagogy of the Holy Spirit in *Discours* 1.36. In this passage Dadisho implicitly marshals Macarius against the Messalians—a strategy we also find taken up explicitly by Isaac of Nineveh.[28] Dadisho also takes Logos III as a treatise against the sort of spiritual pessimism that would deny our capacity to resist sin, and associates this treatise of Macarius with Mark's treatise *On Baptism*, which we know, from Babai the Great, to have been directed

---

[24] *Discours* 1.10 (translated from Draguet's French).

[25] It seems from this notice that the Syriac Macarian corpus was not widely available in the East-Syrian orbit.

[26] Dadisho must have had access to a considerable selection of Macarian material in order to have been able to spot the authorship of this piece. The equivalent of Homily II 19 is not extant in Syriac, yet from the accuracy of Dadisho's references to other works of Macarius that are extant in Syriac, we may assume that this piece did indeed exist in Syriac translation. See Draguet, 'Parallèles macariens'.

[27] *Discours* III.1.

[28] Isaac of Nineveh, *De perfectione religiosa*, Homily 72 (Bedjan, p. 495 = *The Ascetical Homilies of Saint Isaac the Syrian*, Homily 69, p. 336). This passage is later cited by Kallistos and Ignatius Xanthopoulos, *Directions to Hesychasts*, 43 (*Philokalia*, 3rd edn., iv. 242–3). Isaac recognizes that Macarius' stress on the fluctuations of the spiritual life was directed against Messalian claims of inalienable and untroubled *apatheia*.

against the Messalians. It is a good example of Macarius being seen—albeit in this case in the guise of Abba Isaiah—as an opponent of the Messalians. Nevertheless, however interesting and important the *Commentary* of Dadisho is for our understanding of the perception and reception of Abba Macarius in the Church of the East—certainly a topic for further research—we must turn now to the primary concern of this chapter, the Macarian elements within the Logoi of the *Asceticon* of Abba Isaiah.

### 7.3  Logos G25: Τοῦ αὐτοῦ πρὸς τὸν ἀββᾶν Πέτρον τὸν ἑαυτοῦ μαθητήν[29]

Having discussed the Macarian works contained within the Isaian manuscript tradition, we may now turn to a discussion of the Macarian traits perceptible within the Logoi of the Isaian corpus proper. As we have noted, this discussion will have a considerable bearing upon the two-layer thesis posited by Draguet. There is no doubt that the focus of our debate must be Logos G25 (= Sv11). This Logos, which Draguet treats as 'le type même' of the second layer, merits a systematic treatment.[30]

There is a possible connection between G25.1[31] and Macarius, II 21.2. Logos G25.1 observes:

Two matters (δύο ὕλαι) have taken hold of the soul. One comes from the outside and has the care of this world for the repose of the body. The other, from within, is that of the passions which impede the virtues. But the soul does not see the inward one, that of the passions, if it is not freed from (ἐλευθερωθῇ) that of the outside. For this reason the Lord said: 'He who has not renounced his own will in its entirety cannot become my disciple' [cf. Lk. 14: 33].[32] The matter from the outside comes from the will, that from the inside comes from exterior conduct. Knowing that the will was the master of both, our Lord Jesus commanded that it be cut off.

---

[29] 'Of the same [Abba Isaiah] to Abba Peter his Disciple'. The chapter headings are those used by Chitty and should be compared with those provided by Draguet.

[30] Draguet, *Les Cinq Recensions*, i. 84.

[31] Citations from the Greek *Asceticon* (G) give the number of the Logos given in Chitty and the French translation (3rd edn.), followed by the paragraph number drawn from Draguet's edition of the Syriac (S) (also incorporated into the French translation).

[32] This unusual reading of Luke 14: 33 is not found in Macarius.

Macarius, II 21.2 has it that, following the Fall:

Man was bound in two ways and by two chains. [Firstly,] in this life, in the affairs of this life and in the love of the world, that is of fleshly pleasures and passions, riches and glories and possessions, women and children, family, country, places, clothes, and in everything that belongs to the phenomenal world, from which the word of God commands man to be loosed by his own free will—for man is voluntarily bound to the phenomena—to the end that, having loosed and freed (ἐλευθερώσας) himself from all these things, he might perfectly master the commandment. [Secondly,] inside (ἐν τῷ κρυπτῷ), the human soul is surrounded, enclosed, walled-in (περιτετείχισται)[33] and bound in chains of darkness by the spirits of evil, unable to love the Lord as it would, nor believe as it would, nor pray as it would.

Macarius goes on (II 21.3–5) to make it clear that man is first to be loosed from the visible chains of this world, and then to proceed to the inward struggle against the thoughts and the inner passions. So long as the soul remains bound to the things of this world, it will not be aware of the wounds it carries nor perceive the hidden passions. The *Asceticon*'s 'two matters' would seem to be derived from Macarius' 'two chains'. This connection is supported by the shared emphasis on the freely chosen nature of the visible impediments, the Dominical command to free oneself from the ties of this age, and the understanding that man will remain ignorant of the inner struggle until he has so freed himself. The chief difference is that the invisible impediments in Macarius are not said to be freely chosen, whereas Isaiah appears to be hinting at an understanding more in accord with that of Mark and Diadochus, in which such impediments are the product of our own conduct—and not the enduring inheritance of the Fall.[34]

The description of the soul's need to conform to its own nature in G25.10–11 exhibits some similarities with the Macarian writings. The description of the soul as fire when in God is analogous to Macarius' description of the fiery condition of the soul which has received the Lord (II 1.2). The *Asceticon* adds that such a soul will burn its enemies, a point also made by Macarius (I 34.3, 50.2.6; II 12.9, 43.3). It compares the state of the soul in God to iron in the

---

[33] Note Isaiah's description of the inner passions as 'dark walls which surround the soul' in the passage immediately preceding his discussion of the 'two matters' (G25.1). Cf. also the 'walls of evil' that surround the intellect in Macarius, II 50.3.

[34] See Ch. 5.4.3 and Ch. 6.6.2.

fire, as had, after Origen, Macarius (II 4.14). This cathartic fire, says the *Asceticon*, restores the soul to its own nature, the nature it had in the beginning. Macarius has essentially the same understanding of the original purity of the soul (II 46.5), obscured but not destroyed by the Fall (III 26.5.1), and restored by the operation of the Holy Spirit (I 50.1.1–2). He writes that the immaterial fire destroys all evil in the soul and restores to the intellect its natural perceptiveness and limpidity (II 25.9–10). There is a certain difference of emphasis in that the *Asceticon* speaks of the soul's need to conform to its own nature, whereas Macarius stresses the mutual indwelling of God and man, each finding its rest only in the other (II 45.5). Given that, in the *Asceticon*, the soul regains its own nature only in God, the difference is not, in fact, a fundamental one. The Logos goes on in the same section to illustrate the theme:

As animals die if they are plunged into water, because they are of the substance of earth (ἐκ τῆς οὐσίας τῆς γῆς). And again, as fish die if they are brought up onto the earth, because they are of the nature of water. So also birds, which find their rest in the air, fear being hunted when they wish to land. The perfect soul, which remains in its own nature, is similar. If it renounces its own nature, it dies straight away. (G25.10)

Compare Macarius, II 14.7—the same image used to the same end. He begins by drawing an analogy between certain animals who live in volcanoes and eat fire, and Christians who have celestial fire as their food:

If they go out of this [celestial] fire, they are destroyed by evil spirits. Just as those animals die going out of that [earthly] fire, as fish [die when taken] out from water, as four-footed animals thrown in the sea drown, and as birds walking on the land are taken by hunters; so the soul that does not remain in that [celestial] land drowns and perishes.[35]

The imagery is very close: animals dying in water, fish perishing out of water and birds taken by hunters on land. The only difference is that Logos G25 does not take up the myth of the

---

[35] Cf. also III 4.3.1–2, 16.3.2, and 18.2.3: similar analogies used to illustrate essentially the same point. We may also note *AP* (Alph.) Anthony 10 (PG 65 77BC): 'Just as fish die if they stay too long out of water, so the monks who loiter outside their cells or pass their time with men of this world lose the intensity of inner peace. So like a fish going towards the sea, we must hurry to reach our cell, for fear that if we delay outside, we will lose our interior watchfulness.' The basic image of the fish out of water is a commonplace. The imagery is not so developed as it is in Macarius and Isaiah, and speaks of a different subject: the peace of the monk rather than the true home of the soul.

fire-dwelling beasts used by Macarius.[36] The moral is substantially the same: the soul must remain in its own land or in its own nature, or else it will die. It is virtually certain that the Isaian image derives from that of Macarius.

The *Asceticon* then compares the baptized soul to a city occupied by the enemy and re-conquered by Christ (G25.11). This analogy has points of contact with Macarius, particularly with Logos 19 of Collection III.[37] This Logos also treats of the soul-city captured by enemies. In both, the city is described as lawless when occupied by its enemies while the coming of Christ is treated as the restoration of law and order. Both take the imperial image as the guarantee of the rule of law in the city (G25.11; III 19.1) and expand this analogy to encompass the soul's need to carry the image of Christ. In both, the coming of the image of Christ is associated with the soul's acquiring the ability to destroy its enemies. The elements of the image are substantially the same in our two authors. The image has certainly not been simply lifted from Macarius, but has rather been digested by the author of the Isaian piece and given a form more concordant with the *Asceticon* as a whole. This example provides further evidence of the insemination of the thought-world of the author of Logos G25 by Macarian ideas and imagery.

Compare also the analogy of a bird with only one wing and (obviously) unable to fly, introduced by our authors as follows:

καὶ ὥσπερ πετεινὸν οὐ δύναται πετασθῆναι ἑνὶ πτερῷ [ . . . ]. (Logos G25.12)

ἢ ὥσπερ πετεινὸν ἐὰν ἔχῃ πτερὸν ἕν, ἐν τῷ ἑνὶ πετασθῆναι οὐ δύναται [ . . . ]. (Macarius, 11 32.6)

---

[36] This piece of information is rather illuminating in itself. Macarius begins, 'Ὡς δὲ ὁ λόγος τῶν ἔξωθεν λέγει ≪ἔστιν ὄρη πύρινα≫ [ . . . ], providing further evidence of his acquaintance with secular literature. The myth of the fire-dwelling animals is given by Aelian, *Nat. anim.* 11.2 (ed. and tr. Scholfield): 'But that there should spring from the fire winged creatures which men call fire-born, and that they should live and flourish in it, flying to and fro about it, is a startling fact. And what is more extraordinary, when these creatures stray outside the range of the heat to which they are accustomed and take in cold air, they at once perish. And why they should be born in the fire, and die in the air, others must explain.'

[37] The theme of the soul as city is a common one in Macarius. See for example 11 16.12–13, 42.1–2; III 4.3.3–4 (and note). See also I 61.1.4–10, 27.2.2 for the replacement of the image of the evil one with that of Christ. The designation of the soul as a city is in itself a common one. Gregory of Nyssa, for example, treats the soul as the 'city' of the Song of Songs 5: 7, *Cant.*, hom. 5 (GNO 6, pp. 360, 364).

The image is, admittedly, used to different ends. Logos G25 takes it to illustrate the fact that the soul cannot ascend to God if it is attached to anything of this world. Macarius uses it as another depiction of his theme that without intimate communion with the heavenly nature, human nature remains naked and soiled. As we have noted, this is a theme not developed in the *Asceticon*, which prefers to emphasize the soul's need to conform to its own nature. Nevertheless, so far as it goes, the parallel does have weight.

In order to stress our need to look only for spiritual gifts, our authors use a strikingly similar image of a child at his mother's breast:

ἐὰν ἐπιδειχθῇ τῷ βρέφει χρυσὸς ἢ ἄργυρος ἢ μαργαρίται ἢ πᾶν σκεῦος τοῦ κόσμου, προσέχει μὲν αὐτοῖς, ἀλλ᾽ εἰς τοὺς κόλπους τῆς μητρὸς ὑπάρχον πάντα παραβλέπει ἵνα μεταλάβῃ τοῦ μασθοῦ αὐτῆς.　(G25.19)

ἢ ὥσπερ βρέφος περιβεβλημένον μαργαρίτας καὶ ἐνδύματα τίμια, ὅταν πεινάσῃ, ὡς οὐδὲν λογίζεται ἃ φορεῖ, ἀλλὰ καταφρονεῖ αὐτῶν, ὅλην δὲ τὴν μέριμναν ἔχει εἰς τὸν μασθὸν τῆς τροφοῦ, πῶς τὸ γάλα λάβῃ.　(II 45.7)

The image is substantially the same: the infant disregards (παραβλέπει/καταφρονεῖ) pearls and other precious objects when it hungers and looks only to the breast of his mother. It is not a commonplace image. The coincidence of formulation and the similarity of context make it plain that the author of the Isian piece has here drawn directly upon the rich reservoir of Macarian imagery in order to illustrate his theme.

A last instance of Macarian imagery in this Logos is that of the merchant in G25.21. Here the author ends a collection of verses from Proverbs 31 with verse 14: 'She has become like a ship trading from afar.' He continues:

Let us understand this by this word, that the merchant who boards this ship does not put in it only one type [of goods] (οὐχὶ μόνον ἓν εἶδος ἐμβάλλεται) but everything from which he knows he will profit. And if he sees something that will cause him loss, he does not desire it [...]. Such is the perfect soul that wishes to meet God without offence (ἀπροσκόπως) [cf. Phil. 1: 10].

Compare Macarius, II 33.2:

A merchant does not limit his enterprise to one type of operation (οὐ μονότροπον ἔχει τοῦ κέρδους τὴν ἐπίνοιαν) but presses himself to increase and multiply his profit from all sides [...] and he turns away from that which profits nothing and hurries towards that which profits more. In like manner should we make ready our soul in various ways and with ingenuity.

Again we see a very similar image used to a very similar end. The image of the merchant is transposed to the plane of the soul. In each case the reader or listener is encouraged to emulate the merchant, to cultivate all that is profitable—not just this or that thing—and to despise all that is unprofitable. The treatment in G25.21 is rather longer than that of Macarius, yet I would suggest that we have here another example of an image derived from Macarius, dwelt upon and digested by the author of Logos G25, and reproduced by that author as a further illustration of his theme.

We have dealt now with the most striking examples of Macarian imagery found in Logos G25. We may justifiably assert that the thought-world of the author of that Logos was informed and indeed impregnated by Macarius.[38] Let us now attempt to look at the Logos as a whole, in order to make some estimation of the extent of the Macarian element in it.

Draguet doubts the unity of the piece, pointing to the alternative title of MS ξ: λόγοι τοῦ ἀββᾶ Ἰσαΐου.[39] Chitty disagreed, but never had the opportunity to fully develop his argument. The addressee of the Logos fluctuates between the singular and the plural. Overall, it is more homiletic than epistolary. It does, however, stick roughly to its central themes of the need for absolute rejection of the world and for proper repentance. It begins with a sharp distinction between God and Mammon and asserts that preoccupation with things of this world 'darkens the intellect' (G25.1). This may be compared with the descriptions of the intellect 'darkened' by evil in, for example, Macarius, I 6.3.5 and II 26.1.[40] We have discussed the 'two matters' that have taken hold of the soul above. The image of the young wife in G25.2 is only distantly comparable with the various wifely analogies of Macarius (e.g. II 45.5). The

---

[38] This conclusion is, naturally, shared by Draguet (*Les Cinq Recensions*, i. 84). He also reports Villecourt's conclusion that one writer must be relying on the other, 'Grande Lettre', 54–6.

[39] Moscow, Historical Museum 320 = Vladimir 177 (12th cent.). See Draguet, *Les Cinq Recensions*, 12*.

[40] Draguet takes the use of the term νοῦς as characteristic of the second layer. The corpus as a whole speaks far more frequently of 'heart' and 'soul'. Fr Guerric Couilleau has counted 243 uses of the word 'heart', 165 of 'soul' as against 60 of 'intellect'—not counting composites, of which there are many. See his 'Entre Scété et Gaza', 356.

exegesis of 1 Corinthians 2: 7–12 that follows bears no relation to the Macarian exegesis of that passage (II 12.15). G25.3 exhibits great respect for the rebirth in Christ and insufflation of the Holy Spirit effected by baptism. It takes broadly the same approach as Diadochus and Mark, asserting that baptism is received for the eradication of sins and that 'it is impossible for Christ and sin to dwell in the same place'. This is one of the few apparent corrections of Macarius in the Isaian corpus. The author goes on to stress the need for personal effort in a manner entirely consistent with that found in Macarius. The theme of the work of the young child in G25.4–7 contains much that is beautiful, but is not closely paralleled in Macarius. G25.8–9 equally contains little that directly recalls Macarius. We have discussed G25.10–12 above, and found significant parallels there. G25.10–12 contain relatively few scriptural citations, and stand out from what follows in that respect. The treatment of the brazen serpent in G25.17–18 has no significant similarity with that given in Macarius, II 11.8–9. G25.19 is discussed above. G25.20 rapidly becomes a collection of exhortatory sayings linked with a succession of Old Testament figures and concluding with penitence and obedience to God. Throughout G25.20, as in many other places, the audience is addressed in the plural, providing further evidence that G25 is not a unified letter.

G25.21 employs the image of the merchant discussed above. G25.22 takes up a recurrent them of the *Asceticon*, repeated in G25.25–6, of the purified soul as fiancée for the Lord. Macarius also uses this theme, for example in II 32.9 and 45.7, but puts his emphasis on the soul as bride, rather than fiancée, of the Lord.[41] The treatment of baptism that follows in G25.22 is very much that found in Macarius, and indeed in much of the early monastic tradition, in that it has a two-stage approach: baptism has renewed the soul, yet it is repentance that makes the soul a pure virgin for the Lord, quite forgetting its former dilapidation (παλαιότης).[42] The account of the saving work of Christ in G25.23 has some points of contact with Macarius, although these are likely to be the

---

[41] Isaiah also speaks of the soul as bride of God: G25.24–5. This does not, therefore, constitute a significant difference.

[42] Cf. John Climacus, *Ladder* 7 (PG 88 804B): spiritual tears are in a sense greater than baptism; they wash away the defilement of post-baptismal sin. Cf. also *AP* (Alph.) Arsenius 41–2 (PG 65 105C–108B) (tears of repentance), Poemen 119 (353A) (the purifying and perfecting power of tears); and Gregory of Nazianzus, *Or.* 39.18–19 (SC 358, pp. 189–95) (the baptism of tears). See also the discussion of spiritual tears in Ch. 6.7.

product of independent meditation upon Scripture, especially upon Colossians 2: 14. Christ's placing of his image in our heart in that section may be compared with the rather more vivid image of Christ the good painter, painting in us his own image, in Macarius, II 30.4. The reference to the indwelling of the Holy Spirit in G25.25 recalls Macarius, yet is not, of course, his exclusive property. It is one of the few references to the ministry of the Spirit outside of Logos G19. Logos G25 goes on to hold out the great goal of regeneration in Christ and to warn of the danger of rejection by God and of the pains of hell. Of regeneration, it declares of those who have become brides of Christ 'that they are of his essence (οὐσία) through regeneration (or rebirth) and are of his holy body'. This is exactly the sort of bold language we find in Macarius: Anointed with the same oil as he was anointed with, 'we become Christs, [being], so to say, of one essence (οὐσία) and of one body [with him]'. To say we are of one body with Christ is, of course, natural (cf. Rom. 12: 5; Eph. 5: 30). To say, even with the caveat 'so to say' (ὡς εἰπεῖν), that we are of his essence is rather less usual. It may be evidence of a connection. G25 closes with an evocation of God's power to help us and a final reminder to the reader, now addressed in the singular, to apply himself to all this.

In conclusion, we may justifiably assert that much of Logos G25 was written by an author very familiar with some portion of the Macarian writings. He was evidently struck by the graphic imagery of Macarius, and drew upon several of those images in order to illustrate his own arguments. This dependency is clear despite the fact that there are no explicit citations from Macarius, or indeed of any other author, in the Logos (as in the *Asceticon* as a whole). Before drawing any further conclusions, however, we must first examine the remainder of the *Asceticon* and attempt to discern just how distinctive this Logos is in its palpable use of Macarian material.

## 7.4 The Passions and *Apatheia*

The remarkable Logos G2 (περὶ τοῦ κατὰ φύσιν νοός)[43] sets out Isaiah's theory of nature and of the passions. He insists on the

---

[43] This Logos forms part of the most primitive Syriac version (Sa). In Draguet's scheme it is therefore considered as largely first-layer.

essential goodness of nature, arguing that the Fall has perverted
the faculties into a counter-natural state. He goes on to assert that
God has become incarnate precisely to restore to its natural state
that which had become counter-natural (ἕως μεταλλάξῃ τὴν παρὰ
φύσιν εἰς τὴν κατὰ φύσιν διὰ τοῦ ἁγίου αὐτοῦ σώματος) (G2.2).
Isaiah's understanding is, thus far, deeply traditional. It is very
much in accordance with what we find in Macarius. As he puts it
in II 46.5 'The soul is a great and divine and truly wonderful work.
In creating it, God made it such that there should be no evil in its
nature.' Evil is, therefore, counter-natural (II 4.1), a foreign intrusion into our nature stemming from the Fall (II 4.8). The first
and greatest work of the Incarnation is, writes Macarius, 'the re-
establishment of the pure nature of Adam' (I 61.1.1). Where Isaiah
is most original and distinctive is in his development of what
exactly 'natural' passions are, explaining the natural place and
function of desire, anger, jealousy, pride, and hatred (G2.5–10).[44]
He returns to the theme in Logos G17, giving an eloquent description of the need to extinguish all that is counter-natural in us and
thereby to attain not only conformity with our own nature, but
also conformity with the nature of Jesus (G17.5 f.). He goes on to
give a skilful demonstration of the rightful function of natural
anger in the struggle against counter-nature (G17.8). This is not
something that can be readily paralleled in Macarius, in whom we
find references to counter-natural passions (I 49.1.1; *EM* 9.14), but
no developed understanding of what exactly a natural passion
might be. For Macarius, the passions are, by definition, negative.
Thus he labels as 'senseless' those who say that the passions are
natural and God-given (I 40.1.2). There is similarly no significant
development of the concept of the natural passion in Evagrius. It is
clear that Isaiah's theory of the natural passions does not derive
from either Macarius or Evagrius. Isaiah's independence from
Evagrius in this respect is confirmed by the fact that he does not
take up the Evagrian model of the eight principal vices.[45]

---

[44] A parallel for Isaiah's theory of the passions may be found in Theodoret. See Kallistos
Ware, ' "Pathos" in Isaias and Theodoret'.

[45] See Logos G28: περὶ τῶν κλάδων τῆς κακίας. This Logos, largely paralleled by Sxxii,
is regarded by Draguet as, with Svii (= G25), 'le type même de la seconde couche
redactionelle', excepting §2, which is more primitive (*Les Cinq Recensions*, ii. 373). Isaiah's
list of the seven principal vices in G28.1 is clearly unrelated to that of Evagrius.

Isaiah's theory of the passions does not represent any very profound disagreement with Macarius or Evagrius—much depends on how one defines passion in the first place. Elsewhere, the *Asceticon* treats of the passions in purely negative terms, speaking of the 'captivity (αἰχμαλωσία) of the passions' (G17.3), calling for their extinction (G22.4), and declaring that we must flee from them (G21.17). It holds that between us and Jesus there is nothing but the passions (G21.2), and that the Cross consists in abstinence therefrom (G21.25). We are not dealing here with any very fundamental inconsistency. Where the *Asceticon* speaks of the extinction of the passions, it clearly means the extinction of counter-natural passions. This does, however, represent a difference in emphasis, and it does seem that this more negative assessment of the passions is characteristic of the second layer. This change in emphasis becomes most apparent in the teaching on *apatheia*.

The treatment of *apatheia* in the *Asceticon* brings us rather closer to Macarius and Evagrius. Draguet takes the theme as one of the most distinctive signs of the second layer. In Logos G15.86 the reader is warned: 'Do not think yourself impassible so long as sin seduces you. He who has been given freedom (ἐλευθερία) no longer thinks of that which he has done out of counter-nature.' The Logos speaks of *apatheia* as becoming 'immovable' (ἀκίνητος) (G15.92). According to Macarius, charity makes those who aspire to receive it 'impassible and unshakeable (ἀσάλευτος)' (III 28.3.4). Logos G23 (περὶ τελειότητος)[46] advises: 'If you see that when you pray, absolutely nothing evil accuses you, then you are truly free and have entered into [God's] holy repose, according to his will' (G23.2). Note that 'freedom' in the *Asceticon* is essentially a synonym for *apatheia*. This association recalls Macarius' equation of perfection with the freedom of *apatheia*.[47]

The Logos continues: 'But *apatheia* is not subject to warring (ἀπολέμητος), for it has received the prize (τὸ βραβεῖον), and is no longer anxious about the fate of the three that have been split up, when these have been reconciled by God. These three are the soul, body, and spirit, according to the apostle [cf. 2 Thess. 5: 23]'

---

[46] This Logos contains copticisms alongside themes of the second layer. Draguet consequently found it very difficult to classify.

[47] For example the 'calling of perfection and freedom and *apatheia*' in *EM* 13.8.

(G23.11).[48] The *Asceticon* comes close here to asserting that *apatheia* amounts to immunity from temptation. Logos G24 (περὶ ἀπαθείας) confirms this suspicion. The author sketches the undulations of the way of the virtues, and then observes:

> But *apatheia* is far from all these things, and has need of nothing. For it is in God, and God is in it. It has no enemy, nor does it have any more falling, nor lack of faith, nor effort to retain it, nor fear of the passions, nor any desire for anything, nor labour caused by the Enemy. Its glories are great and innumerable. But in so far as there is fear about some passion, it is far away. While accusations rise up from the heart, it is a stranger. It is the body which the Lord Jesus took up. It is the love which he taught to his own to perform in joy. Many simpletons have thought themselves to have reached it, while passions still lived in the soul and the body was not yet wholly purified, and they have fallen away from that which is needful. (G24.1)

It is difficult not to see in the last sentence an attack upon the Messalians. Dadisho indeed treats parts of the *Asceticon* as having been directed against the 'impiety' of the Messalians.[49] But while the author shares Macarius' distrust of hasty declarations of apatheia, and makes use of the Macarian theory of coexistence, he is less circumspect than Macarius, or indeed Evagrius, in his treatment of *apatheia* itself, seeming to suggest that *apatheia* brings about an end to the spiritual struggle, the end not only of yielding to temptation but of temptation itself.[50] If one were looking for the 'Messalian contamination' of which Regnault spoke, this would be a prime example. Like Macarius and Evagrius, the author links

---

[48] The belief expressed in G23.11, quoted above, that impassibility entails the reunification of soul, body, and spirit is also found in G19.3. Here the Isaian text is far clearer on the theme of reunification than is its Macarian model (III 28.2.3), which quotes 1 Thess. 5: 23 as one of the signs of readiness for marriage to the heavenly Bridegroom: 'If "the God of peace" has completely sanctified you such that "your whole spirit, soul, and body are entirely blameless" [...].' The Isaian text (G19.3) reads: 'If you sense that your spirit and soul and body have been unified blamelessly and will rise again stainless on the day of our Lord [...].'

[49] See *Discours* 1.36. Isaiah is presented as at one with 'the solitary fathers', by whom Dadisho means, principally, Macarius, Mark, and Evagrius, in insisting that it is the same Holy Spirit who is received at baptism and to whom we pray. Dadisho is here commenting on a Macarian text (Logos S1).

[50] Macarius insists that there is no immunity from temptation in this life, see, for example II 17.6, 26.23, and 38.4. Evagrius has a similar intuition, see, for example, *Gnostikos* 37 (p. 158) and *Schol. Eccl.* 46 (p. 142).

*apatheia* with love, a further reminder that Christian impassibility does not demand the cessation of emotion. Logos G26.2 goes on to declare: 'To throw yourself before God with knowledge and to obey his commandments in humility leads to love, and love leads to *apatheia*.' In this schema the author follows Macarius, rather than Evagrius, in regarding *apatheia* as the fruit of love (cf. Macarius, II 45.7; III 28.3.4[51]). Both Macarius and the *Asceticon* link *apatheia* to Christ: the *Asceticon* calls it the Lord's body; Macarius treats the indwelling Christ as the source of human *apatheia* (I 40.1.1). Both also associate *apatheia* with the life of God (G24.1; cf. Macarius, I 46.1.10).

The treatment of *apatheia* in the *Asceticon* appears to be in several respects related to that of Macarius. This is particularly true of the warning against presumptuous declarations of *apatheia* on the part of certain inexperienced and over-hasty monks. It does, however, come close to suggesting that *apatheia* constitutes the term of the spiritual struggle, something Macarius could not, in the context of the Messalian controversy, allow.

## 7.5  The Imitation of Christ

The *Asceticon* emphasizes the biblical theme of the imitation of Christ to a degree unusual in the early monastic tradition.[52] This emphasis is most evident in the theme of the ascent of the Cross, an element Draguet takes to be indicative of the second redactional layer. Logos G13 (*passim*) vividly stresses the need to participate in every aspect of Christ's life on earth and especially in every facet of his Passion. As Logos G18.14 declares: 'Blessed is he who has been crucified, has died and been buried, and has risen again in newness [cf. Rom. 6: 4], when he sees himself in conformity with the nature of Jesus and following in his holy footsteps [ . . . ].'[53] Logos G16.126 explains that: 'The Cross of Jesus is the control of

---

[51] Logos G19 follows Logos 28 of Collection III only up to the end of §2. This text does not, therefore, figure in the Isaian version.

[52] For the scriptural roots of this theme, see especially 1 Peter 2: 21. There is some basis for the *Asceticon*'s keen appreciation of the mystery of the Cross in the Scetiote tradition, see *AP* (Alph.), Poemen 144 (PG 65 357B).

[53] See, on the theme of 'newness' in Macarius, the lucid and informative work of Davids, *Das Bild vom neuen Menschen*, *passim*. The only drawback to this work is that it is limited to Collection II.

all the passions, until they are quite cut off.' Logos G21.25 adds
that the Cross the Lord urges us to take up (Matt. 10: 38) demands
the ceaseless vigilance of the intellect, its establishment in the
virtues, and its determination never to descend from the Cross—
which is the control of the passions—until the passions are destroyed and the intellect rises again invincible (or unconquered)
(ἀήττητος).[54] The ascent of the Cross is therefore the acquisition of
the state of *apatheia*. Logos G21.54 asserts that the bearing of the
Cross is the sum of all virtue and adds: 'The Cross is the destruction of all sin, and brings forth love. For there is no Cross without
love.' The extermination of the passions brings man to the true
sabbath and to the resurrection which is in Christ (G22.4–5).

Macarius also gives unusual precedence to the imitation of
Christ and to man's participation in the mystery of the Cross.
With Isaiah he shares the intuition that if one wishes to share in
the glory of Christ, one must be ready to participate in his
sufferings. As Christ passed through sufferings and was crucified,
so also must the Christian be crucified (II 27.1). The Christian is to
be 'nailed to the Cross' (II 18.11), and 'configured to [Christ's]
death' (II 10.4). He is to contemplate Christ's wounds (III 3.1.3);
indeed through his crucifixion to the world he is to carry those
wounds in his own body (I 40.2.10; cf. Gal. 6: 14, 17). Although
there are clearly differences in the two accounts, and no apparent
literal dependence, the very fact that both give such unusual
emphasis to man's participation in the crucifixion enables us to
establish a broad connection between them in this regard.

### 7.6 Prayer

Logos G4 prescribes many prayers for the night, observing that
'prayer is the light of your soul' (G4.7).[55] Isaiah goes on to give an

---

[54] Draguet gives, from the Syriac (Sx1v.25), 'invaincu'. 'Invincible' would certainly fit
with the understanding of *apatheia* discussed in the previous section. The Sa parallel to this
text is the only mention of the theme of the ascent of the Cross in that collection, a theme
generally held by Draguet to be indicative of the second layer. The Sa text does not include
the reference to the unconquered/invincible intellect. This certainly backs up Draguet's
claim that the theme of *apatheia* is a feature of the second layer.

[55] Logos G4 (περὶ συνειδήσεως τῶν καθημένων ἐν τοῖς κελλίοις) is attested in Sa for the
most part. Draguet notes that even the evidence of Sa, in certain places, 'est suspect de ne
plus représenter le texte tout à fait primitif', *Les Cinq Recensions*, i. 151.

example of a prayer to be used in time of combat (G4.75). This prayer is not a short 'arrow' prayer, such as we find in Macarius and others, but a lengthy supplication. He recommends that prayers be made with tears (G9.32) and entreats the reader: 'Love continual prayer, so that your heart should be illumined' (G16.23). Logos G26.40 describes continual prayer as one of the three things, with constant fear and control of the heart, of which a solitary has need. Similarly, continual prayer destroys the state of captivity brought about by the Fall (G16.96). By continual prayer Isaiah seems to understand constant petitionary supplication, as for example in Logos G21.50–2.

There is little in the *Asceticon* on implicit prayer, or prayer as a state of being. It speaks of a hunger for the remembrance of God (G17.3) and regularly refers to the practice of μελέτη. With prayer and manual labour, this is held to be one of the three chief works of the monk (G9.20). The monk is not to abandon his meditation even when engaged in manual labour (G1.10, 15)[56] or on a journey (G3.4). Such meditation will keep the soul from the passions (G16.74). The *Asceticon* gives little indication of what this meditation is to consist of, although it can be presumed from early monastic practice in general that it chiefly means a constant meditation upon Scripture. On only one occasion is the *Asceticon* more specific, advising a constant recollection of the pains of hell interspersed with brief intervals of wailing and intense prayer (G27.7).[57] This is not a practice recommended by Macarius.

Occasionally, the *Asceticon* provides some indications of the nature of prayer. It does, for example, speak of prayer 'in sweetness of love and pleasure of heart' (G25.1). It also touches upon the theme of undistracted prayer. The monk must not allow any illicit pleasure to infiltrate his prayer (ibid.). He must also be careful not to hold any resentment against anyone when praying—otherwise he is merely going through the motions and not praying with the intellect (G18.10). Logos G16.21 recommends a state of interior

---

[56] Isaiah is a great enthusiast for manual labour, thereby clearly distinguishing himself from the Messalians.

[57] Draguet regards this Logos (=Sxxiv.2–18) as second-layer, possibly comprising some more primitive elements. On the recollection of the pains of hell, cf. *AP* (Alph.) Evagrius 1 (PG 65 173ABC). Evagrius recommends, unlike the Isaian text, that the recollection of hell should be balanced by a meditation upon the glories of heaven—an altogether more cheering prospect!

recollection: 'May your thought be one (γένηται οὖν εἷς ὁ λογισμός σου) in God, so that he might guard you.' This is conceivably related to Macarius' understanding of the gathering of the thoughts in prayer εἰς ἕνα λογισμὸν ἔνθεον (III 18.2.2). Overall, it must, however, be admitted that the teaching on prayer contained in the *Asceticon* is by no means as rich as that of Macarius, nor, despite certain similarities, obviously related to it.

### 7.7   Baptism and the Eucharist

We have already noted the *Asceticon*'s apparent rejection of the Macarian theory of coexistence in Logos G25.3 and its two-stage understanding of baptism in G25.22. Elsewhere the teaching on baptism revolves around the intimate connection between baptism and asceticism. Logos G13.2 explains: 'Baptism is this: the suffering of evils in humility, and stillness.'[58] Similarly Logos G18.14: 'everybody who has been baptized should crucify the counter-natural evils which have taken hold of Adam and thrown him down from his glory into bad repute and everlasting shame'. In G16.129–30 Isaiah underlines the seriousness of post-baptismal sin, but allows for the possibility of repentance up to the last breath (cf. G8.65).[59] The insistence that baptism necessarily entails *ascesis* is certainly in harmony with Macarius' theory of baptism. The *Asceticon* does not, however, develop the theme, nor does it take up the Macarian distinction between hidden and revealed grace. Its treatment in comparison with that of Macarius is both jejune and unguarded; it seems far removed from the baptismal controversy sparked by the Messalians.

The theme of the eucharist receives even less attention. In one of his apophthegms, Isaiah says of holy communion: 'They call it union with God. But when we are vanquished by the passions, whether by anger, jealously, seeking to please men, vainglory, hatred, or any other passion, we are far from God. Where is union with God then?' (G8.57). The implication seems to be that

---

[58] This Logos (περὶ τῶν ἀγωνισαμένων καὶ τελειωσάντων) (=Sx1x) is characterized as second-layer by Draguet, *Les Cinq Recensions*, ii. 357.

[59] Cf. also Mark, III 977A (the need for repentance after baptism) and 980B (the debt of repentance right up to death).

the eucharist will not effect union with God while we remain subject to the passions. This is again, to say the least, an unguarded teaching. As with baptism, Isaiah's teaching on the eucharist is considerably less developed and less careful than that of Macarius.

## 7.8 The Heart

Isaiah's grasp of the function of the heart is essentially biblical; he regards it as the thinking centre of the human person and the locus of the spiritual struggle. Frequent mentions of the heart are particularly characteristic of the material classified as first-layer by Draguet. In Logos G6.9, Isaiah describes the way in which the venom of evil spreads outward from the heart to infect the soul. This is the same, traditional, understanding of the relationship between heart and soul we find in Macarius (cf. II 15.20–1).

In Macarius the conscience is charged with 'reproving' the heart, encouraging natural thoughts, and rebuking sinful thoughts (II 15.33–4). In G4.99 Isaiah observes, commenting on Matthew 5: 25: 'They say that the conscience is an accuser ($\dot{\alpha}\nu\tau\acute{\iota}\delta\iota\kappa\sigma$).'[60] It is tempting to think that Macarius is one of those whom Isaiah is thinking of here, but given that Macarius never comments on Mathhew 5: 25, and does not refer to the conscience specifically as an 'accuser', this remains only a distant possibility. Isaiah is more likely to be thinking of Evagrius, who does indeed call the conscience an 'accuser'.[61]

In Logos G17.7 the heart is likened to a field:

Just as a field cannot gainsay the person who is working to cleanse it from tares and to sow in it the natural seed, {so also should he who has given himself to God with knowledge not gainsay him in anything, but love him above all the unnatural things sown in his heart, which are the tares, and throw himself before him with all his heart at all times in knowledge. And it is God's mercy to cleanse him from the tares and to sow in him the

---

[60] Sa9.99 is more specific. Instead of the vaguer 'they say' of G4.99 (=Sx1.99), it gives: 'one of the old ones has said that the thought which reproves man is itself his accuser'. Note that this, older, version gives 'thought' rather than 'conscience'. This example also indicates the greater precision of vocabulary that has crept into the corpus in the redactional process.

[61] *Gnostikos* 39, p. 163.

natural seed,} for natural seeds cannot grow with unnatural ones, because they are suffocated by them.[62]

This is not an obvious borrowing from Macarius. The inspiration is scriptural, rather than Macarian. The passage speaks of the heart as 'field' rather than as 'earth'. Many of the formulations and themes are distinctly Isaian. Notwithstanding the superficial similarity with the Macarian theme of 'working the earth of the heart', the passage does not support a firm connection.

## 7.9   Monastic Life

Much of the *Asceticon* is taken up with practical advice as to the conduct of the monk and the regulation of the monastic community. Logos G1 (ἐντολαὶ τοῖς ἀδελφοῖς τοῖς μετ᾽ αὐτοῦ) sets the conditions for entry into the community and gives some idea of the nature of that community.[63] A regular synaxis is envisaged (G1.7, 11, 16). Contact between the brethren is discouraged except where absolutely necessary (GI 11, 18, 19). A weekly rota of duties is followed (G1.10) and a certain amount of common work is foreseen (G1.12). The brethren appear to eat their meals in common (G1.17). It is a simple, direct piece that would seem to preserve for us the unembellished voice of Abba Isaiah of Scetis. Logos G3 (περὶ καταστάσεως ἀρχαρίων καὶ τῶν κελλιωτῶν)[64] contains a great deal of advice for those beginning monastic life, dealing with contact with strangers, conduct while journeying, behaviour at table, and much else. It provides further insight into the kind of community to which Isaiah addressed himself. Logos G4 (περὶ συνειδήσεως τῶν καθημένων ἐν τοῖς κελλίοις)[65] gives us further information as to the nature and quality of Isaiah's ascetic teaching. For example, you should tell an elder your

---

[62] The bracketed portion is missing in many of the Greek MSS. It is not included in Chitty's provisional text. It is attested in MSS ξ (Moscow, Vladimir 177) (12th cent.) and β¹ β² (Venice, Marcianus 132) (13th cent.). Draguet gives the Greek text and notes that the idea that God alone can eradicate sin or evil is a Macarian trait, also seen in S111.3 (= Macarius, 11 3.4), *Les Cinq Recensions*, ii. 452.

[63] MS ξ tells us that these precepts have been written up by a disciple by a disciple named Peter (G1.2, 28 (ξ)). Draguet classifies the Logos as a slightly modified version of a primitive text, thus an example of the first layer.

[64] This Logos forms part of Sa, and is therefore classified as clearly first-layer by Draguet.

[65] Also attested, for the most part, in Sa.

thought freely 'if you know that he is worthy of confidence and will guard your word' (G4.3). G4.43 warns the monk not to be tempted by demons into excessive ascesis. Throughout, Isaiah is concerned to give the body what is necessary to it in terms of sleep and nourishment. His is a very measured, but strict, ascesis. G4.47 illustrates this nicely with a dialogue between the body and the soul, in which the body is seen as a slightly sluggardly, but well-meaning, helpmate of the soul. It seems from G4.49 that some monks retained slaves on entering the monastery; this practice is abhorred. One should avoid heretics altogether, not even attempting to dissuade them (G4.67–8). Logos G5 (περὶ ἐντολῶν πιστῶν καὶ οἰκοδομῆς τῶν θελόντων μετ᾿ εἰρήνης οἰκῆσαι μετ᾿ ἀλλήλων)[66] appears to be a kind of supplement. In G5.48 Isaiah explains that he had written this Logos 'because the first ones (τὰ πρότερα) have not sufficed for you'. Indeed Isaiah has, so he says, 'forced himself' to write—suggesting a certain reluctance to commit himself to the written word. The Logos is concerned with peaceable communal relations: politeness at table, non-competitiveness at work, the need for humility in attempting to interpret Scripture, and so forth. Isaiah puts particular emphasis on confession—do not, he advises, say one thing for another, or as if it happened to someone else, but simply say the truth (G5.32). Logos G6 (περὶ τῶν θελόντων ἡσυχάσαι ἐν ἡσυχίᾳ καλῇ)[67] contains advice on the reading of Scripture and, again, on the need for discretion in choosing a confessor. Logos G9 (ἐντολαὶ τοῖς ἀποταξαμένοις)[68] contains further advice on the monastic life. In all these Logoi there is little sign of Macarian inspiration. Only in two areas of the *Asceticon's* teaching on the monastic life is there even a distant connection.

The emphasis placed on living in exile (ξενιτεία) in Logos G17 (περὶ τῶν λογισμῶν τῆς ἀποταγῆς καί ξενιτείας)[69] may reflect the experience of one forced to leave his monastic settlement for a more uncertain future. This would certainly fit with Isaiah of

---

[66] Draguet classifies this Logos (=Sx11) as SB, very much in the manner of Sa, yet without correspondence in it. Exceptions to this are sections (12) and (24–5), taken as second-layer by Draguet, *Les Cinq Recensions*, i. 206.

[67] Draguet observes, 'cette pièce comporte des parallèles de contenu avec Sa et son style est coptisant'. He therefore classifies it as SB, *Les Cinq Recensions*, i. 74*.

[68] Largely preserved in Sa.

[69] Predominantly second-layer according to Draguet, with some elements of a more primitive source, *Les Cinq Recensions*, ii. 447.

Scetis, forced to leave that settlement by barbarian incursions. There is however no obvious hint of autobiography in this section, in which ξενιτεία is insisted upon as a necessary feature of the ascetic life. For Isaiah, monasticism implied a clear break of familial and local ties.[70] Macarius also emphasizes this theme in such a manner as to suggest that he himself was leading his monastic life away from his country of origin (1 54.1.2). He also groups ξενιτεία with fasting and vigil as examples of exterior asceticism, contrasting them with the superior works of inward asceticism (1 8.1.1, 53.4.5). The treatments are not especially close.

The short Logos G20 (περὶ ταπεινοφροσύνης) offers a succinct definition of humility as: 'to reckon oneself to be a sinner and one who does nothing good before God' (G20.2). It goes on to detail certain ways in which that humility is to manifest itself.[71] Dadisho explains that in providing this definition, Isaiah is in fact completing and expanding the rather shorter definition given by Abba Macarius:

Now this very humble Abba Isaiah, having seen that Abba Macarius when questioned by the brethren on the subject of humility had written only of humility before men, saying: 'Humility is to suppose oneself to be the least and most insignificant of all men',[72] had the idea to write comprehensively on the two sides of humility—humility before God and humility before men—and in doing so observing very finely the gradations of humility.[73]

Dadisho is here pursuing one of his chief aims, that of situating Isaiah firmly within the context of the spiritual tradition of, in particular, Macarius, Evagrius, and Mark. Isaiah's definition of humility may indeed have been intended as an expansion of the definition of Macarius of Egypt, but for this we have only Dadisho's intuition to rely upon. The example indicates the limits to the Macarian material at Dadisho's disposal. The Greek

---

[70] For *xeniteia* in Isaiah, see Guillaumont, *Aux origines du monachisme chrétien*, 98–100.

[71] A parallel description is found in Logos G26.11

[72] Dadisho is thinking of Epistle 6 of Macarius the Egyptian in the Syriac recension (Macarius, *Syr.* 6, pp. 111–16). This letter is not, in its present form, the work of our Macarius, containing as it does apophthegmata of Poemen and John Kolobos, see Dörries, *Symeon*, 386. The definition of humility is, however, paralleled in Macarius, 11 18.8. Speaking of those exercised by the Spirit, Macarius writes, 'At other times they are so humbled below all men in the humility of the Spirit that they consider themselves the last and least of all men.'

[73] *Discours* IV. 2 (translated from Draguet's French).

Collections contain a great deal more on the subject of humility than do the Syriac, amply dealing with both humility before God and humility before man. Christians are to reckon themselves as nothing before God and as servants of all men (I 16.4.4)—no matter if they have performed ten thousand acts of righteousness (II 10.4). Even if he is an elect of God, the Christian is to consider himself a reprobate (II 41.2).[74] While there is a certain similarity between the definitions of humility proposed by Macarius and Isaiah, it does not, I believe, rise above the level of the commonplace.

## 7.10   The Inner Liturgy

On several occasions the *Asceticon* makes use of the theme of the inner liturgy, all of which belong to Draguet's second layer. Perhaps the most interesting example is G5.25: 'But become rather an altar of God in purity, acting the inner priest, continually offering incense, morning and evening, so that the altar should never be without incense.' This theme of the inner liturgy is taken up again in Logos G7.30: those who have cut off their own will and lost their soul in this world have become 'holy sheep for the slaughter' (cf. Rom. 8: 36). Logos G17.2 has it that, 'he who works and rejects the passions of the body with all its faults by repentance makes his soul precious so that it is an irreproachable offering to God and worthy to become his temple'. Lastly, in Logos G27.7 the monk is advised to be, by his prayer and meditation, 'as if always performing the *synaxis*' (ὡς ἀδιαλείπτως σύναξιν ποιῶν).

This is a theme also developed by Macarius, who sums up his teaching as follows: 'The whole visible dispensation of the Church of God came about for the sake of the living and intellectual essence of the rational soul, made in the image of God, which is the living and true church of God. [ . . . ] For the Church of Christ and the temple of God and the true altar and living sacrifice is the man of God' (I 52.1.1). Macarius also speaks of the good works of the soul as incense (I 63.4.5)[75] and likens the sacrifice of the soul to

---

[74] Elsewhere, humility is treated as the chief distinguishing mark of Christianity (II 15.37, 26.11) and as one of the principal elements involved in the imitation of Christ (I 10.1.8).

[75] Here his point is that the works of the soul must be consummated by the fire of the Holy Spirit to be truly acceptable before God.

those of the Old Testament (II 1.5–6; III 7.2.1). The theme is not, of course, peculiar to Macarius. It is essentially biblical, and became a common theme in Christian writing.[76] The usage of the theme in the *Asceticon* is not sufficiently close to that of Macarius as to support a connection.

### 7.11   Exegesis

The *Asceticon* contains a great deal of interesting exegesis. Broadly speaking, Draguet classifies as second-layer sections which contain an abundance of scriptural quotations or an allegorizing exegesis, especially where introduced by the phrase οὗτός ἐστιν ὁ λόγος. Logos G4 is a good example. In the context of the story of Jacob, the author gives the meaning of the word 'Mesopotamia': the Tigris signifies discernment, the Euphrates humility. Equally, Leah is a type of bodily labours, Rachel of true contemplation (G4.109). There is little in all this interesting exegesis to put us in mind of Macarius. A more straightforward, albeit ingenious, approach to Scripture is to be found in Logoi G11 (περὶ τοῦ κόκκου τοῦ σινάπεως) and G12 (περὶ τοῦ οἴνου). Draguet takes these to be basically first-layer.[77] The explanation of the mystery of the wine is the more developed of the two: every stage of wine-making and wine-keeping has its analogy in the spiritual life. They have no significant parallels in the Macariana.

The treatment of the wise and foolish virgins in Isaiah (G16.131) is not dependent on that given by Macarius (I 49.2.1). The interpretation of the story of Lazarus in Logos G21 is equally distant from that of Macarius; it takes Lazarus as being the intellect, bound by the many 'grave-clothes' (cf. John 11: 44) of its own desires (G21.61). In Macarius, Lazarus is treated rather as a symbol of Adam, 'whose soul had come to stink and was filled

---

[76] On the inner liturgy, see also Ch. 5.4.6 and Ch. 8.12.

[77] *Les Cinq Recensions*, i. 75\*–76\*. His reasoning on this point provides a good example of his methodology in general: 'La sobriété de l'écriture, la simplicité de la typologie bien éloignée de l'allégorisme de SC [i.e of the second layer] et le caractère coptisant du style invite à ranger le fond de ces logoi dans la manière Sa [i.e. as SB]. Qu'ils ne contiennent ni préceptes ni sentences gnomiques implique seulement que la couche la plus archaïque ressortissait à plusieurs registres.' He does, however, admit that they may contain elements of the second layer, *Les Cinq Recensions*, ii. 352. We may justifiably ask whether Draguet himself has taken sufficient account of the different registers of the *Asceticon*.

with blackness and darkness' (II 30.8). The *Asceticon* describes Martha and Mary as being 'mortification and mourning' (G21.61). Macarius, conversely, takes the approach that was to become more or less standard, treating the two sisters of Bethany as representations of work and prayer, both 'springing from the same blessed root' (*EM* 11.9–11).

Logos G22 (περὶ πράξεως τοῦ καινοῦ ἀνθρώπου) begins by revealing the hidden meaning of three aspects of the Old Testament: circumcision, the Passover, and the sabbath. Circumcision is the type of the new man manifested by the Lord in his body, in whom nothing of the old man remains (G22.2). Macarius almost invariably speaks of the 'circumcision of the heart' (cf. Rom. 2: 29). This is a phrase used by Isaiah only very occasionally (e.g. G5.48). Isaiah understands the foreskin as the Pauline 'old man', Macarius as the impurity of sin (II 47.1; III 28.4.2).[78] The approaches are analogous but unrelated. The same may be said of the account of the Passover in G22.3, as compared with that of Macarius in II 47.4–9: the accounts parallel one another only on the most general level. The third exposition is of the meaning of the Sabbath (G22.4–5). Draguet points out that the same theme is developed in Macarius, II 35.1 (he might also have added III 28.4.2). This is true, but there are significant differences in the respective descriptions. Macarius does not, for example, speak of the sabbath of the Passion as the archetype of the soul's sabbath. The similarities that do exist are not weighty.

## 7.12   Other Aspects

The *Asceticon* often makes use of farming imagery, as for example in the following:

If man does not attain conformity to the nature of the Son of God, all his efforts are in vain. [Similarly,] the farmer who sows his seed expects that it will multiply greatly. If it is spoiled by the wind, there is sadness in his heart because of the waste of the seeds and of the labours he expended upon the earth.   (G18.13)

There is a similar image of a saddened farmer in Macarius:

---

[78]  Cf. also I 40.2.1; II 26.23, 32.4.

The farmer scatters his seed everywhere; and he who plants a vine wishes that it should bear fruit all over. If he takes up the sickle and finds no fruit, he is saddened. [ . . . ] As the farmer is saddened at the unproductive land, so the Lord is saddened at the unproductive heart.   (II 32.11)

Macarius' farmer is used to illustrate the sadness of the Lord at the unyielding earth of the human heart. Isaiah's is used to illustrate the fact that if man does not come to conformity to the nature of the Son of God, all his labours are in vain. The difference in context and in formulation makes this a jejune example.

Logos G4.78 offers another farming simile: 'Just as the earth cannot bear fruit of itself, without seed and water, so also it is impossible for man to bear fruit without suffering and humility.' This recalls Macarius, I 50.1.4: 'If the earth abides by itself, receiving neither the attention of the farmers to clear it from tares and thorns and to plant in it the seed, nor rain and winds and sun so that the fruits in it might grow, it is unfit, for the earth of itself is unable to bring forth ripe fruits. [ . . . ] In the same way, human nature [ . . . ] is unable of itself to bring forth the perfect fruits of the virtues [ . . . ].' Although the development of the image in each case is different—Macarius uses it as an illustration of the necessity of divine grace—this does represent a possible connection.

In Logos G14 (πράξεις τοῦ πένθους) we are offered a beautiful description of the soul's recognition of its own weakness, and its struggle with despair.[79] Isaiah laments in G14.3: 'The doctor is good, and does not request payment, but my laziness prevents me from consulting him.' Draguet points out a similarity to Macarius, II 48.4, in which Christ is also portrayed as a doctor.[80] The similarity is a rather distant one, and the image is in any case biblical.

Logos G18.12 declares that 'there is a hidden struggle of the heart in labour and in sweat not to allow his arrow to wound your heart'.[81] This sort of language fits very well with the profoundly militant character of Macarian asceticism, recalling Macarius' call to the Christian to discover the inner 'struggle of the heart, the

---

[79] Draguet believes that the combination of copticisms with certain themes of the second layer suggests that this is a light reworking of a primitive source, *Les Cinq Recensions*, ii. 370.

[80] *Les Cinq Recensions*, ii. 372 n. 9.

[81] Logoi G17 and 18 (=Sxxvi) are classified as predominately second-layer by Draguet, *Les Cinq Recensions*, ii. 447.

hidden battle' (II 21.3), to persevere with 'much labour and sweat of the brow' and to 'remove [himself] far from the arrows of evil' (III 1.2.1).

The gravity of the spiritual struggle is expressed in language which frequently recalls Macarius. The Fall has reduced man to a state of 'bitter servitude' (πικρὰ δουλεία) (G26.8, 35).[82] This is exactly the phrase used of the Fall by Macarius (I 50.1.1, 61.1.8, 61.2.3). The *Asceticon* also speaks of the Fall as a descent into a state of 'captivity' (αἰχμαλωσία) (G17.2), again, as we have seen, a common usage in Macarius (e.g. I 61.1.8). Even after the Incarnation and the gift of baptism, man remains subject to evil, indeed Logos G16.100 has it that 'we are all constrained (βιαζόμεθα) by the enemy'. Macarius is, as we have seen, considerably more circumspect in his use of the language of violence.[83] There are also hints of the theme of indwelling evil in the *Asceticon*. Logos G22.6 observes that we are unaware that 'the enemy is in us and agitates us and makes us go astray every day' (cf. G25.1).[84] The idea that mankind is unaware of indwelling evil is a *leitmotif* of the Macarian corpus.[85] The *Asceticon* describes evil as a 'thick fog (γνόφος) upon the earth' (G25.26) and speaks of the 'terrible mist' (δεινοτάτη ἀχλύς) that surrounds the mind (G29.104).[86] Both of these strongly recall Macarian imagery. The latter, in particular, recalls the δεινὴ ἀχλύς which binds and shackles the intellect in I 18.6.11.

The *Asceticon* has a substantially similar understanding of the importance of the will as does Macarius, and illustrates this importance in similar terms. Isaiah has: 'Every man binds himself for hell, and releases himself. For nothing is more inflexible than the will, whether it inclines to life or to death' (G18.1). Macarius has: 'If somebody wishes, he may become a son of God or again a son of perdition, because free will remains' (II 27.11). Notwithstanding the slight difference in the presentation of this theme,

---

[82] Both examples are classified as second-layer by Draguet, *Les Cinq Recensions*, ii. 425, 427, 434.

[83] Cf. Ch. 5.4.4 and Ch. 6.6.2.

[84] Logos G22 (=Sxx) is regarded as second-layer by Draguet, *Les Cinq Recensions*, ii. 362.

[85] See for example II 16.10: a witty comparison with a group of men submerged by a vast flood-tide who fail to recognize the fact and remark only, 'we heard the sound of water'.

[86] Logos G29 has no Syriac equivalent.

I am tempted to treat this parallel as a plausible suggestion of a connection.

Logos G21 (περὶ μετανοίας) is a substantial piece dealing with many different themes. Some thirty-nine of the sixty-three sections have parallels in Sa, although, as Draguet observes, the Sa elements may themselves represent a development from a more primitive form.[87] Where the Sa elements are compared to G and S, the process of the evolution of the Isaian corpus can often be clearly perceived. The following example, dealing with a theme much used by Macarius, gives some insight into the different qualities of the various recensions.

Sa11.3: He who wants the kingdom, does its works; *and if man tastes the sweetness of the love of God*, he no longer obeys the works of sin of evil passions; he is clad in all the parts of the armour of good works [ ... ].

Sx1v.3: But he who wants to enter the kingdom, does its works, for the kingdom is the destroyer of sin. The enemies do indeed sow, but their thoughts do not germinate; *if the intellect comes to taste the sweetness of the divinity*, their arrows no longer enter it, for it is clad in the armour of the virtues [ ... ].

G21.3: But he who wants to enter the kingdom, does its works, for the kingdom is the destroyer of sin. The enemies sow, but their thoughts do not germinate. *For if the intellect comes to contemplate the sweetness of the divinity*, their arrows no longer enter it. For it is clad in the armour of the virtues [ ... ].

The italicized phrase, particularly as given in S and Sa, does recall Macarius although, of course, the taste of the goodness, if not the sweetness, of God is a biblical image (Ps. 33(34): 8). Conscious experience, expressed as the taste of the sweetness of the divinity, is treated as the foundation of the inviolability of man or, more specifically, the intellect. G21 has omitted the verb 'to taste'.[88] This makes it appear less obviously Macarian, although the guiding principle remains the same. The version in Sa is noticeably simpler than that of G and S: for 'intellect' it has 'man', and for 'divinity', 'the love of God'. The remark is, in fact, rather less circumspect than anything we might find in Macarius. Although Macarius treats the taste of God as an absolutely essential component of the Christian life, the foundation of discernment,

---

[87] *Les Cinq Recensions*, ii. 249.

[88] I say 'omitted' assuming that Sa11 relies on a Greek source more primitive than G.

and the sense of spiritual plenitude,[89] he invariably qualifies such
remarks by insisting on the need never to relax one's efforts, as for
example in III 12.2.1–4, in which it is held to be axiomatic and
indeed necessary that the taste of grace be followed by the taste of
sin in order that the soul can advance in spiritual experience:

> The soul of one who has tasted grace initially rests in a heavenly repose
> foreign to this world, so that it might know the sweetness of the Good by
> experience. But then if the intellect is distracted, or converses [with evil],
> or does some other thing, it is again filled with sin, so that it might be
> afflicted and learn by experience the bitterness of sin.   (III 12.2.1)

If it knew only sweetness, repose, and joy, it would necessarily
become negligent (III 12.2.3). In Macarius the taste of grace is
always a starting-point, hence its intimate connection with the
theme of *epektasis*, particularly clear in I 21.11. The cry taken up
by Farsight the eagle in C. S. Lewis's *The Last Battle*, 'farther up
and farther in!', is heard throughout the Macariana. This is a
dimension that is largely lacking in the *Asceticon*. As was seen to be
the case in our discussion of *apatheia*, the *Asceticon* is considerably
less careful than Macarius in allowing that the conscious experience of grace can usher in an inalienable state of grace. This
suggests that the *Asceticon* is either 'infected' with Messalianism
or, and this is the more likely scenario, distanced from the Messalian controversy, possibly even unaware of it. If the *Asceticon* has
borrowed from Macarius in this instance, it has not sufficiently
heeded the accompanying caveats.

There is, however, a partial qualification in what follows in
G21.3–4 (=SXIV.3–4), a qualification which is, significantly,
absent in Sa. G and S assert that the taste of the sweetness of
God will allow the intellect to concentrate upon 'knowing and
discerning the two ways, [in order] to flee the one and love the
other. Thus if someone has known the glory of God, he will also
have known the bitterness of the enemy'.[90] In other words, one
cannot know the good without experiencing what is evil. This is
very much a Macarian intuition. God has ordered things such
that, 'by its experience of the two natures, tasting frequently both
the bitterness of sin and the sweetness of grace, the soul might

---

[89] For taste and discernment, see I 5.4.4, 33.4.4 and III 12.2.1–4. For taste and plenitude,
see II 14.2 and 15.20.

[90] Note the use of the ancient Jewish metaphor of the 'two ways', cf. *Didache* 1.1.

become more perceptive and more vigilant, so as to flee evil
entirely and to attach itself wholly to the Lord' (III 12.2.2).
Although the version of this theory presented in the *Asceticon* is
less dynamic and graphic, it does appear to be at least partly
dependent upon it. The fact that it does not appear in Sa makes
it very tempting to suppose that it represents a kind of Macarian
qualification of the Isaian text on the part of the composer of the
second layer.

The Logos also contains other elements of a Macarian flavour.
For example: 'Whoever wishes to become a disciple of Christ must
flee from the passions. If he does not cut these off, if he is not
removed from them, he will not be able to become a dwelling
place of God, nor see the sweetness of God's divinity' (G21.17–18).
Sa11 has 'see the light of the divinity'[91] for 'see the sweetness of his
divinity' and has 'cannot be a disciple' (cf. Luke 14: 27) for 'dwelling place of God'. Sx1v has 'taste the sweetness' for 'see the
sweetness' and, like G21, speaks of becoming a 'dwelling place of
God'.[92] Here G and, particularly, S resonate more clearly with
Macarian notes than does the more primitive Sa. While the theme
of divine indwelling is, of course, profoundly biblical, the link
established here between it and conscious 'tasted' experience
does suggest a Macarian influence.


### 7.13  Conclusion

Having examined the *Asceticon* in detail, we may now step back
a little and take an overview of the question before us: Can
the *Asceticon* be regarded as a work composed in the Macarian
tradition?

Let us not underestimate the originality of the Isaian corpus.
Despite the scant regard for originality amongst ancient monastic
writers, the *Asceticon* develops some very striking insights, perhaps

---

[91] One might expect 'light of God' rather than 'light of the divinity' from Sa. Draguet
notes the equally unexpected references to the intellect in Sa, *Les Cinq Recensions*, ii. 256 n.
He has, as we have noted (above, n. 55), warned that even the Sa collection may not be as
primitive as we might like it to be.

[92] The Logos contains other references to divine indwelling, for example: G21.22: 'He
says these things [i.e. John 15: 4–5] to those who renounce the world, because the Spirit is in
them and dwells in their hearts (cf. John 14: 17–18).' See also G21.23 and G15.96.

the most remarkable being the treatment of the ascent of the Cross
and the theory of the natural passions. Nonetheless, the corpus is
in many respects a very traditional piece of work. Besides Scripture, the chief literary and spiritual inspiration of the *Asceticon*,
there are definite affinities between much of the work of Isaiah
and certain sections of apophthegmatic literature. Père Couilleau
in his appendix to the French translation has also pointed out
certain affinities with the *Life* and the *Letters* of Anthony.[93] As for
Evagrius, my own study of the *Asceticon* has convinced me that his
influence is not marked.[94] The *Asceticon's* list of vices is quite
independent of Evagrius, as is its own *Antirrhetikos*. Furthermore,
it does not make use of the Evagrian three-fold schema of the
spiritual life. There are certainly traces of Evagrius, but overall the
*Asceticon* cannot be regarded as a work composed in the Evagrian
tradition.

In what therefore does the Macarian element in the Isaian
corpus consist? Logos G25 has clearly been influenced by Macarius, although the most substantial parallels are on the level of
imagery rather than theology. In the remainder of the corpus,
the theory of the natural passions has been seen to be independent
of either Macarius or Evagrius, although the treatment of *apatheia*
does exhibit certain similarities with both. The themes of the
imitation of Christ and the ascent of the Cross are given in the
Isaian corpus a degree of attention unusual in the fourth and fifth
centuries but, as we have seen, not without precedent in the
Macarian writings. While we have found no very tangible textual
parallels in this area, this does establish a broad connection between our writers. The Isaian treatment of prayer is meagre in
comparison with that of Macarius, and does not appear to be in
any significant way dependent upon it. The treatment of the
sacraments appears as spare and unguarded when set against
that of Macarius. The *Asceticon* does not, moreover, develop the
Macarian distinction between hidden and revealed grace. There
are some general similarities between the respective understand-
ings of the heart, but these do not rise above the level of the
commonplace. Isaiah's extensive precepts on the monastic life

[93] 'Entre Scété et Gaza', 350, 363–4.
[94] There is some scholarly disagreement concerning the extent of Evagrian influence in
Isaiah. It is emphasized by Regnault and Guillaumont, and rather played down by
Draguet, *Les Cinq Recensions*, i. 82*–83*.

are not tangibly paralleled in Macarius. The shared theme of the inner liturgy is not dealt with in a sufficiently close manner to prove dependence. Our examination of exegesis has produced no firm parallels. There are some possible links with Macarius in some of the farming imagery used in the *Asceticon*. The *Asceticon*'s estimation of the grievous captivity brought about by the Fall, and the contrast it makes with the liberation, *apatheia*, newness, and divine indwelling brought by Christ, are in many respects in the tradition of Macarius. The understanding of the seriousness of the struggle of the heart, the metaphors used for evil, and the emphasis on the importance of human free will are also very close to what we find in Macarius. Lastly, the Isaian language of taste and of spiritual experience, albeit both less circumspect and less developed than that of Macarius, does provide some clear signs of Macarian inspiration.

As should be clear, Macarian influence in the *Asceticon* of Abba Isaiah is distinctly uneven. Furthermore, where Macarian influence is clear, it is often not profound, rarely going beyond the level of shared imagery. There are also many aspects of Macarius that are not taken up in the *Asceticon*. There is little use of the language of sense or experience and no reference to spiritual plenitude. The only developed treatment of the role of the Holy Spirit in the *Asceticon* is the Macarian piece Logos G19 (=III 28.1–2). There is equally little nuptial or clothing imagery. Even where aspects of Macarian teaching have been used, such as the language of indwelling sin and the theme of tasted experience, these are generally rather diluted by the time they reach the pages of the *Asceticon*.

There is certainly, as we have seen, a connection between the Isaian and Macarian corpora. It must, however, be acknowledged that on the vast majority of points where a Macarian link is at all firm, these belong to what Draguet has characterized as the second redactional layer. In other words, I have found no firm Macarian parallels in what Draguet has classified as unambiguously first-layer material. This connection helps to explain the almost seamless insertion of Logos G19 into the Greek recension, and of Logoi I and III into the Syriac. The insertion of the Macarian logoi into the Isaian corpus can be regarded as having been eased by the affinity produced between the two corpora by the integration of Macarian material into the body of the *Asceticon* on the part of the composer of the second layer. One might even call it the culmination of a process of 'Macarianization'.

There is much that can and should be said in criticism of Draguet's theory. He does not seem to recognize the fact that because much of Sa is found amongst apophthegmatic literature, it is bound to be restricted in scope and theoretical development. He gives too little weight to the divergence of genre within the *Asceticon* and does not allow sufficiently for the enormous impact of the traditional and oral character of transmission upon its material. His ascription of themes to the second layer can often appear arbitrary and to be over-reliant on the silence of the restricted Sa collection. He is certainly correct in seeing Macarian elements in the second layer, yet his argument runs a certain risk of circularity, defining Macarian elements as features of the second layer and identifying the second layer by its Macarian components—although it must be admitted that his argument does not stand or fall on the Macarian question. While it is not my business here to make any minute judgement upon Draguet's claims as to the genesis of the Isaian corpus, it must be acknowledged that, notwithstanding the flaws noted above, he has presented a very persuasive case that is, broadly speaking, borne out by this study.

The *Asceticon* of Abba Isaiah may therefore be regarded as a work that acquired its present shape within the Macarian tradition. Given the historical obscurity surrounding both Macarius and the *Asceticon*, it is at present impossible to give any precise indication of how and in what manner Macarian material shaped and inspired the *Asceticon*. That it did do so is, I submit, certain.

# 8

# Maximus the Confessor

## 8.1 Introduction

It has become apparent in the course of twentieth-century scholarship that the work of Maximus the Confessor represents not merely a compilation but an original synthesis of the various theological, ascetic, and philosophical traditions in which he himself was nurtured. His is an outstanding example of that creative affirmation that lies at the heart of any truly living tradition. From this perspective it has become possible to approach the analysis of his sources not as an exercise in anatomy, but as an attempt to understand the living sinew of his thought or, to put it another way, the inner dynamic of his thinking.[1]

Maximus was evidently a very erudite and well-read man. His principal reading matter was, naturally, Scripture, of which he had a profound and searching knowledge.[2] He was well grounded in the Hellenic philosophical tradition, in Plato, Aristotle, and Neoplatonism. Perhaps his greatest affinities lay with the Christian Platonists, with Clement of Alexandria, and, notwithstanding his many reservations, Origen, with the Cappadocian Fathers and 'the great Dionysius'. His Christology owes much to Cyril of Alexandria, his anthropology to Nemesius of Emesa. From the monastic tradition, the influence of Evagrius has long been recognized, and more recently the contribution of Macarius and Diadochus has begun to be appreciated.

---

[1] Berthold attacks what I call 'anatomical' and he calls 'reductionist' approaches in his 'The Cappadocian Roots of Maximus the Confessor', 51. Louth, *Maximus the Confessor*, ch. 2, provides an excellent summary of Maximus' sources.

[2] Maximus' approach to Scripture is perhaps best displayed in his *Quaestiones* AD *Thalassium*, a commentary on various, generally obscure, passages of Scripture, selected by his friend Thalassius. Maximus tends to interpret these opaque passages in the light of his own spiritual teaching, an approach that can seem a little forced at times. See, on the *Quaestiones* AD *Thalassium*, the invaluable study of Blowers, *Exegesis and Spiritual Pedagogy*.

Maximus is never confined by his sources, nor does he place any value on repetition.[3] Andrew Louth has shown how much Maximus' work on Gregory Nazianzen involved a rethinking of the Theologian's thought.[4] Maximus has also recast Dionysius, integrating him within a system that is far more overtly Trinitarian and Christocentric.[5]

Most important for our purposes is the debt of Maximus to Evagrius. That Maximus knew and made extensive use of Evagrius has been ably demonstrated by Viller.[6] Viller holds that Maximus owes 'l'essentiel de sa doctrine spirituelle' not to Dionysius or Gregory, but to Evagrius, from whom he has 'toute l'ossature de son système'. Viller sees structure as the principal debt of Maximus to Evagrius. In particular, Viller shows that they share the same tripartite conception of the soul, ultimately derived from Plato, the same understanding of *pathos* and *apatheia*,[7] and the same tripartite division of the spiritual life, with many points of contact on each stage, beginning with faith and culminating in pure prayer. He produces a host of parallels to support his case which, while not all of equal value, add up to a compelling argument. We shall return to many of the themes treated by Viller in the course of our discussion. Viller does not, however, get entirely carried away by the force of his own arguments. He rightly acknowledges that Maximus 'ne copie jamais servilement, il interprète'. Furthermore, he acknowledges that Maximus had 'autres apports', though he says little about what these were. Others have, however, begun to be more specific.[8]

---

[3] This is nicely illustrated in his *Mystagogy*. Maximus writes that he will not repeat what has already been said concerning the divine liturgy by Dionysius, adding that, 'It would be foolish and presumptuous and near madness for those who are not yet able to grasp or understand what he experienced to treat of the same subject, or to bring forward as their own the things that were revealed by the Spirit to him alone' (*Myst.* 660D–661A, tr. Berthold).

[4] 'St Gregory the Theologian and St Maximus the Confessor: The Shaping of Tradition'.

[5] It should noted that Dionysius himself may, in some respects, be drawing on Macarius. Golitzin, in his detailed exploration of Dionysius' possible sources, discusses several points of contact between the two writers, *Et introibo*, 373–85. Certain of these points will be treated in the course of this chapter as they arise.

[6] 'Aux sources de la spiritualité de Saint Maxime: Les oeuvres d'Évagre le Pontique'.

[7] I dispute this claim below, Ch. 8.11.

[8] Dalmais may be credited with having given a certain impetus to this process. Regretting the currency given to Viller's 'massives affirmations', he asked: 'L'orientation n'est elle pas radicalement différente?' 'L'Héritage évagrien dans la synthèse de Saint Maxime le Confesseur', 357.

There has been a growing awareness that Maximus read both Evagrius and Dionysius within the context of a wider spiritual tradition. Attention has been drawn to the possible influence of the Macarian tradition, especially as mediated by Diadochus of Photice.[9] This is particularly the case in the work of Juan-Miguel Garrigues, who sees a distinct Macarian influence in Maximus' understanding of the synergy of divine and human wills and in his approach to the baptismal mystery.[10] Alain Riou broadly follows Garrigues and observes that it was through the Macarian current, probably mediated by Diadochus, that: 'Maxime a reçu l'axe de l'intégration et de synthèse des systèmes origénien et dionysien: la grâce baptismale d'adoption filiale en vue de la synergie des volontés, le primat de la charité dans la divinisation, la prière du coeur et sa dimension pneumatologique, qui sont tous des thèmes typiquement macariens'.[11] Jean-Claude Larchet argues that the Macarian tradition played a key role in Maximus' critique of Origenism. He writes that while the *Centuries on Love* appear, on the level of form, to be strongly marked by Evagrius, in fact they 'rectifient très sensiblement sa doctrine, l'influence de celle-ci étant par ailleurs largement contrebalancée, dans la spiritualité maximienne, par celle de Macaire d'Égypte, de Diadoque de Photicé et de Marc l'Ermite'.[12] He cites Macarius as one of the principal precursors of Maximus' understanding of free will and of the divine and deifying character of the light witnessed in prayer.[13] The thesis of Macarian influence is not, however, without its detractors, notably Lars Thunberg.[14] The question of Macarian influence remains wide open. Viller has shown that Maximus owes the 'ossature' of his spiritual teaching to Evagrius. We must now ask whether a Macarian heart beats within that skeleton. To answer this question we shall examine the relation between our authors under a series of headings, beginning with the Transfiguration.

---

[9] See the references given in des Places, 'Maxime le Confesseur et Diadoque de Photicé'—a short but useful piece.

[10] Garrigues, *Maxime le Confesseur*, 121–3.

[11] Riou, *Le Monde et l'église selon Maxime le Confesseur*, 39–40.

[12] *La Divinisation de l'homme selon Saint Maxime le Confesseur*, 12. Cf. also 678.

[13] *La Divinisation de l'homme*, 140, 510.

[14] See his review of Louth's *Maximus the Confessor*, discussed below, Ch. 8.9.

## 8.2   The Transfiguration

Andrew Louth has noted that in focusing on the Transfiguration, Maximus was picking up on a monastic tradition already found in Macarius.[15] We will take this theme as our starting-point, beginning with a survey of Greek patristic commentaries on the subject.

Irenaeus mentions or alludes to the Transfiguration of Christ only rarely.[16] He writes that the Word was made flesh 'so that the Father's light might come upon the flesh of our Lord, and then go out to us from his resplendent flesh'.[17] Clement of Alexandria is the first patristic writer to give the theme any prominence. For Clement, it represents the revelation of God in a body of flesh. The fleshly eyes of the disciples were empowered by the Saviour to see the divine light that the soul alone could properly perceive.[18] Origen takes the Transfiguration to be not a change in Christ's nature but a revelation of that nature, accessible only to those with eyes able to see his 'wonderful and more divine' condition.[19] He sees Moses and Elijah as representing respectively the spiritual law and prophecy.[20] Origen homes in on the garments of Christ. These are the sayings and letters of the Gospel with which Christ clothed himself, rendered white as light to those with a true understanding.[21] They also prefigure the 'bright garments' (λαμπραὶ περιβολαί) with which the righteous will be clad at the resurrection.[22] Between Origen and Chrysostom, we have relatively few references to the Transfiguration. Gregory Nazianzen declares that its light is the very light of the Godhead.[23] Gregory of Nyssa writes that only he who has put on the bright garments of the Lord and has been transfigured with him can really under-

---

[15] *Maximus the Confessor*, 45. Lars Thunberg in his review of the same, 64, writes that monastic interest in the Transfiguration is not exclusive to Macarius, but he gives no examples. In point of fact, no other monastic writer before Maximus gives the Transfiguration such prominence.

[16] On the theme of the Transfiguration in the patristic tradition see McGuckin, *The Transfiguration of Christ in Scripture and Tradition* and Veniamin, 'The Transfiguration of Christ in Greek Patristic Literature'. Both, disappointingly, omit to discuss the Macarian understanding of the Transfiguration.

[17] *AH* IV.20.2.2 (SC 100, p. 631). This appears to be an implicit reference to the Transfiguration. The only explicit reference is *AH* IV.20.2.9 (pp. 655–7).

[18] *Strom.* VI.16 (GCS 52, p. 503); *Excerpta de Theodoto* 4–5 (GCS 17, pp. 106–7).

[19] *Contra Celsum* IV.16 (GCS 2, pp. 285–6).

[20] *Contra Celsum* VI.68 (GCS 3, p. 138).

[21] *Comm. in Matthaeum* 12.38 (GCS 40, pp. 154–5).

[22] *Fragmenta in Lucam* 140 (GCS 49, pp. 283–4).            [23] *Or.* 40.5–6 (SC 358, pp. 204–8).

stand the soul's yearning for God.[24] Chrysostom explains that at the Transfiguration Christ 'opened out a little of the Godhead and showed them the indwelling God'.[25] Only so much was seen as was possible without damaging the eyes of the disciples.[26] He also holds that the Transfiguration is to be seen as a partial revelation of the nature of Christ's resurrected body.[27]

Cyril of Alexandria takes the Transfiguration as a foreshadowing of the resurrection glory of the body and as a demonstration of the unity of Christ.[28] Proclus of Constantinople, like Chrysostom, takes it as only a partial revelation of the invisible glory of Christ. It was a vision that presented itself to the disciples' 'eyes of the mind'.[29] Dionysius links the Transfiguration squarely to the eschatological vision: 'In most holy contemplation we shall ever be filled with the sight of God shining gloriously around us as once it shone for the disciples at the divine Transfiguration [...] we shall have a conceptual gift of light from him [...] we shall be struck by his blazing light.'[30] Lastly, Anastasius of Antioch also stresses the eschatological dimension—the Thaboric revelation is the revelation of the deification that awaits humanity.[31] Having sketched the background, we may now turn to Maximus.

Maximus deals with the Transfiguration principally in *Quaestiones et dubia* 190–2, *Ambigua* 10 and the *Centuries on Theology and the Incarnate Dispensation of the Son of God* 1.97 and 11.37–8.[32]

---

[24] *Cant.* hom.1 (GNO 6, pp. 14–15).

[25] *Ecloga de imperio potestate et gloria* (PG 63 699).

[26] *Ad Theodorum lapsum* 1.11 (PG 47 292).

[27] *De futurae vitae deliciis* 6 (PG 51 352). Chrysostom's sense of the partial nature of the Thaboric revelation is anticipated by Ephrem. For Ephrem, the Transfiguration took place principally to assure the disciples about both the Resurrection of Christ and the general resurrection. The disciples 'did not see his naked divinity, but only a little of his divinity in the body that came down to them'. *Commentary on the Diatessaron* 14.5–12 (SC 137, pp. 244–50). Similarly *Hymns on Faith* 7.3 (CSCO 154, p. 92 tr. Morris): 'He gleamed a little on the Mount; trembling and aghast were those three whom the Apostle accounted pillars. He granted them a sight of his hidden glory commensurate with their strength.' Macarius, notwithstanding his Syrian background, does not share in this line of interpretation. For the Transfiguration in Ephrem, see also his *Hymns on the Nativity* 1.34–7 (CSCO 186, p. 5): Moses comes up from Sheol and Elijah comes down from heaven to see the Son 'in the middle'.

[28] *Homilia in transfigurationem* (PG 77 1009–16).

[29] *Or. viii in transfigurationem domini* (PG 65 764–72).

[30] *DN* 1.4 (PG 3 592C, tr. Luibheid).

[31] *Sermo i in transfigurationem domini* (PG 89 1361–76).

[32] The works are cited in the chronological order posited by Polycarp Sherwood, *Date-List of the Works of Maximus the Confessor*, respectively 626 (p. 26), 628–30 (pp. 31–2), and 630–4 (p. 35).

In *QD* 190 (p. 132) Maximus links the Transfiguration with our resurrection: 'Thus he glorified the assumed humanity so that in the same way that he was seen transfigured upon the mountain in his passible body, so also shall we be in the resurrection, receiving an incorruptible body.' Maximus goes on in *QD* 191–2 (pp. 132–5) to discuss various aspects of the Gospel accounts in terms of the contemplative ascent that culminates in the Transfiguration of the Lord on the mount of theology, a revelation that can only be expressed apophatically. He observes that the Transfiguration is the manifestation of the hidden nature of the Word. The garments of the Word represent the sayings of Scripture and the created world rendered lucid. The three tabernacles indicate the three stages of the spiritual life as formulated by Evagrius: the practical, natural, and theological, corresponding to Elijah, Moses, and the Lord respectively.

In *CT* 1.97–8 (1121C–1124B) Maximus refers to two forms of the Lord, one obvious, one hidden. The first, to which Isaiah 53: 2 (LXX) refers, is seen by beginners. The second, corresponding to Psalm 44(45): 2, is seen only by those who have become like Peter and John, and have been 'perfected in spiritual knowledge, in so far as such perfection is possible'.[33] Maximus then speaks of the interiorization of this second form, this second *parousia*, within us. *CT* 11.13–16 (1129C–1132C) continues with the double-form theme and goes on, like *CT* 1.97–8, to speak of the interiorization of the mystery of the Transfiguration. The theme of interiorization is one to which we shall return below.

*Ambigua* 10, dealing with Gregory's treatment of the ascent through materiality to God, is woven around the Transfiguration. The theme of the piece is ascent, of which the Transfiguration is the supreme example. The apostles' ascent of Thabor is very much an inward ascent: 'And they passed over from flesh to spirit, before they had laid aside this fleshly life, by the change in the operations of sense that the Spirit worked in them, lifting the veils of the passions (τῶν παθῶν τὰ καλύμματα) from the intellectual power that was in them' (*Amb.* 10.17, 1125D–1128A).[34] They were

---

[33] Note the juxtaposition of the 'beginners' and the 'perfected'. As in Macarius, such distinctions do not presuppose the existence of separate classes of Christians. Maximus is here relying on Origen, see below n. 35.

[34] Gregory Nazianzen had referred to matter and the fleshly as a cloud or veil in the passage from his Oration 21 upon which this *aporia* is centred.

taught that the all-blessed radiance that shone from Christ's face and which overpowered the sight of the eyes was 'a symbol of his divinity which transcends intellect and sense and being and knowledge' (ibid.). Christ's garments, symbols of the words of Scripture, became clear to them, as did the *logoi* of creation (1128BC). This is a mystery in which we too participate: 'Thus ascending the mountain of the divine Transfiguration, we shall see the garments of the Word—by which I mean the words of Scripture and the phenomenal creation—radiant and glorious by virtue of the dogmas that transform them, splendidly set forth by the divine Word for exalted contemplation' (*Amb.* 10.18, 1132C).

*Ambigua* 10.31 returns to the theme. The light that appeared to the senses of the disciples 'is a symbol of what is hidden and unmanifest' (1160C). The light that overwhelmed their senses indicated that God is 'by essence beyond ineffability and unknowability and countlessly raised beyond all infinity' (1168A). Moreover the Transfiguration points to: 'the two universal modes of theology: that which is pre-eminent and simple and uncaused, and through perfect denial alone truly affirms the divine, and fittingly and solemnly exalts its transcendence through speechlessness; and then that which follows it and is composite, and from that which has been caused magnificently sketches out [the divine] through affirmation' (*Amb.* 10.31, 1165B).

Maximus' account draws most obviously on Origen and Dionysius. Völker has neatly summarized the debt owed by Maximus to Origen in respect of the double form of the Logos and the correspondence between Christ's shining garments and the words of Scripture.[35] The Dionysian background is patent in Maximus' use of the distinction between apophatic and cataphatic theology and the language of unknowing, although we must note Ysabel de Andia's argument that while Maximus has drawn certain key structures from Dionysius, he has used these with very different Christological and ontological presuppositions.[36] We shall now turn to Macarius' treatment of the theme.

---

[35] 'Christi Verklärung auf dem Tabor in der Deutung des Maximus Confessor und des Gregorius Palamas'. Appendix to *Scala Paradisi*, 315–27. Origen, developing Philippians 2: 6–7, has the Lord appearing to beginners 'in the form of a servant' and to the perfect 'in the form of God'.

[36] 'Transfiguration et théologie négative chez Maxime le Confesseur et Denys l'Aréopagite'.

The light of the Transfiguration permeates the Macarian writings.[37] It is that light Macarius calls his followers to experience within themselves. Macarius takes the Transfiguration principally as the illustration *par excellence* of the showing-forth of the inner glory in the outward body:

As the body of the Lord was glorified when he ascended the mountain and was transfigured into the divine glory and the infinite light,[38] so too are the bodies of the saints glorified and resplendent. For as the glory that was within Christ covered his body and shone forth, in the same way the power of Christ that is [now] within the saints will overflow outwards upon their bodies.  (II 15.38)[39]

Macarius' account stands in the tradition of Irenaeus, Clement, and Origen, seeing the Transfiguration as the revelation of Christ's divine nature. He takes the Transfiguration as a demonstration of the nature of the resurrection body, that is, of the body that perfectly reflects the state reached by the soul in this life. He equates the garments of Christ with the 'luminous garment' granted to those attaining perfection. Speaking of himself in the third person he recounts:

Another time he was clad in something like a luminous garment such as does not exist on the earth in this age and which cannot be produced by the hands of men. And as when the Lord went up to the mount with John and Peter and James, and his clothes were transfigured and shone, such was this garment.  (II 8.3)

This kind of clothing imagery is an illustration of Macarius' Syrian background, although it must be noted that there are certain precedents in the Greek tradition—notably the example from Origen given above. In his treatments of the Transfiguration, Macarius does not discuss the disciples' apprehension of the vision. Elsewhere he writes, in the context of Paul's blinding vision, that the divine light is beyond the endurance of fleshly eyes (I 58.2.2). For Macarius, the divine light is experienced by means of the spiritual senses, freed from the darkening veil of the

[37] On the Transfiguration in Macarius see Staats's excellent 'Die Metamorphose des Christen. Die Wandlungslehre des Makarios-Symeon im Zusammenhang seiner Anthropologie, Christologie und Eucharistielehre'.

[38] For 'infinite light', cf. Maximus, *CC* II.6, p. 308, cited below.

[39] For the reflection of the state of the soul in the body in the next life, see also Origen, *De Principiis* II.10.8 (GCS 22, p. 182).

passions.[40] One of the most striking and original elements of Macarius' treatment is the connection he sees between the Transfiguration and the Crucifixion:

The Lord shows himself to [the soul] in two aspects, with the stigmata and in the glory of his light, and the soul contemplates the sufferings which he suffered for it, and contemplates the dazzling glory of his divine light and is transformed from glory to glory in this same image [cf. 2 Cor. 3: 18], according to [the action of] the Spirit of the Lord, and grows in both aspects. (III 3.3.2)[41]

It will be obvious to the reader that there are many differences in the two treatments of the Transfiguration. There are, however, also some clear points of contact. Maximus picks up on the theme—central to Macarius but also found in Origen and Cyril—of the Transfiguration as an illustration of the resurrection glory of the body. Both are also united in recognizing the uncreated nature of the light of the Transfiguration, thereby following an established tradition. Maximus also appears to have picked up on Macarius' 'veil of the passions'. Perhaps the theme that connects them most closely is that of the extension of the mystery of the Transfiguration in those held worthy. Maximus' second form of the Logos 'is a prefiguration of the second and glorious advent, in which the spirit [of the Gospel] is apprehended, and which by means of wisdom transfigures and deifies [true] gnostics; because of the transfiguration of the Logos within them, "they reflect with unveiled face the glory of the Lord" [2 Cor. 3: 18]' (*CT* 1.97, 1124A). Similarly:

[40] Maximus, as we have seen, expands upon Gregory's designation of the body as a veil to speak of the Spirit's lifting of the 'veils of the passions' from the intellect. This is an interesting and uncommon phrase. Macarius designates the 'veil of the passions' as the inheritance of the Fall (I 59.1.1; cf. I 25.1.7 and III 26.5.3). This veil—which he also calls the veil of darkness, evil, sin, and the enemy power (II 28.4; I 26.12; III 3.1.4; and II 8.3)—prevents the soul from seeing God (III 26.4.4). The power of the Spirit removes the veil, illumining the intellect with heavenly light (III 26.6.2). Clement of Alexandria makes one reference to a 'veil of the passions' (προκάλυμμα τῶν παθῶν), *Paed.* II.10.99 (GCS 12, p. 216). Origen associates the passions with the veil laid because of evil upon the *hegemonikon* and preventing us from seeing the glory of God, *In Jeremiam* 5.9 (GCS 6, pp. 38–9). We may also mention the solitary reference to the 'veils of passion' (προκαλύμματα τοῦ πάθους) spoken of by Chrysostom, *In epistulam I ad Corinthios* (PG 61 12). Clearly there are other precedents for Maximus' usage, particularly in Origen, but the frequency with which Macarius employs the image, together with the emphasis he places on the role of the Spirit in the removal of the veil, makes him in this respect Maximus' most obvious forerunner.

[41] See also III 12.2.3. For other references to the appearance of Christ in his luminous glory, see II 17.4 and III 3.2.1.

In the worthy, the Logos of God is transfigured to the degree to which each has advanced in virtue, coming to them with his angels in the glory of the Father. For the more spiritual principles in the Law and the prophets—which Moses and Elijah symbolized in their appearance with the Lord at his Transfiguration—manifest the glory that is in them according to the receptive capacity (τὴν χωρητὴν δύναμιν) of the worthy to whom they are revealed. (*CT* 11.15)

Compare the following passages from Macarius:

As one perceives the sun through seeing the brilliance of its rays [ . . . ] so those who bear the heavenly image of Christ and possess in themselves the ineffable light [ . . . ], perceiving the beauty of the ineffable light that is within them, see with the 'unveiled face' of the soul the ineffable variety of the incorruptible glory and how it is transfigured 'from glory to glory' [2 Cor. 3: 18]. (1 10.3.1–2)[42]

[God is able] to change himself, reduce himself and, in embodying himself, to assimilate to himself holy, worthy, and faithful souls, according to [their] capacity (κατὰ χώρησιν) [ . . . ]. As he wishes, he reduces himself, embodies himself and is transfigured, manifesting himself to those who love him in an unapproachable glory of light. (11 4.11–13)

In Maximus, *CT* 1.97 and Macarius, 1 10.3.1–2 the extension of the mystery of the Transfiguration is connected with 2 Corinthians 3: 18. Furthermore, both speak, following Origen, of this mystery being extended to 'the worthy' 'according to capacity'. This gives us grounds to suppose that Maximus was inspired by Macarius in his treatment of the interiorization of the Transfiguration.[43]

On a more general level, we should note that Macarius is the first monastic writer to treat of the Transfiguration at any length. In the monastic tradition he is certainly Maximus' most obvious forebear. He is also one of the foremost propagators of the theology of the divine light that was to flourish so spectacularly in Symeon the New Theologian and the fourteenth-century Hesychasts. Maximus is also very much part of this tradition. This is made clear in his striking description of the sign of the second (higher) state of pure prayer: 'At the very onset of prayer,

---

[42] Golitzin has drawn attention to the parallel between this passage and Dionysius, *DN* 1.4 (PG 3 592C), *Et introibo*, 375 n. 176. It also recalls *DN* 4.4 (697B–700C).

[43] The only other hint of this theme I have found is in the passage from Gregory of Nyssa cited above: we must be 'transfigured with Christ'.

the intellect is ravished by the divine and infinite light and is aware neither of itself nor of any other created thing whatsoever, but only of him who through love has activated such radiance in it' (*CC* 11.6, p. 92). The designation of this light as 'infinite' recalls the 'divine glory and infinite light' of Macarius, 11 15.38, cited above. Our authors' descriptions of the pure intellect also warrant comparison:

ὁ νοῦς τελείως καθαρισθεὶς πάντοτε ὁρᾷ τὴν δόξαν τοῦ φωτὸς τοῦ χριστοῦ. (Macarius, 11 17.4)

νοῦς ἐστι καθαρός, ὁ ἀγνοίας χωρισθεὶς καὶ ὑπὸ τοῦ θείου φωτὸς καταλαμπόμενος. (Maximus, *CC* 1.33, p. 60)

Maximus declares that once the intellect is established in God, it is 'wholly luminous' (ὅλος φωτοειδῆς) (*CC* 111.97, p. 196). Similarly, 'by continual participation in the divine radiance, the intellect becomes wholly luminous (ὅλος φωτοειδῆς)' (*CC* 11.48). This is very reminiscent of the soul that becomes 'all light' (ὅλη φῶς) in Macarius (11 1.2) or the description of all the members becoming ὅλα φωτοειδῆ in deification (11 15.11). It would not be overstating the case to say that Macarius' theology of the divine light should be recognized as one of the foremost contributors to Maximus' own mysticism of light.

To sum up, there are some important points of contact between the two accounts of the Transfiguration—most notably the theme of its interiorization. Perhaps the most important connection, deeper-seated and therefore less easily quantifiable, is in terms of the understanding of the uncreated nature of the light witnessed in prayer. It should be added as a postscript that while Maximus has, as always, taken many elements from the tradition in formulating his own account, he has used these to produce a synthesis that is very much his own.

## 8.3 The Incarnations of the Logos

Related to the theme of the extension of the mystery of the Transfiguration is that of the incarnations of the Logos in the souls of the worthy. Here Maximus draws on a prominent Macarian theme and in so doing appears to take up the controversial 'second soul' teaching of Macarius.

8.3.1   The Incarnation of God in the Worthy

Maximus speaks of the virtues and spiritual principles 'through
which God ever desires to become incarnate in the worthy' (δι᾽ ὧν
ὁ θεὸς ἀεὶ θέλων ἐν τοῖς ἀξίοις ἄνθρωπος γίνεται) (*QT* 22,
p. 143.103–4). Similarly, 'the Word of God [who is] God wishes
eternally to operate the mystery of his embodiment in all things'
(βούλεται γὰρ ἀεὶ καὶ ἐν πᾶσιν ὁ τοῦ θεοῦ λόγος καὶ θεὸς τῆς αὐτοῦ
ἐνσωματώσεως ἐνεργεῖσθαι τὸ μυστήριον) (*Amb.* 7, 1084CD). In
souls that have become 'a translucent abode of the Holy Spirit
[ . . . ] Christ always desires to be born in a mystical way (ἀεὶ θέλων
Χριστὸς γεννᾶται μυστικῶς)' (*LP* 4, p. 50.391–8). Lastly: 'In proportion to our capacity the Logos will become everything for us
who are nourished through virtue and wisdom; and in accordance
with his own judgement he will be embodied differently in each
recipient of salvation while we are still living in this age' (*LP* 4,
p. 59.554–9). This theme of the embodiment of the Logos in the
worthy is, as noted in the previous section, a prominent Macarian
theme. It is most clearly expressed in Homily 11 4.9–13. There is,
however, more to this than simply a shared theme. Maximus
develops the theme of the embodiment of the Logos using a
soul–body analogy and a 'second soul' metaphor in very much
the same way as Macarius.

8.3.2   The Soul-Body Analogy

Macarius introduces his discussion of the embodiment of the
Logos in the saints as a 'subtle and profound' matter:

The infinite, inaccessible and uncreated God has embodied himself
through infinite and incomprehensible bounty and has, so to say, reduced himself from his inaccessible glory so that he might unite himself
to his invisible creations (I mean the souls of saints and of angels),
granting them the capacity to participate in the life of the Divinity.
[ . . . ] The soul, which is a subtle body, has enveloped the eye by which
it sees, the ear by which it hears, the tongue by which it speaks, and the
hands. In short, the soul envelops the entire body and its members and is
commingled with them, and through them accomplishes all the neces-
saries of life. In the same way, the infinite and inconceivable God in his
bounty has reduced himself from his inaccessible glory and has put on
the members of this body and enveloped it; and through clemency and
love for humanity he transfigures himself, embodies himself, mingles
himself with and envelops holy, pleasing and faithful souls. (11 4.9–10)

This is the same analogy we find, albeit less graphically and with
no hint of Stoic materialism, in Maximus: 'God will be the uncircumscribed, permanent, and infinite place of all the saved, becoming all in all in proportion to righteousness, or rather to the
measure of things suffered here for righteousness' sake, giving
himself to each as the soul [gives itself] to the members of
the body (καθάπερ ψυχὴ σώματος μέλεσι) [...]' (*QT* 61,
p. 105.328–33). Furthermore we have in Maximus a version of
the Macarian 'second soul'.

## 8.3.3 The 'Second Soul'

Macarius makes this one of his master themes.[44] In effecting the
mystery of his incarnation in holy souls: '[God] becomes, so to say,
a soul in the soul and a hypostasis in the hypostasis (ψυχὴ [...] εἰς
ψυχὴν καὶ ὑπόστασις εἰς ὑπόστασιν), so that the soul can live in the
divinity, sense immortal life, and become a partaker of incorruptible glory, if it is worthy of and pleasing to him' (II 4.10). Maximus
takes up this very distinctive theme. He writes of Dionysius and
Gregory that they have realized the essence of the soul and
thereby attained the living Christ, or rather Christ 'has become
a soul in their soul' (ψυχὴν αὐτοῖς τῆς ψυχῆς γεγενημένον) (*Amb.*
Prologue, 1033A). Similarly we must strive for the state in which
'the soul becomes to the body that which God is to the soul'
(ἵν' ὅπερ ἐστὶ θεὸς ψυχῇ τοῦτο ψυχὴ σώματι γένηται) (*Amb.* 7,
1092C), or 'God is to the soul what the soul is to the body so that
the soul might receive immutability and the body incorruptibility'
(*Amb.* 7, 1088C). It is difficult not to hear in these passages of
Maximus an echo of Macarius' very characteristic second-soul
theme. Maximus may have been making an allusion which he
would expect John of Cyzicus, and indeed other readers, to pick
up. Furthermore, the fact that Maximus uses this theme, and
indeed the soul–body analogy, in the context of the embodiment(s)

[44] It is condemned in the anti-Messalian list of John of Damascus (J 16): 'They say that
man must acquire two souls, one which is common to men and one which is heavenly.' This
is in itself a perfectly orthodox notion, traditional within the Syriac tradition. It is found, for
example, in the *Demonstrations* of Aphrahat (PS 1, p. 294). See Marriott, 'The Homilies of
Macarius', 261; 'The Messalians and the Discovery of their Ascetic Book', 196. Elsewhere in
Macarius, see I 10.4–5, 63.1.2, 22.2.9; II 1.9, 12.16, 15.22, 15.35, 30.3, 30.6, 32.6, 44.9, 52.5;
III 10.2.4. Desprez justly remarks in a note to III 10.2.4: 'Ces textes expriment simplement
la distinction entre vertus acquises et vertus infuses.'

of the Logos in the saints, provides firm evidence that he is here
consciously developing specifically Macarian themes.

### 8.3.4   The Soul as a Virgin Mother

Macarius exhorts: 'Let the wise virgin know that she must have
Christ in her as did Mary; and as she [carried him] in the womb,
so you [must carry him] in your heart' (III 28.2.1). Maximus writes
of souls that have become dwelling-places of the Holy Spirit: 'In
souls such as this Christ always desires to be born in a hidden way,
becoming incarnate in those who attain salvation, and making the
soul that gives birth to him a virgin mother (μητέρα παρθένον)' (*LP*
4, p. 50.397–400). The theme of the soul as virgin and mother
appears to have been first introduced by Origen, from whom it
passed to Gregory of Nyssa.[45] It is also found in the *Apophthegmata*.[46] Maximus may have found it in any or all of these sources.

### 8.3.5   Becoming Christ

Maximus writes that we should aim: 'to become living icons of
Christ, or rather to be like him by grace, perhaps even to be the
Lord himself' (γενέσθαι ζώσας εἰκόνας Χριστοῦ, καὶ ταυτὸν αὐτῷ
μᾶλλον κατὰ τὴν χάριν ἢ ἀφομοίωμα, τυχὸν δὲ καὶ αὐτὸς ὁ
Κύριος)[47] (*Amb.* 21, 1253D). We have in Macarius some important
precedents for this sort of audacious language: 'As many lamps are
illumined from one flame, so must the bodies of the saints, being
members of Christ become that which Christ is (τὸ αὐτὸ γίγνεσθαι
ὅπερ ἐστὶν ὁ Χριστός)' (II 15.38). Moreover, Christ is called Christ:
'so that we might be anointed with the same oil as he was anointed
with and become Christs, being, so to say, of one essence and one
body [with him] (καὶ ἡμεῖς χρισθέντες γενώμεθα Χριστοί, τῆς μιᾶς,
ὡς εἰπεῖν, οὐσίας καὶ ἑνὸς σώματος)' (II 43.1). To speak of our
becoming 'christs' through baptism and chrismation is not unusual;[48] to speak of our becoming Christ, or what Christ is,
I would suggest, is much less common. This may or may not be

---

[45] See Squire, 'The Idea of the Soul as Virgin and Mother in Maximus Confessor'. Also
Desprez's note to III 28.1.3, citing Origen (*In Ex.* 10.3: GCS 6, p. 248) and Gregory of Nyssa
(*Virg.* 2.2: GNO 8(1), p. 254 and *Cant.* 3: GNO 6, p. 96). *Virg.* 2.2 is very similar to Macarius,
III 28.2.1: what happened bodily in Mary also happens inwardly within every virginal soul.
See also Miquel, 'La Naissance de Dieu dans l'âme'.

[46] See (without, however, an explicit reference to *virgin* motherhood) *AP* (Alph.) Longinus 5 (PG 65 257B) (cited above, Ch. 7 n. 21).

[47] For 'living icon' in Macarius see I 4.30.5; III 26.4.4.          [48] See Lampe 1532 (J).

a connection between our authors. It is certainly evidence of their shared audacity.

To conclude this section, we may assert that Maximus has almost certainly picked up on Macarius in respect of the extension of the mystery of the Incarnation, the soul–body analogy, and the theme of the second soul. As regards the soul as virgin mother and becoming Christ, the connections are less certain but nonetheless significant. We may now turn to another related theme: the depiction of the image of God within the soul.

## 8.4 The Depiction of the *Imago Dei*

Macarius, Diadochus, and Maximus use the analogy of wax to illustrate the soul's taking on of the divine:

ὥσπερ ἵνα ᾖ κηρὸς οὗτος ὢν ἐν ψυχρῷ ἀέρι ἀπόσκληρός ἐστιν, ὅταν δὲ βληθῇ εἰς πῦρ καὶ ἄρχηται μαλάσσεσθαι καὶ ἁπαλύνεσθαι, τότε λαμβάνει τύπον καὶ εἰκόνα τελείαν τῆς σφραγῖδος οὕτω καὶ αὐτὴ ἡ ψυχὴ πολλάκις εἰσερχομένη εἰς πῦρ καὶ δοκιμαζομένη χρῄζει παιδαγωγίας πολλῆς, ἵν' οὕτω δυνηθῇ τὴν τελείαν εἰκόνα ἐντυπωθῆναι τοῦ Χριστοῦ καὶ σφραγῖδα ἐπουράνιον. (Macarius, III 1.1.2–3)

ὃν τρόπον μὴ θερμανθεὶς ἢ μαλαχθεὶς ὁ κηρὸς ἐπὶ πολὺ οὐ δύναται τὴν ἐπιτιθεμένην αὐτῷ σφραγῖδα δέξασθαι, οὕτως οὐδ' ὁ ἄνθρωπος, ἐὰν μὴ διὰ πόνων καὶ ἀσθενειῶν δοκιμασθῇ, οὐ δύναται χωρῆσαι τῆς τοῦ θεοῦ ἀρετῆς τὴν σφραγῖδα. (Diadochus, *GC* 94)

ἡ δὲ ψυχή, ἢ κηρὸς ὡς φιλόθεος ἢ πηλὸς ὡς φιλόϋλος [...] πᾶσα δὲ φιλόθεος, ὡς κηρὸς ἁπαλύνεται, καὶ τοὺς τῶν θείων τύπους καὶ χαρακτῆρας εἰσδεχομένη, γίνεται ≪θεοῦ κατοικητήριον ἐν πνεύματι≫ [Eph. 2.22]. (Maximus, *CT* 1.12, 1088в)

The only other use of this image I can trace is in St John Chrysostom. He uses the analogy in the context of preaching: one can either harden the soul with cold homilies or fire it up and soften it so that it takes on whatever imprint you wish, even the royal image.[49] His use of the analogy has some points of contact with that of Macarius and provides further evidence of their shared background. Diadochus' use of the image is certainly derived from

---

[49] *In epistulam ii ad Thessalonicenses* (PG 62 478): Ὥσπερ γὰρ κηρός τίς ἐστιν ἡ ψυχή· ἂν μὲν γὰρ ψυχρὰς ἐπαγάγῃς ὁμιλίας, ἐπώρωσας αὐτὴν καὶ ἐσκλήρυνας· ἂν δὲ πεπυρωμένας, ἐμάλαξας· μαλάξας δέ, τυποῖς πρὸς ὅπερ ἂν θέλῃς, καὶ τὴν εἰκόνα τὴν βασιλικὴν ἐγχαράττεις.

that of Macarius—note especially the context of trials in both. Maximus' usage is closer to that of Macarius and Diadochus than to that of Chrysostom. This looks, therefore, very like a case of Macarian influence. The fact that Macarius and Maximus, and not Diadochus, use the verb ἀπαλύνω and speak in terms of types suggests that, in this case, we are dealing with an example of direct Macarian influence.

The theme of the depiction of the *imago Dei* within us is a common one in Maximus: 'Making God himself the type and paradigm of the virtues, [Moses] modelled himself on him, like a picture beautifully reproducing the archetype (καθάπερ γραφὴν εὐφυῶς τοῦ ἀρχετύπου τὴν μίμησιν σώζουσαν)' (*Amb.* 10.5, 1117C). He who, like Moses, enters the darkness (γνόφος) which embraces knowledge of the prototypes of created things, 'through this knowledge depicts in himself (ἐν ἑαυτῷ ζωγραφήσας) the beauty of the divine virtues, as if painting a picture which is a faithful copy (ἀπεικόνισμα) of the archetypal beauty' (*CT* 1.85, 1120A). Christ is present in the perfect, 'hiddenly pre-delineating in them the features of his future advent as if in an icon' (προδιαγράφων αὐτοῖς κρυφίως τῆς μελλούσης αὐτοῦ παρουσίας ὡς ἐν εἰκόνι τοὺς χαρακτῆρας) (*CT* II.28, 1137C).

This sort of language and imagery bears comparison with a passage in Macarius in which, using the analogy of an earthly artist, Macarius observes:

Just as the portraitist attends to the face of the king and paints it, and if the face of the king is turned towards the painter and attends to him, then he is able to depict the image well and with ease. But if the king turns his face away, he cannot be painted because he does not rivet his attention upon the painter. In the same way Christ, the good artist, depicts directly in those who believe in him and rivet their attention upon him a heavenly man after his own image (ὁ καλὸς ζωγράφος Χριστὸς τοῖς πιστεύουσιν αὐτῷ καὶ ἀτενίζουσι διαπαντὸς πρὸς αὐτὸν εὐθέως ζωγραφεῖ κατὰ τὴν εἰκόνα αὐτοῦ ἐπουράνιον ἄνθρωπον). With his own Spirit, with his own substance, the inexpressible light, he paints a heavenly image. (II 30.4)[50]

---

[50] Macarius uses this kind of pictorial imagery with some frequency. He compares the authority conferred by the imperial portrait with the authority enjoyed by the soul that bears the 'glorious and heavenly and luminous' image of the Lord (I 23.1.9–10). As we adorn our houses with beautiful pictures, so God wishes to depict in the house of the body the heavenly image of the life of the Spirit (I 26.5). We may note that he regards painted images as dead. The only true icon is, therefore, the living divine image in man (I 4.30.5).

Again, Diadochus takes up the same theme. When the intellect begins to taste the Holy Spirit in full awareness, we should realize that grace has begun as it were to paint (ἐπιζωγραφεῖν) the divine likeness onto the image. As artists first draw the outline and then add the colours, so grace first restores the image and then depicts the divine likeness, virtue by virtue (*GC* 89). The divine likeness in Diadochus equates to the heavenly image—itself equivalent to the 'second soul'—in Macarius. I have traced only one other proximate[51] example of this kind of imagery, in the *Ecclesiastical Hierarchy* of Dionysius the Areopagite:

Virtuous conformity to God can only appear as an authentic image of its object when it rivets its attention on that conceptual and fragrant beauty. On this condition—and only on this condition—can the soul impress upon itself and reproduce within itself an imitation of loveliness. In the domain of perceptible images, the artist keeps an eye constantly on the original and never allows himself to be side-tracked or to have his attention divided by any other visible object. [ ... ] It is thus with those artists who love beauty in the mind. They make an image of it within their minds. The concentration and the persistence of their contemplation of this fragrant, secret beauty enables them to produce an exact likeness of God. (*EH* 473BCD, tr. Luibheid)

Note the earthly artist analogy, found in Macarius and Diadochus but not in Maximus. Note also the stress on the riveted attention of the sitter, as in Macarius. It is not to be excluded that Macarius is amongst Dionysius' sources here. The fact that Dionysius speaks of the soul's impressing upon itself the image makes it likely that he is Maximus' principal source in the first two Maximian examples given above. The references to the virtues in these two examples also recall Diadochus. The last example, referring to Christ's artistic work, is most clearly paralleled in Macarius. All the examples given from Maximus are, however, insufficiently close to any of the three main possible sources to warrant the suggestion of anything more than rather broad connections in this particular instance.

---

[51] We might also mention a rather more distant parallel in Basil: 'And in general, just as painters in working from models constantly gaze at their exemplar and thus strive to transfer the expression of the original to their own artistry, so too he who is anxious to make himself perfect in all the kinds of virtue must gaze upon the lives of the saints as upon statues, so to speak, that move and act, and must make their excellence his own by imitation' (*Ep.* 2: Courtonne, vol. i, p. 9).

## 8.5   Baptism

The understanding of baptism represents one of the most fundamental connections between Macarius and Maximus. This connection, particularly between the Macarian *Logos* 1 43 and
Maximus' *QT* 6, was noted by le Guillou in 1974.[52] It has since
been characterized by Garrigues as one of the most important
*rapprochements* between our authors.[53]

In *QT* 6, Maximus gives an answer to a question concerning the
apparent paradox between the fact of post-baptismal sin and statements such as 1 John 3: 9.[54] He states: 'The mode of birth from God
is double to us. One gives all the grace of filial adoption present in
potential ($\delta\upsilon\nu\acute{a}\mu\epsilon\iota$) to those who are born; the other makes it entirely
present in act ($\kappa a\tau'$ $\acute{\epsilon}\nu\acute{\epsilon}\rho\gamma\epsilon\iota a\nu$), transforming the free choice of the
one that is born towards God who has begotten him' (*QT* 6,
p. 69.8–13).[55] This second mode of birth is the work of the Spirit,
co-operating with the human will in the revelation of hidden grace.
Maximus goes on to argue that he who has had experience ($\pi\epsilon\hat{\iota}\rho a$) of

---

[52] Le Guillou, 'Remarques sur la notion macarienne de "subtilité"', with a translation of
*Logoi* 43 and 25 of Collection I: 'Deux homélies inédites du Pseudo-Macaire sur la
"subtilité" physique de l'Esprit'. Of the link with Macarius, Le Guillou observes: 'Saint
Maxime ayant assumé en le corrigeant tout le positif de la mystique macarienne, peut
exprimer la doctrine de la synergie avec l'Esprit, non plus en termes physiques mais dans
l'ordre intentionnel de la liberté' (ibid., 342). Le Guillou's criticism of the excessive
physicality of the Macarian *Logoi* is due in part to the tendentious translation by Manfred
Kniewasser. For instance, Kniewasser translates $\tau\grave{\eta}\nu$ $\mathring{a}\rho\chi\grave{\eta}\nu$ $\tau\hat{\eta}s$ $\mathring{\upsilon}\pi\sigma\sigma\tau\acute{a}\sigma\epsilon\omega s$ $\tauo\hat{\upsilon}$ $\pi\nu\epsilon\acute{\upsilon}\mu a\tau\sigma s$
(1 43.2 (line 5)) as 'le commencement de la substance de l'Esprit', which le Guillou takes to
imply a physical acquisition of the Spirit. A better translation would be 'real existence',
meaning, as Macarius puts it later, 'the life of the Spirit' (1 43.6 (line 26)). It is related by
Macarius to Hebrews 3: 14b: 'if we hold the beginning of [our] confidence ($\tau\grave{\eta}\nu$ $\mathring{a}\rho\chi\grave{\eta}\nu$ $\tau\hat{\eta}s$
$\mathring{\upsilon}\pi\sigma\sigma\tau\acute{a}\sigma\epsilon\omega s$) steadfast to the end'. This correspondence should perhaps be preserved.
Similarly, he translates $a\mathring{\iota}\sigma\theta\eta\sigma\iota s$ (43.2 (line 10)) as 'perception sensible'. $A\mathring{\iota}\sigma\theta\eta\sigma\iota s$ in Macar-
ius does not denote merely physical perception. 'Perception' would suffice. Lastly, Le
Guillou takes the 'subtlety' ($\lambda\epsilon\pi\tau\acute{o}\tau\eta\tau\sigma s$) of grace (43.6 (line 17)) to imply its materiality.
This is an absurd interpretation: what Macarius is saying here is simply that grace operates
in a very subtle manner, that is to say with great finesse, care, and accuracy.

[53] Garrigues, *Maxime le Confesseur*, 45 n. 10. Blowers, *Exegesis and Spiritual Pedagogy*, 6,
concurs with Garrigues on this point. Similarly Riou, *Le Monde et l'église*, 39. None of these
has, however, actually demonstrated the point. On baptism in Maximus see especially
Larchet, 'Le Baptême selon Saint Maxime le Confesseur'.

[54] 'No one born of God commits sin; for God's nature abides in him, and he cannot sin
because he is born of God.'

[55] Larchet, 'Le Baptême', n. 34, notes, quite rightly, that this twofold schema is also
found in Mark. He does not, however, point out that Mark himself has it from Macarius, as
we have shown in Ch. 5.

this process of revelation, this second birth, will not fall: 'those who are born of the Spirit have their free choice (προαίρεσις) entirely seized' and are 'rendered clearly impeccable (ἀναμάρτητος)' (ibid., pp. 69–71.28–36). Baptism has this twofold character precisely to bring into play man's free will. It is up to us to keep the incorruption conferred by baptism spotless by giving ourselves to good works and dying to our own will (*CT* 1.87, 1112B). In the *Mystagogy*, Maximus is careful to underline the ecclesial dimension of this second mode of birth: it is the Church that 'brings to light the grace of adoption which was given through holy baptism in the Holy Spirit and which makes us perfect in Christ' (*Myst.* 24, 712B). Similarly, Maximus asserts that the various baptisms mentioned in Scripture refer to a single reality (*CT* 11.63, 1152CD).

Maximus is here drawing upon the two-fold schema found in Macarius. Baptism, according to Macarius, confers the 'beginning of the life of the Spirit', a life which becomes manifest in proportion to the practice of the virtues (I 43.2), 'for baptism is the perfect pledge of the coming inheritance' (III 28.3.2; cf. Eph. 1: 14). Maximus borrows this idea of baptism as a pledge: 'The pledge of all good things and of eternal life is the grace given in baptism, of which we become partakers by the grace of our Lord Jesus Christ' (*QD* II. 9, p. 167).[56] Macarius explains that the grace of the Holy Spirit operates with such subtlety that it is initially 'neither known nor grasped' (ὡς μηδὲ νοεῖν μηδὲ καταλαμβάνειν) (I 43.6). This grace is manifested only slowly (I 43.5), until such time as 'active grace' (ἡ ἐνεργὴς χάρις) (I 25.1.9) is experienced. Grace operates in this double manner in order to embrace the self-determining free will (ἡ αὐτεξούσιος προαίρεσις) of man (*EM* 2.5). Only in this way does one grow in communion with grace to the perfect measure of man, 'which is the total liberation from passions and the active and complete inhabitation of the Holy Spirit' (I 25.2.5), and divine filiation (I 43.2).

The accounts are fundamentally symphonous. Baptism has a twofold character; this is so as to allow the exercise of human free will, which necessarily entails the possibility of post-baptismal sin. Both, however, hold out the possibility of such a perfect conjunction of free will and grace as to produce, in effect,

---

[56] Maximus may also have found this image in Mark and/or Diadochus, both of whom, as we have seen, have it from Macarius.

impeccability—neither fall into the trap of treating freedom and necessity as opposites. If anything, Macarius is more cautious on this point, consistent with his position as a reformer of the Messalian tendency. Lastly, this twofold schema precludes the confusion of the presence of grace with the sensation thereof.[57]

There are compelling grounds for treating Maximus' baptismal teaching as a development of the Macarian tradition. The influence may, however, be largely indirect. Diadochus and Mark have, as we have seen, the same intuition of the double character of baptism, in each case drawn from Macarius.[58] The point which most clearly associates Diadochus and Maximus is the connection they make between the revelation of hidden grace and the acquisition of the divine likeness (*QT* 6, p. 71.39–40; *GC* 89). Moreover Diadochus shares the emphasis on human co-operation we find in Macarius and Maximus. The prominence of the theme of filial adoption consequent upon the synergy of wills, the possibility of *de facto* impeccability, and the image of baptism as a pledge, however, link him more obviously to Macarius.

Whilst it is impossible to entirely unravel the various threads contributing to Maximus' understanding of baptism, it can be claimed with good assurance that the Macarian understanding, produced against the background of the Messalian controversy, and mediated by Diadochus and Mark, was seminal.


## 8.6   Free Will

As we have seen, the twofold understanding of baptism treated above indicates a fundamentally symphonous understanding of free will in Macarius and Maximus. We may also note certain other aspects of their respective teachings on free will that demonstrate their deep affinity in this area.

---

[57] Like Macarius, Maximus is clear that unfelt grace belongs only to the earlier stages of the spiritual life. See *Myst.* 24 (704A): the invisible grace of the Holy Spirit is especially present at the time of the synaxis even if this is not felt (using αἰσθάνομαι) by the spiritually immature.

[58] According to von Balthasar, *Kosmische Liturgie*, 318, This 'shows how orthodoxy and heterodoxy can be reconciled. For the Messalians, the invisibility of the sacramental grace (of baptism) signifies the descent into the soul of a seed of life which must develop experientially. Diadochus would be able to take up this idea virtually unchanged, and it reappears in Maximus.' For 'Messalians', read Macarius.

## 8.6.1 The Intellect in Balance

Both Maximus and Macarius stress man's self-determining nature and speak of his being in balance, poised between a good and evil angel. Maximus writes: 'Our intellect lies between two things (μέσος ἐστὶ δύο τινῶν), an angel and a demon, each of which works its own ends, the one virtue, the other vice. The intellect has both the power and authority to follow or resist whichever it wishes' (*CC* III.92, p. 188).[59] Compare, from Macarius:

> God and his angels wish every man to dwell with them in the Kingdom. Likewise, the devil and his angels wish him to dwell with them. The soul thus lies between these two realities (μέση οὖν ἐστιν ἡ ψυχὴ τῶν δύο ὑποστάσεων) and becomes the possession and son of whichever party the will of the soul inclines towards. (II 26.24)

> Two angels accompany (παρέπονται) man, one good and one bad. (I 34.3)[60]

> After the Transgression, the soul finds itself placed between two spirits, one good and one bad. (I 18.4.10)[61]

> Our intellect is equally matched (ἀντίπαλός ἐστιν), having the power to subdue evil assaults and base desires by the strength of its thought. (II 15.23)

> If someone wishes, he becomes a son of God, or again a son of perdition, because free will remains. (II 27.11)

These examples provide some very tangible points of contact. The close proximity of our authors' understanding can be further illustrated in their understanding of the co-operation of grace and free will.

---

[59] This is an ancient idea, with Jewish roots. It is found, amongst Christian sources, in The *Shepherd of Hermas*, Mandate VI.2 (SC 53bis, p. 173) and the *Epistle of Barnabas* 18.1 (PG 2 776c–777A). Both are quoted by Origen in *De Principiis* 3.2.4 (GCS 22, p. 251). Hermas speaks of the two angels, one of righteousness and one of evil, that are with man; the *Epistle of Barnabas* speaks, after the *Didache*, of the two roads, one guarded by the angels of God and the other by the angels of Satan.

[60] The passage begins, 'There is a revelation which says that [ . . . ]'. Dörries, in *Symeon*, 218 n. 2, suggests that Macarius may be referring to something like the *De exitu animae* ascribed to Macarius of Alexandria in PG 34 385 ff. Cf. also the short Logos preserved as Homily 22 of Collection II.

[61] The Messalians were accused of teaching that 'a demon is essentially joined immediately to each person who is born, this being inherited from the condemnation of Adam' (T 1). This is clearly not the teaching of Macarius, *pace* Villecourt.

### 8.6.2 Free Will and Grace

Grace is not given without the activity of man:

The grace of the Holy Spirit does not work wisdom in the saints without the intellect which receives it, nor knowledge without the receptive power of the reason, nor faith without the full assurance (πληροφορία) in reason and intellect of the coming good things hidden up to now to all, nor the gift of healing without the natural love of man, nor any of the charismata without the receptive disposition and inclination of each [...] neither does man possess any of these by natural capacity without divine power. (*QT* 59, pp. 47‒9.55‒62)

This is the same principle we find in Macarius: God does nothing without the exercise of the free will of man (II 37.10); equally man is incapable of achieving any good thing by his own activity alone (II 37.9). It is, of course, the classic tradition of συνέργεια, worked out by writers such as Irenaeus and Origen in reaction to the various deterministic religious systems of the late antique world. It illustrates the close convergence within the tradition of our authors' ways of thinking, but does not allow us to posit any very specific connection.

### 8.6.3 Free Will and Human Nature

Macarius declares: 'Man has the ability to apply himself (ἡ ἐπιτήδευσις) by nature (κατὰ φύσιν) [...]. The will of man is therefore a part of his very being (παράστασις ὑποστατική)' (II 37.10).[62] This linking of free will to nature, and not to person, may be one of Maximus' sources for his defence of the full human nature and hence the human will of Christ. Again, it illustrates the very close correspondence in our author's understanding of human free will.

## 8.7 Language of Sense and Experience
### (Πεῖρα **and** αἴσθησις)

For both Macarius and Maximus man is to exercise his free will so as to reveal and to experience the grace conferred at baptism. Maximus is, like Macarius, a deeply experiential theologian,

---

[62] Macarius regards the will as one of the four ruling faculties of the soul (II 1.3).

appealing, as Miquel informs us, to *peira* upwards of the thirty times in his works.[63] This is an element in his teaching that distinguishes him from the traditions of Evagrius and Dionysius, in whom *peira*—the conscious experience of grace (or sin)—has no prominence. Maximus speaks of the experience of evil (*CC* 11.67, p. 126), the experience of divine power (*CC* 11.39, p. 112), and the experience of rebirth in the Spirit (*QT* 6, pp. 69, 71). His appeal to experience associates him far more closely with the experiential tradition of Macarius and Diadochus which we have discussed above.[64] The importance of this tradition within Maximus' theology is particularly evident in his understanding of the experiential character of knowledge. He distinguishes two types of knowledge: 'One is relative, lying in word and concepts alone, and does not have active perception (αἴσθησις) through experience (διὰ πείρας) of the object of cognition [ . . . ]. The other, properly true, confers perception by participation of the whole of the object of cognition in active experience alone, without [recourse to] word and concepts' (*QT* 60, p. 77.63–9).[65] True knowledge is participatory knowledge, knowledge gained through the unmediated experience and perception of the thing which is known. Such knowledge suppresses relative, discursive, knowledge about the said thing (ibid., p. 77.74–86). Maximus defines experience as 'this active knowledge which comes about beyond all thought' (αὐτὴν τὴν κατ᾿ ἐνέργειαν γνῶσιν τὴν μετὰ πάντα λόγον ἐπιγινομένην) (ibid., 87–8) and perception as 'experience by participation of supernatural good things' or 'this participation in the object of cognition [that comes about] beyond all conception' (αὐτὴν τοῦ γνωσθέντος τὴν μέθεξιν τὴν μετὰ πᾶσαν νόησιν ἐκφαινομένην) (ibid., 81–2, 88–90). He also writes of the insufficiency of 'mere knowledge' (γνῶσις ψιλή) of divine things, and the

---

[63] See his *Le Vocabulaire de l'expérience spirituelle*, 120-7. See also his 'Peîra: Contribution à l'étude du vocabulaire de l'expérience religieuse dans l'oeuvre de Maxime le Confesseur'. Maximus disclaims his own experience, appealing rather to that of the saints, as in *Amb*. 10.29–30 (1157B–1160B). In this respect he anticipates the approach of Gregory Palamas, in contrast to that of, say, Macarius or Symeon the New Theologian.

[64] See Ch. 6.2.

[65] See also the distinction between academic knowledge, knowledge about the *logoi* of created things, which serves no purpose, since not directed towards the execution of the commandments, and 'actively effective knowledge which confers a true experiential apprehension of created beings (κατ᾿ ἐνέργειαν πρακτικήν, αὐτὴν ἀληθῆ διὰ τῆς πείρας τῶν ὄντων κομίζουσα τὴν κατάληψιν)' (*CT* 1.22, 1092BC).

need rather for the 'blessed passion of holy love' (*CC* III.67, pp. 174–6) in order to bind the intellect to spiritual contemplation. The emphasis throughout is upon the immediate apprehension of the thing known. This epistemology stands squarely within the Macarian tradition.[66]

Macarius distinguishes between 'mere knowledge' (γνῶσις ψιλή) and 'knowledge of truth in the mysteries of God'. He is no obscurantist, and allows that the former does offer some indications of the righteousness of God; he does insist, however, that it is superseded by the latter (I 38.2.9). The former is ἀφανὴς καὶ ἀνυπόστατος (I 18.4.13) whereas only the latter is knowledge ἐν ὑποστάσει (I 58.2.4). God is known only by experience of him, not by merely rational and discursive means but directly, in the heart ἐν πάσῃ αἰσθήσει καὶ ἐπιγνώσει (I 5.2.7). He makes very clear his exasperation with merely rational theology, theology that depends upon worldly wisdom and not upon the inspiration of the Spirit (III 16.3.3). Knowledge of the mysteries of the Spirit comes about πείρᾳ καὶ αἰσθήσει (I 50.2.1). The apostles, prophets, and martyrs, for example, experience divine love and goodness, 'not in word only, or in mere knowledge, but in word and in act through [experience of] these very things (οὐ λόγῳ μόνον ἢ γνώσει ψιλῇ, ἀλλ᾽ ἐν λόγῳ καὶ ἔργῳ δι᾽ αὐτῶν τῶν πραγμάτων)' (II 37.2).

Diadochus shares a similar understanding, albeit one expressed less explicitly. He comments that the wisdom of the world is 'unable to produce any good effect through an experience of perception (πείρᾳ αἰσθήσεως)' (*GC* 11). Elsewhere he observes that the gnostic is established above the passions 'by active experience' (ἐκ τῆς κατὰ τὴν ἐνέργειαν πείρας) (*GC* 72). Maximus has clearly picked up the experiential theory of knowledge developed by Macarius and built upon by Diadochus.

Maximus' use of the term αἴσθησις is important. In his works, the term usually refers to the physical sense or senses, often in a negative context.[67] This contrasts with Macarius, who tends to use the term αἰσθητήριον to denote the physical senses. Maximus, however, also uses αἴσθησις to denote understanding (*QD* 78, p. 59) and in reference to the spiritual senses (*QD* 43, pp. 36–7;

---

[66] The experiential epistemology of Macarius and Diadochus is discussed above, Ch. 6.2.

[67] See for example the call to mortify sense (i.e. sensuality) (*LP*, pp. 35–6.161–2) or to restrain sense activity (*LP*, p. 56.496–7).

cf. Macarius, 1 58.3.3). The most interesting example for our purposes is Maximus' reference to the faculty of intellectual or spiritual perception, the αἴσθησις νοερά: 'The Word enables us to participate in divine life by making himself food, as those who have received from him this intellectual perception (αἴσθησις νοερά) know. It is by the taste of this food that they truly know in full knowledge that the Lord is good' (*LP*, p. 34.128–32). Maximus is here clearly drawing upon the language of Macarius and Diadochus.[68]

All three of our authors insist that there can be no knowledge of God unless granted by God. Maximus writes:

A soul can never attain (ἐκταθῆναι) the knowledge of God unless God himself in his condescension takes hold of it and raises it up to himself. For the human intellect does not have the capacity to soar aloft and to share in divine illumination unless God himself draws it up—in so far as it is possible for the human intellect to be drawn up—and illumines it with rays of divine light (ταῖς θείαις αὐγαῖς κατεφώτισεν). (*CT* 1.31, 1093D–1096A)

As a rider to his discussion of the ineffable light that shines in the worthy soul, Macarius observes:

The things of God are known in truth only by the experience (τῇ πείρᾳ μόνῃ γινώσκεται) of those in whom these hidden realities operate worthily. When these operations of the mysteries of grace are realized in you, you can hear the word of God and understand beyond your knowledge, beyond your intellect, and beyond your consciousness (καὶ νοεῖν ὑπὲρ τὴν γνῶσιν σου, ὑπὲρ τὸν νοῦν σου, ὑπὲρ τὴν συνείδησίν σου). (1 10.3.3)[69]

Diadochus shares this understanding, defining knowledge as a form of ecstasy (Defn. 5, p. 84.10–11) and clearly regarding both theology and gnosis as divine charismata (*GC* 72).

Furthermore, all hold that experience is a prerequisite for speaking about the action of grace. Macarius holds that spiritual realities: 'are not to be understood through mere words; they must be achieved in the intellect in a mysterious way through the activity of the Holy Spirit (ἐργασίᾳ ἁγίου πνεύματος ἐν μυστηρίῳ

---

[68] See our discussion of the term αἴσθησις νοερά above, Ch. 6.1. Note also Maximus' use of the language of *taste*, again a distinctly Macarian theme.

[69] A striking foreshadowing of Dionysian apophatic terminology, cf. *DN* 1.5 (593A); *MT* 1.3 (1001A); *Ep.* 1 (1065A).

ἐν τῷ νῷ ἐπιτελούμενα), only then can they be spoken about'
(1 16.3.3). Maximus for his part writes: 'Only those who have
received in abundance from God in great purity of intellect all
the grace of the Holy Spirit accessible to men can speak of those
things with exactitude' (*QT* 55, p. 481.15–18). Diadochus holds that
illumination is a necessary precondition for spiritual discourse and
that 'nothing is so destitute as a mind that is outside God philoso-
phising about the things of God' (*GC* 7).[70]
   The experiential dimension of the Maximian synthesis is firmly
rooted in the Macarian–Diadochan tradition. This is particularly
evident in respect of its epistemology. Maximus has clearly drawn
on Macarius both directly and, through Diadochus, indirectly.

## 8.8 *Πληροφορία*

To express the experience of grace, Maximus uses the term
πληροφορία. This has been noted by von Balthasar and picked
up by des Places.[71] Maximus uses the term in the following ways:

[...] the higher and true intelligence which is the product of the full
assurance of heart (ἡ τῆς καρδίας πληροφορία) of those who address
themselves to the spiritual understanding of that which causes difficulties
[in Scripture]. (*QT* intro., p. 23. 96–8)

The grace of the Holy Spirit does not work [...] faith without the full
assurance (πληροφορία) in reason and intellect of the coming good things
hidden up to now to all. (*QT* 59, p. 47.57–9)

The word of grace was preached [...] to men to give them full assurance
to confess (πληροφορῶν ὁμολογεῖν) that the one God is the Creator and
Judge of all. (*QT* 64, p. 203.258–9)

[The wind experienced by Elijah at Horeb was a sign of] zealous faith
in full assurance (τὴν ἐν πληροφορίᾳ πρόθυμον πίστιν). (*Amb.* 10.12,
1121C)

---

[70] See our discussion above, Ch. 6.2. It should also be noted that Evagrius' understanding of theology certainly involves an experience of God—even if this dimension is not
stressed and the vocabulary of experience not used.

[71] Von Balthasar, *Kosmische Liturgie*, 65 n.1: 'For the assurance of the intellect and the faith
linked to reason worked by the grace of the Holy Spirit, Maximus uses the famous term
πληροφορία, which the Messalians and, on the Orthodox side, Diadochus of Photice, had
used for the unmediated and blessed certainty of heart and spiritual instinct.' Des Places,
*Maxime et Diadoque*, 34–5.

It is difficult to be precise about the exact meaning attached by Maximus to the terms πληροφορία and πληροφορέω in these instances. The first does seem to indicate something akin to Macarian plenitude, an impression reinforced by the fact that Maximus speaks specifically of the πληροφορία of the heart. The second example in its anticipatory character and association with faith can certainly be paralleled in Macarius, but is likely to be simply the product of meditation on the πληροφορία of hope and of faith spoken of in Hebrews 6: 11 and 10: 22. It is more in accord with the Basilian use of the term. The use of the verb πληροφορέω as an active transitive in the sense of to convince, to satisfy, is, according to Stewart, a usage not found in the New Testament, but pioneered by Macarius.[72] The last example seems to be an allusion to Hebrews 10: 22. Thus Maximus appears to make only very limited use of the Macarian motif of spiritual plenitude expressed by the term πληροφορία. Maximus may also have found the motif in Diadochus and/or Mark. Maximus does not make use of the (in)famous phrase ἐν πάσῃ αἰσθήσει καὶ πληροφορίᾳ.

## 8.9 The Heart

The experiential dimension discussed in the preceding sections brings us on to the locus of spiritual experience, that is, to the heart. Lars Thunberg, in his review of Andrew Louth's *Maximus the Confessor*, pours cold water on Louth's suggestion of Macarian influence, stating that, 'The reference to the Macarian metaphor "the earth of the heart" in *Opuscula* 7 is isolated and might well be a commonplace.'[73] We have shown above (Ch. 6.5) that the metaphor is not a commonplace and is, in Greek writings, directly related to the Macarian tradition. Furthermore the usage is not, in fact, isolated in the works of Maximus, as the following (beginning with the citation already mentioned) will indicate:

You have the whole warmth of the Spirit, and possess fire in the earth of the heart. (*Opuscula* 7, 69C)

---

[72] Stewart, '*Working the Earth of the Heart*', 100.
[73] Review of Louth, *Maximus the Confessor*, 64.

[We are] required to struggle always against the shameful counter-natural passions abiding in us in the earth of the heart, until we root them out and occupy this earth alone and henceforth unperturbed, all foreign passions expelled.   (*QT* 51, pp. 403–5.167–71)

God examines the earth of each heart.   (*QT* 63, p. 169.367–8)

[ . . . ] so that God might hear the earth of the heart and grant us the rain of his charismata.   (*QT* 65, p. 293.654)

After the accomplishment of ethical philosophy all the earth of the heart is filled with divine knowledge.   (*QD* 80, p. 63.85–7)

[ . . . ] the earth of his own heart is dry.   (*QD* 80, p. 63.89)

[ . . . ] the earth is Adam's heart, deprived of heavenly good things, cursed because of the Transgression.   (*QT* 5, p. 65.27–8)[74]

The four general virtues take hold of the heart of the faithful like earth.   (*QT* 63, p. 175.463–5)

He has made our earth, that is to say the heart, to quake and has rent it open.   (*Exp. Ps. LIX*, p. 9.104–5)

With the plough of the Logos we are to:

cut open the stones of the heart, to root out the tares of the passions and open up the earth of the heart to receive the divine Logos.   (*QD* 17, pp. 36–40)[75]

The metaphor is certainly not 'isolated'. The last-cited example is a particularly striking example, using as it does the Macarian theme of 'working the earth of the heart'.[76]

Maximus routinely interprets scriptural references to earth as indicating the heart: 'For earth in the Gospel means the heart' (*QD* 148, p. 105.6–7). In *Centuries on Love* he makes a straight equation between heart and intellect: 'Strive to cleanse the intellect—which the Lord calls heart—from hatred and dissipation' (*CC* IV.73, p. 226). This is exactly the equation found in Origen.[77] Elsewhere, Maximus focuses on the heart as the seat

---

[74] Macarius describes the post-lapsarian earth of the heart of Adam as a 'desert' (1 4.30.2).

[75] For the Lord's ploughing of the earth of the heart in Macarius, see 1 4.30.2. Cf. also Cassian, *Conf.* 1.22 (SC 42, pp. 106–7): the Gospel plough with which we are to work the earth of the heart.

[76] Compare the working of the field of the heart in *CC* IV.71 (p. 224) (cf. Matt. 13: 44). This may also be compared to Origen's reference to one who 'cultivates the fields of his soul' (*Homilies on the Psalms*: SC 411, p. 75).

[77] *De Principiis* 1.1.9: GCS 22, pp. 26–7.

of knowledge, no doubt in an effort to balance the bias towards the intellect evident in Evagrian spirituality. Consider the following:

All the treasures of wisdom and knowledge are hidden in our hearts. (*CC* IV.70, p. 224)

[ . . . ] in the place of divine knowledge, by which I mean the heart. (*QT* 65, p. 297.712–13)

I suppose paradise to mean the heart of man planted in the East of the knowledge of God. (*QD* 44, p. 37.3–4)

Gathering the diverse *logoi* [of creation] in the productive and contemplative part of the heart, one *logos* of God is born. (*QD* 64, p. 51.27–9)[78]

[ . . . ] he who fills the heart with theological contemplations. (*Amb.* 48, 1364c)

This is the theme of the 'knowing heart' rooted in the Bible and given particular prominence in the Macarian writings. Maximus allots to the heart a special role in contemplation, both natural and theological. By doing so he has corrected the tendency towards excessive intellectualism in Evagrian contemplation.

Furthermore, Maximus follows Macarius in seeing the heart as the locus of the spiritual struggle, the place where man encounters God and evil:

[ . . . ] having the Logos dwelling in the depths of the heart. (*QT* 56, p. 13.153–4)

The house of this thief and liar [the devil] is the heart of everyone who is inclined to love sin. (*QT* 62, p. 127.206–8)

Compare Macarius on the heart: in the heart one finds God and all the workings of evil (II 43.7, 15.32–3). Note also the vocabulary of indwelling in Maximus, again a prominent feature of Macarian spiritual teaching.

Perhaps the most arresting parallel is Maximus' reference to hearing certain accusations:

in the hidden workshop of the heart (ἐν τῷ κρυπτῷ τῆς καρδίας ἐργαστηρίῳ). (*QT* 62, p. 135.331)[79]

---

[78] Compare Macarius, III 18.2.2: 'and gathers the thoughts into one divine thought'.

[79] Elsewhere, Maximus calls our nature a 'workshop' (*QD* 1, p. 3.6); cf. Macarius, II 15.32.

This is a phrase that almost certainly originated with Macarius. It is also found in the *Vita Hypatii*, and I have argued above (Ch. 1.4) that it is a sign of Macarian influence in that work. I would submit that it puts the thesis of Macarian input in this area beyond reasonable doubt.

Maximus has used the Macarian understanding of the place of the heart to balance the primacy of the intellect found in Evagrius. This gives his anthropology a far more holistic quality. He has grounded Evagrian spirituality in the earth of a Macarian heart.

## 8.10   Love and Ecstasy (Ἀγάπη, ἔρως and ἔκστασις)

The dimension of the heart contributes to the decidedly affective tone of Maximus' spiritual teaching. This affective quality is patent in his teaching on ecstasy and love, to which we may now turn.

Gregory of Nyssa is the first Christian writer to use the theme of ecstasy with no reticence whatsoever, in marked contrast to Clement, Origen, and Evagrius.[80] Gregory uses an abundant metaphorical repertoire to describe the essential passivity of the soul's ecstatic departure from its own nature, speaking, for example, of drunkenness, vertigo, erotic desire, madness, and the wound of love. The presence of God draws the soul out of itself and renders

---

[80] Clement refers to ecstasy only pejoratively, to criticize certain false prophets, by whom he doubtless means the Montanists (*Strom.* 1.17.85: GCS 52, p. 55). He does not draw on Philo in this respect. Origen shows a similar reticence, again reacting to the Montanists. He insists that possession by the Holy Spirit, as in the case of the Hebrew prophets, enhances rather than abolishes the faculties. The intellect should not be alienated but rather rendered clearer and more perceptive when taken up into God (*De Principiis* 3.3.4: GCS 22, pp. 260–1). Even where Origen uses imagery such as the wound of love, he does not ascribe to these the ecstatic quality found in Philo or Gregory of Nyssa. The whole concept of ecstasy is similarly alien to the Evagrian system, in which the intellect by a process of elimination ascends to reunion with God. The term 'ecstasy' is used in Evagrius to describe a falling away from the human condition, such as the loss of one's wits brought about by the demons (*Praktikos* 14, p. 532). Where he speaks of the soul's 'rapture', for example, he is essentially speaking of its separation from the sensible, not of its transcending itself (*Praktikos* 66, p. 650; cf. *OP* 52: PG 79 1177C). He does suggest a certain loss of self-awareness in contemplation, comparing it to sleep (*Selecta in Psalmos*: PG 12 1644ABC) and also hints at the disappearance of the subject–object distinction in the state of true theology (*KG* IV.87, p. 175). His teaching is, however, like that of Origen, firmly centred on the discovery–recovery of the primal state of the intellect and not on self-transcendence; that is to say, on (*apo*)*katastasis*, not *ekstasis*.

it unaware of either itself or its surroundings, being wholly caught up in God.[81] Macarius makes use of Gregory's teaching on ecstasy, employing all the Gregorian metaphors mentioned save vertigo. He shares a sense of the loss of normal consciousness brought about when the soul is rapt by God. Many of Macarius' descriptions of prayer have a decidedly ecstatic quality. For example the following:

A man may be occupied throughout the day, and give but one hour to prayer and yet be carried away by it in the inner man, entering into the infinite depths of the other world in intense delight. His intellect is then wholly removed [from this world], raised up and carried away in such a way that it forgets all earthly thoughts, its thoughts rather being filled with and captivated by divine and heavenly things, by boundless and incomprehensible realities, by marvels which cannot be uttered by the mouth of man. In that hour he prays saying, 'would that my soul be taken up with my prayer'. (I 4.8)

Macarius goes on to recount, once again speaking of his own experiences in the third person:

Another time the man entered in prayer as it were into ecstasy (ὡς ἐν ἐκστάσει γέγονεν) and found himself standing before the altar of the church and three breads were brought to him, leavened as with oil, and which expanded and grew the more he ate of them. [...] Another time the very light that shines in the heart opened to the more inward, deeper, and hidden light such that the whole man was as though submerged in that sweetness and contemplation and no longer possessed himself (μηκέτι ἔχειν ἑαυτόν), but became like a fool and a barbarian to this world, because of this superabundant light and sweetness and because of the hidden mysteries [...]. (II 8.3)

Macarian ecstasy is a departure from this world, something which involves a loss of normal consciousness but which yields to a heightened awareness of divine reality.

Diadochus also uses the theme of ecstasy. He defines knowledge as 'to lose awareness of oneself through going out of oneself to God' (ἀγνοεῖν ἑαυτὸν ἐν τῷ ἐκστῆναι θεῷ) (Defn. 5, p. 84.10–11).[82] He also gives a startling description of ecstatic love. A man transformed by the love of God:

---

[81] On ecstasy in Gregory see Daniélou, 'Mystique de la ténèbre chez Grégoire de Nysse'.

[82] This and *GC* 14 are the only uses of the verb ἐξίστημι by Diadochus. In *GC* 14 he also quotes 2 Cor. 5: 13. Diadochus never uses the noun ἔκστασις. The only example of the noun or verb in Macarius in the sense of divine rapture is that given above (II 8.3).

is both in this life and not in it, for while still living in his own body, he yet migrates (ἐκδημεῖ)[83] ceaselessly from it towards God through love by the movement of his soul. Then his heart burns constantly with the fire of love and cleaves to God with a kind of irresistible longing, since he has once and for all stood outside of (ἐκστάς) self-love in his love for God.   (*GC* 14)

The soul here is brought out of self-love by the impelling force of its love for God. Ecstasy in Diadochus is a movement into true from false love. It enhances rather than erases the personalistic character of union with God.

Dionysius expresses the double movement of love between God and man in terms of ecstasy. The human person is brought out of himself such that he belongs no longer to himself but to his beloved, that he no longer lives but God lives in him. Equally, by his desire and care for his creation, God goes out of his transcendence to become immanent within it, while remaining entirely within himself (*DN* 4.13, 712AB). He goes on to write that the soul by the way of negation comes to stand outside of its own finite nature (*DN* 13.3, 981B). Detailing this process, he explains:

Here, renouncing all that the mind may conceive, wrapped entirely in the intangible and the invisible, he belongs completely to him who is beyond everything. Here, being neither oneself nor someone else, one is supremely united to the completely unknown by an inactivity (ἀνενεργησία) of all knowledge, and knows beyond the mind by knowing nothing.   (*MT* 1.3, 1001A, tr. Luibheid)[84]

---

[83] Compare the use of the term ἐκδημία in Gregory of Nazianzus and Evagrius to describe the intellect's journey to God: Gregory, *Ep.* 6 (PG 37 29C) and Evagrius *OP* 46, 142 (PG 79 1176D, 1197A). In both the term denotes the migration or return of the intellect to God, a process that does not entail ecstasy. It is a journey out of the material world, not out of oneself. Diadochus has given the term an ecstatic quality absent in either of these writers. Diadochus' approach is developed by Dionysius, who equates the verbs ἐκδημέω and ἐξίστημι (*DN* 3.2, 681D). Maximus' use of the term also has an ecstatic quality, as in *CC* 1.10 (p. 52): 'When the intellect in the intensity of its love (τῷ ἔρωτι τῆς ἀγάπης) migrates (ἐκδημῇ) towards God then it is no longer aware either of itself or of any created thing whatsoever.' Similarly *CC* 11.28 (p. 104).

[84] Roques, in 'Contemplation chez les orientaux chrétiens (Denys)', 1899, characterizes this ecstasy as 'une véritable sortie de la condition humaine', an abandonment of all recognizably human activity whether intellectual, rational, or emotional, a surrender to the divine darkness. Sheldon-Williams, in 'The Greek Christian Platonist Tradition', 470, is more sympathetic, and indeed more just, observing: 'By ecstasy the ps.-Dionysius means not the abandonment of will and intellect but an extension of their capacities beyond their natures such that they can no longer rely upon themselves but, encountering the Divine Power which comes to meet them [ . . . ], become merged with it.' See also Vanneste, *Mystère de Dieu*, 206–14.

Maximus uses the theme of ecstasy to express the union of God and man. He values the theme as indicative of the passive quality of our relationship to God. Thus he defines the love that moves us to ecstasy as a passion in that it is produced not by us, but by the Good in us (*Amb.* 7, 1073B).[85] Elsewhere, he declares that mystical theology is entrusted to the pure intellect alone 'in ineffable ecstasy' through which the intellect becomes 'unutterably conversant with God' (*Amb.* 10.22b, 1149B). It is through an 'ecstasy of desire' that the soul is clothed in God and becomes immovable in him (*CT* 1.39, 1097C). He describes ecstasy as a 'madness' in which the sober intellect goes out from the realm of created beings (*QT* 55, p. 499.320–2). Note the adjective 'sober'. Maximus has little time for the psychological epiphenomena of ecstatic experience— unlike Gregory of Nyssa. Ecstasy for Maximus clearly does not involve the suspension of the faculties. This is well illustrated by his deliberate and bold use of the language of sexual ecstasy, in which consciousness of the other is never lost and is indeed, in a sense, heightened (*Amb.* 7, 1073C; 23, 1260BC; *Scholia*, PG 4 265D–268A). Ecstasy thus involves not the suspension of the faculties but their enhancement and fulfilment in God. Human freedom is never abnegated even in the highest states of mystical experience, since it has, by nature, an immutable foundation in God (*Amb.* 7, 1076B).[86]

The theme of ecstasy in Maximus is a prime example of the subtle play of influences at work in his thought: influences that do not submit to precise dissection. He is very wary on the question of the suspension of the faculties, demonstrating considerably more reserve than Gregory of Nyssa or Dionysius.[87] His reserve is, in

---

[85] Cf. the 'impassible passion' that is the soul's attraction to God in Gregory of Nyssa (*Cant.* 1: GNO 6, p. 23). Cf. also Dionysius' description of Hierotheos 'suffering divine things' (παθὼν τὰ θεῖα) (*DN* 2.9, 648AB). For this phrase in Maximus see Thunberg, *Microcosm and Mediator*, 431–2.

[86] The maintenance of will in the highest states of mystical experience is also an intuition of Macarius. In II 40.2 he explains that perserverance in prayer is so important because: 'through prayer there comes to the worthy communion in the holiness of God and in spiritual energy, and the conjunction of the dispositions of the intellect with the Lord in ineffable love'. This sense of the conjunction of human and divine wills is essentially the same as that which governs Maximus' Christology.

[87] Sherwood, *The Ascetic Life*, 96, also makes this point, arguing that Maximus can be distinguished from Dionysius in that his notion of ecstasy is not ecstasy in the full Dionysian sense of 'an irrational, supra-rational estrangement of the mind in the divine darkness. The overall sense is that of an outgoing of the volitive power, which effects the final gnomic unity and unity in love.' Supra-rational is a more accurate term than irrational. Sherwood is right

fact, more in the tradition of Gregory Nazianzen or Evagrius. He does, however, also bring in an element of ecstasy absent in these writers, drawing most obviously on Dionysius in order to express the insufficiency of human nature to apprehend the divine. Maximus, however, insists on the personal, volitive, and affective character of ecstasy far more clearly and consistently than does Dionysius. In this respect his approach is more obviously related to that of Macarius and Diadochus.

As with ecstasy, the place of love in Maximian spirituality distinguishes his teaching from that of Evagrius.[88] Although love plays a key role in Evagrius' spiritual teaching, it belongs to the stages of *praktike* and natural contemplation, and not to the final stage of theology.[89] Maximus' goal is not the perfect contemplation of the simple intellect, but union in love: 'Love is therefore a great good, and of goods the first and most especial good, since through it God and man are joined together in a single embrace, and the Maker of man appears as man, through the undeviating likeness of the deified to God in the good, so far as this is possible to mankind' (*Ep.* 2, 401C). He also speaks of 'This reciprocal disposition which on one side deifies man by his love for God and on the other humanizes God by his love for man; and by this beautiful reciprocal conversion, man is made God by the deification of man and God man by the humanization of God' (*Amb.* 7,

to stress the more personal and volitive character of Maximian ecstasy, but overlooks the affective element within Dionysian ecstasy evident in *Divine Names* 4, albeit not in the *Mystical Theology*.

[88] As Dalmais argues: 'The summit of spiritual life is no longer a perfect transference of the contemplative intellect to the divine light in which it itself becomes luminous, but in a loving identification of the human will to the divine will, such that there occurs between them that exchange known as charity.' 'L'Héritage évagrien', 358.

[89] Spiritual love (ἀγάπη) in Evagrius controls the passions of the soul (*Praktikos* 35, p. 580). It is the offspring of *apatheia* (*Praktikos* 81, p. 670) and the term of *Praktike* (*Praktikos* 85, p. 676). Love is 'the excellent state of the rational soul, in which the soul can love nothing which is amongst corruptible things more than the knowledge of God' (*KG* I.86, p. 57). It is necessary within natural contemplation (*KG* III.58 (p. 121)). Evagrius also speaks, rather more rarely, of ἔρως, for example *OP* 52 (PG 79 1177C): 'The state of prayer is one of dispassion which by virtue of the most intense love transports to the noetic realm the intellect that longs for wisdom.' Here again love controls the passible part of the soul and channels its energies towards primary natural contemplation. Neither ἔρως nor ἀγάπη are referred to in the context of the final recapitulation of the intellect in God. While Viller is right to point out the debt of much of Maximus' teaching on love to Evagrius—*CC* I.1 and 2, for example, are modelled on *KG* I.86 and *Praktikos* 81 respectively—he fails to recognize the very essential difference between the place of love in the two systems.

1084C).[90] Similarly: 'They say that God and man are exemplars of one another, that in as much as God is humanized to man by love for mankind, to that degree is man able to be deified to God through love' (*Amb.* 10, 1113B).[91]

The primacy of love in deification is also a prominent Macarian theme. It is through love that the gap between uncreated and created nature is closed (II 49.4).[92] Similarly, through prayer, man comes to participation in God 'in ineffable love' (II 40.2). Of course, Macarius is not the only writer to speak in such terms. Diadochus also holds that the motive force of man's union with God is love, as is clear in the passage from *GC* 14 cited above. Love also plays a very significant role in the Areopagitica. Dionysius takes both ἔρως and ἀγάπη to signify 'a capacity to effect a unity, an alliance, and a particular commingling in the Beautiful and the Good' (*DN* 4.12, 709CD, tr. Luibheid).[93] It is that which causes the superior to provide for the subordinate and stirs the subordinate to return to the superior; it is that which unites man and God.

Other aspects of Maximus' teaching on love can also be distinguished from that of Evagrius. Maximus' reworking of *OP* 60 is perhaps the most eloquent illustration of his very different priorities:

If you are a theologian, you will pray truly. And if you pray truly, you are a theologian. (Evagrius, *OP* 60, 1180B)

He who truly loves God prays entirely without distraction (ἀπερισπάστως). And he who prays entirely without distraction, loves God truly. (Maximus, *CC* II.1, p. 50)

Maximus has neatly substituted love for theology, a personal encounter of the whole man with God for the intellect's contemplation of the divine unity. Maximus holds knowledge and faith to be dependent on love: 'faith without love does not actualize the

[90] The theme of reciprocal love in Maximus bears comparison with the 'iconic love' (εἰκονικὴ ἀγάπη) that exists, or should exist, between the soul and its Maker, the image and the Prototype (Macarius, I 3.5.8).

[91] The theme of the reciprocity between the deification of man and the humanization of God is part of the common tradition. Macarius sums it up rather neatly: the Lord became 'that which we are according to the dispensation, so that we might become that which he is' (I 3.4.2, after Irenaeus, *AH* v Prologue: SC 153, p. 15).

[92] This gap is the first of the five divisions of the Maximian universe (*Amb.* 41, 1304D ff.).

[93] Dionysius refuses to separate ἔρως and ἀγάπη (*DN* 4.12, 709AB). In this he is in accord with Gregory of Nyssa's definition of ἔρως as ἐπιτεταμένη ἀγάπη (*Cant.* hom. 13 (GNO 6, p. 383)).

light of knowledge in the soul' (*CC* 1.31, p. 60). The pure soul, freed
from the passions, is 'constantly delighted by divine love' (*CC* 1.34,
p. 60). Maximus frequently expresses this love with fiery language.
For example, the New Testament forces one towards God 'flying
by the fire of love' (τῷ πυρὶ τῆς ἀγάπης πτερούμενον) (*QT* 63,
p. 165.318–19).[94] This sort of fire imagery has almost innumerable
parallels in Macarius. A good example is the following: 'Indeed, he
who daily constrains himself to persevere in prayer is enflamed by
spiritual love in divine desire and fiery yearning (εἰς ἔρωτα θεῖον
καὶ πόθον ἔμπυρον ὑπὸ τῆς πνευματικῆς ἀγάπης ἐκκαίεται)'
(II 40.2). This kind of language is also found in Diadochus, in
whom we find the arresting notion of the 'fire of impassibility'
(*GC* 17) and the reference to the 'fire of love' cited above (*GC* 14).
This may be yet another example of the mediation of the Macarian tradition to Maximus by Diadochus.

Maximus' debt to Evagrius is here, as elsewhere, one of form
not of substance. His teaching on love is difficult, if not impossible,
to pin down to any particular source precisely because it runs so
deep in his thinking. We can, however, say that it clearly distinguishes his work from that of Evagrius and closely associates him
with the more affective and holistic Macarian–Diadochan
tradition.

## 8.11   The Passions and *Apatheia*

Maximus' understanding of the passions is another aspect in
which he differs significantly from Evagrius. Evagrius speaks of
the perfect soul as one in which the passible part of the soul
(ἡ παθητικὴ δύναμις) acts according to nature, but regards
the passions themselves as entirely negative and prefers to call
for their eradication rather than for their transformation, for
*apatheia* rather than for *metriopatheia*.[95] Evagrius defines *apatheia* as

---

[94] For the inner liturgy in Maximus, see below, Ch. 8.12.
[95] *KG* III.16 (p. 103). Cf. *OP* 37 (PG 79 1176A): 'First pray to be purified from the
passions.' Where Evagrius does speak of *metriopatheia* this would seem to designate, as in
Philo, a stage inferior to *apatheia*. See *Schol. Prov.* 3 (p. 93) in which he takes *paideia* to indicate
'the moderation of passions which is observed around the passionate or irrational part of
the soul'. This builds on Clement, who had made the same connection between *paideia* and
*metriopatheia* (*Strom.* 11.8.39.4-5: GCS 52, p. 134). Evagrius' negative approach to the passions
is very much in the tradition of Clement and the Stoics. Clement calls the passions 'illnesses'

'a peaceful condition of the rational soul arising from humility and temperance'.[96] This condition is not to be confused with impassivity, as indicated by his description of the state of prayer as 'one of *apatheia* which by virtue of the most intense love (ἔρως) transports to the noetic realm the intellect that longs for wisdom' (*OP* 52 1177C).[97]

Maximus has a more positive approach to the passions than does Evagrius.[98] Whereas in the *Centuries on Love* he defines passion in a purely negative way, as 'an impulse of soul contrary to nature' (*CC* II.16, p. 96), in the *Ambigua* he offers a broader definition of passion as 'motion from one [state] to another, having for its end the impassible' (*Amb.* 7, 1072B).[99] This wider sense of passion refers not to the corruption of the powers of the soul, but to the natural passivity of all beings within the realm of becoming (ibid., 1073B).[100] Maximus argues that the passions are evil not in themselves but by misuse. They too have their part to play in the spiritual life (*QT* 1, pp. 47–9).[101] Like Isaiah, he distinguishes between natural and counter-natural passions, the former being

---

(*Prot.* XI.115.2: GCS 12, p. 81), defining them as 'a counter-natural movement of the soul' (*Strom.* II.13.59.6: GCS 52, p. 145). His aim is therefore *apatheia*, the extinction of all such counter-natural movements. The truly good man 'stands outside the passions, having risen above the whole life of passion by the habit or disposition of the virtuous soul' (*Strom.* VII.11.65.4: GCS 17, p. 47). On the passions in the Stoics, see Rist, *Stoic Philosophy*, esp. 22–36. Rist points out that Stoic *apatheia* constitutes not impassivity or the total suppression of the emotions but rather the extinction of all *disordered* movements of the soul. This also holds true for Evagrian *apatheia*. Of course, whether one aims at *apatheia*, *eupatheia*, or *metriopatheia* largely depends upon the definition of *pathos* that one begins with. A more positive view of the passions (including a different definition thereof) and their potential transformation is adumbrated in Plato and developed by Aristotle, see Kallistos Ware, '"Pathos" in Isaias and Theodoret', 316.

[96] *Skemmata* 3, p. 374.

[97] See also his advice that, 'The soul which has *apatheia* is not one which is insensible to things but one which remains unperturbed by their remembrance' (*Ad Anatolium* 39: PG 40 1232B).

[98] Viller, 'Aux sources de la spiritualité de S. Maxime', 168–80, overlooks the very real differences that exist between Evagrius and Maximus with respect to the passions.

[99] Some MSS of *CC* II.16 have not simply 'passion' but 'blameworthy passion'. This would certainly fit with the more positive understanding of passion developed elsewhere by Maximus.

[100] This is presumably the semantic basis of the arresting phrase 'the blessed passion of holy love' (*CC* III.67, p. 176).

[101] Maximus does allow, on the authority of Gregory of Nyssa, that the passions are not part of man's original constitution. Gregory outlines this teaching in *Virg.* 12 (GNO 8 (1), p. 298). This understanding can only be squared with the rest of Maximus' teaching if we assume that he is speaking here of counter-natural passions.

perfectly proper and the latter reprehensible ($QT$ 21, p. 127). It is
the latter that obstruct the law of nature and divide soul and body
($QT$ 62, p. 131), exercise tyranny over us ($CC$ II.30, p. 106), and
corrupt our nature ($QD$ 63, p. 49). These may properly be called
'alien passions' ($QT$ 51, p. 405). It is these that must be killed ($CC$
IV.54, p. 216), these that God wishes to destroy, and not the
natural movements of the soul ($QD$ 69, p. 53). Maximus speaks
in detail of the transformation ($QT$ 27, p. 197) and recapitulation
($QT$ 47, p. 321) of the passions. Our task is to bring the counter-
natural passions back into accord with nature, to harness these
powerful motive forces in our journey towards God.[102] This channelling of the passions produces *apatheia*, the state in which the
passible aspect of the soul is re-integrated, in which the *epithumia*
(the desiring part) is transformed into *eros* for God and the *thumos*
(the irascible part) into divine *agape* ($CC$ II.48, p. 116; $QT$ 55,
p. 499.310–15).[103]

Macarius does speak of 'counter-natural passions' (*EM* 9.14; II
4.1), but does not develop an understanding of natural or blameless passions. Thus passion in Macarius always means counter-
natural passion. In this respect his teaching is very like that of
Evagrius. Macarius regards the passions as the inheritance of the
Fall (I 29.2.8, 50.1.9).[104] They are not ours but alien (I 40.1.5), not
natural but accidental to us (I 40.1.10). Our aim therefore is to be
the 'perfect liberation from the passions' (I 19.3.3), a condition
brought about by perfect love (II 45.7; III 7.4.3) and described
elsewhere as the 'state of health according to nature' (I 25.2.3), the
restitution of the pre-lapsarian impassibility of Adam (I 7.2–3,
50.1.1–2).[105] There are few signs in Macarius of the more positive

---

[102] $CC$ IV.45 (p. 212): 'The intellect functions in accordance with nature when it keeps the
passions under control [...].'

[103] In $QT$ 55 Maximus also distinguishes four degrees of *apatheia*. The first is abstention
from all evil actions; the second, total rejection of every thought tending towards evil; the
third, perfect absence of passionate impulses in secondary natural contemplation; the
fourth, the perfect purification of even the mere imagination of passion (p. 493.200–11).
Maximus' understanding of *apatheia* shares many features with that of Evagrius. The
definition of *apatheia* in $CC$ 1.36 (p. 60), for example, is clearly derived from *Skemmata* 3
(p. 374). Viller draws attention to the echoing by Maximus of Evagrius' assertion that the
perfect one has no need of *encrateia* ('Aux sources de la spiritualité de S. Maxime', 177). This
understanding, although Viller does not mention this, derives from Clement, *Strom.*
IV.22.138 (GCS 52, p. 309).

[104] Like Maximus, Macarius follows Gregory of Nyssa in this regard.

[105] Macarius has inherited this understanding of Adam's impassibility from Basil, *Longer
Rules* 55.1 (PG 31 1044D).

understanding of the passions evident in Maximus. There is, however, one tangible connection: the designation of the passions as 'alien' (ἀλλοτρία) (*QT* 51, p. 405.171. Cf. Macarius, I 40.1.5; III 19.5).[106]

Mark and Diadochus follow both Evagrius and Macarius in their negative appraisal of the passions. There are adumbrations of Maximus' approach to the passions in Dionysius,[107] but the most obvious forebear of Maximus in this regard is the *Asceticon* of Abba Isaiah, especially the teaching contained in Logos G2.[108] The fact that Maximus appears to borrow the Isaian apophthegm concerning the sparrow tied by the leg would suggest Maximus' acquaintance with the *Asceticon*.[109]

## 8.12 The Soul as Church

In his *Mystagogy*, Maximus describes the church as a representation of man and man as a representation of the church. He sees a correspondence between body and nave (moral wisdom), soul and sanctuary (natural contemplation), and mind and altar (mystical theology) (*Myst.* 4, 672B).[110] He goes on to speak of the reciprocal symbolic relationship between soul and church:

Whoever has been able to have been intelligently and wisely initiated into that which is celebrated in church has established his own soul as a true and divine church of God. It is perhaps for this reason that the church made by hands, *which has the soul as its symbolic model*, has, because of the variety of divine things in it, wisely been handed down to us for our

---

[106] Clement calls sin, but not passion, 'alien' (*Strom.* VII.13.82.3: GCS 17, p. 58). Mark, as we have seen, took exception to Macarius' designation of the passions as 'alien', see Ch. 5.4.3.

[107] For example *DN* 4.25, 728B.

[108] See above, Ch. 7.4. Theodoret had also developed a very positive understanding of the utility and indeed the necessity of the passions. See Kallistos Ware, ' "Pathos" in Isaias and Theodoret'.

[109] *CC* 1.85 (p. 82) cf. *Asceticon* Logos G8.49. Maximus: 'When a sparrow tied by the leg tries to fly, it is held back by the string and pulled down to the earth. Similarly when the intellect that has not yet attained *apatheia* flies upward towards heavenly knowledge, it is held back by the passions and pulled down to earth.' Isaiah: 'I am like a sparrow whose leg has been tied by a child; if he lets it go, it thinks itself freed; but if the child pulls, he makes it descend. And what I mean is that nobody should slacken, right up to their last breath.' Maximus has made the unusual Isaian metaphor his own with characteristic aplomb.

[110] Cf. Clement, *Paed.* 1.6 (GCS 12, p. 113): church as man, consisting of body and soul.

guidance towards the greatest good. (*Myst.* 5, 681D–684A, emphasis mine)

Compare the opening of Macarius' treatise on the Church and its ministry: 'The whole visible arrangement of the Church of God came to pass for the sake of the living and intellectual essence of the rational soul, made according to the image of God, which is the living and true church of God' (1 52.1.1). Conversely: '[The word] "church" has two meanings, the assembly of the faithful and the uniting of the soul. When it is taken in a spiritual sense and applied to man, "church" designates the whole composite structure (σύγκριμα) [of man]' (11 37.8). Similarly: '[The word] "church" applies both to many and to one soul; for the soul gathers all the thoughts and is thus a church for God' (11 12.15). This reciprocal symbolic relationship between soul and church is very much what we find in Maximus' *Mystagogy*. Origen does call the soul church, but not the church soul.[111] No other writer to my knowledge has the same sense of the reciprocity of this symbolic relationship as do Macarius and Maximus.

This intuition of the soul–church reciprocity gives rise to many metaphors of what can be called the 'inner liturgy'. This is a theme that, as we have seen, has a long heritage in Christian usage.[112] Evagrius, for example, declares that: 'The intelligible temple is the pure intellect which now possesses in itself the "wisdom of God, full of variety"; the temple of God is he who is a beholder of the sacred unity, and the altar of God is the contemplation of the Holy Trinity.'[113] Maximus speaks of the altar as the symbol of God, where we sacrifice ourselves spiritually (*QT* 36, p. 243.19–20). It is there that we are to 'offer up to God as his due our morals which are in accord with philosophy and all our natural powers, consecrated to God as a burnt offering by the fire of grace in the Spirit' (*QT* 65, p. 287.571–5). Similarly, Macarius speaks of making the body an altar, laying upon it all our thought and invoking the

---

[111] Origen, *Scholia in Cant.* 71 (PG 17 280C): 'The bride of the Logos is the soul, which is the church of Christ.'

[112] Cf. our discussions of the theme in Ch. 5.4.6 and Ch. 7.10.

[113] *KG* v.84 (p. 213). Cited Golitzin, 'Hierarchy versus Anarchy', 156–7. A number of other examples may also be mentioned. *KG* v.53 (p. 199). 'The spiritual sacrifice is the pure conscience which places the state of the intellect as if on an altar.' *Skemmata* 6 (p. 374): 'The censer is the pure intellect which at the time of prayer touches upon no sensory thing.' *Skemmata* 34 (p. 377): 'The intellect is the temple of the Holy Trinity.'

heavenly and invisible fire (II 31.5).[114] This is in accord with his principle that 'the Church of Christ and temple of God and true altar and living sacrifice is the man of God' (I 52.1.1).[115] In respect of the inner liturgy, then, our authors are inextricably linked within a shared tradition.

## 8.13 Conclusion

The evidence given in this chapter provides a compelling argument to support the thesis that Maximus was acquainted both directly and indirectly with the Macarian tradition. His teaching on the Transfiguration has definite points of contact with Macarius, particularly on the understanding of its interiorization in the worthy and on the theology of the divine light. Maximus has also drawn upon Macarius in his teaching of the extension of the mystery of the Incarnation, employing the soul–body analogy and even, albeit somewhat toned down, the controversial 'second soul' theme. Maximus' use of the analogy of wax in the context of the depiction of the *imago Dei* looks very like a borrowing from Macarius. There is a palpable Macarian input into Maximus' understanding on baptism, very probably mediated by Mark and Diadochus. This link is confirmed by the very substantial affinity evident between Macarius and Maximus on the question of human free will. The experiential dimension of Maximus' teaching certainly draws from the Macarian–Diadochan tradition, most notably in respect of the theory of knowledge and the αἴσθησις νοερά. Maximus' mystical theology is grounded in the heart, a grounding we can confidently ascribe, at least in part, to Macarius. His teaching on ecstasy has certain points of contact with that of Macarius and Diadochus, with whom he is clearly associated in his teaching on love. Lastly, the reciprocal symbolic relationship between soul and Church unmistakably recalls Macarius.

---

[114] Cf. also Dionysius, *EH* 4.3.12 (484D): 'It is on Jesus himself, our most divine altar, that there is achieved the divine consecration of our intellectual essences. In whom, consecrated and consumed as a burnt offering, as Scripture says, "we have access" [to the Father].'

[115] Logos I 52 develops the idea that the earthly liturgy is a symbol of the inner liturgy of the soul. A similar understanding is shown by Dionysius in *CH* 1.3 (121C–124A), cited Golitzin, 'Hierarchy versus Anarchy', 149–50.

Maximus' debt to Macarius—both direct and indirect—should not surprise us; he was an erudite and widely read man, well versed in the traditions of monastic spirituality. The Macarian writings formed, by the seventh century, part of the common stock of monastic teaching, on which Maximus was free to draw. The debt is remarkably thoroughgoing—there are few significant aspects of Macarian teaching that Maximus does not, in some way, pick up. Naturally, the Macarian legacy is only part of the rich tapestry of Maximus' teaching. It nonetheless represents a vital component of that teaching. With its emphasis on the heart and the gradual manifestation of baptismal grace, the Macarian tradition enabled Maximus to balance the overly intellectualist Evagrian tradition, while the Macarian intuition of the synergy and conjunction of divine and human wills, coupled with a profoundly Christocentric spiritual vision, supplied a volitive and personalistic emphasis lacking in Dionysian ecstasy. The Macarian influence in Maximus is difficult to pin down precisely because it runs so deep. I have nevertheless attempted to point out areas in which it is obviously manifest. Viller has ably demonstrated that Maximus owes the 'ossature' of much of his system to Evagrius. I hope to have shown that a significant part of his inner dynamic is derived from Macarius. The Macarian tradition must, I submit, be recognized as a major contributor in any evaluation of Maximus' sources.

# Conclusion

In seeking to establish the place of Macarian writings within the Eastern Christian tradition during the first three hundred years of their existence, the Messalian question has, naturally, proved central. The connection between the writings and the anti-Messalian lists that has clouded so much twentieth-century Macarian scholarship has been shown to be much less straightforward than previously supposed. I have argued that if, as seems most likely, the Messalian *Asceticon* condemned at Ephesus did indeed contain a selection of Macarian material, then this material was condemned because of its superficial affinities with a body of anti-Messalian propositions already built up by the earlier councils of Antioch, Side, and Constantinople. Thus not only must we avoid a facile equation of Macarius with Messalianism—the circularity warned of by Stewart—but must also recognize that the Macarian elements within the anti-Messalian lists represent an additional layer of material, inconsistent with the primary layer and derived, ironically, from a writer who addresses precisely the same concerns as those reflected in the primary layer.

The tragedy of the Ephesine condemnation is that it implicitly rejected the Macarian approach to the reform of the Messalian tendency. This approach should be seen as essentially analogous to the Cappadocian model of monastic reform, a model governed not by the condemnation of half-imagined foes, but by the harnessing and assimilation of the extreme ascetic tendencies. Gregory of Nyssa's reworking of Macarius' *Great Letter* is an eloquent testimony to the Cappadocian approval of Macarius' ascetic teaching. Imitation is, after all, the sincerest form of flattery. The association with the Cappadocians was to prove fundamental for the subsequent history of the Macarian writings within the Eastern Christian tradition.

I asserted in my opening chapter that the exploration of the Macarian legacy in the later Christian tradition will help elucidate the real nature of Macarius' relations with the Messalian tendency—thereby allowing us to escape from the 'swamp' which has trapped and hindered so many earlier studies of this question. This assertion has, I believe, been borne out. We have found that both Mark and Diadochus, generally regarded as anti-Messalian writers, inherit and build on Macarius' reforming programme. This inheritance is particularly clear in their respective theologies of baptism, the central plank of their anti-Messalian arguments. Both depend upon Macarius' two-fold theory of baptism and concomitant understanding of the complex relationship between divine grace and human freedom. Neither, however, accept Macarius' teaching passively: both, for example, revise his theory of the coexistence of sin and evil, itself an anti-Messalian position. Mark and Diadochus are clearly operating at some distance from the Messalian controversy, not attacking Messalianism directly, but refining and thereby strengthening Macarius' own thorough-going critique. The works of Mark and Diadochus thus confirm the profoundly anti-Messalian character of the Macarian writings. This confirmation was to open the way for the assimilation of the Macarian teaching within the mainstream Christian tradition, notwithstanding the Ephesine condemnation.

In examining the legacy of the Macariana, I have found it necessary to review the opposition customarily perceived between the Evagrian and Macarian spiritual traditions. This perceived dichotomy needs wholesale revision, but not outright rejection. Evagrius and Macarius can legitimately be contrasted, but not simply as representatives of, respectively, intellective and affective spiritualities. The most significant contrast is, in fact, that while both are aware of the complementary dimensions of heart and intellect, this complementarity is far more successfully realized in the work of Macarius than in that of Evagrius.

In Mark we see the rudimentary beginnings of a synthesis between the Macarian and Evagrian traditions. This synthesis, however, only reaches maturity in the work of Diadochus. Diadochus' synthesis builds on the fine intellective–affective balance evident in the Macarian writings and uses this as the axis on which to integrate the Evagrian tradition. The *Asceticon* of Abba Isaiah contains elements of both Evagrius and Macarius, but does not integrate them in any very profound manner. The Evagrian inheritance in the *Asceticon* is slight, while the Macarian rarely goes deeper than the level of imagery and metaphor. Both are, moreover, largely contained within the second redactional layer of the *Asceticon*. Maximus the Confessor is the principal heir to Diadochus' synthesis. Maximus, as we have demonstrated, is deeply influenced by the Macarian tradition, being aware of the teaching of Macarius both directly and, through Diadochus and Mark, indirectly.

The later tradition preserved many of the most significant features of the Macarian writings. The writers that drew upon Macarius were attracted by the finesse of his observations on the workings of grace and by his insistence on the need for a lived experience of that grace, by his Christocentric and Pneumatic spirituality, and by his holistic anthropology. None, however, draws from Macarius uncritically. Apart from the aforementioned revision of the theory of coexistence, we may also note that certain of the more esoteric aspects of Macarius' teaching tended to fall by the wayside in the later tradition, as, for example, the feminine character of the Holy Spirit and the materialism latent in the concept of the 'subtle body'. The writers surveyed preserve the most valuable and lasting features of the Macarian vision, providing a fine example of the operation of a living tradition.

The Macarian writings rapidly attained a wide circulation. From an origin on the borders of the Greek and Syriac worlds, the writings had reached the hands of Gregory of Nyssa in Asia Minor during the 380s. They were present in the Constantinopolitan region by 426, possibly brought to Hypatius' monastery by Alexander the Acemite. They were also, regrettably, exhibited in some form at the Council of Ephesus in 431. During the subsequent course of the fifth century the writings reached Mark, wherever he may have been, and Diadochus in Epirus. The writings were certainly used by the author of the second layer of the Isaian *Asceticon*, a work that appears to have taken shape in Palestine during the latter half of the fifth century. Lastly, Maximus the Confessor's use of the Macariana points to their having become, by the seventh century, part of the common store of the Eastern Christian spiritual tradition.

This study has traced the process whereby the Macarian writings were established as an integral component of the mainstream Christian tradition. This having been done, its work is over. It is, however, in another sense, only a beginning. Many other avenues remain to be explored: the Syriac tradition; the factors that governed the explosion of activity out of which the four principal Greek collections emerged; the use of Macarius by Symeon the New Theologian and the fourteenth-century Hesychasts; and, finally, the remarkable odyssey of the Macariana in the Christian West. Far from closing the book on the Macarian legacy, I hope to have provided a firm basis on which that legacy may be explored still further.

# BIBLIOGRAPHY

## Primary Sources

Note: [=] indicates conventions of abbreviated citation in the text.

### ALEXANDER THE ACEMITE

Stoop, E. de, *La Vie d'Alexandre l'Acémète* (PO 6 (5); Paris 1911).

### AMMONAS

Nau, F., *Ammonas, successeur de saint Antoine* (PO 11 (4); Paris 1915).
Kmosko, M., *Ammonii eremitae epistulae* (PO 10 (6); Paris 1915).

### ANTHONY THE GREAT

Rubenson, S., (tr. on the basis of extensive MS research), *The Letters of St Anthony* (Studies in Antiquity and Christianity; Minneapolis 1995).

### APOPHTHEGMATA PATRUM

Alphabetical Collection in PG 65 72–440. [= *AP* (Alph.)]
Anonymous Collection, ed. F. Nau, *Revue de l'Orient chrétien* 12–14, 17–18 (1907–9, 1912–13).
Systematic Collection, ed. J.-C. Guy, *Les Apophtgmes des Pères, Collection Systématique, I–IX* (SC 387; Paris 1993).
Guy, J.-C., 'Recherches sur sur la tradition grecque des *Apophthegmata Patrum*' (Subsidia Hagiographica 36; Brussels 1962).
Budge, W., *The Book of Paradise: Being the Histories and Sayings of the Monks and Ascetics of the Egyptian Desert*, 2 vols. (London 1904).
Regnault, L. (tr.), *Les Sentences des pères du désert*, vol. iii (Solesmes 1976). [pp. 159–91 = *Virtues of Saint Macarius*]
Ward, B. (tr.), *The Sayings of the Desert Fathers* (Oxford/Kalamazoo 1975).

### ATHANASIUS OF ALEXANDRIA

Bartelink, G. J. M, *Vie d'Antoine* (SC 400; Paris 1994). [= *VA*]
Other texts in PG 25–8.

### BASIL OF CAESAREA

Courtonne, Y., *Lettres*, 3 vols. (Paris 1957–66). [= *Ep.*]
*De baptismo* (PG 31 1513–1628). [= *On Baptism*]
*Regulae fusius tractatae* (PG 31 889–1052). [= *Longer Rules*]

*Regulae brevius tractatae* (PG 31 1082–1305). [= *Shorter Rules*]
*Liber de Spiritu Sancto* (PG 32 68–217). [= *On the Holy Spirit*]
Other texts in PG 31–2.

CALLINICUS

Bartelink, G. J. M., *Vie d'Hypatios* (SC 177; Paris 1971). [= *VH*]

CLEMENT OF ALEXANDRIA

Stählin, O. *et al.*, *Protrepticus* (GCS 12.3; Berlin 1972). [= *Prot.*]
—— *Paedagogus* (GCS 12.3; Berlin 1972). [= *Paed.*]
—— *Excerpta ex Theodoto* (GCS 17.2; Berlin 1970).
—— *Quis dives salvetur?* (GCS 17.2; Berlin 1970).
—— *Stromata* I–VI (GCS 52.4; Berlin 1985). [= *Strom.*]
—— *Stromata* VII–VIII (GCS 17.2; Berlin 1970). [= *Strom.*]

DADISHO QATRAYA

Draguet, R., *Commentaire du Livre d'Abba Isaïe par Dadisho Qatraya* (CSCO 326–7; Louvain 1972).

DIADOCHUS OF PHOTICE

Des Places, É., *Diadoque de Photicé. Oeuvres spirituelles* (SC 5.3; Paris 1966). [*Gnostic Chapters*= *GC*]
Palmer, G., Sherrard, P., and Ware, K. T. (tr.), *The Philokalia*, vol. i (London 1979). [tr. of *GC*]
Rutherford, J., *One Hundred Practical Texts of Perception and Spiritual Discernment from Diadochos of Photike: Text, Translation and Commentary* (Belfast 2000).

DIONYSIUS THE AREOPAGITE

*De divinis nominibus* (PG 3 585A–984A; PTS 33 (1990)). [= *DN*]
*De mystica theologia* (PG 3 997A–1048B; PTS 36 (1991)). [= *MT*]
*De ecclesiastica hierarchia* (PG 3 369–569A; PTS 36). [= *EH*]
*De cælesti hierarchia* (PG 3 120A–340B; PTS 36). [= *CH*]
*Epistulae* (PG 3 1065A–1120A; PTS 36). [= *Ep.*]
Luibheid, C. (tr.), *Pseudo-Dionysius: The Complete Works* (Classics of Western Spirituality; New York/Mahwah 1987). [tr. of *DN, MT, EH, CH, Ep.*]

ECCLESIASTICAL COUNCILS

Mansi, G., *Sacrorum conciliorum nova et amplissima collectio*, 31 vols. (Florence 1759–93).
Tanner, N., *Decrees of the Ecumenical Councils*, vol. i: *Nicaea I to Lateran* (Washington, DC 1990).
Schwartz, E., *Acta conciliorum oecumenicorum* (Berlin 1914–). [=*ACO*]

## EPHREM THE SYRIAN

Beck, E., *Hymnen de fide* (CSCO 154–5; Louvain 1955). [= *Hymns on Faith*]
—— *Hymnen de nativitate* (CSCO 186–7; Louvain 1959). [= *Hymns on the Nativity*]
—— *Contra haereses* (CSCO 169–70; Louvain 1957). [= *Against the Heresies*]
—— *Hymnen de virginitate* (CSCO 233–4; Louvain 1962). [= *Hymns on Virginity*]
Leloir, L., *Commentaire de l'Évangile concordant ou Diatessaron* (SC 121; Paris 1966). [= *Commentary on the Diatessaron*]
Brock, S. P. (tr.), *The Harp of the Spirit* (Studies Supplementary to Sobornost 4; London 1983). [tr. of selected hymns]
McVey, K. (tr.), *Ephrem the Syrian: Hymns* (Classics of Western Spirituality; New York/Mahwah 1989). [tr. of *Hymns on the Nativity, On Virginity, against Julian*]
Morris, J. B. (tr.), *Select Works of St Ephrem the Syrian* (Oxford/London 1847).

## EPIPHANIUS OF SALAMIS

Holl, K., *Ancoratus* (GCS 25; Leipzig 1915).
—— *Panarion* (GCS 37.2; Berlin 1985).

## EVAGRIUS OF PONTUS

Brock, S. P. (tr.), *The Syriac Fathers on Prayer and the Spiritual Life* (Kalamazoo 1987).
Driscoll, J., *The 'Ad Monachos' of Evagrius Ponticus: Its Stucture and a Select Commentary* (Studia Anselmia 104; Rome 1991). [= *Ad Monachos*]
Gressmann, H., *Nonnenspiegel* (TU 39 (4); Leipzig 1913), 146–51. [= *Advice to a Virgin*]
Frankenberg, W., *Euagrius Ponticus* (Berlin 1912).
Guillaumont, A., *Les Six Centuries des 'Kephalaia Gnostica' d'Évagre le Pontique* (PO 28; Paris 1958). [All citations from the new Syriac version $(S^2) = KG$]
Guillaumont, A. and C., *Traité pratique ou le moine*, 2 vols. (SC 170–1; Paris 1971). [= *Praktikos*]
—— *Le Gnostique* (SC 356; Paris 1989). [= *Gnostikos*]
Géhin, P., *Scholies aux Proverbes* (SC 340; Paris 1987). [= *Schol. Prov.*]
—— *Scholies à l'Ecclésiaste* (SC 397; Paris 1993). [= *Schol. Eccl.*]
Géhin, P., with A. and C. Guillaumont, *Sur les pensées* (SC 438; Paris 1998). [= *Thoughts*]
Muyldermans, J., 'Note additionelle à Evagriana', *Le Muséon* 44 (1931), 374–80. [= *Skemmata*]
—— 'Evagriana: Le vatic. Barb. Graecus 515', *Le Muséon* 51 (1938), 200–3. [= *Ad Monachos* (Add.)]
*De oratione capitula* (PG 79 1165–1200). [= *OP*]

## GREGORY NAZIANZEN

Bernardi, J. *et al.*, *Orationes* 1–12, 20–43 (SC 247, 309, 405, 270, 284, 250, 318, 358, 384; Paris 1978–95). [= *Or.*]
*Orationes* 13–19, in PG 35. [= *Or.*]
Moreschini, C., *Poemata arcana* (Oxford 1997).

## GREGORY OF NYSSA

Series: *Gregorii Nysseni Opera* (gen. ed. W. Jaeger; Leiden 1960–). [= GNO]
Callahan, J., *De oratione dominica* (GNO 7 (2)).
Cavarnos, J., *De virginitate* (GNO 8 (1)). [= *Virg.*]
Gebhardt, E., *In suam ordinationem* (GNO 9).
Langerbeck, H., *Homiliae in Canticum canticorum* (GNO 6). [= *Cant.*]
Mühlenberg, E., *Oratio catechetica* (GNO 3 (4)). [= *Or. cat.*]
Staats, R., *Makarios-Symeon: Epistola Magna* (q.v.). [= *De instituto christiano*]
Other texts in PG 44–6.

## HISTORIA MONACHORUM IN AEGYPTO

Festugière, A.-J., *Historia monachorum in Aegypto* (Subsidia Hagiographica 34; Brussels 1961). [= *HM*]
Russell, N. (tr.), *The Lives of the Desert Fathers* (Oxford/Kalamazoo 1981).

## IRENAEUS OF LYONS

Rousseau A. *et al.*, *Contre les hérésies* 1–v (SC 263–4 (i), SC 293–4 (ii), SC 210–11 (iii), SC 100 (iv), SC 152–3 (v); Paris 1965–79). [= *AH*]

## ISAAC OF NINEVEH

Bedjan, P., *Mar Isaacus Ninivita: De perfectione religiosa* (Paris 1909).
Brock, S. P., *Isaac of Nineveh (Isaac the Syrian): 'The Second Part', Chapters IV–XLI* (CSCO 554–5; Louvain 1995).
Holy Transfiguration Monastery (Dana Miller) (tr.), *The Ascetical Homilies of St Isaac the Syrian* (Boston 1984).
Wensinck, A. J., *Mystic Treatises by Isaac of Nineveh. Translated from Bedjan's Syriac Text with an Introduction and Registers* (Wiesbaden 1969).

## ABBA ISAIAH

Draguet, R., *Les Cinq Recensions de l'Ascéticon syriaque d'abba Isaïe* (CSCO 289–90 (text), 293–4 (translation)). [= S (the common Syriac recension) and Sa (the earliest Syriac recension)]
Augustinos Monachos, Τοῦ ὁσίου πατρὸς ἡμῶν ἀββὰ Ἡσαΐου λόγοι κθ′ (Jerusalem 1911; repr. Volos 1962).
Guillaumont, A., *L'Ascéticon copte de l'abba Isaïe. Fragments sahidiques édités et traduits* (Bibliothèque d'études coptes 5; Cairo 1956).

Chitty, D. J., Working text of the Greek *Asceticon*, MS held in the Library of the House of SS Gregory and Macrina, Oxford. [= G]

Broc, H. de (tr.), *Abbé Isaïe: Recueil Ascétique*, 3rd edn. (Spiritualité Orientale 7 bis; Bellefontaine 1985). [tr. of Greek *Asceticon*]

## JOHN CASSIAN

Pichery, E., *Conférences* (SC 42 (i–vii), SC 54 (viii–xvii); SC 64 (xviii–xxiv); Paris 1955–9). [= *Conf.*]

Guy, J.-C., *Institutions cénobitiques* (SC 109; Paris 1965). [= *Inst.*]

## JOHN OF DAMASCUS

Kotter, B., *De haeresibus* (PTS 22; Berlin 1981), 41–8. [= J]

## LIBER GRADUUM

Kmosko, M., *Liber graduum* (PS 3; Paris 1926). [= *LG*]

## MACARIUS-SYMEON

Baker, A., 'Corrections in *Macarii Anecdota*', *JTS* 22 (1971), 538–41.

Berthold, H., *Makarios/Symeon, Reden und Briefe. Die Sammlung I des Vaticanus Graecus 694 (B)*, 2 vols. (GCS 55–6; Berlin 1973). [= 1]

Dörries, H., Klostermann, E., and Kroeger, M., *Die 50 Geistlichen Homilien des Makarios* (PTS 4; Berlin 1964). [= ii (1–50)]

Desprez, V., *Pseudo-Macaire: Oeuvres spirituelles*, i: *Homélies propres à la Collection III* (SC 275; Paris 1980). [= iii]

Jaeger, W., *Two Rediscovered Works of Ancient Christian Literature: Gregory of Nyssa and Macarius* (Leiden 1954).

Klostermann, E. and Berthold, H., *Neue Homilien des Makarius/Symeon*, i: *Aus Typus III* (TU 72; Berlin 1961). [= iii]

Nicodemus the Haghiorite and Macarius of Corinth, Φιλοκαλία τῶν ἱερῶν νηπτικῶν πατέρων, 5 vols. (3rd edn. Athens 1957–63), iii. 169–234. [= The 150 Chapters]

Marriott, G. L., *Macarii Anecdota: Seven Unpublished Homilies of Macarius* (Harvard Theological Studies 5; Cambridge, Mass. 1918). [= ii (51–7)]

Staats, R., *Makarios-Symeon: Epistola Magna. Eine messalianische Mönchsregel und ihre Umschrift in Gregors von Nyssa 'De Instituto Christiano'* (Göttingen 1984). [= *EM*]

Strothmann, W., *Makarios/Symeon: das arabische Sondergut* (Göttinger Orientforschungen, Series 1: Syriaca 11; Wiesbaden 1975). [= TV]

—— *Die syrische Überlieferung der Schriften des Makarios*, 2 vols. (Göttinger Orientforschungen, Series 1: Syriaca 21; Wiesbaden 1981). [= Syr.]

—— *Schriften des Makarios/Symeon unter dem Namen des Ephraem* (Göttinger Orientforschungen, Series 1: Syriaca 22; Wiesbaden 1981).

Strothmann, W., *Textcritische Anmerkungen zu den geistlichen Homilien des Makarios/Symeon* (Göttinger Orientforschungen, Series 1: Syriaca 23; Wiesbaden 1981).

Cremaschi, L. (tr.), *Pseudo-Macario: Spirito e fuoco. Omelie spirituali (Collezione II)* (Magnano 1995). [tr. of 11]

Deseille, P. (tr.), *Les Homélies spirituelles de saint Macaire* (Spiritualité Orientale 40; Bellefontaine 1984). [tr. of 11]

Fitschen, K. (tr.), *Pseudo-Macarius, Reden und Briefe, eingeleitet, übersetzt und mit Anmerkungen versehen von Klaus Fitschen* (Bibliothek der griechischen Literatur 52; Stuttgart 2000). [tr. of 1]

Haywood, T. (tr.), *Primitive Morality or the Spiritual Homilies of St Macarius the Egyptian; Full of very profitable instructions concerning that Perfection which is Expected from Christians and which it is their Duty to Endeavour after. Done out of Greek with several considerable emendations and some enlargements from a Bodleian MS, never before printed* (London 1721). [tr. of 11 ]

Maloney, G. (tr.), *The Fifty Spiritual Homilies and Great Letter* (Classics of Western Spirituality; New York/Mahwah 1992). [tr. of 11 and *Great Letter* (PG 34 version)]

Mason, A. J. (tr.), *Fifty Spiritual Homilies of St Macarius the Egyptian* (London 1921). [tr. of 11]

Palmer, G., Sherrard, P., and Ware, K. T. (tr.) *The Philokalia*, vol. iii (London 1984). [tr. of The 150 Chapters]

Penn, G. (tr.), *Institutes of Christian Perfection* (London 1816). [tr. of the *Opuscula*]

Touraille, J. (tr.), *Philocalie des Pères neptiques* (fascicule 5) (Bellefontaine 1984). [tr. of the 150 Chapters]

## MARK THE MONK

Durand, G. M. de, *Marc le Moine: Traités*, 2 vols. (SC 445, 455; Paris 1999, 2000). [= *Opuscula* I–V, VII–VIII, X–XI]

Kunze, J., *Marcus Eremita* (Leipzig 1895), 6–30. [*Op.* XI]

Papadopoulos-Kerameus, A., Ἀνάλεκτα Ἱεροσολυμιτικῆς Σταχυολογίας, vol. i (St Petersburg 1891), 89–113. [*Op.* XI]

Rocchi, A., in Cozza-Luzi, J. (ed.), *Nova Patrum bibliotheca*, vol. x (Rome 1905), 201–47. [*Op.* XI]

Ware, K. T., Provisional MS text of *Op.* I–V, VII–VIII, X–XI.

Palmer, G., Sherrard, P., and Ware, K. T. (tr.), *The Philokalia*, vol. iii (London and Boston 1984). [tr. of *Op.* I–II, V]

Zirnheld, C.-A. (tr.), *Marc le Moine: Traités spirituels et théologiques* (Spiritualité Orientale 41; Bellefontaine 1985). [tr. of *Op.* I–V, VII–VIII, X–XI]

## MAXIMUS THE CONFESSOR

Ceresa-Gastaldo, A., *Capitoli sulla carità* (Verba seniorum 3; Rome 1963). [= *CC*]

Laga, C., and Steel, C., *Quaestiones ad Thalassium* (CCSG 7, 22; Louvain 1980, 1990). [= *QT*]

Declerck, J., *Quaestiones et dubia* (CCSG 10; Louvain 1982). [= *QD*]

Van Deun, P., *Opuscula exegetica duo: Expositio in Psalmum LIX; Expositio orationis dominicae* (CCSG 23; Louvain 1991). [= *Exp. Ps. LIX; LP*]

*Ambigua* (PG 91 1031–1418). [= *Amb.*]

*Capita theologiae et oeconomiae* (PG 90 1033–1176). [= *CT*]

*Epistulae* (PG 91 362–650). [= *Ep.*]

*Mystagogia* (PG 91 658–718). [= *Myst.*]

Other texts in PG 90–1.

Berthold, G. C. (tr.), *Maximus the Confessor: Selected Writings* (Classics of Western Spirituality; New York/Mahwah 1985). [tr. of *CC, CT, LP, Myst.*, and the *Trial of Maximus*]

Louth, A. (tr.), *Maximus the Confessor* (London 1996). [tr. of *Ep.* 2; *Amb.* 1, 5, 10, 41, 71; *Opuscula theologica et polemica* 3, 7]

Palmer, G., Sherrard, P., and Ware, K. T. (tr.), *The Philokalia*, vol. ii (London 1981). [tr. of *CC, CT, LP*, and other texts]

Sherwood, P. (tr.), *St Maximus the Confessor*, The Ascetic Life, The Four Centuries on Charity (Ancient Christian Writers 21; London/ Maryland 1955).

Ponsoye, E. (tr.), *Saint Maxime le Confesseur: Ambigua*, with introduction by J.-C. Larchet and notes by D. Staniloae (Paris 1994).

—— *Saint Maxime le Confesseur: Questions à Thalassius*, with introduction by J.-C. Larchet (Paris 1992).

## ORIGEN

Series: *Origenes Werke* in GCS (Berlin 1899–).

Prinzivalli, E., *Homélies sur les Psaumes 36 à 38* (SC 411; Paris 1995).

## PACHOMIUS

Halkin, F., *Sancti Pachomii vitae Graecae* (Subsidia hagiographica 19; Brussels 1932).

## PALLADIUS

Butler, C., *The Lausiac History of Palladius* (Cambridge 1898–1904). [= *LH*]

## PHOTIUS

Henry, R., *La Bibliothèque de Photius*, 5 vols. (Collection Byzantine; Paris 1959). [= *Bibliotheca*]

## SEXTUS

Chadwick, H., *Sentences of Sextus* (Cambridge 1959).

266 Bibliography

TIMOTHY OF CONSTANTINOPLE
*De iis qui ad ecclesiam ab haereticis accedunt* (PG 86 12–68). [48A–52C = T]

THEODORET OF CYRRHUS
*Haereticarum fabularum compendium* (PG 83 336–556). [= *Haer. fab. comp.*]
Parmentier, F., *Historia ecclesiastica* (GCS 44; Berlin 1954). [= *HE*]
Canivet, P., and Leroy-Molinghen, A., *Histoire des moines de Syrie*, 2 vols.
(SC 234, 257; Paris 1977, 1979).

## General and Secondary Sources

Abou-Zayd, S., *Ihidayutha: A Study of the Life of Singleness in the Syrian Orient from Ignatius of Antioch to Chalcedon 451 AD* (Oxford 1993).
Ahrens, K., and Krüger, G., *Die sogenannte Kirchengeschichte des Zacharias Rhetor in deutscher Übersetzung* (Leipzig 1899).
Alfeyev, H., *St Symeon the New Theologian and Orthodox Tradition* (Oxford 2000).
Andia, Y. de, 'Transfiguration et théologie négative chez Maxime le Confesseur et Denys l'Aréopagite' in ead. (ed.), *Denys l'Aréopagite et sa postérité en Orient et en Occident* (Études Augustiniennes; Paris 1996), 293–328.
Baker, A., 'Pseudo-Macarius and the Gospel of Thomas', *VC* 18 (1964), 215–25.
—— 'The Great Letter of Pseudo-Macarius and Gregory of Nyssa', *Studia Monastica* 6 (1964), 381–7.
—— 'Pseudo-Macarius and Gregory of Nyssa', *VC* 20 (1966), 227–34.
—— 'Syriac and the Scriptural Quotations of Pseudo-Macarius', *JTS* 20 (1969), 133–49.
Balthasar, H. von, *Présence et pensée: Essai sur la philosophie religieuse de Grégoire de Nysse* (Paris 1942).
—— *Kosmische Liturgie. Das Weltbild Maximus' des Bekenners* (2nd edn. Einsiedeln 1961).
Bank, J. H. van de, *Macarius en zijn invloed in de Nederlanden* (Amsterdam 1977).
Bardy, G., 'Apatheia', *DS* i. 727–46.
Bartelink, G. J. M, 'Text Parallels between the *Vita Hypatii* of Callinicus and the Pseudo-Macariana', *VC* 22 (1968), 120–36.
Beulay, R., *La Lumière sans forme: Introduction à l'étude de la mystique chrétienne syro-orientale* (Chèvetogne 1987).
Bellini, E., 'Maxime interprète de Pseudo-Denys l'Aréopagite. Analyse de L'Ambiguum *ad* Thoman 5', in F. Heinzer and C. Schönborn (eds.), *Actes du Symposium sur Maxime le Confesseur* (Paradosis 27; Fribourg 1982), 37–49.

Benz, E., *Die protestantische Thebais: zur Nachwirkung Makarius des Ägypters in Protestantismus des 17. und 18. Jahrhunderts in Europa und Amerika* (Mainz 1963).

Berthold, G., 'The Cappadocian Roots of Maximus the Confessor', in F. Heinzer and C. Schönborn (eds.), *Actes du Symposium sur Maxime le Confesseur* (Paradosis 27; Fribourg 1982), 51–9.

Berthold, H., 'Frühe christliche Literatur als Quelle für Sozialgeschichte', TU 120 (1977), 43–63.

—— 'Die Ursprünglichkeit literarischer Einheiten im Corpus Macarianum', TU 125 (1981), 61–76.

Beyer, H.-V., 'Die Lichtlehre der Mönche des vierzehnten und des vierten Jahrhunderts, erörtert am Beispiel des Gregorios Sinaïtes, des Evagrios Pontikos und des Ps.-Makarios/Symeon', *Jahrbuch der österreichischen Byzantinistik* 31 (1981), 473–512.

Bianchi, U. (ed.), *La tradizione dell'Enkrateia* (Rome 1985).

Blowers, P., *Exegesis and Spiritual Pedagogy in Maximus the Confessor: An investigation of the Quaestiones ad Thalassium* (Christianity and Judaism in Antiquity 7; Indiana 1991).

Bousset, W., *Apophthegmata. Studien zur Geschichte des ältesten Mönchtums* (Tübingen 1923).

Bouyer, L., *Histoire de la spiritualité chrétienne*, i: *La spiritualité du Nouveau Testament et des Pères* (Paris 1960).

Brock, S. P., 'St Isaac of Nineveh and Syriac Spirituality', *Sobornost* 7.2 (1975), 79–89. (Also in (idem) *Studies in Syriac Christianity*.)

—— *The Holy Spirit in the Syrian Baptismal Tradition* (The Syriac Churches Series 9; Poona 1979).

—— 'The Prayer of the Heart in the Syriac Tradition', *Sobornost/ECR* 4.2 (1981), 131–42. (Also in (idem) *Studies in Syriac Christianity*.)

—— *The Luminous Eye: The Spiritual World Vision of St Ephrem the Syrian* (Placid Lectures 6; Rome/Kerala 1985; 2nd edn. Kalamazoo 1992).

—— 'Clothing Metaphors as a means of Theological Expression in Syriac Tradition', in M. Schmidt (ed.), *Typus, Symbol und Allegorie bei den östlichen Vätern und ihre Parallelen im Mittelaltern* (Regensburg 1982), 11–40.

—— *Syriac Perspectives on Late Antiquity* (London 1984).

—— *Spirituality in Syriac Tradition* (Kerala 1989).

—— *Studies in Syriac Christianity: History, Literature and Theology* (London 1992).

Bunge, G., *Akèdia: La doctrine spirituelle d'Évagre Pontique sur l'acédie* (Spiritualité Orientale 52; Bellefontaine 1983).

—— 'Évagre le Pontique et les deux Macaire', *Irénikon* 56 (1983), 215–26, 323–60.

—— 'On the Trinitarian Orthodoxy of Evagrius Ponticus', *Monastic Studies* 17 (1986), 191–208.

Bunge, G., *Das Geistgebet. Studien zum Traktat De Oratione des Evagrios Pontikos* (Cologne 1987).

Burton-Christie, D., *The Word in the Desert: Scripture and the Quest for Holiness in Early Christian Monasticism* (Oxford 1993).

Canévet, M., 'Le "De Instituto Christiano" est-il de Grégoire de Nysse?', *Revue des études grecques* 82 (1969), 404–23.

—— 'Sens spirituel', *DS* xiv. 598–617.

Chadwick, H., Review of Staats, *Gregor von Nyssa und die Messalianer* (q.v.), *JEH* 20 (1969), 319–20.

—— 'The Identity and Date of Mark the Monk', *ECR* 4 (1972), 125–30.

Chitty, D. J., *The Desert a City* (Oxford 1966).

—— 'Abba Isaiah', *JTS* 22 (1971), 47–72.

Clark, E. A., *The Origenist Controversy: The Cultural Construction of an Early Christian Debate* (Princeton 1992).

Cleve, F., and Ryökäs, E., *Makarios-Symposium über den Heiligen Geist: Vorträge der zweiten Finnisch-deutschen Theologentagung in Karis 1984* (Åbo 1989).

Couilleau, G., 'Entre Scété et Gaza, un monachisme en devenir: l'abbé Isaïe', in H. de Broc (ed.), *Abbé Isaïe: Recueil Ascétique*, 3rd edn. (Spiritualité Orientale 7 bis; Bellefontaine 1985), 337–67.

Csányi, D. A., 'Optima Pars. Die Auslegungsgeschichte von Lk 10, 38–42 bei den Kirchenvätern der ersten vier Jahrhunderte', *Studia Monastica* 2 (1960), 5–78.

Dagron, G., 'Les Moines et la ville: Le monachisme à Constantinople', *Travaux et mémoires* 4 (1970), 229–76.

Dalmais, I.-H., 'L'Héritage évagrien dans la synthèse de saint Maxime le Confesseur', *Studia Patristica* 8 (1966), 356–62.

—— 'Maxime le Confesseur', *DS* x. 836–47.

Daniélou, J., *Les Anges et leur mission d'après les Pères de l'Église* (Chevetogne 1953).

—— *Platonisme et théologie mystique: Essai sur la doctrine spirituelle de saint Grégoire de Nysse* (2nd edn. Paris 1954).

—— 'Mystique de la ténèbre chez Grégoire de Nysse', *DS* ii. 1872–85.

—— 'Grégoire de Nysse et le Messalianisme', *Recherches de science religieuse* 48 (1960), 119–34.

—— *From Glory to Glory* (New York 1961).

—— Review of Staats, *Gregor von Nyssa und die Messalianer* (q.v.), *Recherches de science religieuse* 57 (1969), 123–6.

Darrouzès, J., 'Notes sur les Homélies du Pseudo-Macaire', *Le Muséon* 67 (1954), 297–309.

Davids, E. A., *Das Bild vom neuen Menschen. Ein Beitrag zum Verständnis des Corpus Macarianum* (Salzburger patristische Studien 2; Salzburg/Munich 1968).

—— 'Eine Illustration zur Textüberlieferung des Corpus Macarianum', *Byzantinische Zeitschrift* 61 (1968), 10–18.

—— 'Von der Anonymität zur Pseudonymität. Der Liber Graduum und der Corpus Macarianum', in W. Voigt (ed.), *XVII Deutscher Orientalistentag* (Wiesbaden 1969), 375–9.

Des Places, E., 'Maxime le Confesseur et Diadoque de Photicé', in F. Heinzer and C. Schönborn (eds.), *Actes du Symposium sur Maxime le Confesseur* (Paradosis 27; Fribourg 1982), 29–35.

—— 'Diadoque de Photicé et le messalianisme', in P. Granfield and J. Jungmann (eds.), *Kyriakon: Festschrift Johannes Quasten* (Münster 1970), 591–5.

Deseille, P., 'Épectase', *DS* iv. 785–8.

Desprez, V., 'Le Pseudo-Macaire'; 'Pseudo-Macaire: L'âme et l'église'; 'Les Relations entre le Pseudo-Macaire et S. Basile', in J. Gribomont (ed.), *Commandements du Seigneur et libération évangélique* (Studia Anselmiana 70; Rome 1970), 175–200, 201–7, 208–21.

—— 'Les Citations de Rom. 1–8 dans les "Homélies macariennes"', *Parole de l'Orient* 3 (1972), 208–17.

—— 'Le Baptême chez le Pseudo-Macaire', *Ecclesia Orans* 5 (1988), 121–55.

—— 'L'Eucharistie d'après le Pseudo-Macaire et son arrière-plan syrien', *Ecclesia Orans* 8 (1990), 191–222.

—— 'Le Pseudo-Macaire, I. Perfection, communauté et prière dans la Grande Lettre', *Lettre de Ligugé* 252 (1990), 11–24.

—— 'Le Pseudo-Macaire, II. Combat spirituel, prière et expérience', *Lettre de Ligugé* 254 (1990), 23–40.

—— *Le Monachisme primitif: Des origines jusqu'au concile d'Éphèse* (Spiritualité Orientale 72; Paris 1998).

—— 'Diadoque de Photicé et le Pseudo-Macaire: Du débat vers un bilan?' (as yet unpublished).

Desprez, V., with Canévet, M., 'Pseudo-Macaire (Syméon)', *DS* x. 20–42.

Desprez, V., with Miquel, P., 'Plèrophoria', *DS* xii. 1813–21.

Disdier, M.-T., 'Une oeuvre douteuse de saint Maxime le Confesseur: Les cinq Centuries théologiques', *Échos d'Orient* 30 (1931), 160–78.

Dodds, E. R., *Proclus: The Elements of Theology* (2nd edn. Oxford 1963).

Dörr, F., *Diadochus von Photike und die Messalianer* (Freiburg im Breisgau 1937).

Dörries, H., *Symeon von Mesopotamien. Die Überlieferung der messalianischen 'Makarios'-Schriften* (TU 55; Leipzig 1941).

—— *Geist und Geschichte bei Gottfried Arnold* (Göttingen 1963).

—— 'Das Verhältnis der κεφάλαια γνωστικά zum Messalianismus', in idem, *Wort und Stunde*, vol. i (Göttingen 1966), 352–422.

Dörries, H., 'Die Beichte im älten Mönchtum', in *Wort und Stunde*, vol. i (Göttingen 1966), 225–50 (= 'The Place of Confession in Ancient Monasticism', *Studia Patristica* 5 (= TU 80; Berlin 1962), 298–311).

—— 'Eine altkirchliche Weihnachtspredigt', in *Wort und Stunde*, vol. i (Göttingen 1966), 302–33.

—— 'Urteil und Verurteilung. Kirche und Messalianer: Zum Umgang der alten Kirche mit Häretikern', in *Wort und Stunde*, vol. i (Göttingen 1966), 334–51.

—— 'Die Messalianer im Zeugnis ihrer Bestreiter: Zum Problem des Enthusiasmus in der spätantiken Reichskirche', *Saeculum* 21 (1970), 213–27.

—— *Die Theologie des Makarios-Symeon* (Göttingen 1978).

Draguet, R., 'Une section "isaïenne" d'apophtegmes dans le Karakallou 251', *Byzantion* 35 (1965), 44–61.

—— 'Notre édition des recensions syriaques de l'Ascéticon d'abba Isaïe', *Revue d'histoire ecclésiastique* 63 (1968), 843–57.

—— 'Parallèles macariens syriaques des logoi I et III de l'Ascéticon isaïen syriaque', *Le Muséon* 83 (1970), 483–96.

Drijvers, H., 'Hellenistic and Oriental Origins', in S. Hackel (ed.), *The Byzantine Saint* (Studies Supplementary to Sobornost 5; London 1981), 25–33.

Durand, G. M. de, 'Études sur Marc le Moine I: L'Épitre à Nicholas', *Bulletin de littérature ecclésiastique* 85 (1984), 259–78.

—— 'Études sur Marc le Moine II: Le Traité sur l'Incarnation', *Bulletin de littérature ecclésiastique* 86 (1985), 5–23.

—— 'Études sur Marc le Moine III: Marc et les controverses occidentales', *Bulletin de littérature ecclésiastique* 87 (1986), 163–88.

—— 'Études sur Marc le Moine IV: Une double définition de la foi', *Bulletin de littérature ecclésiastique* 89 (1988), 23–40.

Elm, Susanna, *'Virgins of God': The Making of Asceticism in Late Antiquity* (Oxford 1994).

Festugière, A. J., *Les Moines d'Orient*, vol. i: *Culture ou sainteté. Introduction au monachisme oriental* (Paris 1961).

Fitschen, K., *Messalianismus und Antimessalianismus. Ein Beispiel ostkirchlicher Ketzergeschichte* (Forschung zur Kirchen -und Dogmengeschichte 71; Göttingen 1998).

Fitschen, K., with R. Staats (eds.), *Grundbegriffe christlicher Ästhetik: Beiträge des V. Makarios-Symposiums Preetz 1995* (Göttinger Orientforschungen, Series 1: Syriaca 36; Wiesbaden 1997).

Flew, R. Newton, *The Idea of Perfection in Christian Tradition* (Oxford 1934).

Fowden, E. Key, *The Barbarian Plain: St Sergius between Rome and Iran* (Berkeley/London 1999).

Fraigneau-Julien, B., *Les Sens spirituels et la vision de Dieu selon Syméon le Nouveau théologien* (Théologie historique 67; Paris 1985).

Garrigues, J. M., *Maxime le Confesseur: La Charité, avenir divin de l'homme* (Théologie historique 38; Paris 1976).

Gatier, P. L., 'Un moine sur la frontière: Alexandre l'Acémète en Syrie', in A. Rousselle (ed.), *Frontières terrestres, frontières célestes dans l'antiquité* (Perpignan/Paris 1995), 435–57.

Géhin, P., 'Un recueil d'extraits patristiques: les Miscellanea Coisliniana (*Parisinus Coislinianus* 193 et *Sinaiticus graecus* 461)', *Revue d'histoire des textes* 22 (1992), 89–139.

—— 'Evagriana d'un manuscrit Basilien', *Le Muséon* 109 (1996), 59–85.

—— 'Le Dossier Macarien de l'Atheniensis 2492', *Recherches Augustiniennes* 31 (1999), 89–147.

Golitzin, A., *Et introibo ad altare Dei: The Mystagogy of Dionysius Areopagita with Special Reference to its Predecessors in the Eastern Christian Tradition* (Thessalonica 1994).

—— 'Hierarchy versus Anarchy? Dionysius Areopagita, Symeon the New Theologian, Nicetas Stethatos, and their Common Roots in Ascetical Tradition', *SVQ* 38 (1994), 131–79.

—— 'Temple and Throne of the Divine Glory: "Pseudo-Macarius" and Purity of Heart', in H. Luckman and L. Kulzer (eds.), *Purity of Heart in Early Ascetic and Monastic Literature* (Minnesota 1999), 107–29.

Gouillard, J., 'Constantin Chrysomallos sous le masque de Syméon le nouveau théologien', *Travaux et mémoires* 5 (1973), 313–27.

—— 'Quatre procès de mystique à Byzance (vers 960–1143)', *Revue des études byzantines* 36 (1978), 5–81.

Gould, G., *The Desert Fathers on Monastic Community* (Oxford 1993).

Grant, R. M., *Irenaeus of Lyons* (London 1997).

Gribomont, J., 'Le Monachisme au IVe siècle en Asie Mineure: De Gangres au Messalianisme', *Studia Patristica* 2 (= TU 64; Berlin 1957), 400–16.

—— 'Eustathe le Philosophe et les voyages du jeune Basile de Césarée', *Revue ecclésiastique* 54 (1959), 116–24.

—— 'Le *De instituto christiano* et le Messalianisme de Grégoire de Nysse', *Studia Patristica* 5 (= TU 80; Berlin 1962), 312–22.

—— 'Mystique et orthodoxie: Évagre et Syméon', in idem (ed.), *Commandements du Seigneur*, 106–19.

—— 'Le Dossier des origines du Messalianisme', in J. Fontaine and C. Kannengiesser (eds.), *Epektasis: Mélanges J. Daniélou* (Paris 1972), 611–25.

—— 'Saint Basile et le monachisme enthousiaste', *Irénikon* 53 (1980), 123–44.

Gribomont, J., *Saint Basile: Évangile et église*, 2 vols. (Spiritualité Orientale 36; Bellefontaine 1984).

—— 'Marc le Moine' *DS* x. 274–83.

—— 'Marc l'Ermite et la christologie évagrienne', *Cristianesimo nella storia* 3 (1982), 73–81.

—— 'Encore Marc l'Ermite: l'union selon l'hypostase', *Cristianesimo nella storia* 5 (1984), 463–73.

Gribomont, J. (ed.), *Commandements du Seigneur et libération évangélique* (Studia Anselmiana 70; Rome 1970).

Grillmeier, A., *Christ in Christian Tradition*, i: *From the Apostolic Age to Chalcedon* (2nd edn. London 1975).

—— 'Markos Eremites und der Origenismus' (TU 125; Berlin 1981), 253–83 (= 'Marco Eremita e l'origenismo', *Cristianesimo nella Storia* 1 (1980), 9–58).

Gross, J., *Geschichte des Erbsündendogmas*, 4 vols. (Munich 1960–72).

Guillaumont, A., 'Une notice syriaque inédite sur la vie de l'Abbé Isaïe', *Analecta Bollandiana* 67 (1949), 350–60.

—— 'Les Sens des noms du coeur dans l'Antiquité', *Études carmélitaines: Le Couer* (1950), 131–8.

—— *Les 'Kephalaia gnostica' d'Évagre le Pontique et l'histoire de l'origénisme chez les Grecs et chez les Syriens* (Patristica Sorbonensia 5; Paris 1962).

—— 'Situation et signifiance du Liber Graduum dans la spiritualité syriaque', in *Symposium Syriacum 1972* (OCA 197; Rome 1974), 311–22.

—— 'Le Coeur chez les spirituels grecs à l'époque ancien', *DS* ii. 2. 2281–8.

—— 'Messaliens', *DS* x. 1074–83.

—— *Aux origines du monachisme chrétien: pour une phénoménologie du monachisme* (Spiritualité Orientale 30; Bellefontaine 1979).

—— 'La Vision de l'intellect par lui-même dans la mystique évagrienne', in *Mélanges de l'Université Saint-Joseph* 50 (Beirut 1984), 255–62.

—— *Études sur la spiritualité de l'Orient chrétien* (Spiritualité Orientale 66; Bellefontaine 1996).

Hatzopoulos, A., *Two Outstanding Cases in Byzantine Spirituality: The Macarian Writings and Symeon the New Theologian* (Thessalonica 1991).

Hausherr, I., 'Les Grands Courants de la spiritualité orientale', *OCP* 1 (1935), 114–38.

—— 'L'Erreur fondamentale et la logique du Messalianisme', *OCP* 1 (1935), 328–60.

—— (as J. Lemaître), 'Contemplation chez les Grecs et autres Orientaux chrétiens', *DS* ii. 1762–1872.

—— 'L'Imitation de Jésus-Christ dans la spiritualité byzantine', in *Mélanges offerts au R.P. Ferdinand Cavallera* (Toulouse 1948), 231–59.

—— *Philautie: De la tendresse pour soi à la charité selon S. Maxime le Confesseur* (Rome 1952).

—— *Les Leçons d'un contemplatif* (Paris 1960).

—— *Noms du Christ et voies d'oraison* (OCA 157; Rome 1960).

—— *Hésychasme et prière* (OCA 176; Rome 1966).

—— 'Les Orientaux connaissent-ils les "nuits" de saint Jean de la Croix?' in idem, *Hésychasme et prière* (OCA 176; Rome 1966), 87–128.

—— *Études de spiritualité orientale* (OCA 183; Rome 1969).

Heinzer, F., and Schönborn, C., *Actes du Symposium sur Maxime le Confesseur* (Paradosis 27; Fribourg 1982).

Hesse, O., 'Markus Eremita in der syrischen Literatur', in W. Voigt (ed.), *XVII Deutscher Orientalistentag* (Wiesbaden 1969), 450–7.

—— 'Markos Eremites und Symeon von Mesopotamien: Untersuchung und Vergleich ihrer Lehren zur Taufe und zur Askese' (doctoral dissertation; Göttingen 1973).

—— 'Was Mark the Monk a Sixth-Century Higumen near Tarsus?' *ECR* 8 (1976), 174–8.

—— 'Vom Paradies der Kirche und vom Paradies im Herzen. Zur Deutung der Paradiesesgeschichte bei Makarios/Symeon und Markos Eremites', in K. Fitschen and R. Staats (eds.), *Grundbegriffe christlicher Ästhetik* (Wiesbaden 1997), 23–6.

Horn, G., 'Sens de l'esprit d'après Diadoque de Photicé', *RAM* 8 (1927), 402–19.

Hornschuh, M., *Studien zur Epistula Apostolorum* (PTS 5; Berlin 1965).

Ivanka, E. von, *Plato Christianus* (Paris 1990).

Jaeger, W., *Early Christianity and Greek Paideia* (Oxford 1961).

Janin, R., *Géographie ecclésiastique de l'empire byzantin* (2nd edn. Paris 1969).

—— 'La Banlieue asiatique de Constantinople IV: Rufinianes', *Échos d'Orient* 22 (1923), 182–90.

Kemmer, A., *Charisma maximum. Untersuchung zu Cassians Volkommenheitslehre und seiner Stellung zum Messalianismus* (Louvain 1938).

—— 'Gregor von Nyssa und Ps. Makarius. Der Messalianismus im Lichte östlicher Herzenmystik', in B. Steidle (ed.), *Antonius Magnus Eremita* (Studia Anselmia 38; Rome 1956), 268–82.

Kirk, K. E., *The Vision of God* (London 1932).

Kittel, G. (ed.), *Theologisches Wörterbuch zum Neuen Testament*, 10 vols. (Stuttgart 1932–79).

Klijn, A. F. J., 'Some Remarks on the Quotations of the Gospels in Gregory of Nyssa's *De instituto christiano* and Macarius' *Epistola Magna*', *VC* 19 (1965), 164–8.

Klostermann, R. A., *Die slavische Überlieferung der Makariusschriften* (Göteborg 1950).

Kunze, J., *Marcus Eremita. Ein neuer Zeuge für das altkirchlichen Taufbekenntnis* (Leipzig 1895).

Kvist, H.-O., *Bibelauslegung und Gruppenidentität: Vorträge der vierten Finnisch-deutschen Theologentagung (Makarios-Symposium) im Kloster Neu-Valamo 1991* (Åbo 1992).

Lampe, G. W. H, *A Patristic Greek Lexicon* (Oxford 1961). [= Lampe]

Le Guillou, M.-J., 'Remarques sur la notion macarienne de "subtilité"', *Istina* 3 (1974), 339–42. Followed, 343–9, by Kniewasser, M. (tr.), 'Deux homélies inédites du Pseudo-Macaire sur la "subtilité" de l'Esprit'.

Larchet, J.-C., 'Le Baptême selon saint Maxime le Confesseur', *Revue des sciences religieuses* 65 (1991), 51–70.

—— *La Divinisation de l'homme selon saint Maxime le Confesseur* (Paris 1996).

Lethel, F.-M., *Théologie de l'agonie du Christ. La liberté humaine du Fils de Dieu et son importance sotériologique mises en lumière par saint Maxime le Confesseur* (Théologie Historique 52; Beauchesne 1979).

Liddell, H., and Scott, R., *A Greek–English Lexicon* (9th edn. revised and augmented by H. Stuart Jones and R. McKenzie, Oxford 1940; with supplement, 1968). [= LS]

Lossky, V., *The Vision of God* (London 1963).

—— *The Mystical Theology of the Eastern Church* (London 1957).

Lot-Borodine, M., *La Déification de l'homme selon les Pères grecs* (Paris 1970).

Louth, A., *The Origins of the Christian Mystical Tradition: From Plato to Denys* (Oxford 1981).

—— 'Messalianism and Pelagianism', *Studia Patristica* 17 (Oxford 1982), 127–35.

—— 'St Gregory the Theologian and St Maximus the Confessor: The Shaping of Tradition', in S. Coakley and D. A. Pailin (eds.), *The Making and Remaking of Christian Doctrine: Essays in Honour of Maurice Wiles* (Oxford 1993).

—— 'St Denys the Areopagite and St Maximus the Confessor: A Question of Influence', *Studia Patristica* 27 (1993), 166–74.

—— *Maximus the Confessor* (London 1996).

—— 'Recent Research on St Maximus the Confessor: A Survey', *SVQ* 42 (1998), 67–84.

McGuckin, J. A., *The Transfiguration of Christ in Scripture and Tradition* (Studies in the Bible and Early Christianity 9; Lewiston/Queenston 1986).

Malone, E. E, *The Monk and the Martyr* (Washington 1950).

Marriott, G. L., 'Macarius of Egypt: His Epistle *Ad filios Dei* in Syriac', *JTS* 20 (1918), 42–4.

—— 'Gennadius of Marseilles on Macarius of Egypt', *JTS* 20 (1919), 347–9.

Bibliography 275

—— 'The Homilies of Macarius', *JTS* 22 (1921), 259–62.

—— 'The Messalians and the Discovery of their Ascetic Book', *Harvard Theological Review* 19 (1926), 191–8.

Martikainen, J., 'Das Böse in den Schriften des Syrers Ephraem, im Stufenbuch und im Corpus Macarianum', in W. Strothmann (ed.), *Makarios-Symposium über das Böse* (Wiesbaden 1983), 36–46.

Martikainen, J., with Kvist, H.-O. (eds.), *Makarios-Symposium über den Heiligen Geist: Vorträge der dritten Finnisch–Deutschen Theologentagung in Amelungsborn 1986* (Åbo 1989).

May, G., 'Die Datierung der Rede *In suam ordinationem* des Gregor von Nyssa und die Verhandlungen mit die Pneumatomachen auf dem Konzil von Konstantinopel 381', *VC* 23 (1969), 38–57.

Mengus, C., 'Le "Coeur" dans les "Cinquante homélies spirituelles" du Pseudo-Macaire', *Collectanea Cisterciensia* 58 (1996), 3–18; 59 (1997), 32–43, 118–31.

Messana, V., 'San Diadocho di Fotica', *Strumenti della corona Patrum* 4 (Turin 1995), 425–42.

Meyendorff, J., *A Study of Gregory Palamas* (London 1964).

—— *Christ in Eastern Christian Thought* (Washington 1969).

—— 'Messalianism or Anti-Messalianism? A Fresh Look at the "Macarian" Problem', in P. Granfield and J. Jungmann (eds.), *Kyriakon. Festschrift Johannes Quaesten* (Münster 1970), 585–90.

—— *Byzantine Theology: Historical Trends and Doctrinal Themes* (London 1975).

—— 'St Basil, Messalianism and Byzantine Christianity', *SVQ* 24 (1980), 219–34.

Miquel, P., 'La Naissance de Dieu dans l'âme', *Revue des sciences religieuses* 35 (1961), 378–406.

—— 'Les Caractères de l'expérience spirituelle selon le Pseudo-Macaire', *Irénikon* 39 (1966), 496–513.

—— 'Peîra: Contribution à l'étude du vocabulaire de l'expérience religieuse dans l'oeuvre de Maxime le Confesseur', *Studia Patristica* 6 (= TU 92; Berlin 1966), 355–61.

—— *Le Vocabulaire de l'expérience spirituelle dans la tradition grecque du IVe au XIVe siècle* (Théologie historique 86; Beauchesne 1989).

—— *Lexique du désert: Étude de quelques mots-clés du vocabulaire ancien* (Spiritualité Orientale 44; Bellefontaine 1986).

Miquel, P., with Desprez, V., 'Plèrophoria', *DS* xii. 1813–21.

Murray, R., *Symbols of Church and Kingdom: A Study in Early Syriac Tradition* (Cambridge 1975).

Nieto Ibáñez, J.-M., 'Orthodoxos, humanistas y protestantes ante la espiritualidad bizantina: el enigma de San Macario', in M. Morfakidis and I. García Gálvez (eds.), *Estudios neogriegos en España e Iberoamérica*, i: *Historia, literatura y tradición* (Granada 1997), 31–9.

Nieto Ibañez, J.-M., (with A.-M. Martín Rodríguez) *Pedro de Valencia: Obras completas*, ix.1: *Escritos espirituales: San Macario* (León 2001).

Obolensky, D., *The Bogomils: A Study in Balkan Neo-Manichaeism* (Cambridge 1948).

——— *The Byzantine Commonwealth* (London 1971).

Outler, A. C. (ed.), *John Wesley* (Oxford 1964).

Outtier, B., 'Un Patericon arménien', *Le Muséon* 84 (1971), 299–351.

Palmer, A., *The Seventh Century in the West-Syrian Chronicles* (Liverpool 1993).

Pargoire, J., 'Rufinianes', *Byzantinische Zeitschrift* 8 (1899), 429–77.

——— 'Autour de Chalcédoine', *Byzantinische Zeitschrift* 11 (1902), 333–57.

——— 'L'Église de Sainte-Euphémie et Rufinianes à Chalcédoine', *Échos d'Orient* 4 (1911), 107–10.

Parys, M. van, 'La Liturgie du coeur selon S. Grégoire le Sinaïte', *Irénikon* 51 (1978), 312–37.

Payne-Smith, J., *A Compendious Syriac Dictionary* (Oxford 1903; repr. 1990). [= Payne-Smith]

Peterson, E., 'Die Schrift des Eremiten Markus über die Taufe und die Messalianer', *Zeitschrift für neutestamentliche Wissenschaft* 31 (1932), 273–88.

Piret, P., *Le Christ et la Trinité selon saint Maxime le Confesseur* (Théologie historique 69; Beauchesne 1983).

Plested, M., 'The Christology of Macarius-Symeon', *Studia Patristica* 37 (2001), 593–6.

Pseftogas, V., *Ἡ γνησιότης τῶν συγγραμμάτων Μακαρίου τοῦ Αἰγυπτίου* (Thessalonica 1967).

Quasten, J., *Patrology*, 4 vols. (Utrecht/Westminster, Md. 1950–86).

Quispel, G., *Makarius, das Thomasevangelium und das Lied von der Perle* (Leiden 1967).

——— 'The Syrian Thomas and the Syrian Macarius', *VC* 18 (1964), 226–35.

——— 'Macarius and the Diatessaron of Tatian', in R. H. Fischer (ed.), *A Tribute to Arthur Vööbus* (Chicago 1977), 203–9.

Rahner, K., 'Le Début d'une doctrine des cinq sens spirituels chez Origène', *RAM* 13 (1932), 113–45.

——— 'Ein messalianisches Fragment über die Taufe', *Zeitschrift für katholische Theologie* 61 (1937), 258–71.

Refoulé, R., 'Rêves et vie spirituelle', *La Vie Spirituelle* (Suppl. 5) (1961), 470–516.

Regnault, L. 'Isaïe de Scété ou de Gaza', *DS* vii.2. 2083–95.

——— Introduction to H. de Broc (tr.), *Abbé Isaïe: Recueil ascétique* (3rd edn. Bellefontaine 1985).

Resch, P., *La Doctrine ascétique des premiers maîtres Égyptiens du quatrième siècle* (Beauchesne 1931).

Riou, A., *Le Monde et l'église selon Maxime le Confesseur* (Théologie historique 22; Paris 1973).

Rist, J. M., *Stoic Philosophy* (Cambridge 1969).

Roques, R., 'Contemplation, extase et ténèbre chez le Pseudo-Denys', *DS* ii. 1885–1911.

—— *L'Univers dionysien* (Paris 1954).

Rorem, P., *Biblical and Liturgical Symbols within the Pseudo-Dionysian Synthesis* (Toronto 1984).

Rousseau, P., *Ascetics, Authority and the Church* (Oxford 1978).

—— *Basil of Caesarea* (Berkeley 1994).

Runciman, S., *The Medieval Manichee* (Cambridge 1947).

Sauget, J. M., 'La Double Recension arabe des Préceptes aux novices de l'abbé Isaïe de Scété', in *Mélanges E. Tisserant*, iii (*Studi e Testi* 233; Rome 1964), 299–336.

Schulze, U., 'Die "geistigen Sinne" der Seele. Eine kurze Skizze zur Anthropologie des Makarios/Symeon', in K. Fitschen and R. Staats (eds.), *Grundbegriffe christlicher Ästhetik* (Wiesbaden 1997), 12–15.

Sheldon-Williams, I. P., 'The Greek Christian Platonist Tradition from the Cappadocians to Maximus and Eriugena', in A. Armstrong (ed.), *The Cambridge History of Later Greek and Early Medieval Philosophy* (Cambridge 1967), 423–533.

Sherwood, P., *Date-List of the Works of Maximus the Confessor* (Studia Anselmiana 30; Rome 1952).

—— *The Earlier Ambigua of Saint Maximus the Confessor and his Refutation of Origenism* (Rome 1955).

Solignac, A., ' "Noûs" et "mens" ', *DS* xi. 459–69.

Sophrony, Archimandrite, *Saint Silouan the Athonite* (Tolleshunt Knights 1991).

Spanneut, M., *Le Stoïcisme des pères de l'église* (Patristica Sorbonensia 1; Paris 1957).

Špidlík, T., *La Spiritualité de l'orient chrétien* (OCA 206; Rome 1978).

Squire, A. K., 'The Idea of the Soul as Virgin and Mother in Maximus Confessor', *Studia Patristica* 8 (= TU 93; Berlin 1966), 456–61.

Staats, R., 'Die Asketen aus Mesopotamien in der Rede des Gregor von Nyssa *In suam ordinationem*', *VC* 21 (1967), 165–79.

—— *Gregor von Nyssa und die Messalianer: Die Frage der Priorität zweiter altkirchlicher Schriften* (PTS 8; Berlin 1968).

—— 'Die törichten Jungfrauen von Mt. 25 in gnostischer und antignostischer Literatur', in W. Eltester (ed.), *Christentum und Gnosis* (*Zeitschrift für die neutestamentliche Wissenschaft* Suppl. 37 (1969)), 98–115.

Staats, R., 'Die Basilianische Verherrlichung des Heiligen Geistes auf dem Konzil zu Konstantinopel 381', *Kerygma und Dogma* 25 (1979), 232–53.

—— 'Beobachtungen zur Definition und zur Chronologie des Messalianismus', *Jahrbuch der österreichischen Byzantinistik* 32 (1982), 235–44.

—— 'Messalienerforschung und Ostkirchenkunde', in W. Strothmann (ed.), *Makarios-Symposium über das Böse* (Wiesbaden 1983), 47–71.

—— 'Messalianism and anti-Messalianism in Gregory of Nyssa's *De virginitate*', *Patristic and Byzantine Review* 2 (1983), 27–44.

—— 'Chrysostomus über die Rhetorik des Apostels Paulus. Makarianische Kontexte zu *De sacerdotio* IV 5–6', *VC* 46 (1992), 225–40.

—— 'Die Metamorphose des Christen. Die Wandlungslehre des Makarios-Symeon im Zusammenhang seiner Anthropologie, Christologie und Eucharistielehre', in K. Fitschen and R. Staats (eds.), *Grundbegriffe christlicher Ästhetik* (Wiesbaden 1997), 16–22.

Stewart, C., *'Working the Earth of the Heart': The Messalian Controversy in History, Texts and Language to AD 431* (Oxford 1991).

Stiglmayr, J., *Sachliches und Sprachliches bei Makarius von Ägypten* (Innsbruck 1912).

—— 'Die Agrapha bei Makarius von Ägypten', *Theologie und Glaube* 5 (1913), 634 ff.

—— 'Pseudomakarius und die Aftermystik der Messalianer', *Zeitschrift für katholische Theologie* 49 (1925), 244–60.

Stoffels, J., *Die mystische Theologie Makarius des Aegypters und die ältesten Ansätze christlicher Mystik* (Bonn 1908).

—— 'Makarius der Aegypter auf den Pfaden der Stoa', *Theologische Quartalschrift* 92 (1910), 88–105, 243–65.

Strothmann, W., 'Makarios und die Makariosschriften in der syrischen Literatur', *Oriens Christianus* 54 (1970), 96–105.

Strothmann, W., (ed.), *Makarios-Symposium über das Böse. Vorträge der Finnisch-deutschen Theologentagung in Goslar 1980* (Göttinger Orientforschungen, Series 1: Syriaca 24; Wiesbaden 1983).

*Thesaurus Linguae Graecae Workplace 6.0* (CD-ROM Silver Mountain Software 1997). [= TLG]

Thunberg, L., *Microcosm and Mediator: The Theological Anthropology of Maximus the Confessor* (Lund 1965).

—— *Man and the Cosmos: The Vision of St Maximus the Confessor* (New York 1985).

—— Review of A. Louth, *Maximus the Confessor* (q.v.), *Sobornost/ECR* 19.2 (1997), 61–5.

Vanneste, J., *Le Mystère de Dieu* (Brussels 1959).

Veniamin, C., 'The Transfiguration of Christ in Greek Patristic Literature' (doctoral dissertation; Oxford 1991).

Villecourt, L., 'La Date et l'origine des "Homélies spirituelles" attribuées à Macaire', in *Comptes Rendus de l'Académie des Inscriptions et Belles-lettres* (Paris 1920), 250–8.

——'La Grande Lettre grecque de Macaire, ses formes textuelles et son milieu littéraire', *Revue de l'Orient chrétien* 22 (1920), 29–56 (includes 'Note sur une lettre de l'abbé Isaïe à l'abbé Pierre', 54–6).

Viller, M., 'Aux sources de la spiritualité de S. Maxime. Les oeuvres d'Évagre le Pontique', *RAM* 11 (1930), 156–84, 239–68, 331–6.

Voicu, S., 'Frammenti di un palinsesto greco di Efrem (Sinaiticus Syr. 30, f. 171e e seguenti)', *Scriptorium* 38 (1984), 77–8.

Völker, W., *Scala Paradisi. Eine Studie zu Johannes Climacus und zugleich eine Vorstudie zur Symeon dem Neuen Theologen* (Wiesbaden 1968). (Including, 315–27: 'Beilage: Christi Verklärung auf dem Tabor in der Deutung des Maximus Confessor und des Gregorius Palamas'.)

——*Maximus Confessor als Meister des geistlichen Leben* (Wiesbaden 1965).

Vööbus, A., *On the Historical Importance of the Legacy of Pseudo-Macarius: New Observations about its Syriac Provenance* (Papers of the Estonian Theological Society in Exile 23; Stockholm 1972).

——*A History of Asceticism in the Syriac Orient*, 3 vols. (CSCO 184, 197, 500/ Subs. 14, 17, 81; Louvain 1958, 1960, 1988).

Ware, K. T., 'The Sacrament of Baptism and the Ascetic Life in the Teaching of Mark the Monk', *Studia Patristica* 10 (= TU 107; Berlin 1970), 441–52.

——'The Jesus Prayer in St Diadochus of Photice', in *Aksum-Thyateira: A Festschrift for Archbishop Methodios of Thyateira and Great Britain* (Athens 1985), 557–68.

——'Diadochus von Photice', *Theologisches Realenzyklopädie*, viii. 617–20.

——' "Pathos" in Abba Isaias and Theodoret of Cyrrhus', *Studia Patristica* 20 (Louvain 1989), 315–22.

——Introduction to C.-A. Zirnheld (tr.), *Marc le Moine* (Bellefontaine 1985).

——'Prayer in Evagrius and the Macarian Homilies', in R. Waller and B. Ward (eds.), *Introduction to Christian Spirituality* (London 1999).

Wenger, A., 'Grégoire de Nysse et le Pseudo-Macaire', *Revue des études byzantines* 13 (1955), 145–50.

Williams, N. P., *The Ideas of the Fall and of Original Sin* (London 1927).

Wilmart, A., 'L'Origine véritable des Homélies pneumatiques', *RAM* 1 (1920), 361–77.

Wimbush, V. L. (ed.), *Ascetic Behaviour in Graeco-Roman Antiquity: A Sourcebook* (Minneapolis 1990).

Zeller, E., *The Stoics, Epicureans and Sceptics* (London 1870).

# INDEX

*Epistula apostolorum* 119, 136 n. 18
eucharist 39–40, 42, 114–15, 197–8
Euphrates 13, 203
Eusebius of Nicomedia 47
Eustathius of Sebaste, Eustathians 19, 46–8
Evagrius of Pontus 30, 31, 59–71, 97 n. 65, 103, 104, 105, 110, 111, 112, 126, 132, 134, 135–6, 138 n. 22, 139–40, 142 n. 33, 147, 149, 150, 160 n. 71, 164, 165, 169–70, 171, 174, 175, 191, 192, 194, 198, 210, 214, 215, 218, 241, 242, 244 n. 83, 246, 247, 248, 250, 252
exegesis 32, 70 n. 26, 93, 101, 108 n. 89, 109, 115–19, 203–4
experience (πεῖρα and related terms) 38, 113–14, 139, 140–4, 207–9, 230–1
evil 36–7, 78–9, 92–95, 100, 125, 157–60, 161, 191; *see also* indwelling
Ezekiel 31, 32

Fall 35–6, 65, 66, 77–81, 83–4, 89, 96, 115–16, 191, 206
fire 24, 108, 171–3, 184–5, 248, 252–3
Fitschen, K. 13 n. 18, n. 20, 17, 23 n. 52, 25 n. 58, 179
Flavian of Antioch 20, 21
Fowden, E. Key 20
Fowden, G. 13 n. 19
Fraigneau-Julien, B. 32 n. 4, 134 n. 9
free will, freedom etc. 42, 90–2, 95–6, 97, 98–9, 100, 101–2, 155, 163, 184, 206–7, 230–4, 245

Gangra, council of 46–7
Garrigues, J. M 215, 230
Géhin, P. 12–13
Golitzin, A., 61–2, 222 n. 42, 252 n. 113
Goths 14

grace 36–7, 42, 44, 52, 53, 81–9, 90–2, 96, 97, 100, 112–15, 138–9, 150–6, 157, 158, 159, 231–2, 234–8; *see also* coexistence
St Gregory of Nazianzus 56, 62–3, 105, 128, 170 n. 95, 214, 216, 218, 244 n. 83
St Gregory of Nyssa 9, 15, 46, 50–8, 69–70, 79 n. 13, 80, 84, 103, 108 n. 90, 147 n. 40, 154 n. 60, 186 n. 37, 216–7, 226, 242–3, 245, 249 n. 101
St Gregory Palamas 3, 27 n. 60
Gribomont, J. 17 n. 35, 27–28, 46, 47 n. 6 n. 8 n. 9, 51, 53, 58 n. 38, 75 n. 1, 76, 128 n. 141
Grillmeier, A 76
Gross, J. 78 n. 10
Guillaumont, A. 17 n. 35, 33 n. 5, 63 n. 11, 68 n. 21, 178 n. 13, 176 n. 2, 210 n. 94
le Guillou, M. –J. 230

Hatzopoulos, A. 3 n. 5
Hausherr, I. 27 n. 61, 59–60, 87, 154, 170, 171
Haywood, Thomas 10 n. 4
heart 33, 35, 61–2, 65–6, 67–8, 70, 106–7, 108, 109, 110, 115–16, 154, 158, 162, 198–9, 205–6, 241–2
'earth of the heart' 154 n. 60, 239–42
*Henotikon* 129–30
Hesse, O. 76 n. 6, 81, 84, 101 n. 70, 115, 116, 117, 118, 119, 123 n. 127, 124, 126–7
Hesychasts 61, 70, 222
*Historia monachorum* 105, 147 n. 44
Holy Spirit 25, 32, 39, 40, 42–5, 50, 54, 55, 83, 85–8, 109, 114, 118, 141, 154
Homer 147 n. 40
Horn, G. 134 n. 9
Hornschuh, M. 136 n. 18